Trauma, Religion, and Spirituality in Germany during the First World War

Trauma, Religion, and Spirituality in Germany during the First World War

Jason Crouthamel

BLOOMSBURY ACADEMIC
LONDON • NEW YORK • OXFORD • NEW DELHI • SYDNEY

BLOOMSBURY ACADEMIC
Bloomsbury Publishing Plc
50 Bedford Square, London, WC1B 3DP, UK
1385 Broadway, New York, NY 10018, USA
29 Earlsfort Terrace, Dublin 2, Ireland

BLOOMSBURY, BLOOMSBURY ACADEMIC and the Diana logo are
trademarks of Bloomsbury Publishing Plc

First published in Great Britain 2021
Paperback edition first published 2023

Copyright © Jason Crouthamel, 2021

Jason Crouthamel has asserted their right under the Copyright, Designs and
Patents Act, 1988, to be identified as Author of this work.

For legal purposes the Acknowledgments on pp. x–xi constitute an extension
of this copyright page.

Cover image: *Liller Kriegszeitung*. © With the illustrated supplement: Kriegs-Flugblaetter
from the Bundesarchiv-Militärarchiv, Freiburg

All rights reserved. No part of this publication may be reproduced or transmitted in
any form or by any means, electronic or mechanical, including photocopying, recording,
or any information storage or retrieval system, without prior permission
in writing from the publishers.

Bloomsbury Publishing Plc does not have any control over, or responsibility for, any
third-party websites referred to or in this book. All internet addresses given in this
book were correct at the time of going to press. The author and publisher regret any
inconvenience caused if addresses have changed or sites have ceased to exist, but
can accept no responsibility for any such changes.

Every effort has been made to trace copyright holders and to obtain their permissions for
the use of copyright material. The publisher apologizes for any errors or omissions and
would be grateful if notified of any corrections that should be incorporated in future
reprints or editions of this book.

A catalogue record for this book is available from the British Library.

Library of Congress Cataloging-in-Publication Data
Names: Crouthamel, Jason, author.
Title: Trauma, religion and spirituality in Germany during the
first World War / Jason Crouthamel.
Description: London ; New York : Bloomsbury Academic, 2021. |
Includes bibliographical references and index.
Identifiers: LCCN 2021023366 (print) | LCCN 2021023367 (ebook) |
ISBN 9781350083707 (hb) | ISBN 9781350083714 (epdf) | ISBN 9781350083721 (ebook)
Subjects: LCSH: Psychic trauma–Religious aspects. | Soldiers–Religious life. |
World War, 1914–1918–Germany–Psychological aspects.
Classification: LCC BL65.M45 C76 2021 (print) | LCC BL65.M45 (ebook) |
DDC 940.3/1–dc23
LC record available at https://lccn.loc.gov/2021023366
LC ebook record available at https://lccn.loc.gov/2021023367

ISBN: HB: 978-1-3500-8370-7
PB: 978-1-3502-7048-0
ePDF: 978-1-3500-8371-4
eBook: 978-1-3500-8372-1

Typeset by Newgen KnowledgeWorks Pvt. Ltd., Chennai, India

To find out more about our authors and books visit www.bloomsbury.com
and sign up for our newsletters.

To Grace and Max
… it's just a shot away

Contents

List of Figures	viii
Acknowledgments	x
A Note on the Text	xii
List of Abbreviations	xiii
Introduction	1
1 "*Gott mit Uns*": Hegemonic Religious Ideals, Emotions, and Mobilizing for War	15
2 God and the "Spirit of 1914": Religiosity of Ordinary Soldiers and Civilians at the Outbreak of the War	35
3 Processing Trauma: Nerves, Religious Language, and Coping with Violence	61
4 "Where Is God?" The Brutalization of Faith in the Front Experience	81
5 Diagnosing Religious Beliefs: Contemporary Scientific and Popular Debates over the Spiritual-Psychological Effects of the War	109
6 Alternative Beliefs in the Trenches: Superstitions, Gods and Monsters, and Religious Humor	135
7 Spiritual Subjectivities: Constructing New Beliefs Out of Total War	161
Epilogue: Defeat, Revolution, and Aftermath	183
Conclusion	197
Notes	203
Bibliography	239
Index	253

Figures

1.1 "*Gott mit Uns*—1914" ("God is on our side—1914"), 1914.   18
1.2 "Durchhalten! Im Vertrauen auf Gott!" ("Hold Through—Trust in God!"), 1915.   20
2.1 "Weihnachten," Drawing, *Kriegsflugblätter—Beiblatt zu Liller Kriegszeitung*, December 23, 1917, PH 23/202.   46
2.2 "Sein Schutzengel—Der Engel, er schützet mit sicherer Hand/Die Kinder, du schützest das Vaterland" ("His guardian angel—the angel, he protects with a sure hand/Children, you protect the fatherland"), 1915.   51
2.3 "Der Kriegers Schutzengel—Es mögen Dich in Kriegeszeiten Schutzengel immerdar geleiten" ("The warrior's guardian angel—May guardian angels always guide you in times of war"), 1915.   52
2.4 Sterbebild, Franz Xaver Heudorfer, von Schönebürg, fürs Vaterland gestorben am 7. Februar 1917.
4.1 "Leutnant Gontermann," from the popular Sanke postcard series, 1918.   89
6.1 Arnold (artist), "Der Beherrscher des Meeres," *Liller Kriegszeitung*, No. 29, October 25, 1916, PH/23/200.   150
6.2 E. George (artist), "Trommelfeuer," *Liller Kriegszeitung*, No. 82, April 1, 1918, PH/23/202.   151
6.3 "Leutnant Josef Jacobs, Führer der Jagdstaffel 7 (48 Luftsiege), Flandern 1914/18" (Lieutenant Josef Jacobs, Leader of Fighter Squadron 7 (48 aerial victories), Flanders 1914–18), 1950s.   153
6.4 "Startbereite Schlachtstaffel—Die Flugzeuge sind mit Maschinengewehren, Signalpatronen und Handgranaten ausgerüstet" (Ready to Start Battle Squadron—The aircraft are armed with machine guns, signal flares and hand grenades), "Brünhilde," from the popular Sanke postcard series, 1918.   154
6.5 Cartoon of St. Peter giving a gas mask to an angel, *Kriegszeitung der 4. Armee*, Weihnachten 1916, PH/5/II.   158

6.6 Drawing of baby Jesus in No Man's Land, *Kriegszeitung der 4. Armee*, December 24, 1917, PH/5/II. 159

8.1 "Unser erfolgreicher Kampfflieger—Leutnant Röth" ("Our successful battle flier, Leutnant Röth") from the popular Sanke postcard series, 1918. 191

Acknowledgments

It's a pleasure to reflect, at the end of a project, on all the friends and colleagues who gave me encouragement at different stages of thinking and writing. Undertaking research brings great personal and intellectual fulfilment, but it is often challenging to preserve a psychological zone where this can take place. As a pandemic and an increasingly tense political atmosphere swirled around outside and as my family and I hid in our work and hobby cave to shield ourselves from reality, I became more aware of how lucky I was to have so much love and support. I've been very fortunate to find a network of trauma specialists who generously shared their minds, food, and living rooms. I'm grateful to Peter Leese for helping me think about religion through the lens of trauma. The insightful feedback that he provided for various chapters pushed me to consider broader questions that were essential to moving the project forward. Julia Köhne gave me invaluable critiques at crucial junctures, and her generosity in sharing her expertise in wartime psychiatry is a model for collegiality. I want to thank her for her tireless work and comradeship in the trenches of editing this book and other projects. Ville Kivimäki's encouragement is also much appreciated, and I thank him for bringing me on board to collaborate at various conferences and workshops that allowed space to reflect on the traumatic impacts of war with a diverse array of colleagues.

The number of colleagues who shared their knowledge, time, and good cheer are too many to list. But I want to give particular thanks to Michael Geheran for his feedback on chapters and for sharing his extensive expertise on sources about German Jewish soldiers. Conversations with Mark Micale and Jay Winter at conferences and workshops sparked new ways of thinking about trauma inflicted on belief systems, and I'm indebted to them for pushing me to think differently about how to approach letters and diaries. Jeremiah Cataldo's willingness to read chapters and ask thought-provoking questions is most appreciated. Bruno Schmäling kindly corresponded and shared his notes and memories about interviews with veterans in the 1970s that helped illuminate otherwise lost stories. I'd also like to thank Steven Crouthamel for sharing his expertise in anthropology, as well as experiences as a veteran, yielding critical questions that helped me to bridge disciplines and reconsider approaches. When gathering a list of colleagues, inevitably someone may be inadvertently omitted, but for their vigorous conversations and sharing of intellects at conferences, workshops, and cafes, I'd like to thank Devlin Scofield, Brian Feltman, Heather Perry, Erika Kuhlman, Anne Freese, Philipp Rauh, Gundula Gahlen, Dagmar Herzog, Steven Schouten, Kamil Ruszała, Andrea Sinn, Laurie Marhoefer, Karen Hagemann, Susan Grayzel, Thomas Kühne, Gerald Lamprecht, Joanna Bourke, Robin May Schott, Daniel Brandl-Beck, Pumla Gobodo-Madikizela, Max Alexandrin, Paul Murphy, and Ann Carmichael. Special thanks to Keny Hernandez for sharing his thoughtful perspectives on the nature and meaning of religious faith, which gave me insight into sources in ways that I would not have otherwise considered. Thanks also to the peer reviewers whose detailed suggestions for revision are most appreciated. Most importantly, to my *Doktorvater* Jim Diehl I'd like to give my gratitude for his friendship and ongoing discussion about the legacy of the Great War and the lessons of the past.

The support that I've received from various institutions reminds me how much a book depends on collaboration and cooperation. One of the most rewarding experiences for German historians is the great joy found in working in Germany's federal and regional archives and libraries. The staff at the Bundesarchiv-Militärarchiv in Freiburg was incredibly helpful as I carried out research there, and I would like to give my thanks for permission to use images from front newspapers. I am also grateful to archivists at the Bayerisches Hauptstaatsarchiv (Kriegsarchiv) in Munich as they made documents available despite the COVID-19 crisis. Christian Westerhoff and Irina Renz generously helped me navigate their collection of letters and diaries from the Württembergische Landesbibliothek and the special archive on the world wars. I would also like to thank the Deutscher Akademischer Austauschdienst (DAAD) for ongoing support over the years in funding my archival research. Grand Valley State University's Center for Scholarly and Creative Excellence (CSCE), and Robert Smart in particular, have been instrumental in making my research come to fruition. I am also grateful to my university's dean, Fred Antczak, for financial support behind a number of my endeavors, and to our department chair Mike Huner for his zeal in valuing scholarship. Finally, thanks to editor Rhodri Mogford at Bloomsbury for his support, enthusiasm, and expertise from the outset. He, along with other editors at Bloomsbury including Laura Reeves, are ideal collaborators who have made it a real pleasure to work with Bloomsbury.

Finally, on a personal note, I'd like to thank my mom and dad, Steven and Kathy, and my brother Erik for putting up with my neurotic obsession with a century-old war. Shell-shocked veterans Hermann (*SMS Seydlitz*) and Fritz (*Jasta* 22) inspired me with their goal-oriented routines and disciplined personalities that kept me sane even when they drove me mad. I can't thank my secret-sharer Grace Coolidge enough for escaping with me through travel, debates about history in between everything else in life, and for heroically pushing through her own surgical annoyance this time, which didn't disrupt her awesome resilience and production of her book. Our son Max, in sharing a cult-like obsession with twentieth-century machines that are now safely located in museums rather than battlefields (as they should be) has sparked an epiphany for another project. To Grace and Max, I dedicate this book for all those other self-referential things that cannot be encapsulated in an acknowledgments page.

Grand Rapids, 2021

A Note on the Text

All English-language translations are the author's own, unless otherwise stated.

Abbreviations

BHStArch, Abt. IV	*Bayrisches Hauptstaatsarchiv, Abteilung IV, Kriegsarchiv* (Bavarian State Archive, IV, War Archive)
BArch	*Bundesarchiv Berlin-Lichterfelde* (Federal Archive, Berlin Lichterfelde)
BArch-MA	*Bundesarchiv-Militärarchiv, Freiburg i.Br.* (Federal Archive-Military Archive, Freiburg)
LBINY	Leo Baeck Institute Archive, New York
OHL	*Oberste Heeresleistung* (Supreme Army Command)
SPD	*Sozialdemokratische Partei Deutschlands* (Social Democratic Party of Germany)
WLS	*Württembergische Landesbibliothek Stuttgart* (Württemberg Regional Library, Stuttgart)
WLS/SZdW	*Württembergische Landesbibliothek, Sondersammlung Zeit der Weltkriege* (Württemberg Regional Library, Special Collection of the World Wars)

Introduction

Volunteering for war in 1914, Wilhelm S. reassured his wife Lisette and their three daughters that he would survive if they all kept up their belief in God. He developed a kind of symbiotic religious relationship with his family, in which they maintained their connections with each other through their mutual faith. After his first experiences with combat on the Eastern Front in November 1914, he intimated, "Was twice in battle, but God had his protective arm over us. Just pray diligently (to comfort you, I'll do it for you too)."[1] However, only a few weeks later, he expressed worry that believing in God was inadequate. In one letter to his wife he oscillated between confidence and insecurity about God's protective capability, until he finally speculated: "You will think that in times of need one recognizes God. This is not the case and I think you have already realized that for quite a while."[2]

After several more months of combat, Wilhelm S. could not understand why God was waiting so long to intervene and stop this catastrophic war. A few days after that first wartime Christmas, he wrote to his wife that God's silence in the face of such carnage was unbearable.[3] He admitted that he was on the brink of a psychological breakdown: "My love, forgive my weakness. As I write this letter here, tears have started to flood … I have the confidence that I have a good wife and children at home, who pray for me, when I imagine this, then I regain courage and the future does not look so bleak. But sometimes the thoughts come and overwhelm me."[4] Wilhelm S. continued to seek resilience in his faith, but the nervous stress and physical deprivations that he encountered were almost too much to bear. He continued asking God for help, but by the summer of 1915 he was so frustrated with God's silence that he could only find comfort in the fact that his comrades were suffering as much as he was:

> We have put up with a lot the last few days. And who knows what we are facing? Indeed, I'd like to be able to endure the tremendous strain (*großen Strapazen*), if only God allows me to tolerate it. I ask him daily many times about it … My legs hurt so much that I can barely stand. But almost everybody is like that. That is the only consolation.[5]

Wilhelm S.'s writing suggested that while he still asked God for help to survive the trauma of war, the certainty he felt when he first mobilized had begun to evaporate. These doubts made him feel embarrassed, and when he confessed his ambivalence in a letter to his wife, he asked her to keep all this confidential: "Please don't give my letters to everyone."[6] However, he still asked his wife to keep taking the children to church so they could pray for him.[7]

The religious language used by Wilhelm S. offers a glimpse into the complex ways in which ordinary individuals narrated psychological trauma in the First World War. The function of faith in assuaging nervous stress and the liminal state in which Wilhelm S. fluctuated between certainty about his prewar beliefs and a sense of uncertainty are central themes of this book. What exactly did religious beliefs do for Wilhelm S. and his family and for other Germans on the combat and home fronts? Wilhelm S.'s letters home exemplify how many individuals used religious language to diagnose the effects of traumatic experiences. They ruminated on the damage that the war would inflict on an aspect of their deeper selves that many struggled to define but were obsessed with—their souls and spirits. Religious language, beliefs, and rituals enabled individuals to share the complex, often contradictory emotions generated by trauma. In turn, trauma, defined here as an experience that damaged belief systems rather than solely a category of medical diagnosis, altered the ways in which individuals perceived religion.

The impact of the war on religious beliefs would fall along a broad spectrum that was ever-changing and difficult to categorize, posing a unique challenge to historians. Using letters, diaries, memoirs, and popular media produced by individuals engulfed in the experience of total war, this book explores the effects of traumatic violence and psychological stress on the religious beliefs of primarily front soldiers in combat, and it also examines civilians suffering from stress on the home front. Inspired not only by trauma studies but also by the history of emotions and the social and cultural history of religion, this book moves away from the history of religious authorities and institutions.[8] It turns the spotlight away from the perspectives of clerics, especially military chaplains and their views on nationalism and the compatibility of killing with Judeo-Christian theology, which has already generated substantial scholarship.[9] Instead, this book concentrates on the history of religion and trauma "from below," focusing on the religiosity of ordinary people, an approach that has only recently generated interest from scholars, especially those studying British and American soldiers, who investigate the degree to which dominant religious ideals actually reflected the views of ordinary individuals.[10] The questions explored in this book include the following: What were the effects of psychological trauma on ordinary Germans' religious beliefs, broadly defined to include Judeo-Christian traditions, popular beliefs, or "superstitions" (*Aberglaube*, or "alternative beliefs" in German) as well as more subjective or hybrid belief systems? How did religious belief function as a language for narrating traumatic experiences? What were some of the "new" belief systems, beyond the framework of preexisting Judeo-Christian and popular beliefs, generated as a result of the collision between human beings and industrialized killing and dying?

The central argument of this book is that religion was the primary prism through which German soldiers in the Great War articulated and processed trauma. More than just a mechanism for coping with traumatic experiences, religious beliefs and language also provided front soldiers a framework for comprehending and explaining the otherwise indescribable universe of the trenches. On one hand, men tried to use religion to achieve a kind of stasis, a continuous act of psychological or emotional rebalancing, to counter the stress of the trench experience. But at the same time, beliefs themselves were not static, as individuals were constantly adapting to brutalizing environments. They embraced new and hybrid ideas to cope with these environments, both physically and emotionally. Belief systems were, as a result of encounters with trauma, in a state of constant flux. Just as the war was, as Benjamin Ziemann observes, a "laboratory for violence,"[11] it was also a laboratory for religion.

Psychological trauma inflicted by modern war allows a glimpse into the "lived religion" of front soldiers as they drew from everyday life to modify their belief systems to make sense of their experiences.[12] As traumatic stress challenged preexisting belief systems, men reached for a psychological toolbox that included a hybrid of ideas stitched together using prewar concepts mixed with images or experiences derived from the combat and home fronts. Many constructed new spiritual-religious language and concepts, utilizing the immediate environment filled with industrialized weapons, death, and surreal scenes of destruction to forge subjective religious structures. In many ways, wartime trauma thus enables us to see how religion is invented.

One of the key functions of religion in war for both soldiers and civilians, as a number of scholars who have focused on religion and everyday life have demonstrated, is that it served as a source of psychological comfort to help cope with stress.[13] However, religion and popular beliefs, I argue, were not always a source of comfort. The beliefs that individuals brought into the war experience could also generate tremendous anxiety. What did men, as well as women, do when preexisting, traditional belief systems were no longer adequate for coping with mass death? Protestant, Catholic, and Jewish religious leaders asserted that traditional beliefs were still useful in modern industrialized war, if not as a means to fully explain God's mysterious plan, then at least as a coping mechanism. To a degree, the stress of total war did reinforce religious faith, and ordinary men and women continued to see religion as a useful tool for coping with a frightening, if inexplicable, world. However, front soldiers in particular modified beliefs and rituals to serve more diverse functions. Beyond helping men to cope with trauma, religious language and beliefs also became the lens through which front soldiers narrated concepts of psychological renewal, rebirth, or transformation. Religious concepts enabled men at war, as well their wives, girlfriends, and mothers at home, to envision new internal or external worlds that would replace the shattered physical and psychological landscape that overwhelmed them.

The focus here is on the experiences of front soldiers and the traumatic effects of the trench experience. But their experiences were of course not isolated, and this book examines the interactions between front soldiers and civilians. Religious beliefs, whether drawn from prevailing institutions or more subjectively forged, were often reinforced and constructed in symbiotic relationships, communicated through letters, with civilians on the home front, who were also trying to cope with the effects of loss, anxiety, separation, and physical deprivation.[14] Religious language enabled soldiers and civilians on the two fronts to build a spiritual-psychological bridge between their separate spheres, generate mutual emotional support, and integrate imagined spaces between the combat front and the *Heimat* (homeland). Religious concepts and language also gave front soldiers a means for expressing love and compassion, the "feminine" characteristics that men had to incorporate into their front experience to help deal with stress.[15]

Soldiers and civilians converged as they sought mutual emotional support, but they also diverged as their disparate experiences shaped their perceptions in distinct ways. In exchanges of letters between the two fronts, men often claimed that the intensity of violence on the combat front had a more dramatic impact on their religious beliefs, one that loved ones at home might not necessarily understand. After the war, men would remember their own experiences and sacrifices as exceptional and privileged, pushing women back into traditional roles as mothers and housewives.[16] This narrative was already emerging during the war in letters home, in which men constructed the idea that they endured a psychologically and spiritually extraordinary front experience. At the same time, letters, diaries, and memoirs by women reveal religious responses to trauma that were similar to narratives written by men at the combat front. In particular, women recounted how, as a result of the loss of their loved ones, their prewar religious beliefs were reinforced, challenged, or even collapsed, in ways that mirror men's experiences.[17] While men often saw their religious trauma as distinct, the difficulties women faced in explaining suffering through the lens of prewar religious beliefs suggest that, as historians have found in other sectors of society shattered by total war, the boundaries between home and combat fronts were often blurred.[18]

This book does not claim to be an exhaustive study of the content of religious beliefs during the First World War. There are simply too many strands of thought, including complex debates among Christian theologians about the impact of the war, the proliferation of "superstition" or popular beliefs, as well as experimentation with spiritualism.[19] In Germany, the war experience would stimulate increased fascination with pagan mythology, especially Nordic culture, as well as interest in a curious mixture of supernatural and occult rituals and beliefs that would have a lasting influence on political movements, including National Socialism, as historian Eric Kurlander has recently investigated.[20] Instead of examining the content of these diverse systems of thought, this book concentrates on the function of religion for individuals under extreme stress. This introduction will suggest paths for historians to explore the religious imaginations of ordinary individuals, and it will propose approaches to the diverse ways in which traumatic experiences impacted the beliefs and emotions of soldiers and civilians in the First World War.

Uncovering Religious Imaginations at the Front

For social and cultural historians, reconstructing the religious imagination of ordinary people poses immense challenges, yet it also offers the possibility of uncovering what individuals considered to be the most important and meaningful concepts that defined their lives. As Jay Winter has suggested, the religious beliefs of soldiers and civilians, one of the most crucial dimensions of the war experience, are still relatively unexplored by historians.[21] This book uses an empirical approach, focusing on the voices of front soldiers, and to some extent also civilians, to uncover the varieties of religious beliefs and practices conveyed through their letters, diaries, memoirs, and front newspapers.

This is extremely difficult to reconstruct. Language used to formulate memories of trauma is diverse, subjective, and mediated through varied social and cultural contexts, requiring historians to be sensitive to the different forms of language in which narratives are constructed.[22] Further, language, along with symbols and images, is the primary portal into the psychological landscape of historical subjects, but the degree to which language reflects religious thinking is limited.[23] This is a problem that has been recognized by gender historians who deal with tensions or inconsistencies between language and practice,[24] and in the case of religion, the problem is exacerbated when even historical subjects admit that language falls short in encapsulating their perceptions and experiences regarding spirituality.

Sources that provide a glimpse into the spiritual universe of front soldiers as well as that of civilians are also challenging because their backgrounds and beliefs fall across such a broad spectrum. At the outbreak of the war, nearly 60 percent of Germans identified as Protestant (mostly Lutheran and Calvinist backgrounds). Nearly 40 percent identified as Catholic, and just under 1 percent of Germans came from Jewish backgrounds.[25] Unfortunately, archival files of letters[26] from the front (*Feldpostbriefe*) rarely provide information about the religious background of individuals, though this can often be inferred from their letters, making it difficult to reconstruct the context behind narratives of religious crisis experienced at the front. Further, there are significant demographic limitations to available letters and diaries produced by front soldiers, which have been recognized by social and cultural historians.[27] Examples of letters from working-class men and women, the majority of German society, can be found in archive collections, but most available letters were written by officers from the middle class, many of whom had some university education. In addition, the letters available in archives often include only one side of the conversation. We find individuals unburdening their conscience, which offers intriguing possibilities for analysis, but letters of response are usually missing, and collections have possibly been edited by families who submitted them.[28] Another potential limitation that needs to be considered is military censorship, as the Supreme Army Command (*Oberste Heeresleistung*, OHL) officially reviewed correspondence. However, the OHL had to deal with an average 6.8 million letters sent every day between soldiers and civilians on the Western and Eastern Fronts. With only 8,000 censorship officials, much got through the post without being reviewed.[29] Men and women were thus surprisingly candid about their religious perceptions, and their letters included criticism of chaplains, irreverence toward religious institutions, and disillusionment with hegemonic religious ideals.

Despite potential challenges with letters from the front, these sources nevertheless provide a remarkable snapshot into how their writers constructed religious beliefs and emotions. War diaries (*Kriegstagebücher*) tended to concentrate on logistics, though as we will see there were some instances where men and women felt more comfortable sharing with their diaries than with their loved ones. Letters, in many cases, contained more emotional intimacy.[30] Letters from the front were often written under artillery and machine gun fire, and they thus provide a raw glimpse into soldiers' complex and contradictory emotional reactions to traumatic violence and the impact of stress on their religious beliefs.[31] In these cases, men sometimes poured their emotions and religious feelings out on the page with little analysis, in self-referential style, and without any intention to publish after the war. Letters written after their encounters with violence, often after men were rotated behind the lines or in hospitals, also provide insight into how individuals used religious language to process trauma and ruminate on the meaning of their beliefs. In many ways, correspondence allowed performance of self, as soldiers assured loved ones that they adhered to prevailing masculine and religious norms. At the same time, men saw their loved ones at home as a kind of safe zone for confessing feelings and intimate psychological transformations that were difficult to encapsulate into words. As Michael Roper demonstrated in his study of emotions shared between British soldiers and their wives and mothers, letter writing was an essential part of the relationships in which men and women, traumatized by mass violence, provided each other with emotional support, as they confessed how the war affected them.[32] German front soldiers were thus comparable to their counterparts on the other side of the trenches in how they related to their wives, mothers, and children on the home front.

Religious beliefs, rituals, and attitudes in the imperial German army can also be analyzed through front newspapers, which were widely distributed to soldiers on both the Western and Eastern Fronts.[33] These front newspapers have been closely studied for the insights they provide into a number of aspects of soldiers' daily lives, including motivations for fighting, perceptions of the enemy and civilians in occupied territories (including racial views of "the other"), views of the home front, and constructions of gender roles.[34] However, the topic of religion, which was discussed in articles and visual media in virtually every issue of front newspapers, has so far been largely underexplored. Front newspapers were diverse and reflected different perceptions depending on who produced them. The largest in terms of circulation were the army newspapers (*Armeezeitungen*), which included among others the *Kriegszeitung der 4. Armee* (the *War Newspaper of the Fourth Army*) and the *Liller Kriegszeitung* (*War Newspaper of Lille*). These were produced at the army corps and at a divisional level, and around 80,000 copies were circulated in editions produced several times per month.[35] These army newspapers published articles mostly by officers and also pieces by civilians, including pastors and theologians, who disseminated religious ideals, as well as dominant ideals of masculinity, heroism, and sacrifice. Though they were less widely circulated, the trench newspapers (*Schützengrabenzeitungen*), which were produced at the regimental and company level and edited by enlisted men and noncommissioned officers, were more dissonant and irreverent.[36] The military imposed censorship on army and trench newspapers, but control was not aggressive, and they contained rather candid descriptions of the traumatic effects of the war, including the religious crises of individuals coping with violence and psychological stress.

It is perhaps impossible to reconstruct exactly what individuals "believed." But from letters, diaries, and soldiers' media, it is possible to delineate how soldiers and civilians perceived religious beliefs that were part of their cultural toolbox. Studying expressions of religious belief in war inevitably leads to the crucial question: how do we define religion? From an historical perspective, scholars working on early modern European society have offered some of the most careful definitions of religion, which can also be applied to a modern framework, including Protestant, Catholic, and Jewish cultures in the First World War. Historian Keith Thomas, focusing on early modern British culture, argues that in addition to being a set of beliefs and practices, religion is a source for providing explanation, moral injunctions, social order, and the promise of immortality. Religion, according to Thomas, is also used for "the prospect of a supernatural means of control over man's earthly environment."[37] Within the context of monotheistic Judeo-Christian cultures, an important part of religion is the assumption that God, an all-powerful supernatural creator of the universe, can be influenced by prayer or rituals. These represent the essential form of communication between humans and the Supreme Being that are developed to ensure psychological stability and self-preservation.[38] Even into the twentieth century, this was a crucial element in the lives of a majority of soldiers and civilians who struggled to cope with the trauma of total war. Men and women desperately sought to exert some level of agency in their chaotic lives through communication with a supernatural being who they hoped could intercede in and alter the escalating physical and psychological destruction that surrounded them.

Considering the challenges of dealing with language and the meaning of belief systems, it is useful to consider anthropological approaches, which help illuminate historical analysis. As Clifford Geertz has argued, religion is not just a set of rituals, sacred texts, hierarchies, and normative dogmas. Religion is also a complex set of beliefs and behaviors with specific cultural functions and structural relationships.[39] These complex cognitive domains are most often translated into written sources, art and literature, and such media can reinforce and give justification to social and cultural institutions, or function as sites of dissonance that represent tension between cultural elites and laypersons.[40] In looking at diverse expressions of religiosity, anthropologists have highlighted the malleability of religion, which gets modified and retooled when existing beliefs prove inadequate in the face of changing conditions. In many cases, rather than an erosion or reinforcement of traditional beliefs, trauma causes individuals to revitalize belief systems with new rituals or ways of seeing.[41] The traumatic environments produced by the Great War dramatically illustrate the fluctuating nature of religiosity that has been analyzed by anthropologists. Extraordinary psychological pressures and physical deprivation drove many front soldiers to alter their religious culture, in terms of content, paraphernalia, and norms. Soldiers' writings, the symbols they employed, and the rituals they modified or freshly constructed, reveal the flexible or resilient character of religious belief, which individuals would replenish or adapt when hegemonic or traditional ideals eroded. As Michael Snape found in the case of British soldiers, men responded to stress by developing a much more "diffusive," nondogmatic, and utilitarian approach to Christian beliefs,[42] especially when preexisting institutions, rituals, or beliefs seemed ineffective. This can also be seen in the case of German soldiers who adopted a nimble or flexible approach to religion.

As cultural historians influenced by anthropology and sociology have shown, the concept of "God" is in many ways a reflection of the cultural environment, used to reinforce social hierarchies and power agendas.[43] That is certainly the case for power elites, including military and religious authorities in the early twentieth century, who weaponized religion to bolster nationalism and instill conformity behind the social, political, and economic status quo.[44] However, while religious beliefs were weaponized, modern weapons had uncontrollable effects on religion, breaking down feelings of obligation to authorities and connections to prevailing structures. Thus, looking at the function of religion for ordinary people on the front lines of war, the focus shifts away from its role in reinforcing power of the nation and authorities to its role in finding psychological homeostasis or stability for traumatized individuals. Under stress, religion became primarily a language for describing existential crisis, resilience, psychological and physical suffering, the effects of violence, and the breakdown or fragmentation of the self. As sociologists have emphasized, religion's promise of salvation, transcendence, or comfort, and thus an ultimate escape from the horrors of earthly existence, including oppressive power hierarchies and violence, is perhaps one of its most powerful attractions.[45]

Historians and anthropologists have recently collaborated in interesting ways to explore the effects of trauma on individual identity. In their interdisciplinary study of neurophysiological responses to trauma in the First World War, historian Stefanos Geroulanos and anthropologist Todd Meyers argue that in both physical and psychological terms, "individuality—and indeed, individuals' very corporeality, their wholeness—was almost certainly collapsing."[46] This can also be applied to an analysis of traumatized religious beliefs, where the individual sense of self, the whole spiritual identity and belief system of front soldiers, became fragmented or disintegrated. Traumatized men struggled with language to describe these feelings of disintegration, which they often articulated as a "spiritual" experience, requiring reconstruction of their sense of self or meaning using available psychological tools drawn from their prewar structures and the environment of the trenches.

Violence splintered religious beliefs as well as bodies and minds. Industrialized weaponry, explosions, mud, and corpses invaded and took hold of the mental universe, and religious beliefs, of front soldiers, who blended together imagery from the front environment with the language of prewar religious orthodoxies to explain, or at least describe, their powerful emotions and experiences. In response to violence, deprivation, and stress, men and women experimented with diverse systems of thought. This could involve utilizing preexisting popular beliefs or "superstition," which included a wide range of devices and rituals like numerology, talismans, amulets, charms, and other objects. Men dabbled with iconography borrowed from outside Judeo-Christian mythology. They played with images of the Valkyrie and Norse goddesses, which allowed them to incorporate an element of the feminine into their psychological-religious landscape. Fascination with spiritualism, magic, ghosts, and the occult also proliferated. In many ways, the stress of modern war, as historian Owen Davies recently demonstrated, stimulated even greater interest in "premodern" popular beliefs. Religion, magic, and science mingled as soldiers and civilians eagerly sought both "traditional and novel ways of coping with the realities of warfare."[47] The hybridization of Judeo-Christian and popular beliefs would become a crucial part of the arsenal used by soldiers and civilians who developed rituals to help them imagine some semblance of control over an increasingly unbearable reality.

Perhaps most interestingly, one sees that in the case of front soldiers in particular who struggled with a chaotic environment in which existing belief systems seemed inadequate or ineffective, men constructed entirely new belief systems. Historian Patrick Houlihan recently suggested that scholars need to further explore and uncover this dimension of thinking.[48] This is one of the most exciting spheres of religious beliefs that emerges from soldiers' letters and diaries, where they generated from their immediate environment, especially their close psychological relationships with comrades, as well as their encounters with weapons and death, belief systems that were not directly related to preexisting Judeo-Christian or popular traditions. Front soldiers were convinced that war gave them new insights and metaphysical knowledge. These were often loose, self-referential, and undogmatic sets of beliefs that were malleable and adaptable. Such subjectively constructed spiritual universes helped to not only reassure fragile minds and crumbling psyches in the chaos of the front experience, but they also became the basis for individuals to mentally rebuild themselves and explain how they were spiritually transformed or reborn by the trauma of war.

Religion, Emotions, and Psychological Trauma

Religious experiences shed greater light on the complexities of psychological trauma in war. In a recent afterword to her seminal work, *Unclaimed Experience: Trauma, Narrative and History*, Cathy Caruth called on scholars to develop more innovative approaches to uncover more subjective ways in which individuals narrate psychological trauma.[49] In response, scholars are moving trauma scholarship forward by seeking new approaches to trauma narratives that are often hidden from state, medical, and political spheres of diagnosis, where categories like "shell shock," "war hysteria," and later "posttraumatic stress disorder" (PTSD) were used to define mental trauma.[50] Religious language reveals more subjective expressions of trauma and the ways in which trauma was described and self-treated by individuals and families outside medical spheres. The shift in focus to more subjective ways in which trauma is communicated, especially through the lens of religion, also highlights the problematic concepts of "cultural trauma" or "collective trauma," which have come under fire from scholars for concealing more complex individual experiences with violence that are shaped by diverse cultural contexts.[51] It is important to avoid overgeneralizing about a collective "religious trauma." There was no singular "religious crisis." Rather, individual narratives require more nuanced approaches that listen to the diverse ways in which trauma impacted religious beliefs and perceptions.[52]

Traumatic experiences caused individuals to be in a constant state of emotional instability, with historical subjects often struggling to categorize or concretely articulate their contradictory, ever-changing feelings.[53] Trauma was often so overwhelming that individuals relied on religious metaphors or indirect references to describe their emotions. In the act of narrating experiences, religion thus became a means for self-therapy, which helped men and women to psychologically regroup. This self-therapy was practiced through the act of writing itself, which enabled individuals to reclaim a sense of psychological balance as they processed the meaning of their experiences through the prism of religion, often seeking advice from families at home who bolstered their psyches with familiar, reassuring religious concepts.[54] Writing home thus gave front soldiers several therapeutic paths, including a return to a core sense of (prewar) identity; a reminder of childhood stability, rituals, and authority, which could provide a sense of security; a pause from other more disturbing states of mind; and a chance to reorder thoughts and perceptions, or restructure new observations and understanding. Writing about religion also provided men a language for expressing their emotions. Similar to how shell shock (or "war hysteria" as it was categorized by German doctors) was, as historian Elaine Showalter argued, an outlet for men to express otherwise repressed or socially unacceptable emotions,[55] religion also gave traumatized men a language for venting allegedly "feminine" feelings like anxiety, fear, love, and vulnerability.

Religious language enabled men and women to confront physical and psychological pain, but it had limitations. In the Christian traditions in which most Germans were raised before the war, pain was widely constructed as a reminder of the need to cleanse the soul of sin in order to prepare for the afterlife. Pastors and priests thus preached the idea that pain was spiritually necessary.[56] Children from both Protestant and Catholic backgrounds who would become part of the 1914 generation were socialized with this idea that pain would bring them closer to Christ, helping them to understand his suffering and respect his sacrifice. Front soldiers, especially early in the war, often carried this thinking into the trenches and interpreted their first encounters with trauma as a "gift" that opened their eyes to God's blessings.[57] However, such prewar religious interpretations of pain collided dramatically with the sheer scope of suffering encountered in the war. Soldiers dealing with the physical and psychological effects of violence, and women at home coping with loss and anxiety, asked the fundamental questions: what was God's purpose in creating a world with so much cruelty and pain? Why did God not intervene to stop the carnage? Many struggled with these questions and could not find an answer. Front soldiers in particular sought religious and spiritual mechanisms and beliefs outside the boundaries prescribed by prewar authorities. Their lived environment, advice from comrades, and subjective feelings triggered by traumatic experiences seemed more reliable or authentic to them as they tried to find meaning and explanation for pain. Many began to trust their experiences rather than pre-inscribed assumptions, making them willing to experiment with alternative ways of thinking or being religious.

Emotional responses to pain, especially the psychological mechanisms for coping, have been a central part of historiography dealing with the religious feelings of ordinary soldiers and civilians. This can be seen in one of the first major works to look at religion in the wake of the cultural turn in First World War Studies in the late 1990s, Annette Becker's *War and Faith: The Religious Imagination in France, 1914–1930*, which examined how religion motivated men and women to both sacrifice and endure suffering as the war bogged down into industrialized slaughter.[58] More recently, in his essential work on the resilience of front soldiers, Alexander Watson points to religion as a crucial factor in providing men a sense of hope for survival, which enabled them to face day-to-day stress. Belief in an omnipotent God allowed men to relinquish a sense of responsibility, and in turn resign themselves to their fate, as they imagined a Supreme Being who would either protect or abandon them, or decide whether they would live or die.[59] Soldiers could derive feelings of control, Watson argues, from a wide range of rituals, devices, and beliefs, whether originating from Christian or popular religious traditions, which gave them a sense of order in an otherwise incomprehensible environment.[60]

In his definitive study of Catholicism in Germany and Austria–Hungary during the Great War, which deftly integrates both an institutional history of the church at war as well as insightful analysis of the importance of religious belief for ordinary men and women, Patrick Houlihan also stresses the centrality of religion as a tool for psychological resilience. Houlihan challenges prevailing assumptions that the war broke down religious faith. He persuasively argues that the war actually reinforced traditional beliefs, as many Catholics fell back on their religious traditions and rituals, which he observes were more effective than Protestant traditions in helping men and women cope with varieties of pain and survive the war.[61] Houlihan's work is inspiring because he acknowledges there was a wide range of religious responses to the war and he tackles a wealth of letters by soldiers and civilians to uncover what he describes as a broad spectrum of perceptions of and experiences with Catholic faith.[62] At the same time, Houlihan also makes a crucial observation for any scholar trying to take on the daunting challenge of reconstructing the complexity of religious beliefs as a means of coping with stress: "[a] focus on religion and everyday life will inevitably fall short of any adequate representation of personal religiosity."[63]

Acknowledging how these historians have been instrumental in carving a path for scholars to approach the religiosity of ordinary people, I propose that it is possible to move the conversation forward in at least two significant ways. First, historians would benefit from moving beyond the bifurcated question of whether the war "broke down" or "reinforced" prewar religious beliefs. Instead, ego documents reveal the complicated ways in which war transformed religiosity. Even psychologists during the war insisted that religious beliefs had to be much more carefully deconstructed. Those who kept their faith in God often did so in a way that was increasingly detached from existing authorities, structures, and dogmas, where individuals constructed subjective connections to God based on their own interpretations of personal experiences. In turn, many who become disillusioned did not necessarily "lose" religion, but rather retooled, modified, or completely reconstructed belief systems with their own rituals and devices that more effectively reflected their immediate psychological needs in response to extreme stress.

Second, much of the scholarship on religion and soldiers' resilience focuses on men as passive victims trying to survive unimaginable violence. As historians Stéphane Audoin-Rouzeau and Annette Becker warned, this offers only one dimension into the daily life of front soldiers.[64] There is a more difficult question that also needs to be explored: what role did religion play in justifying and motivating the act of killing? This is challenging because front soldiers rarely confronted this directly, though historians like Joanna Bourke and Benjamin Ziemann have brilliantly found ways to approach narratives of violence that reveal how men became fascinated with, and even addicted to, the act of killing.[65] Beyond motivating men to rationalize killing within the context of state-sanctioned violence combined with the notion of a "holy war" or "crusade,"[66] religion also played a role in giving men a language to describe the ways in which they became enamored of violence. The act of killing produced complex psychological effects that included the worship of violence, as men celebrated their roles as perpetrators and even reveled in the experience of trauma as a spiritually purifying event.[67] Most famously, veterans like Ernst Jünger would construct themselves as "new men" with quasi-supernatural capabilities who, instead of being passive victims of violence and industrialized technology, cultivated a sense of power over it as they internalized war as a kind of quasi-religious experience in itself.[68]

Recent approaches by psychologists provide a path for empirical historians to expand their analysis of trauma and religion beyond paradigms generated so far by historians. Ursula Wirtz, a clinical psychologist, argues that there are multifaceted responses to trauma, in which religious beliefs and language play a central role, which still need to be explored. This includes looking at the ways in which trauma alters how individuals perceive their own psyches, imagination, and consciousness. For example, by producing a shock moment, trauma severs ties between the individual and preexisting beliefs. In shattering one's belief systems, trauma thus sparks what Wirtz, influenced by Jungian ideas about self-actualization and expansion of consciousness, characterizes as a "spiritual transformation." Because of the "elastic" nature of identity and the "fluid character of the psyche," the traumatized individual goes through a process in which they turn the experience of death and destruction into a kind of psychological and spiritual breakthrough.[69] This process can be found in letters and diaries of front soldiers who would sometimes characterize trauma as liberating. Men would narrate violence as an experience that gave them a deeper understanding of the world, and they portrayed themselves as transformed by their new awareness of their minds and conception of reality. Such trauma narratives can be found in postwar memoirs of veterans from diverse backgrounds and cultural-political orientations, including left-wing veterans like Ernst Toller, as well as right-wing veterans like Ernst Jünger. Though they would use their experiences and memories of the war to fuel opposing agendas in the fragmented sociopolitical landscape of the Weimar Republic, both narrated what they described as a profound spiritual experience in which trauma, whether victimizing or ennobling, transformed their sense of self and their worldviews. Though famous figures like Toller and Jünger suggested a "road to Damascus" level of certainty and fervor, most individuals who survived the war described a psychological and emotional zone that reflected a much greater sense of flux.

Finally, studying the religious experiences of ordinary soldiers and civilians pushes us to expand how we conceptualize trauma in war. "Trauma" involves not only injury to the body and the psyche but also wounded belief systems. This has been addressed recently by psychologists dealing with "moral injury," especially in the treatment of veterans returning from Vietnam, and, more recently, Iraq and Afghanistan. Moral injury occurs when soldiers are traumatized by their own actions that transgress their religious values and conception of a moral universe. It can result in feelings of betrayal, whether from the realization that one's government is waging an immoral war, or a sense of betrayal stemming from the break one feels with one's self for the "sin" of transgressing moral norms.[70] Evidence of this form of psychological injury can also be seen in the letters and diaries of soldiers from 1914 to 1918. While religion was quite effective in mobilizing men to rationalize the act of killing, the tension between wartime behavior and Christian moral precepts could also generate tremendous anxiety. Men wrote about their fears that the war had betrayed God's laws. This was a central trauma for many as the war experience triggered questions about their own responsibility in the breakdown of moral structures, fear over what the war revealed about their essential nature, and anxiety over God's existence. Religion could help numb the pain caused by trauma and suffering, but traumatic experiences also inflicted wounds on faith that could not be healed.

Organization

This book explores the myriad religious responses to trauma and how, following a loosely chronological approach over the course of the war, religious beliefs were reinforced, modified, or reconfigured. Chapter 1 focuses on collaboration between military and religious authorities at the outbreak of the war to build an ideal warrior. The central argument of this chapter is that authorities considered religion essential to managing the emotions and behavior of soldiers and civilians, especially Germans' willingness to subsume their own sense of self into the collective, national project of war. Chapter 2 shifts away from the history "from above" to focus on how ordinary men and women in the early stages of the war perceived the religious ideals prescribed during the "spirit of 1914." This chapter argues that hegemonic religious ideals had only limited appeal, especially after front soldiers began to encounter traumatic violence. Nationalism conflated with religion permeated narratives, but letters and diaries reveal much more complicated layers and functions of religious belief.

Chapter 3 uncovers how language about God and nerves was ubiquitous in letters and diaries, where men and women ruminated on the unbearable psychological effects of total war. Front soldiers in particular integrated the language of "nerves" with the language of religion using religious concepts to combat the psychological crisis caused by modern war. This chapter looks at how soldiers defined concepts like "*Geist*" ("mind" or "spirit") and "*Seele*" ("psyche" or "soul"), which had dual meanings that were perceived differently by lay persons versus medical professionals. There was a broad spectrum of religious responses to traumatic stress, and Chapter 4 uses case studies to dissect the wide-ranging impact of war on individual belief systems. Religious responses to trauma do not fit into clear categories, as individuals rarely identified themselves as belonging to a particular group (e.g., as "agnostic" or "atheist"). Rather, letters and diaries focus on often contradictory emotions triggered by the collision between traumatic violence and religious beliefs.

Chapter 5 turns to contemporary psychologists and other secular scholars and their theories on the impact of the war on religious beliefs. Soldiers' beliefs were extremely complex and constantly changing, psychologists argued, as men occupied a kind of unique, liminal state in which they oscillated between faith, cynicism, and irreverence, reflecting their constantly changing emotions, environments, and experiences at the front. Struggling in this twilight psychological dimension, men at the front developed ad hoc explanations, solutions, or distractions that met their immediate psychological and emotional needs under stress. Chapter 6 argues that these hybrid or "alternative" systems of thought were not just an opiate against stress. They were also an attempt to construct a different imagined reality out of the surreal environment of the trenches.

Beyond reinforcing or eroding traditional religious and popular beliefs, modern war was producing "something else" entirely.

Chapter 7 examines these subjective beliefs that departed from preexisting Judeo-Christian and popular belief systems. Weapons, death experiences, comradeship, and war itself became objects of worship. Exploring these subjective spiritual worlds is enlightening because they offer a glimpse into how religion itself is generated, as material and experiential support systems from the trench environment were forged into an elaborate *cultus*. Though the focus of this book is on the period 1914–18, it contains an epilogue that examines the diverse ways in which religious belief shaped encounters with defeat and revolution. While many perceived Germany's catastrophe, and escalating political radicalism, through the same religious lens through which they processed the trauma of the war, four years of industrialized slaughter had profoundly altered the ways in which many Germans perceived God and spirituality.

1

"*Gott mit Uns*": Hegemonic Religious Ideals, Emotions, and Mobilizing for War

Writing for the army newspaper *Liller Kriegszeitung* in October 1914, noncommissioned officer (*Unteroffizier*) and theology student Georg Guertler argued that the weapons of war were not the only important instrument in the nation's arsenal. Faith in God enabled Germany's ultimate victory:

> Yes, not only our weapons, but also the old belief in God, deeply rooted in the German people, has made a triumphant march through all German lands. All of them. Those who were otherwise estranged from church now fill the churches. Crisis teaches you to pray (*Not lehrt beten*) ... Like a man, all of Germany has risen, and a unified Germany has found its way back to the one true God.[1]

Guertler celebrated prayer as the foundation for not only personal religious renewal but also a collective national awakening, giving both men and women the strength to fight and sacrifice for their fatherland. Focusing on men streaming to the front lines, Guertler gave anecdotes about soldiers facing fire and experiencing a "fresh new religious life," articulated through prayer, which was their natural inclination to ease their fear of death. Ecstatic that soldiers would turn pious, he repeated several times the popular cliché that "crisis teaches you to pray" (*Not lehrt beten*, the German equivalent of the Anglo-American proverb, "there are no atheists in foxholes").[2]

Like Georg Guertler, many theologians and laypersons welcomed a short and decisive war that would stimulate religious conviction and bolster patriotism.[3] Seemingly grateful for a crisis that would shore up belief in God, religious leaders eagerly tried to demonstrate the usefulness of faith as a weapon of war. Protestant and Catholic leaders writing for army newspapers saw the outbreak of the war as the opportunity to cement their devotion to nationalist aims by equating soldierly ideals with Christian virtues of self-sacrifice, discipline, and devotion to a larger cause.[4] They emphasized faith in God as the foundation for the nation's victory. In turn, military authorities were eager to harness Christianity as an instrument for managing the emotions, resilience, and fighting resolve of front soldiers and civilians. These efforts to manage soldiers' emotions through religious faith are the focus of this chapter. How did authorities use religion to try to control the spiritual and psychological health of German soldiers and civilians?

The central argument of this chapter is that military and clerical authorities collaborated to weaponize religion as an indispensable tool for reinforcing ideals of masculine discipline and sacrifice for soldiers. Religion was also utilized to prescribe women's roles, which were to provide loyalty and emotional support from the home front. Religious leaders pointed to faith, and in particular the belief in an afterlife, as a key tool in the psychological arsenal of both soldiers and civilians to counteract anxiety caused by separation as well as apprehension about the looming danger of combat and possible death. In addition to helping men deal with anxiety over the possibility of getting killed, religious concepts were also employed to help manage ambivalence over the act of killing. However, by the end of 1914, military and religious leaders had already begun to recognize some emerging tensions: to what degree was prayer a path for national victory or primarily a tool for personal psychological survival? Did hatred of the enemy and the act of killing that was central to the war experience contradict Christian ideals? Despite the potential dissonance, religious authorities assured soldiers and their loved ones at home that wartime violence and nationalized hatred were perfectly compatible with Christianity and that these factors did not threaten the purity of the soul (*Seele*) or spirit (*Geist*).

The tactics used to weaponize religion can be analyzed in three key sites where religious concepts and language were used by officers, military chaplains, and civilian clergy to manage frontline emotions. First, mass media for soldiers and civilians was an important platform where military and church leaders attempted to merge Christian ideals of loyalty, redemption, and sacrifice with nationalism. Civilian newspapers, publications by Protestant and Catholic congregations, army newspapers and other popular media promoted religious faith as an ideal psychological and emotional tool for "holding through" the rigors of modern war. Second, military and religious authorities used popular media to emphasize that the warrior image not only conformed to Christian ideals but also that the front soldier was most effective when he was devoted to his religious faith. Real men were good Christians, the military insisted, conflating masculine soldierly ideals of emotional discipline and comradeship with Christian prescriptions for manhood, which mirrored feminine ideals of religiosity and emotional support maintained on the home front.[5] Finally, the military collaborated with Protestant, Catholic, and Jewish leaders to provide worship services that were seen as critical to the psychological health of soldiers at the front. Organized just behind the lines, these services were geared to bolster resilience, reinforce continuity between prewar life and the front experience, as well as to build spiritual bridges between the combat front and home fronts. Through these services, military chaplains tried to manage soldiers' psyches and emotions, which were seen as vulnerable because men were in a fragile psychological zone between home and the front, separated from loved ones and preparing for combat. Soldiers' spiritual lives, and in turn fighting fitness, were now considered a priority and placed under military supervision.

Exploring sources "from above," especially media directed at front soldiers, this chapter focuses on hegemonic religious ideals constructed by military and religious authorities as they tried to mobilize the minds of German men and women. The solidification of these ideals represented an attempt to centralize and control spiritual life, and to create a monolithic image of the German soldier's spirit or mind (*Geist*, the most frequently used term, means "spirit" and "mind" in German, depending on the context). As will be touched upon here, and explored in greater depth in subsequent chapters, the responses of ordinary soldiers and civilians to these officially sanctioned ideals were much more complex and diverse than dominant prescriptions would suggest.

Forging Christian Soldiers: Weaponizing God and "Holding Through"

As with so many sectors of German society transformed by total war, religion became increasingly militarized.[6] Similar to other nations at war, German military and religious authorities collaborated to mobilize minds and provide a bulwark for coping with traumatic violence.[7] Military officers, chaplains, and pastors contributed to popular media and merged together nationalistic and religious ideals of loyalty, redemption, and sacrifice. Historian Phillip Jenkins, in his analysis of religious institutions and their responses to the war, argues that Germany was exceptional in the degree to which it militarized religion, as Protestant clergy in particular, compared to England and France, were enthusiastic in characterizing the war as God's will, and they actively spearheaded a form of patriotic fervor that was tinged with religious language.[8] The Catholic clergy, though it had a more tense relationship with the state stemming from decades of discrimination against Catholics as second-class citizens, also largely supported mobilization and the notion of a "just war" in an effort to demonstrate national loyalty.[9] The merging of religious faith and nationalism is epitomized in the ubiquitous slogan "God is on our side" or "God is with us" (*Gott mit Uns*), which was a centerpiece of sermons throughout Germany.[10] One of the most popular forms of mass media that fused faith in God with faith in the nation included postcards. The message "God is on our side" was frequently delivered through the German mail system (see Figure 1.1). The well-known slogan, along with the emperor's crown, also appeared on each German soldier's belt buckle.

Militarized religious ideals were defined and celebrated in one of the most popular forms of media consumed by soldiers, army newspapers, of which there were various examples, including the *Kriegszeitung der 4. Armee* (*War Newspaper of the 4th Army*) and the *Liller Kriegszeitung* (*War Newspaper of Lille*), which circulated in total around 80,000 copies in editions produced several times a month.[11] Army newspapers published articles, cartoons, and poems mainly by officers and military chaplains, but they also included contributions by a mix of civilians, including pastors and theologians.[12] Christian faith was a central topic in these newspapers, and authors of articles carefully prescribed the relationship they imagined between front soldiers and God. The Kaiser modeled this relationship, writers emphasized, but it could be emulated by ordinary men, with faith in God providing a spiritual connection that bound the emperor to his loyal soldiers. The *Liller Kriegszeitung*, which was published by Paul Oskar Hoecker, a professional editor and popular publisher who served as a captain in the imperial

Figure 1.1 *"Gott mit Uns—1914"* ("God is on our side—1914"), 1914. Postcard, personal collection of the author.

army, proclaimed in numerous articles that there was a symbiotic and hierarchical relationship between God, the Kaiser, and the front soldier, which provided the nation with strength essential to victory. One article from 1915 emphasizes the unique relationship between God and the Kaiser, and in turn the German nation:

> God, who is always on lonely watch with our emperor, finds him again in storms, death and wounds, and prays with his emperor and for him. The God of the Germans (*Der Gott der Deutschen*) continues to give the emperor strength to care for his army and his people. He blesses him and gives him a long life, and gives our country victory and honor.[13]

"The God of the Germans" is portrayed as a supreme ally of "his Kaiser," as both stand watch for each other and the nation. Numerous clerics celebrated what they called the "German God" and characterized German culture as the soul of Christianity.[14] The *Kriegszeitung der 4. Armee* also celebrated God's specific love for the Kaiser. Poems in the army newspaper reassured Germans that they had nothing to fear because "God is with our Kaiser, and with you."[15]

This idea that God favored Germans was pervasive in army newspapers. Editors for the *Liller Kriegszeitung* conceded that the notion that God took the side of a particular nation might not stand up under the scrutiny of Christian faith, but it fulfilled what Germans desired to believe. In a preface by Paul Oskar Hoecker to the 1915 edition of the *Liller Kriegszeitung*, he wrote that, "lawyers should focus on criminal matters and war-time law (*Kriegsrecht*), but it is up to the front chaplains to speak about He who is with us, because the old God is still alive, and he does not abandon Germans and their struggle for the cause."[16] God's preference for German victory was a bit of a self-fulfilling prophecy. One pastor wrote that men could be reassured that God would "bless our weapons on the battlefield" as long as front soldiers prayed hard enough. Field chaplain August Jaeger promised that if men followed prescribed prayers for victory, God would then also send his angel of peace.[17]

Chaplains and military leaders were confident that if front soldiers, as well as civilians at home, displayed the prescribed faith and piety, Germany's home and combat fronts would be psychologically able to endure the test of war. Perhaps the most frequently used term in popular media and discourse on physical and psychological perseverance was "*durchhalten*" ("hold through," or "persevere"), which was also widely disseminated in postcards and other visual media. These popular media often emphasized God as the foundation for this resilience (Figure 1.2). In a poem that appeared in the army newspaper *Die Somme-Wacht* (*The Watch on the Somme*), which was published by the 1st Army, faith in Jesus and reliance on the Holy Spirit was essential for psychological endurance:

We hold through in the strength of Jesus
Who saved us on the cross ...

We hold through in the Holy Spirit,
The spirit of discipline and strength
The spirit that shows us the way to victorious accomplishments.[18]

Similar to pieces from other army newspapers, this poem envisioned God as a path to victory. But it also prescribed a regimen for protection against fear. The promise of eternal salvation alleviated fear of death, and faith provided the resilience needed to endure stress. On the home front, church leaders also disseminated this idea that God was the backbone for resilience. A leaflet published by the Protestant church in Bietigheim, in Baden-Württemberg, equated service to God with service to the nation, and it called on congregants to remember that Germany's military technology was only one component for victory: "Our people (*Volk*) have a 'good set of weapons and defense' at the ready, but now the nation reaches for its best [weapon], its God."[19]

Army newspapers revealed concern among religious leaders that Christian soldiers might experience some cognitive dissonance. Perhaps it was understandable if good Christians were hesitant about going off to war, especially considering that the act of killing might be perceived as contravening Christian moral teachings, but military and religious authorities asserted that Christian ideals and wartime emotions and behavior, including hatred for the enemy and the act of killing, were perfectly compatible. Protestant pastors emphasized that men could still be good Christians if they maintained, at least privately, their ethical standards of "love for one's neighbor," even if they had to engage in, and were sometimes tainted by, the sinful public world.[20] For example, Julius Schiller, the Royal Municipal Protestant Pastor (*Koenigliche protestantischer Stadtpfarrer*) from Nuremberg, argued in an article for the *Kriegs-Zeitung der 4. Armee* that it was moral and consistent with Christian values to hate the enemy, despite Christian rhetoric about love and forgiveness. "It was previously

Figure 1.2 "Durchhalten! Im Vertrauen auf Gott!" ("Hold Through—Trust in God!"), 1915. Postcard, personal collection of the author.

considered immoral to hate," he admitted, but "today we know only one thing, and that is that we are allowed to hate. We must hate." Schiller reflected on this tension: "Is holy hate (*heiliger Hass*) a paradox?" He concluded that the German emotion of hatred was distinct and morally pure: "German hate is different than that of the Sons of Albion [the British]. We Germans hate honestly, and we're on the side of right. England's hate is driven by lies, envy, resentment and jealousy." Consequently, Schiller believed the emotion of hatred would be accepted by God, and thus "we can hate with a pure conscience, as strange as it sounds, even though religion seems to reject anything that smacks of hatred as unethical." He further rationalized that hate was natural and acceptable because it sprang from the same internal source that produced love and was guided by the same Holy Spirit:

> Moral love (*sittlichen Liebe*) corresponds necessarily from moral hatred. That means hate comes from a moral foundation for moral purposes. Hatred, which comes from the natural self, also comes from the Holy Spirit. Yes, there is even hate that comes from the Holy Spirit. That is spiritual hatred, which is the antipathy of carnal or selfish zeal and hatred.[21]

Here Schiller tried to reconcile emotions that may seem separate from or antithetical to Christian values. In case anyone felt ashamed about feelings of hatred that emanated from the "natural self," Schiller reassured readers that these instincts were ultimately governed by the Holy Spirit and thus remained pure compared to the "carnal" emotions condemned by religious authorities.

The dichotomy between love and hate, and anxiety about whether it was sinful for Christians to feel the latter, was a popular theme in religious leaders' advice for Christian soldiers. Will Vesper, a Protestant writer who published poetry and stories that retold the legends of Parsifal, Tristan, and Isolde that were popular before he volunteered as an infantryman in 1914, contributed regularly to army newspapers with poems on the spiritual experience of war. After the war he became a devoted member of the Nazi Party and was one of the writers to give a speech praising the May 1933 book burning. During the Nazi years, he published books like *Warriors for God* (*Kämpfer Gottes*, 1938), in which he narrated stories of devout and idealistic Christian soldiers who sacrificed themselves for the German nation and Adolf Hitler.[22] In one of his poems for the *Liller Kriegszeitung* in 1915, he reflected on how even though Jesus preached against hate and sacrificed himself on the cross out of love, the war required German soldiers to reject this teaching. Vesper imagined confronting Jesus with a new reality in which hatred and love allegedly sprang from the same source:

> And so I write here: I hate, Lord!
> From the bottom of my soul (*Seele*) I hate, Lord!
>
> And when I look straight into your [Jesus's] face:
> My hate does not give way to your love.
>
> Because, Lord Jesus Christ, this hatred
> Is the fruit of the highest form of love.

And when my fatherland is in deep crisis:
Hate alone will send my enemies to their death.[23]

This kind of self-justification of hatred was a common theme in army newspapers, especially in the first two years of the war, as the drives toward hatred, power, and violence needed for victory were rationalized as consistent with God's will.[24]

The bellicose, hypernationalistic religious rhetoric found in soldiers' media was not universally embraced, even in the first months of the war. Instead of finding in Christianity justification for hatred, some religious leaders argued that God should only be a source of comfort. For example, in January 1915 the Protestant congregation in Bietigheim published a pamphlet with an article critical of the prevailing aggressive rhetoric, which they suggested was un-Christian:

> The newspapers are reporting that our fighting troops use as a greeting or farewell the wrathful phrase "God punish England!" This report also indicates that it has been recommended that this "war greeting" also be used at home, and that it be answered with the counter-greeting, "He is punishing it [England]!" We cannot agree with this suggestion, even if it reflects the general mood. Greetings means wishes, not curses! We think it should remain that way even in this war year, 1914–15.[25]

The author of this article added a poem proposing that citizens should not call on God to punish anyone, but only to bless them, and that God's call for love and forgiveness was no different in war. Instead of condemning England, greetings should be confined to "God bless Germany," as God sees through man's arrogance and desire for power. The article also suggested that the military's goals and Christian values should be compartmentalized. God could not condone hatred and violence. Instead, the article emphasized, God was strictly a provider of comfort to increasingly stressed individuals.[26]

Though army newspapers and popular media were dominated by articles and poems by Christian chaplains and soldiers who rationalized war, these periodicals also offered the voices of Jewish religious leaders. The Kaiser's promise that he recognized "only Germans" regardless of political or religious background, and the ideal of "comradeship," gave many Jews who volunteered a sense of optimism that the war experience would open the door to integration.[27] Despite the persistence of antisemitic stereotypes, which culminated in the infamous "Jew Count" in 1916, where Jews were falsely accused of avoiding frontline service, Jewish front soldiers' letters and diaries are filled with anecdotes about how they felt acceptance from their comrades in the shared front experience.[28] One of the experiences they shared with Christians was the struggle to reconcile war with religious faith, a problem with which rabbis, like pastors and priests, wrestled. This can be seen in a February 1915 issue of the *Liller Kriegszeitung*, which published an article titled "War and Religion" by Rabbi Dr. Leo Baerwald, a field rabbi (*Feldrabinner*) who served on the Western front.[29] Dr. Baerwald began his essay with a personal anecdote. He recounted a visit to a field hospital where he met a wounded man that he knew. The wounded soldier had lost his faith shortly before the war but was now going through a religious experience and he asked, "Why didn't you speak to me about God yesterday?" The rabbi deduced that in the face of bullets and stress, men yearned for God's meaning. This yearning provided an ideal opening for religion, which he believed was perfectly suited as a spiritual antidote to trauma. He concluded his essay with rhetoric that echoed Christian sentiments about God, the nation, and the war. He saw religion and "love for the fatherland" as perfectly compatible: "What is the main purpose of religion?—to promote goodness on earth. And that is the same goal as the fatherland. Thus we should give our best strength to the fatherland and promote the progress of goodness and nobility."[30] Quoting a passage from Psalms 94:2 about the "Judge of the World" calling on his followers to rise up, he conflated this with the Kaiser's call to arms, which he said was just in God's eyes.[31] Interestingly, Rabbi Baerwald, who would serve after the war as a rabbi for the main synagogue in Munich before he was arrested by the Nazis in the wake of the 1938 *Reichspogramnacht* and then emigrated to the United States in 1940, did not differentiate between Jewish and Christian soldiers. Rather, he suggested that soldiers' longing for God, and the rapport between religion and the fatherland, was felt universally.

Despite Rabbi Baerwald's emphasis on shared values between Jews and Christians, Christian leaders often emphasized the exceptionalism of Christians as ideal soldiers. Pastors pointed to Christ's sacrifice as the model for selflessness that would inspire men to give up their lives for the nation. This emphasis on Christ's self-sacrifice appeared in the rhetoric of pastors and priests throughout the duration of the war. As late as March 1918, a few days after the German army's last major offensive, one chaplain wrote for an army newspaper that men should find inspiration from Christ's suffering, and that like Jesus, "the brave man only thinks of himself last." The Christian soldier, this chaplain argued, was equipped with an exceptional "German soul" (*deutsche Seele*), which enabled him to put the nation and God above all other concerns. Through prayer and reflection on Christ's sacrifice, the front soldier would be reminded of selflessness as the core of Christian faith.[32]

Christians on the home front could also weaponize prayer. According to religious leaders, women and children at home could fight the enemy by praying for their loved ones. If front soldiers knew their loved ones were praying for them, it would help fortify their psychological strength. Thus schoolchildren were taught how to pray for their fathers and brothers. The previously mentioned Protestant writer Will Vesper, whose articles frequently appeared in soldiers' newspapers, prescribed a prayer for children to say every morning: "Protect our soldiers at the front/who stand against the whole world/Be their defense in the great battle/Stand with them when they are on watch."[33] Children were also mobilized to send care packages, and these were often supplemented with letters that promised faithfulness and prayer. One group of Sunday school students wrote several letters each week in August–October 1914 to their former teacher, Wilhelm W., which reflected the rhetoric prescribed by Vesper. One letter, signed by a whole class of children, promised, "We were all happy to hear the news that the dear Lord has protected our dearest teacher up until now."[34] In another, one girl named Maria H. wrote, "May God continue to protect you in all peril and return you to us soon, healthy and victorious."[35] Their former teacher wrote back to individual students about the sermons he heard at front services, and he assured the children that their prayers protected him and gave him courage.[36]

God, Masculinity, and the Warrior Ideal

If there were some tensions over wartime rhetoric and whether it was consistent with Christianity, religious leaders also felt compelled to explain how the image of soldierly masculinity matched the image of the ideal Christian husband and father. Many religious authorities were eager to conflate Christianity and the masculine soldierly ideal. They claimed that religious faith was vital because it made men real men, and they asserted that the same traits they acquired as good Christians equipped them for the masculine enterprise of war.

In the decades before the war, the concept of masculinity became increasingly aligned across Europe with a militarized notion of the heroic ideal, which dictated personal sacrifice and absolute loyalty to the nation.[37] In Germany, this prevailing model of masculinity was reinforced by conservative teachers in the school system, and it required men to be fierce and aggressive soldiers, yet also capable of controlling their emotions in an effort to stay focused on making sacrifices for the nation.[38] Emotional restraint and self-discipline was a cornerstone of the masculine ideal, but many medical authorities and civilian morality organizations feared that the male character was being eroded by "degenerate" sexual promiscuity, socialism, and a modern culture that corrupted Germany's youth.[39] Doctors and conservative critics welcomed the idea of a war that they believed would regenerate decaying masculinity and resuscitate traditional values threatened by rapid social, political, and economic change.[40]

Before 1914, there was a prevailing assumption that religion was an essentially "feminine" enterprise. Though men were expected to be pious, psychiatrists associated fervent religious belief primarily with women, and fanaticism could be linked to mental illness, including "religious mania" or "hysteria."[41] However, a "muscular Christianity" movement, which had been gaining steam in the decades before the war, especially in literary and theological circles in Britain, tried to counteract this stereotype.[42] After the war broke out, religious authorities in Germany insisted that religion was not only "masculine" but also a key component of the psychological strength men needed to be effective front fighters. For example, the Catholic professor of Church history Georg Pfeilschifter, who at the end of the war edited a collection of Catholic soldiers' letters from the front, and in 1933 publicly professed his support for Hitler, made the case that Christian faith lay the groundwork for courage and thus success in battle. He wrote:

> The Christian religion has once again proved its worth as a heroic religion, which creates heroes in battle and in conflict and also fosters individual endurance. War shows us that Christianity is by no means a religion only for women and children, for weak and soft people, but it's a religion that unleashes the highest active and passive psychological [or soul] forces (*höchsten aktiven und passive Seelenkräfte*) in courageous and strong men.[43]

Reinforcing the argument that Christianity was masculine rather than "soft," Pfeilschifter further emphasized that religion sparked the essential psychological characteristics, or "psychological/soul forces" (*Seelenkräfte*) needed for success in war. These included the propensity for both active courage and passive obedience of authority and subservience to hierarchy. This idea was adopted by military leaders, including Field Marshal von Mattonowich, who saw the war as a kind of "Reformation," where men discovered the inherent value and applicability of religious ideals, turning abstract theories about spiritual strength into practical reality, to be exhibited on the battlefield.[44]

The image of God constructed by religious authorities was in many ways a reflection of the militarized, masculine, and nationalistic self. The idea that God, and religion in general, is a projection of prevailing social and cultural structures and values, including masculine ideals, has been emphasized by gender historians.[45] In this light, "God" in 1914 was arguably a projection of militarized notions of masculinity and national identity, as evidenced by religious leaders who saw their warrior ideals in the image of the Supreme Being. This can be seen in an article for the *Kriegszeitung der 4. Armee* by a field division pastor (*Felddivisionspfarrer*) named Barchewitz, who made the case that, based on close analysis of figures from the New Testament, Christian values were perfectly in unison with the warrior ideal. Barchewitz observed that the New Testament of the Bible was "the most widely read book at the front," and that it was a treasured possession often gifted to soldiers by wives and mothers at home.[46] Like other pastors eager to convince front soldiers that there was no tension between their Christian values and their military duty, Barchewitz explained that men should not feel like sinners because they put on a uniform and went to war. Rather, he insisted that disciples like John and Luke were themselves "people of war" (*Kriegsleute*) who fought the Romans and preached "on orders from God." John the Baptist's rituals at the Jordan River, Barchewitz argued, were essentially ancient versions of "front worship services" (*Feldgottesdienste*). God himself, Barchewitz claimed, was the commander-in-chief who oversaw his loyal soldiers.[47] Looking at Christian history through the lens of military culture, built on an edifice of obedience and rituals where violence was normalized, Barchewitz projected the norms of the imperial German army on to Jesus's disciples and the all-powerful, heavenly field marshal.

One particular cornerstone of the masculine ideal that was refracted through the prism of Christian values was the notion of "comradeship." Comradeship was seen as a central component of the male experience that gave soldiers a sense of meaning and belonging to counteract the psychological stress of trench warfare. The memory of comradeship would evolve into a quasi-religious experience in postwar memoirs and literature, and it was glorified as the most spiritually and psychologically important experience of the war.[48] Comradeship was widely embraced by many Christian leaders who argued that it was a natural extension of Christian values. This linkage between militarized warrior masculinity and Christianity was made explicit in a sermon published by chaplain B. Pfister for *Der Dienstkamerad* (*The Service Comrade*), the front newspaper for the 3rd infantry division of the Prussian army. Speaking to soldiers just behind the front lines, Pfister argued that the "friendliness and selfless love of brothers" learned from Christian teachings was the essential basis for comradeship, and in turn military fitness. He called on front soldiers to become "real men" through faith in God:

> Be a man who trusts in God, from whom you generate your greatest strength. This, comrades, is my third point, and it is the crown of true manhood. Without looking towards God, who is the source of life, without the connection to him, from whom comes all that is good and all perfect gifts, we cannot be men who are inwardly strong and victorious, fighting with our own egos (*Ich*), and at the same time full of love and mutual devotion against the nights, ruthlessly advocating for truth and justice and yet doing this with tender softness (*weichem Zartgefühl*), taking pity on the suffering and unhappiness of brothers.[49]

Pfister's sermon provides rich imagery that juxtaposes the dichotomy between the "masculine" (hard) warrior and "effeminate" (soft) Christian values of love and mercy. He painted an image of men struggling with their sense of self, between their roles as warriors and Christians. These two poles, he argued, were not mutually exclusive. Rather, they were symbiotic, and he reiterated that "the ideal manly character is to fight hard and to win, but also to love tenderly and with devotion."[50] Pfister thus also recognized that there was a "softer side" of comradeship, rooted in Christian ideals, which incorporated and normalized "feminine" characteristics of love and compassion needed to survive the psychological strain of the front experience. Sermons by other pastors also began to reflect this mixture of toughness with compassion. The image of "gentle Jesus" was expanded by Protestant preachers to portray him also as the "hero and standard-bearer for our time, and our Volk."[51]

Army newspapers published testimonies from soldiers who agreed that the "masculine" arena of war and "feminine" Christian ideals could be combined to mold a more effective comrade. For example, the *Kriegszeitung der 4. Armee* published a prayer by a sailor, K. Kirmse, who called on God to give him strength and comfort in times of stress. The prayer portrays the German soldier, though willing to perform his duty, as in a lonely state of anxiety on the brink of battle. Kirmse imagined God "taking my rough warrior hands with child-like gentleness," and giving him courage before the moment of truth. He asks for God's blessing, "Then I can be free in the storm and crisis."[52] Kirmse integrated soft compassion with the soldier's tough, steel-like nerves. The binary gender ideals, the "feminine" emotion of love and the "masculine" warrior image, were thus balanced and synchronized for battle.

Christianity, religious leaders insisted, was also essential in building comradeship because it provided the foundation of discipline that was an essential part of the front soldier's character. The hegemonic masculine ideal emphasized emotional discipline and self-control as the basis for military fitness and loyalty to the nation. The Prussian tradition in particular emphasized *Manneszucht* ("male discipline") as essential to preserving military obedience and order.[53] Religious leaders argued that Christian piety was the basis for this self-discipline. The *Kriegszeitung der 4. Armee* asserted that this idea had deep roots by publishing an excerpt from *Catechism for the German Soldier* (*Katechismus für den deutschen Wehrmann*), originally written during the Napoleonic wars by nationalist writer and poet Ernst Moritz Arndt. In his catechism, Arndt conflated Christian piety, loyalty to the nation, and manly character. According to Arndt, German soldiers were "known in history for their respectability, piety, and fidelity," but war threatened to "turn them hollow with its ferocious and inhuman activities."[54] Nevertheless, Arndt believed that the discipline that men learned as Christians, where they preserved their faith and loyalty to God despite the depravations of the world, prepared them for battle, where they could maintain "the discipline of a Christian soldier" against hunger, cold, and violence.[55]

Christian values also reinforced comradely virtues by teaching men the spirit of sacrifice for others. Protestant pastor Heinrich von Hausen argued that sacrifice for the fatherland came naturally to soldiers who were true to their Christian upbringing. "Dear comrades," he wrote in the *Somme-Wacht*, "it's not the number of men that's important, but rather the spirit (*Geist*) of the army. In order to become a good, brave soldier, it's not enough to just pray. Prayer alone has no value if the words don't follow the act, and prayer is hollow without soldierly virtue (*Soldatentugend*)."[56] Von Hausen defined "soldierly virtue" as closely related to Christian virtues, in particular "bravery," defined by the willingness to "constantly sacrifice oneself and be ready to die for the fatherland." Von Hausen further emphasized this notion of bravery and sacrifice as holy and sacred virtues by referring to John 3:16 ("For God so loved the world, he gave his only son, so that whoever believes in him shall not perish but will have eternal life"). Men could emulate Jesus's self-sacrifice, a central tenet of Christianity, and apply it to their endeavors and comrades who sacrificed for the nation.[57]

In addition to conflating Christian and soldierly ideals of self-sacrifice, von Hausen claimed that Christian values were essential to helping men survive psychological stress.[58] If political and medical authorities saw the war as a test of nerves and willpower,[59] religious leaders like von Hausen believed faith held the solution to this challenge.[60] Von Hausen lamented that many men, especially those who were impious, would rely on alcohol and prostitutes to calm their nerves before combat. But he prescribed Christian piety and prayer as more effective, arguing that God was more reliable in bolstering nerves than booze and promiscuity. This required considerable self-restraint. "Men had to have courage not only against the enemy," von Hausen claimed, "but also against themselves." To help men through this inner battle, God was both a friend who gave comfort and the ultimate authority figure to be feared. Von Hausen warned men that God knew whether they were loyal to faith and virtue, or slipping into weakness and sin, because God was the ultimate "leader in battle" (*Schlachtenlenkers*) and the "greatest army leader" (*groessest Heerfuehrers*). Obedience to God's will, he concluded, was the ultimate expression of masculine virtue and soldiers proved they were "complete men" (*ganze Männer*) if they could conquer the temptation toward immoral behavior.[61]

The appeal of militaristic and nationalistic rhetoric that conflated Christian ideals and the masculine soldierly image would gradually erode for a number of men over the course of the war, as will be seen in subsequent chapters. But for some, even before they experienced combat, it was impossible to reconcile Judeo-Christian values with militarism. Religious convictions, especially opposition to killing in any context, motivated some individuals to protest the war. As in other nations at war, there was a small population of conscientious objectors (*Kriegsdienstverweigerer*) in Germany, though the number of those who protested joining the military were lower than in Britain, for example, where religious minorities like Quakers and Mennonites organized more sustained protests against the war. There were approximately 16,000 conscientious objectors in Britain during the war, but, though numbers are not exactly known, it is estimated that there were fewer in Germany.[62] As historian Rebecca Bennette demonstrates, German psychiatrists who were assigned to evaluate conscientious objectors struggled with how they should be categorized and treated. In some cases, these individuals were labeled "paranoid psychotics," as in one of the cases studied by Bennette, that of Wilhelm W., a member of the Bible Student Movement, who refused to carry a weapon because it went against God's commandment against killing. As with most other conscientious objectors, Wilhelm W. avoided prison and instead was given treatment for mental illness in a psychiatric hospital.[63] For many psychiatrists and the military, the fact that men refused to fight was in itself evidence that they were mentally unstable, as doctors could not fathom that a real man would not be willing to fulfill his masculine duty and sacrifice himself for the nation. One of Germany's leading psychiatrists, Robert Gaupp, who treated "war hysterics" and published extensively on conscientious objectors, struggled to understand why anyone would declare himself to be a conscientious objector, as their refusal to fight, for whatever reason, revealed that individual's masculine shortcomings. From the point of view of the military, he wrote, even if a potential soldier refused to fight on "moral or religious grounds," any individual who had a sense of his manly responsibilities should be aware that the fatherland needed him, and this should trump any religious feelings that might make him reluctant to fight.[64]

Worship in the Trenches: Maintaining the Moral and Spiritual Health of Frontline Troops

One of the most important ways in which the military tried to ensure spiritual care for soldiers was through worship services at the front (*Feldgottesdienste*). Worship services were seen by religious and military authorities as a way to reinforce continuity between prewar life and life in the trenches, and to cement bonds between front and *Heimat*, as civilians were supposed to feel reassured that their loved ones continued to adhere to traditional social and cultural structures. Religious services varied in size and proximity to the front. Military chaplains from Protestant, Catholic, and Jewish backgrounds led services that were usually organized just behind the front lines and in the reserve units, often in staging areas where men were being transported en route to the trenches, or near hospitals. Catholic military chaplains often operated in the front lines, even bearing arms, in order to provide the sacraments, including last rites, to men in the front and reserve trenches.[65] Masses organized by Catholic priests just behind the lines could be simple, ad hoc events with a handful of congregants, or, less often, much larger events, especially when it involved visits from high-ranking officers or clergy. The military actually required Catholic troops to attend services on Christmas and Easter, and they were expected to do so each Sunday, unless military duties made it impossible. Leadership from officers in each unit, depending on their level of interest, set the tone for how often men attended services.[66]

Often at the same locations where a mass had just ended, Protestant and Jewish services would also be organized, with pastors and rabbis rotating services at the same improvised altar where a priest had just given sacraments to Catholic soldiers.[67] Pastors often had to improvise as they tended to their flock under the ever-changing conditions of life at the front. Wilhelm Z., for example, was able to hold a Protestant service in a Catholic church, Russian and Greek Orthodox churches, and "even in the synagogue in Kolno, I was able to schedule a service," though the synagogue's representative (*Synogogenrat*) begged him at the last minute to not proceed with a service there. The pastor concluded, "You have to seize the opportunity to worship wherever you find it, in the woods, in the field, on the roadside, on a farm."[68]

The rotating services reinforced the spirit of the *Burgfrieden* ("peace within the fortress," or social-political truce), promised by the Kaiser at the beginning of the war.[69] Many front chaplains eagerly supported this spirit of unity, and they pointed to the rotating Catholic, Protestant, and Jewish services as proof of solidarity. One officer, Freiherr von Berlepsch, recorded how moved he was to see a service with Protestant and Catholic soldiers standing side by side, alternating between singing "A Mighty Fortress Is Our God" and "God, We Praise You." He claimed that in this shared experience, prewar religious divisions evaporated:

> All the petty inter-confessional conflict was forgotten in the face of danger to the fatherland. Just as there were no longer political parties, there were no longer any [religious] denominations. There was only one God, *the* God, who is to be a mighty fortress against a world of enemies.[70]

Mirroring the alleged disappearance of political party conflict, von Berlepsch claimed, men at the front also no longer recognized religious divisions. He went on to describe the front services in which he saw Catholic and Protestant soldiers who became quite emotional at the interfaith experience. Because they recognized a common belief in the same God, von Berlepsch argued, soldiers felt they could also overcome any social or cultural conflicts.[71] To at least some degree, this spirit of unity was shared by front soldiers who, if they were interested, could see multiple services and enjoy the commonalities they had with other faiths. Many experienced religious rituals and liturgy that they had never before personally encountered, breaking down barriers between, or at least demystifying, the differences between religious communities. For example, Christian front soldier Rudolf V. wrote to his wife Julie at the end of August 1914 about how one of his Jewish comrades invited him to a Sabbath service where his new friends there made him feel welcome. He told his wife that the Jewish service was "beautiful and relaxing."[72]

Part of the spiritual arsenal disseminated to soldiers by church authorities were hymn and prayer books. In their letters and diaries, soldiers often described these as cherished belongings and indeed many of these religious publications were preserved with their collections of letters that were delivered by family members decades later to archives. For example, Willy L.'s file in the federal archive in Freiburg includes his *Field*

Hymn Book for Protestant Soldiers in the Army (*Feldgesangbuch für die evangelischen Mannschaften des Heeres*) with his diary and letter writing equipment. The book, which included over thirty hymns, "spiritual folk songs," and prayers, was originally published in 1897. He also kept a little black book containing the Gospel According to John. In the front cover of the Gospel According to John, he wrote his last will and testament in bold letters for his parents: "This book, dear parents, is to be your last memory of your son Willy, who now stands under God's counsel, and joyfully gave his blood for his beloved fatherland—written on October 16, 1914."[73] Willy L. survived that first baptism of fire in the fall of 1914, but his letters and diary entries ceased in the spring of 1915, and his exact fate is unknown.

Prayer books and worship services were also an important part of the front experience for Jewish soldiers. Jewish soldiers recorded in letters and diaries how deeply moved they were to see rabbis stand side by side next to Catholic and Protestant chaplains, and Christian comrades often stayed respectfully after Christian services as rabbis led prayers and blessings for the troops.[74] Similar to Protestant and Catholic communities, Jewish home front organizations, often led by women, mobilized to support their husbands and sons with "field books" (*Feldbücher*) that provided spiritual sustenance in the trenches.[75] For example, Paul Plaut, who volunteered in 1915, brought with him to the front his *Field Prayer Book for Jewish Men* (*Feldgebetbuch für die jüdischen Mannschaften des Heeres*), which was edited by the Association of German Jews (*Verband der Deutschen Juden*) and published in 1914. The details of Plaut's personal religious beliefs are largely hidden, but he wrote an extensive academic study of the psychological effects of the front experience that included a scientific analysis of the spiritual impact of the war on front soldiers, which will be analyzed in a later chapter. However, his field prayer book shows signs of being used, and its presence in his estate belongings in his archival file at the Jewish Museum in Berlin suggests it held at least some significance for him.[76]

The spiritual "arming" of soldiers also took place through sermons they heard at front services. Sermons emphasized the importance of faith in a front soldiers' life, and they reassured men that God stood by their side as they prepared for battle. Chaplains delivered a message that men were not alone, but that God was ever-present, a kind of good comrade who protected soldiers from enemy fire.[77] One chaplain, Otto Riemann, informed his congregants that Jesus was the greatest comrade, because loyalty to him held the promise of eternal life. He told soldiers to imagine Jesus saying to them: "Be faithful unto death, and I will give you the crown of life." Thus the militarized language of sacrificing one's life for the nation was reinforced with similar Christian language, but in this case with the guarantee of salvation from death. When officers called out "Prepare your rifles," Riemann sermonized, "God is with you … We must ride to victory, to death, as is God's will."[78] In this way, Christianity complemented and enhanced sacrifice for the nation with an added reward of God's approval.

Army newspapers reported confidently that front services had their intended effect. One corporal named Nickel wrote a poem for an army newspaper about a service given just behind the lines near Jonkershofe, Belgium, in early 1915. During prayer, as artillery fell nearby, men continued defiantly: "Stay with us your grace, Lord Jesus Christ, so that the enemy will do us no harm!" According to Nickel, after the prayers, men felt great resolve and courage with the knowledge that Jesus was with them through danger and stress.[79] Whether or not Nickel's poetic interpretation of his comrades' feelings during the service is accurate, this was the image that authorities tried to disseminate. The army newspapers frequently painted positive images about the effects of front services on morale. These services gave men an escape from the mud and filth of the trenches, reported one article for the *Kriegszeitung der 4. Armee*, giving them a brief encounter with the familiar beauty and ritual of a worship service.[80] A similar sentiment was echoed in the *Liller Kriegszeitung*, which published a poem titled, "Church Service" ("*Gottesdienst*"), which celebrated an idealized, if improvised, house of God in the forest, where soldiers could find respite amidst the chaos and stress of the war.[81]

Chaplains used front services to assure men that through their Christian faith they could still find joy even while they endured the most stressful situations. One chaplain named Arnold gave a sermon in 1917 in which he insisted that even if men felt "an inner storm and the pain of the world (*Weltschmerz*)," this could be masked with a "happy outlook on life." Jesus wanted men to be optimistic: "Jesus does not like sour faces." Chaplain Arnold compared the stress of the trenches to fasting, and he made the case that just as the fasting Christian forgets food and drink while he focuses on cleansing his soul, so should the front soldier find spiritual contentment despite the physical deprivations of everyday life at the front.[82] This emphasis on maintaining a happy countenance also reinforced conformity to military obedience, with religious leaders discouraging any dissent or grumbling.

Beyond building a spiritual and psychological bulwark, front services also provided a practical function in giving men a sense of belonging and creature comforts. In the case of Paul Lebrecht, for example, religious services were most important in providing familiar German cultural rituals and food. Lebrecht was a liberal (reform) Jew who kept an extensive war diary that detailed everyday life at the front.[83] He was called up as an infantryman in the summer of 1916 to serve with the 28th Bavarian Infantry Regiment, and he served on both the Western and Eastern Fronts in 1916–18. Lebrecht saw himself as a popular, well-liked comrade, and he wrote that he wanted to simply "do my duty" at the front and not be treated as different because he was Jewish.[84] By being a good comrade, he felt he could win respect just as any other soldier serving his fatherland. At the same time, he also tried to maintain his Jewish cultural identity. While on the Eastern Front, he visited synagogues several times, but he felt alienated from the Jewish communities there.[85] He wrote that Romanian Jews were suspicious of German soldiers. They could not believe that there could be a Jewish soldier in the supposedly cruel German army, and they were surprised to find that he was quite civilized. Lebrecht expressed pride that he gave a civilized face to German culture.[86]

Lebrecht wrote in his war diary that he tried to remain pious, but he was not particularly strict, and his diary does not offer much reflection on God or spirituality.[87] When he was invited by Christian comrades, he sometimes attended Christian church services. However, he did not find these services particularly interesting, and he actually fell asleep during sermons. He complained that the synagogue services he went to while in Romania were also "boring."[88] Lebrecht admitted that he sometimes only went to worship services for the food, and he preferred Christian services because they offered better meals, including bratwurst, after all the rituals. He also recorded that his favorite time was Christmas because the men would set up Christmas markets and they got special care packages with extra chocolate and baked goods, all of which improved the good mood of his Christian comrades.[89] Gastronomical nourishment and comradeship, rather than spiritual sustenance, were his top priority.

Paul Lebrecht's diary gives a glimpse into the how ordinary front soldiers actually perceived religious services in the field, which will be explored further in the next chapter. But to foreshadow the voices of men and women on the combat and home fronts, it is interesting to note the strain experienced by religious authorities themselves, especially chaplains serving in the front lines, who were shattered by the trauma they experienced in the trenches. The war experience seemed to overwhelm them, despite their prescriptions of piety. For example, Kaspar G., a Catholic chaplain with a Bavarian battalion who also drove an ambulance, wrote to a fellow chaplain in May 1915 about a worship service that had to be moved from a church to a grove of trees to make room for the wounded overflowing from the field hospital. He took comfort reflecting on the tribulations of Jesus's twelve apostles who had to "fight for their faith in order to be victorious," and he predicted that despite the horrors of war "German faith and German justice will not be annihilated by our enemies."[90] He reassured his friend that he could weather the stress with a positive outlook and faith in victory. But only two months later, he wrote, "I'm sick of this wretched war and mass murder (*Massenmord*) … all my sense of humor has disappeared, like smoke in the air."[91] Overwhelmed by the numbers of wounded, Kaspar G. was in despair because he and his fellow chaplains were unable to deliver last rites and holy sacraments to all the dying. By September, after being transferred to the Russian front, he was dying of cholera. In a letter to his mother he said he was praying more than he ever had in his life, and he asked forgiveness for unspecified transgressions: "When I was young and stupid I was to blame (*verschuldet*). Forgive me, for those things I was guilty of, so I can look to the future."[92] Kaspar G. died a few weeks later, before he could be transported back home.

Conclusion

Military and religious authorities who prescribed religious ideals used army newspapers and other popular media to promote faith as an ideal tool for mobilization and "holding through" as total war engulfed combat and home fronts. They conflated the ideal warrior image with the idealized Christian, merging masculine soldierly ideals with Christian conceptions of manhood. The military eagerly collaborated with religious leaders to help maintain the psyches and emotions of front soldiers, and spiritual life was prioritized as key for ensuring victory. Ideally, the pious, spiritually resilient front soldier was to be bolstered by emotional support from loyal, faithful women on the home front.

However, the image of spiritually resilient front soldiers and civilians generated by military and religious authorities proved fragile. Religious ideals prescribed for men and women would quickly seem less efficacious as the war bogged down into stalemate and industrialized violence. As will be revealed in subsequent chapters, which shift away from a history of religion "from above" to a history "from below," there was much greater complexity and diversity of beliefs about God and his role in the front experience. Front soldiers gradually detached from dominant conceptions of God as the nationalistic supreme commander dedicated to the collective victory of the nation. Instead, men in the trenches, under unimaginable stress, would compartmentalize their relationship with God. Often in symbiotic spiritual relationships constructed through correspondence with their loved ones, they assigned God a more subjective role as a personal comrade who might help them to escape an increasingly unbearable and surreal world.

2

God and the "Spirit of 1914": Religiosity of Ordinary Soldiers and Civilians at the Outbreak of the War

Language that emphasized "God is on our side" (*Gott mit Uns*) was a key component of media produced for soldiers at the outbreak of the war, as discussed in the previous chapter. However, perceptions of God's presence, like perceptions of the "spirit of 1914," were much more diverse and complex than army newspapers, sermons, and religious pamphlets would suggest.[1] This chapter explores the following questions: To what degree did hegemonic concepts of religion, prescribed by religious leaders, resonate with the men and women mobilizing for war? What was God's function for front soldiers as they mobilized for the trenches, and how did their first experiences with trench warfare impact their religious beliefs?

The central argument of this chapter is that dominant religious ideals had only limited or temporary appeal for ordinary men and women, especially after encounters with traumatic violence. To some degree, language that conflated nationalism and religion was pervasive in letters and diaries in the first months of the war. However, especially for many men at the front, initial experiences with violence pushed them to reflect intensely on their existing beliefs and assumptions. Reactions to God's signs or silence would result in increasingly complicated and fragmented religious beliefs that fell across a broad spectrum. While their responses to violence were disparate, one pattern that emerges is that language in letters began to shift focus away from nationalistic, collectivist rhetoric and more toward religion's function in providing individual emotional comfort and support.

Men, as well as women on the home front, quickly discovered that subsuming oneself into the collective national spirit, as prescribed by religious and military authorities, was not an entirely adequate tactic for coping with stress. Letters and diaries reveal how many needed to imagine God more subjectively, as a personal companion who had the power to provide emotional comfort, or to protect their families who were vulnerable, especially in the absence of patriarchal authority. Further, God was yearned for by soldiers and civilians not just to cope with, but also to help escape, at least spiritually, the stress of modern war. Religion provided men and women a mutually constructed, imagined zone that was safe from the unbearable material world. Religious language also gave front soldiers a means for sharing love and compassion with women at home. The religious-framed language of love and healing provided access to and a framework for expressing "feminine" emotions that helped them to process and absorb stress.

The increasing disparity between military and religious authorities' nationalistic conceptions of God and the more complex and diverse subjective perceptions of ordinary soldiers and civilians can be explored through several key sites of spiritual language, experience, and imagination. First, the language used by men and women in letters to describe their relationship to God reveals that although officially sanctioned religious language sometimes appeared in personal correspondence, it was defined in more complex ways. One can trace a distinct shift over the first year of the war, as rhetoric about the national religious significance of mobilization dissolved into more individualized reflection focused on resilience and survival. God evolved from an abstract national symbol to a utilitarian, ideal comrade in the trenches. Second, this chapter explores the experience of religious services and rituals from the perspective of front soldiers, focusing on how men perceived these organized events, especially during the crucial first Christmas at the front. While religious authorities prescribed front services, as discussed in the previous chapter, as a ritual that built connection with the home front and continuity with prewar life, the actual experience had a different effect. Worshipping in the front lines, and the experience of Christmas while separated from their families in particular, actually reinforced for many a feeling that they were detached and remote from the home front. Nevertheless, as the third section here analyzes, men and women desperately reached out to each other and used faith, and their religious imagination, to build a bridge between combat and home fronts. This was not so much as a motivator to fight in defense of the threatened homeland, a pervasive image in front newspapers,[2] but rather this spiritual connection was crucial for building an emotional connection between both spheres, and in turn a bulwark against stress. Believing in God as a source of protection gave soldiers and civilians a sense of agency and control that allowed them to reach, at least in their imaginations, across spatial and experiential lines.

Finally, this chapter examines the complex feelings of fatalism related to the religious imagination. As the mass slaughter of industrialized warfare unfolded, and religious language became increasingly divorced from nationalistic conceptions of God as a force for courage, patriotism, and sacrifice, language about God focused on the capriciousness of life and death as well as God's will and role in this irrational front experience. An interesting tension can be found in the correspondence between the home and combat fronts. While men and women often struggled to exert agency through their imagination of God as a savior and protector, the sense that one did not actually have any control also pervaded letters and diaries. For many, God was not so much "with us," as the dominant rhetoric promised. Rather, he seemed to be a remote, incomprehensible, and mysterious arbiter of a colossal, apocalyptic accident. The importance of fatalistic religious language has been analyzed by a number of historians because of its function as a coping mechanism for soldiers who struggled with an increasingly chaotic environment.[3] However, beyond its role as a coping mechanism, fatalistic thinking also signaled a shift to more personal and increasingly subjective thinking about religion. If God is remote and capricious, perhaps other spiritual-religious tools were needed to protect one from danger? The breakdown of the spirit of 1914 would lay the groundwork for religious experimentation, improvisation, and invention that will be explored in further chapters.

Religious Language in Letters and Diaries at the Outbreak of the War

Many who mobilized for war embraced prevailing ideals that conflated nationalism and religion. Front soldiers, like Christian religious leaders, often celebrated the outbreak of the war as a spark that would intensify religious faith and piety. However, especially as the brutality of trench warfare unfolded, narratives about religion shifted away from reflections on the collective meaning of the war for the nation. The nationalistic, bellicose language about the "God of the Germans" gradually eroded. Letters and diaries of terrified front soldiers began to focus instead on God as a companion or ideal comrade who was with them individually, helping to at least spiritually escape the stress of industrialized violence. Though combat soldiers are the focus of this section, narratives by women on the home front suggest a similar pattern in which they sought more subjective understanding of God's protective role. Rather than a weapon to help mobilize national fervor and fighting resolve, religion would become an individual instrument of survival.

The famous belt buckle worn by every German soldier that professed *"Gott mit Uns"* seemed to echo the sentiments of many men preparing for battle. As Europe plunged into war at the end of July 1914, Rudolf Berthold, who started the war as an infantryman but in the coming years would become one of Germany's most decorated fighter pilots,[4] described those days in religious terms. He recorded in his diary:

> The bells toll! A serious reminder, but the noise that bursts through the air is also joyful. Crowds of people stream towards war. The German people once again feel their God (*Das deutsche Volk fühlt wieder seinen Gott*), and they become aware that only in God's true strength—that only in faith alone—do weak people find the strength to be strong in times of need. We will be strong, because God and justice are with us.[5]

Berthold equated the outbreak of the war with a kind of religious revival, with the dormant faith of Germans waking up to the call of war. He believed that individuals derived strength from faith, and he was fortified by the promise that God allied himself with the German people.

Religious responses to the outbreak of the war were also reconstructed in memoirs long after the "spirit of 1914," as volunteers later recalled their emotions through the lens of faith. This can be found in the postwar recollections of one individual who, struggling in Munich in the years before 1914, would find in the war experience a sense of meaning and belonging that he had not yet discovered. Recalling his feelings a decade later, he perceived the outbreak of the war as a revelation, even a form of salvation from his empty prewar existence:

> To me those hours seemed like a release from the painful feelings of my youth. Even today I am not ashamed to say that, overpowered by stormy enthusiasm, I fell down on my knees and thanked Heaven from an overflowing heart for granting me the good fortune of being permitted to live at this time.[6]

Adolf Hitler thus later reconstructed August 1914 as a spiritual revelation in which God had awakened nationalist resolve. Hitler wrote further that God revealed to him that Germany was engaged in a struggle for its existence, and he considered himself blessed to be part of events governed by God's will. He interpreted God's will as a trigger for the latent, collective desires of the German people: "The struggle of the year 1914 was not forced on the masses—no, by the living God—it was desired by the whole people."[7]

The idea that the nation was collectively unified and that God bestowed his blessings on the German people was not just a postwar recollection. It also reverberated in letters from the front in the first months of the war, especially as men tried to reassure loved ones that they could "hold through" their first baptism of fire. For example, Gustav K., the son of a master carpenter from Halberstadt who volunteered at the outbreak of the war, wrote in 1915 to his brother Walter, who was also in the trenches, about his terrifying experiences at the front. At the end of a long letter detailing the effects of French artillery attacks, with shrapnel and debris flying through the air and killing comrades, he concluded, "But in spite of all this we'll hold through, with God, for the *Kaiser* and the *Reich*."[8] Gustav K. used similar rhetoric in letters to his parents. He wrote, "We've been dealt a heavy hand here on the extreme right flank, but we all trust in the God of the Germans (*aber wir vertrauen alle auf den Gott der Deutschen*) and our good cause."[9] Giving his gratitude for safe deliverance from enemy shells, Gustav K. also told his parents that he was inspired by the sermon of a field chaplain at a worship service just behind the lines. He was particularly impressed that the chaplain was a veteran from the 1870/71 Franco-Prussian War, which made him feel that the chaplain knew what he was talking about, and thus his blessing was all the more sincere.[10]

Women on the home front also refracted their religious faith through nationalist ideals and militarized language about "heroic death." For example, sacrifice for the nation was often described as a path to salvation, with "heroic death" celebrated as a supreme sacrifice that was rewarded with redemption and eternal life. This can be seen in the case of Ruth N., who gives her condolences to her friend Uta von S., whose cousin died in battle in October 1914. Ruth N. wrote:

> I feel your pain and kiss you deeply. Dearest Uta, God has helped you and him: what you shyly conceal in your hearts with pride and supreme courage has now become so fine and sweet, without being marred by suffering according to human laws that have to be renounced.
>
> My Uta, if you think about Germany's greatness, you will be able to think of him [your cousin]. One day you will go to the place where the sea washes over German heroes' tombs and calls to all those who are at rest that they have died in salvation and honor of the great and honorable fatherland. Heroic death

in battle—that was his last wish! Your eyes are crying, but your soul will find peace.[11]

Religious language used by Ruth N. mixed Christian concepts with militarized ideals of "heroic death," which is held up here as a transcendent experience. The soldier's sacrifice subsumes him into something larger than himself, the "great and honorable fatherland," which is rewarded with eternal life and, Ruth N. tells her friend, should help her overcome her grief.

Perhaps one of the most common ways in which religious language was employed by women was in their beseeching God to be a protector over their men on the combat front. Similar to the phrase *Gott mit Uns,* the militaristic phrases "watch over" (*behüten*) and "protect" or "defend" (*schützen*) were ubiquitous in popular media and army newspapers, which emphasized that front soldiers stood watch over the home front. In turn, seeking an entity that would protect those who protected them, women called on God to watch over their husbands and fathers. For example, Berliner Hedwig V. wrote in her diary that every night she and her little son Gotthard prayed to God to "watch over" her husband at the front.[12] This kind of language also permeated the diary of Käthe L., who wrote that when she read news of an offensive in her husband's sector of the front, she was overwhelmed with thoughts of his death, but prayed "God protect him!" (*Gott schütze ihn!*).[13] This kind of language gave women a sense of agency as they waited for news on the home front.

God's role as a protector and consoler also resonated in men's writings, which often contained a synthesis of religious and nationalistic language. This can be seen in the case of Hermann T., who volunteered in 1914 and quickly joined an aerial reconnaissance unit. He wrote extensively to his family about his feelings of loneliness at the front. He reflected on how he was deeply moved by the stress of separation and thought of his family and their love for him. Hermann T. intimated to his stepdaughter, Irmagard, that while he felt incredibly lonely, he found consolation in his faith.[14] He included in this letter to Irmagard a "wartime flyer" (*Kriegsflugblätter*), published by a Christian organization called "Christianity and the Present Day" (*Christentum und Gegenwart*) for soldiers in the field. The flyer included an article that particularly inspired him titled "The Peace of God in Battle" (*Gottesruhe im Kampf*), which gave recommendations on how soldiers should deal with stress. The author was purportedly an unnamed forty-year-old officer "who experienced tremendous pressure" at the front, but considered stress to be a God-given blessing that helped men rediscover their religious faith. The officer said that when the war broke out he realized, "So, your life is now over, whatever you experience and suffer henceforth is not about you as an individual, but rather you as a part of the German people." He described this evaporation of his individuality as God-ordained, and he took solace in the idea of sacrificing and subsuming himself into something larger: "I've thus concluded that every day that happens is now a gift from God. In this way, everything that happens—work, stress, danger—has become something that no longer concerned me, but only the fatherland and God." He went on to describe this approach to danger as a "new life," celebrating the war as a spiritual education that brought him closer to God.[15]

The author of the article sent by Hermann T. further suggested that by relying on God, one could build the internal resilience needed to survive. The war taught him that the Supreme Being was not to be sought outside himself, but rather God was to be discovered within, a source of power who gave him the strength to endure:

> I do not pray outwards from myself, but rather into myself, because I find traces of God with the innermost star of my being (*mit meinem innersten Wesenstern*). All actions, even the heaviest, become easy; there are no more decisions to be made, but only instructions that come from within me, and which will be executed as certainly as an electrical current is sure to be conducted. And all my life is a gift from God.[16]

In this vein, God lifts the burden of responsibility, enabling men to become like tools plugged into an "electrical current," presumably controlled by a higher power, that directs their behavior. His discovery of this "innermost star of my being" was a kind of revelation that made him feel "reborn." At the same time, it also caused some anxiety, as he realized that he was only an instrument of God's larger plan, the purpose of which was obscure.[17] Nevertheless, giving up responsibility calmed his fears. Imagining himself as a minuscule part in the machinery of God's indecipherable plan enabled him to detach and let go of his individuality. He reflected on how this allowed him to face otherwise unbearable violence:

> Eight days later we came under shell fire. Three artillery batteries fired on our company.
> The effect was tremendous. When the thunder of the batteries roared outside, when the screaming shells shrieked ominously and inescapably … that was when men stood powerless under the threat of absolute annihilation. Our thoughts were completely dominated by these scenes. Each projectile flies its course according to a certain will, the will of God. No object functions outside of this. It's been this way since even before it was born. But this tremendous destructive power is, compared to God, weaker than the adhesive strength of a particle of dust, which man breathes away without even being aware of it.[18]

Belief in God's all-powerful divine will allowed him to withstand overwhelming violence because he imagined himself, and this war, as ultimately insignificant in the larger scheme of God's plan. Including this officer's article in his letter home suggests that it struck a real chord with Hermann T. Shortly before he died in a crash at his flight training school, he wrote to his mother that this was how he saw the world, as one in which he was only a trivial speck, subject to God's will.[19]

While sublimation into the larger national spirit and God's plan held appeal for some individuals, there are also many cases where men reflected early in the war on their personal relationship with God, but they made no allusions to Germany's collective spiritual destiny. In these instances, language about sacrifice focused exclusively on the individual's salvation, and they were often marked by anxiety about their fate and the afterlife. This is especially the case when contrasting letters home with personal diaries, as one finds that the image presented to families could often be rosier than intimations in diaries, which might contain more ambivalence. Willy L., for example, whose inscription to his parents in a copy of The Gospel According to John was mentioned in the previous chapter, took comfort in reflecting on Jesus's sacrifice, without mention of nationalist sentiment. As the "spirit of 1914" bogged down into the reality of stalemate and trench warfare by October, Willy L. wrote to his parents about the harsh realities of the front, the strain of sleep deprivation, constantly being soaked in the rain, and wretched food. He took inspiration from Jesus's suffering, which he compared to his own stresses endured at the front. He assured his parents in October 1914, "I am always praying to God, who constantly stands with me."[20]

Willy L. also kept a diary, which contained views similar to those expressed in his letters to his parents, but his diary suggests he was a bit more apprehensive than he let on to his elders. He expressed confidence that Jesus was protecting him from bullets and shells, and he reiterated his belief that God was with him.[21] However, he also noted in his diary that he was anxious about his path to redemption. He believed Jesus was his Savior who gave him hope for salvation, but after his first battle, he expressed worry about whether God would forgive him for his sins. Though he also confessed this anxiety in his letters to his parents, he was not concrete about what those sins were, whether he was concerned about the act of killing, or something else. Despite his trepidation, he shared with his parents his hope that whatever his fate, he would be reunited with his family and that God would show him the way to avoid sin:

> God willing, other times will come again, where I will see you again, my dears. So far, my dear God has mercifully protected me from committing sin; he will, I am sure, continue to do so. As bad as things really are here, I could have never imagined a war such as this ... I trust in our dear Lord God.[22]

Willy L. did not make any mention of God in nationalistic terms. Rather, his entire focus was on his own individual relationship with God as his personal protector and savior, and whether the war experience endangered his chances for salvation. By the spring of 1915, his letters home started to change in tone. Instead of reflections on forgiveness, sin, and redemption, he focused on practical needs and the deprivations of everyday life in the trenches. In his last letters available in his file, written to his parents in February and March 1915, he joked after rotating to a rest area behind the lines, "Whenever one gets a chance to sleep on straw, one can thank God for that!"[23] He also quipped that his most valuable possession was his waterproof vest.[24] Loftier concerns about his spiritual well-being had all but disappeared. Willy L.'s fate is not recorded.

Building Resilience through Worship: Religious Services at the Front

As demonstrated in the previous chapter, religious authorities saw worship services as essential for reinforcing feelings of psychological strength and resilience, as well as patriotism and connection to home. However, for many front soldiers, even if the experience of communing with God was emotionally powerful, the actual experience of worship while under fire had a different effect. Instead of establishing continuity with prewar life, many men felt remote from their familiar religious environment and *Heimat*. Their experience of religious worship, often while in an atmosphere of extreme physical and emotional stress, reinforced a sense that they were detached from the real world and going through a unique spiritual experience that might or might not be translated through the prism of prewar rituals and beliefs. For some, the experience of religious services just before battle stirred emotions that transcended the nationalistic passions that frontline services were supposed to buttress, even creating transnational spiritual feelings that vexed military and religious authorities.

The sense of community that men found in religious rituals was vital in helping them endure the shock they felt when they encountered unimaginable violence in those first months of the war. One soldier compared his experience to that of the early Christians, and he wrote home about a church service with comrades, held inside the cave of a mineshaft just behind the lines, which made him feel an exceptional sense of bonding with other men at war. He wrote:

> Truly, I have never seen anything so touching, so moving in my life. Yesterday there was a short devotional service followed by confession and communion. I would compare the whole thing to a scene from the novel *Quo Vadis* (about the persecution of Christians under Nero). Just like the Christians gathered in caves for the holy miracles of healing, we gathered in a cave, in a small mine. And just as the Christians back then went to these places in times of greatest stress and danger, so too have we hurried to this place in circumstances of great danger.[25]

Though a religious service promised continuity with the prewar world, the actual experience of worship in the atmosphere of war was distinct. It made him feel like he was returning to the origins of the Christian movement, where a community under threat bonded and gave each other consolation. The essential appeal and function of Christianity as a movement that provided emotional support for the downtrodden became apparent.

The experience of worship was not always through front services organized by the German military. German soldiers in France and Belgium sometimes went to local services in these occupied territories, standing among civilians, which had unpredictable and emotionally powerful results. One unknown German infantryman recorded in a letter home how moved he was by the prayers given at a French mass on All Saints' Day (November 2) 1914. However, nationalist stereotypes shaped his perceptions of the local congregants. He was repulsed by the French civilians, who he said did not attend church diligently, but rather drank and made disrespectful jokes: "One 62 year-old Frenchmen said, 'Here is my heaven!' while pointing to his beer-filled bottle and sugar beets. We were amazed to find such hardhearted, non-religious people in such times." Touting the superiority of German piety, he proudly wrote that the church service was "densely occupied by our military, a company of our comrades." In the middle of the service, one of his comrades led in saying the Lord's Prayer, "which made hot tears roll down some warriors' cheeks," especially when the

French civilians stood reverently to hear the Germans' prayers and singing. "It made us feel a little easier about our fate," he wrote.[26] The experience of a church service gave him more than just a sense of spiritual reassurance or connection to prewar rituals and structures. His unabashed reference to the heartrending response of soldiers who were moved to tears reveals how within the framework of religion, "real men" could express their emotions.

The extraordinary circumstances of frontline worship services, especially with "enemy" civilians, sometimes had an unintended emotional effect. Men found the experience so transcendent and sacred that it seemed to eclipse their nationalist sentiments. Even if men sometimes complained about French and Belgian civilians, the experience of going to mass with people whose husbands and fathers were fighting them across the lines made a powerful impact that they tried to convey in letters and diaries. This was particularly true for Catholic German soldiers, who experienced a tension between their animosity toward the French as national enemies and their sense of common religious identity. For example, infantryman Wilhelm S. witnessed a Catholic mass given by a French priest in October 1914, and he was deeply moved by how the priest handled the potentially awkward situation of German soldiers and French civilians praying side by side. Wilhelm S. wrote to his family:

> Last Sunday I was in the Church with my comrades and could see that almost nobody was inside, despite the big Church. There were more German soldiers than civilians. My comrade, who speaks good French, understood the deeply moving words of the old pastor very well. He first prayed for all those who were at the front, without exception for any nation .... He thanks us many Germans coming to visit Church, because otherwise only the civilians who had loved ones at the front showed up. One hears nothing but complaints and crying. I was deeply moved in a way that I never have been before in my life.[27]

Wilhelm S. was shocked by the French clergyman. The priest's transnational compassion, and the experience of witnessing firsthand the pain suffered by French congregants who lived in chronic fear about their loved ones at the front, made such an impression that he struggled to put it into words.

Experiences worshipping with people who were "enemies" could also be tense. Even if men like Wilhelm S. were moved by the spirit of compassion across national boundaries, some realized how difficult it was for French civilians to have the occupiers in their houses of worship. But national loyalty was not easily dented by common religious identity. Tense interactions between French congregants and Catholic German soldiers can be found in the case of Joseph R., an infantryman who wrote home in November 1914 about his experience at a mass where the priest and women in the congregation were angered about the presence of men who might soon kill their husbands, brothers, and fathers. Joseph R. wrote home about German soldiers in the pews who recited "Great Lord we praise you!" drowning out the mostly older women congregants, after the priest read from the gospel. It brought the service to a standstill when French congregants heard the German language ring out, and he noticed that "it hit the priest pretty hard—he had tears in his eyes." Despite the awkward tension,

Joseph R. described it as extremely moving when he and his comrades tried to show that they could be both German soldiers and devout Catholics: "What a feeling went through us, that we could show the Frenchmen, what it is to be a German Catholic and a German soldier—it will remain in my memory for all my life." Sensitive to the reactions of his fellow Catholics, he added that, "Germans must be compassionate with the French clergymen," especially after witnessing the emotional responses to German soldiers in their midst.[28]

German chaplains were worried that some men might feel too much transnational religious spirit, and authorities tried to control potentially problematic sentiments. Otto B., who volunteered at the age of eighteen and served in a Baden-Württemberg regiment, wrote in his diary about training in Germany for a few weeks in August 1914 before he was sent to the front. Bright and early one Sunday morning, he and his new comrades were woken up and sent to different church services, depending on whether they were Catholic or Protestant. He wrote that his pastor emphasized the righteousness of the German cause and exhorted them not to forget that first and foremost they were Germans, even if they shared religious denominations with the enemy.[29] Otto B. did not reflect on what he thought about this, but it clearly made enough of an impression to be entered into his diary.

While a number of men recorded in their letters and diaries how deeply moved they were by religious services, this was not the universal response. For some front soldiers, religious worship made little impression, and it was even seen as a bit of a distraction, or even trivial, compared to the practical daily challenges they faced while preparing for combat. One soldier writing home tried to describe the unbearable stress of life in the trenches, getting stuck in the mud, drinking schnapps to fight the cold. He mentioned that he went to a religious service but recorded nothing about how it affected him. Asked by his family what he wanted for Christmas, his mind was on physical survival: "Would it be possible to get rubber covers for my boots?—please look for some. My Christmas prayer, if I make it to Christmas, is: a new pair of good boots and maybe a sleeping bag."[30] Spiritual issues seemed to be of little consequence to this soldier. For many, that first Christmas seemed almost surreal and the experiential gap intensified the distance they felt from home.

Christmas at the Front: Isolation and Distance from the *Heimat*

Christmas was perhaps the most important religious event that was utilized by the military to heal loneliness and build bridges between front and *Heimat*. Military and religious authorities put tremendous resources into replicating a German Christmas experience at the front, with an avalanche of Christmas trees, ornaments, food packages, and even Christmas market stalls and other reminders of home set up just behind the lines.[31] By pouring so much energy into Christmas rituals at the front, the military tried to incorporate "home" into the other-worldly experience of the trenches, and familiar Christmas traditions were employed to help console and assuage the stress triggered by separation, deprivation, and combat. But how did men perceive the experience of a frontline Christmas, and to what degree did it ease the stress of the front experience? While Christmas was intended to be a catalyst for cementing connections between men and their families, it actually intensified feelings of isolation, helplessness, and remoteness. In many cases, Christmas paradoxically reinforced a sense of spiritual disruption and distance from God, family, and home.

Military and religious authorities tried to utilize the powerful emotions that dominated the holidays to bolster morale. Military chaplain Dr. Aufhauser assigned Christmas a dual function. He linked the spirit of love that permeated Christmas to love of nation, and he saw Christmas as an ideal way to cement the bond between civilians and their loved ones fighting on the front. Christmas, Aufhauser observed, was a "holy night in which men on their watches could see glimmering stars send a golden bridge to the *Heimat*." Christmas provided "spiritual threads" (*geistige Faeden*) between home and the front, with "strong loyal love" as the common bond between the two. Since Christmas bolstered that love between men and their families, it in turn strengthened the home front's support for men in the trenches, giving them "renewed courage" and the resolve to fight. The Christmas season also reminded men of Jesus's "unfailing love," which inspired comradeship and self-discipline, and motivated them to defend their families and nation. "There in the redeemer's love found in the trustworthy crib [of baby Jesus]," Aufhauser wrote, "we find strength for the greatest sacrifice, and the ability to devote our own self to our friends!"[32] Artwork in army newspapers reinforced the importance of baby Jesus inspiring front soldiers, with one cover of the *Liller Kriegszeitung* in December 1917 depicting two steel-helmeted enlisted men who pray and hold watch over Jesus in his crib with a Christmas tree nearby (Figure 2.1).

While military and church authorities prescribed Christmas as a spiritual experience that reinforced military and nationalistic ideals, ordinary soldiers had a much more complicated relationship with the memories triggered by the sacred holiday. As early as December 1914, homesickness became particularly acute as men realized they would miss Christmas with their families. Despite the flood of care packages and Christmas trees arriving in the front lines, letters and diaries reveal how emotionally painful it was for many men to be separated from their families on this day that was so sacred for Christians and of profound importance in German culture.[33] Infantryman (*Fusilier*) Bach, who served in a Prussian regiment in France, wrote a letter to his family on Christmas Day 1914 in which he placed his faith in God to reunite him with his wife and children:

> It will be God's will that the Christ child soon brings peace and we can return home. We just have to trust God. Then everything will be right. I prayed a lot when I was in the *Heimat* and now I pray even more. And these days teach us that we should pray again, whereas previously nobody wanted to think about such things. It will be God's will if we are together at home next Christmas and freed from this misery.[34]

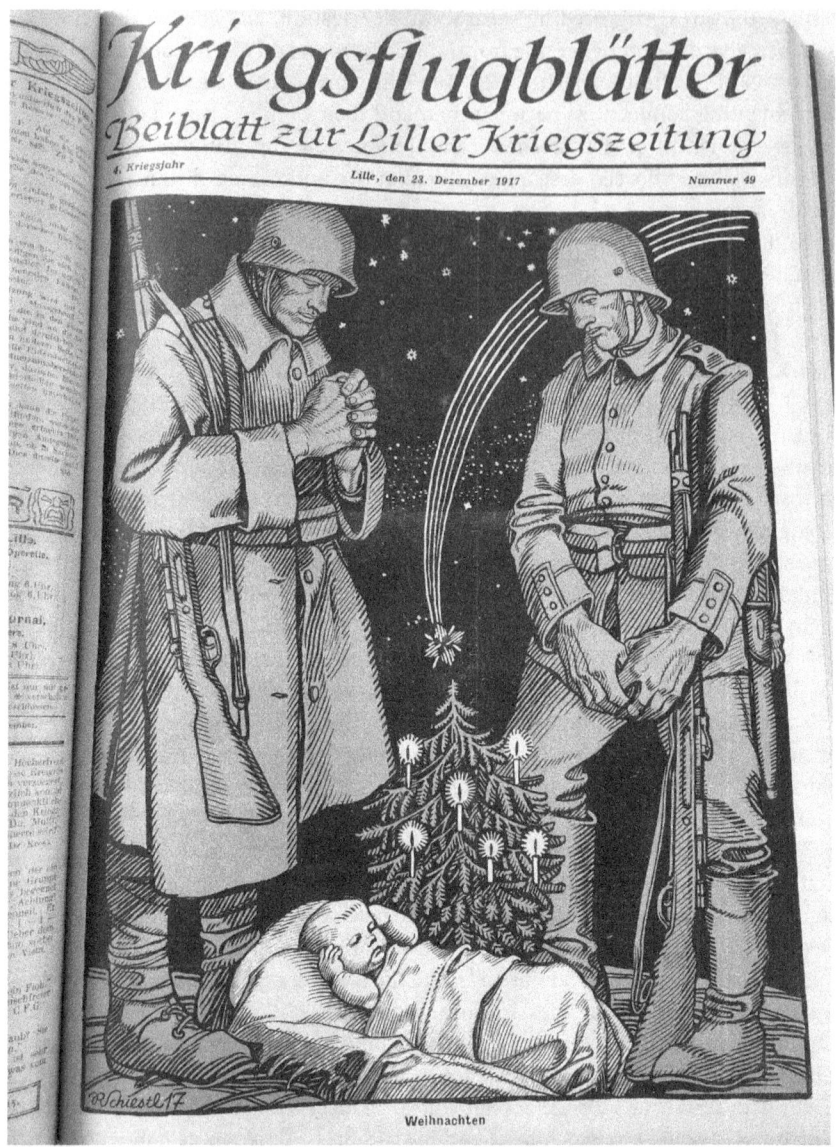

Figure 2.1 "Weihnachten," Drawing, *Kriegsflugblätter—Beiblatt zur Liller Kriegszeitung*, December 23, 1917, 4. Kriegsjahr, No. 49, PH 23/202, *Source*: BArch-MA.

Bach put all his hope in God's will to return to his family by Christmas 1915. On one hand, Christmas reinvigorated his will to pray and thoughts of God, but only in the context of pain caused by separation. His piety was stimulated by a desire to end the war and go home.

For many soldiers, Christmas was indeed a tradition with tremendous spiritual weight. However, they did not always see it as something that supplemented their sense of duty and national sacrifice. Rather, they often perceived Christmas as a separate entity that cut through the horrors of war, or that reminded them of another world that stood in stark contrast to the immediate environment of the trenches. This was most famously reflected in the Christmas truce of 1914, when German and British soldiers briefly suspended fighting to fraternize in No Man's Land. Men on both sides saw the sacred holiday tradition as something that transcended, or at least briefly interrupted, the catastrophe of war, and there were a number of instances in different parts of the front lines where opposing soldiers organized football matches and gift exchanges.[35] Even if they were banned from repeating the informally organized cease-fire on that holy night in December 1914, many German soldiers continued to fantasize about the Christmas spirit inspiring an end to war. Josef Peterhans, a young theater actor at the front who was on the verge of a film career that would later include roles in infamous Nazi propaganda pieces like *Jüd Süss* (1940), envisioned soldiers on both sides moved to tears by the baby Jesus, who he imagined visiting the trenches and bringing the killing to a temporary halt. Writing a poem for an army newspaper in December 1916, Peterhans dramatically described the horrors of the front: "A sea of flames—a scream, thunder and a crash/The battle rushes past, crushing the strong and the weak/The earth bursts open and as if in an earthquake its skeletons quiver."[36] Suddenly, in the midst of this surreal scene, a sound breaks through the chaos, and on the horizon he sees, "A looming cross and God's holy son/Extends his hands through the bloody, pale haze." Like Moses parting the Red Sea, Jesus, who appears as a baby, breaks through the fire and destruction until someone calls out to the soldiers on both sides of No Man's Land: "The Christ Child wants to go through your lines!/So stop! Give him just a narrow space/A little lane for his feet!/ He also brings you a Christmas tree, and holy, warm greetings from home." Upon the arrival of baby Jesus at the front, all the noise goes silent and the soldiers, "both friends and enemies," lower their weapons. "Memories return back from blood and night," Peterhans writes, "Everybody laughs and cries."[37] The Christ child thus brings not only the message of Christmas but also memories of life before the war. Interestingly, considering this was for an official army newspaper, the poem echoes more than just familiar nationalistic imagery of bonds between front and *Heimat*. Cutting through the material carnage of the war, Jesus also invades the consciousness of front soldiers on both sides, reminding them of their common humanity.

If military and religious authorities hoped that Christmas would bolster men's spirits with support from home and inspiration from Christian ideals of love and sacrifice, letters home revealed that in many ways the opposite was the case. Especially by Christmas 1915, all the care packages filled with miniature Christmas trees, chocolate, and other trappings of the season seemed a bit artificial and only reminded men of how far they were from home and their families. Christmas made front soldiers more homesick, fueling spiritual malaise. Two days before Christmas in 1915, Wilhelm L. wrote to his pastor about the Christmas festivities in the trenches. Soldiers decorated Christmas trees, sang, and held a feast of food and drink collected from care packages, with each soldier getting their own box marked "Christmas greetings from Baden," all while "under the serious warning of heavy guns, which thundered almost continuously." With all the food and gifts from home, he wrote wistfully, "I believe that we live better at the front than our loved ones do at home." But he could not help but feel like this was all just going through the motions. "It seems to me," he added, "as if the joyful mood was somewhat forced." All the Christmas paraphernalia reminded him of just how long he had been away from his family, and he concluded his letter with the wish, "In the hope that the war will soon come to an end with God's help."[38] For noncommissioned officer Bruno C., Christmas in 1915 intensified his sense of loneliness, as he remembered past Christmases and lamented his absence from home. But he found comfort in the avalanche of letters and care packages, "each one a precious treasure."[39]

In other cases, Christmas reinforced how cut off men felt from their wives and children. Infantryman FL wrote to his wife in December 1915 that he was ecstatic to get so many packages from home, but he felt a bit helpless that he could not send more than money and best wishes. The responsibility for making the kids happy, he wrote, fell on his wife, and he promised to make up for his absence in the next year, leaving him to put his "trust in God and hope for the best."[40] Their forced passivity during the Christmas season fueled men's feelings that the war had paralyzed them as they relinquished patriarchal roles over to their wives and children. To counteract their gloom at being ripped away from family and Christmas joy, soldiers tried to replicate Christmas celebrations, but this often only reinforced a sense of isolation. Franz W., posted as a guard at a prisoner of war (POW) camp in December 1915, lamented, "Since I'm not able to celebrate Christmas at home with my loved ones, I have to spend it with Russian POWs, 19,000 in number." He made do by having prisoners build a Christmas market with a theater, music, and folk dances. But he wrote that the more work he put into creating a German Christmas, the more distant he felt from home.[41] Hermann S., for example, wrote in December 1914 to his wife Elly from the naval base in Cuxhaven that "I will celebrate Christmas with you in spirit (*Geist*)."[42] Interestingly, this was the extent of spiritual rhetoric in Hermann's letters to his wife. His letters contained no reference to the religious significance of Christmas, making no mention of God or the birth of Jesus. Rather, the connection he felt to home came solely through the care packages he received and the Christmas markets in Cuxhaven, though he complained that "the Christmas punch was unfortunately a bit watery."[43]

Most letters home about Christmas focused on care packages and how much soldiers missed their families. But in a number of instances, men intimated how spending Christmas at the front affected their relationship with God. Contrary to the military's prescription, the Christmas season seemed to amplify their sense of spiritual dislocation. For example, writing to his pastor from the Russian front in January 1916, Catholic soldier Karl H. reported that Christmas was a miserable experience. From a practical standpoint, he felt he was not able to engage the proper rituals. Services had been set up just behind the front, but for some reason he could not get access to a Catholic chaplain: "For five months we have not yet been able to go to a Church where one could go to confession and take the blessed sacraments." From a spiritual standpoint, he wrote that he felt remote from God, and that he did not feel comfortable talking about religion with his comrades: "It's such a shame that things are so bad here in our column—on the topic of religion, nobody even talks about it." The "content-rich and edifying writings" from his pastor, he wrote, were the only things that "were good for my soul in lonely Russia." He concluded his letter by saying that he was desperate to come home to his parish church, where he could "prostrate on my knees before the Blessed Sacrament and worship God who is hidden there in the tabernacle."[44] Though military and religious leaders had promised they could give men a Christmas experience that would strengthen their spirits and fighting morale, for at least some front soldiers, Christmas at the front only amplified their sense of remoteness and frustration.

God as a Bridge between Combat and Home Fronts

The Christmas season brought into sharp focus the stress that separation inflicted on families. Faith in God was a common language used by men and women to try to bridge that gap. Similar to case studies of British soldiers studied by historian Michael Roper, religious language was central for German soldiers who reached out to mothers, wives and girlfriends for emotional support, even if they felt they could not describe the terrifying scenes they witnessed in the trenches.[45] The linguistic and psychological tools used to build these connections between home and combat fronts were diverse. The subjective and self-referential language found in correspondence, which became increasingly detached and decentralized from hegemonic religious language, can be challenging to reconstruct. But a common denominator in correspondence between the two fronts was that religion provided a language that helped soldiers and civilians find an imagined space separate from the increasingly traumatic material world.

Though an experiential gap widened between the two fronts, belief in God helped bind stressed families together psychologically. "God" was a kind of shorthand between men and women as they expressed love and support for each other. Imagining God's protective hand, and trying to influence that hand through faith and prayer, gave men and women a sense of control over the destiny of their loved ones, which helped them achieve some level of psychological homeostasis. Further, the belief in God as an all-powerful protector helped men feel like a benevolent eye was watching over their families. At the same time, families at home imagined that God took care of their husbands and fathers while they faced danger at the front.

The idea that a spiritual bridge existed between combat and home fronts permeated letters and diaries. For example, infantryman Max M. recorded in his 1914–15 diary entries that he felt his family's presence and that their prayers worked.[46] His family frequently sent him care packages, which reinforced his feeling that at least spiritually, his loved ones at home were with him. In an October 1914 diary entry, he wrote:

> The French can't hold out much longer, as their artillery is pretty much shot up and ours is already bombarding their trenches all day long. Every evening we also receive care packages: cigars, cigarettes, chocolate, bacon and clothes. As a result, our stamina is strengthened. One fights much better in the awareness that in spirit (*Geist*) our loved ones at home are always with us at the front.[47]

This concept of "spirit" (*Geist*) was widely used by men and women to reassure loved ones that they were still present in their imaginations, if not in body. This was often closely linked to the idea that God oversaw and facilitated these spiritual connections. When he returned from patrols, Max M. carefully recorded in his diary his belief that he had survived because of God's intervention, which was made more certain because of his family's spiritual strength and piety.[48]

This image of mutual spiritual support through faith was reinforced by popular media. Postcards, for example, were one of the most common forms of communication used during the war and an important part of the over six million pieces of mail exchanged between home and combat fronts each day.[49] Photographic technology was used to represent soldiers' psychological universe in which they imagined guardian angels and their families accompanying them on the battlefield (Figures 2.2 and 2.3).

Though images in such popular media of guardian angels looking over loved ones might have reassured some, households were often consumed with anxiety. For example, Minna F.'s husband and son both served, and throughout 1914 and 1915 she wrote letters to them that were filled with assurances that their faith would protect them. However, in 1916 her son was killed. Shortly after his death, she wrote to her husband Karl that she was overwhelmed with fear and could not bear the thought of his death. She begged him to apply for sick leave, implying that he fake an illness, like the husband of one of her friends, so he could escape the trenches and be sent home. In one letter, after imploring her husband to convince his officer that he was too sick to fight, she included a prayer to God to protect her man and return him home:

> Dear God, stand by me and help me, send my dear husband home. My son is gone and soon I will lose my husband. Oh God, how do I keep going, I can't remain in the world. What will happen to me if I have no one left by my side. Oh God, help me in my great anxiety. At Pentecost (*Pfingsten*), when everyone else is usually so happy, I went into my little room and cried my eyes out.[50]

Despite her efforts to implore God for protection and look over her men at the front, the psychological stress of waiting, worrying, and imagining the death of her loved ones was too much to endure. As subsequent chapters will show, Minna F. tried just about everything to alleviate her anxiety, from traditional prayer and rituals to reliance on superstitions that promised to shield her husband and son from harm.

Men reassured anxious loved ones that God was still with them, despite feelings of isolation and stress. For example, Hans S., a printer who volunteered shortly after the outbreak of the war, wrote in 1915 from the Eastern Front to his wife Ida about fighting off depression.[51] In his letters from his mobilization in 1915 through the end of the war, he regularly asked his family to pray for him to help ensure God's protection. In August 1918, he told his parents to take solace in their mutual faith because no matter how much stress he endured, he had a "curious feeling" that his family was always with him and that their prayers kept him protected and in God's hands.[52] He was confident that his parents understood this feeling of God's presence, and he emphasized that the more he and his family prayed, the more he felt this uplifting support from God.

God and the "Spirit of 1914"   51

Figure 2.2 Postcard, "Sein Schutzengel—Der Engel, er schützet mit sicherer Hand/Die Kinder, du schützest das Vaterland" ("His guardian angel—the angel, he protects with a sure hand/Children, you protect the fatherland"), 1915. Postcard, personal collection of the author.

Though men assured their families that God helped them survive stress, the bridge between home and combat fronts could also feel tenuous. Belief in God gave them a sense of comfort, and a kind of refuge when they felt cut off from familial sources of emotional support, but they struggled to convey their traumatic experiences when they felt it would be a burden on their family. For example, corporal (*Gefreiter*) David

Figure 2.3 "Der Kriegers Schutzengel—Es mögen Dich in Kriegszeiten Schutzengel immerdar geleiten" ("The warrior's guardian angel—May guardian angels always guide you in times of war"), 1915. Postcard, personal collection of the author.

A. wrote to his pastor in October 1914 that he could not tell his parents about the pain and suffering that surrounded him, but his faith still sustained him. He confessed:

> So if we retrieved the wounded at night, it was very dangerous for us. The patrols and the artillery always bombarded the streets of Vermelles, where we had to fetch the wounded … A private named Geiger got a belly shot and died shortly thereafter … Please do not tell my parents, as I don't want them to be worried about me; I do not always write to them about how things are really going right now. We are now hoping and praying to God that there will be peace soon and that we will be able to return healthy to our dear *Heimat*.[53]

Shielding his parents from the horrifying images of war, David A. put his faith in God to end the carnage and bring them home. He thus started to develop a closer relationship with his pastor, with whom he could intimate the terror of combat, than with his family.

Nurses in field hospitals, with a foot in both combat and home fronts, often tried to buttress the bridge between those two worlds. In one case, a mother received a letter from her son's nurse, who was with her boy as he died. The nurse tried to reassure the mother that God remained by her son's side, despite the boy's tormented last moments. According to the nurse, who only signed her name "Gisela," the son scribbled a few lines of poetry just before he died. She pried the poem out of his hand when he passed away and sent it to the mother. The poem, a dream-like and confusing stream of consciousness that the nurse said was produced in a "feverish delirium," suggested that the young man was tormented with guilt after killing. "Great God, there's such terrible anguish (*schwere Not!*)," the son wrote, "I used to kill every fly/But now I think about it: they are suffering." The young soldier signed his poem, "A tired infantryman (*Landesknecht*)." Perhaps fearful of how the mother would take the delirious last lines written by a dying son, Nurse Gisela intervened and tried to provide some comfort:

> Dear poor mother, he was so tired, your son; the artist whom the war had made an infantryman, and who with noble enthusiasm gave his life for his fatherland. He died as an artist: steel struck him from the clouds. One piece [of steel] that hovered above him ultimately caused his death. God gave you a falcon of mourning to comfort you and lift you up.[54]

The nurse counterbalanced the son's last descent into a "terrible anguish" with reassuring images of a compassionate God, "noble" sacrifice of the fatherland, and a fateful death over which no one has any control. Portraying God as caring and present, Nurse Gisela offered some hope that the mother could cling to as she imagined her son's death. Whether the nurse's efforts at consolation were effective is unknown.

Though their experiences diverged, in many cases men and women were still able to share their fears, anxieties, and the impact of the war on their spiritual health. This can be seen in the case of Rudolf V., a middle-class Protestant mentioned in the previous chapter who was moved by the experience of being invited to a synagogue. Rudolf V. volunteered as a lieutenant at the outbreak of the war and for two years he sent letters virtually every day to his wife, Julie. He was emotionally very close to her. He told her in graphic detail about the violence that he witnessed, and he documented how these experiences affected him. Within the first few weeks after he mobilized, he wrote to her about how the stress of war profoundly changed him, making him feel like he was living a kind of dual existence, strong on the outside, but internally fragile. "There are sometimes strange moods in me," he wrote, "when a horn sounds, that causes me to cheer and sing for war, war and war again, but one also wants to flee all this loud hustle and bustle—it's just that nobody sees where the lonely people like me want to sneak away to feel a loving, soft hand. Julie be proud and brave."[55]

Rudolf V. processed his traumatic experiences through the lens of his religious beliefs, though these were tested after he was wounded in September 1914. He shared his inner spiritual turmoil with Julie and wrote to her about how he could not get out of his mind the moment in which a bullet struck him in the lung and he believed he would die.[56] He told her about the deaths of comrades and detailed their last moments as well as the different injuries suffered by men in the hospital beds around him. Most traumatic for him was witnessing men call out for God, though they could not find respite from all the pain.[57] Rudolf V. insisted that he maintained his faith, but he shared with Julie that his most reliable spiritual support came from the love and support of his comrades. He described the importance of comradeship in a poem called "My Dead Comrades from Chilly," where he recounted "tears that streamed into my hands" when he reflected on the terrible wounds they suffered.[58] Rudolf V. told her that he was inspired by Christian self-sacrifice, expressed through comradeship, and what he called "selfless love" that men displayed in their friendships and compassion for fellow soldiers: "I've never seen more examples of selfless love than there at the front, where in blood and desperation we fight through the most difficult days."[59]

The "selfless love" that Rudolf V. found in comradeship suggested that he was finding as much spiritual sustenance from fellow soldiers as he did from home. Comradeship also caused him to broaden his views about religion, and he shared this change with his wife. In particular, when he found such support from Jewish comrades, whom he described as friends that were as close-knit as his family, he had to reevaluate the antisemitic stereotypes that shaped his attitudes before the war. One of his friends, Schumacher, was given the chance to go home on leave to mourn his dead brother, but chose instead to stay with his comrades at the front. German Jewish soldiers, he told Julie, were, contrary to the stereotypes he had been raised to believe, just as courageous, patriotic, and willing to fight as Christian comrades. Finding spiritual support and what he described as Christ-like "selfless love" from his new family of comrades at the front, Rudolf V.'s world-view had been broadened as he realized that his values of love and compassion were universal, transcending the social and cultural structures in which he had been socialized at home. His letters reveal the willingness of men to share their profound experiences with women at home, even while they were at the same time suggesting that their closest spiritual bonds were gradually being developed with fellow front soldiers.

Fatalism: Relinquishing Control to a Higher Power

As the enthusiasm of the "spirit of 1914" began to break down into stalemate, attrition, and the drudgery of survival, so did the sense that God had a specific plan to guide the German army to victory. Men become focused on individual, rather than national, destiny. Historian Peter Knoch observes that in many cases, men "privatized" their relationship with God, thanking him for the inexplicable, seemingly miraculous moments that enabled them to survive.[60] This privatized relationship was often expressed through a lens of fatalistic language. Fatalism, the belief that events are predetermined and inescapable, became a powerful mechanism for men who struggled with day-to-day uncertainty and terror. It allowed them to process the stress of combat and pain resulting from the loss of comrades by relinquishing a sense of control or responsibility.

Fatalistic emotions fell across a wide spectrum, ranging from contentment to resignation, or submission, and even joy that God had everything under control, even if it was unknowable. As Alexander Watson argues, many front soldiers found solace in the notion that they could relinquish control to a higher power.[61] For other soldiers, the sense of not knowing whether the next bullet or shell was destined for them produced tremendous anxiety. Fatalism could also be invoked by soldiers coping with impatient loved ones at home as tensions mounted over the duration of the war. Finally, feelings about God's control or capriciousness were not static over time. For those who survived for several years in the trenches, their language sometimes evolved from carefully constructed beliefs about their private relationship with God to more vague feelings or ambivalence about the mysteriousness or even oppressive nature of fate.

Fatalism could provide a sense of calm and even awe for God's power. Eduard F. wrote to his priest in December 1914 that he believed his Catholic faith was particularly effective in helping him accept God's will, which enabled him to keep going: "Unfortunately, I was wounded and was completely ripped away from my effective circle of control (*aus meinem Wirkungskreise herausgerissen*). But you have to submit to God's will. He will do everything for the best. This shows how the Catholic religion is so sublime and beautiful."[62] Eduard F.'s expression of admiration for Catholicism specifically is interesting, as he suggested that this particular faith system was ideally suited for alleviating frontline stress, though he does not elaborate on how Catholicism was exceptional from a theological perspective.[63] However, he was convinced that Catholic faith was optimal for his emotional health. Submission to God's will, he intimated, counterbalanced his anxiety that he had become helpless and ineffective after he was wounded.

Eduard F.'s careful reflection on his fatalistic emotions was relatively exceptional. Men more often avoided intricate descriptions of emotions related to fatalism, but rather merely stated matter-of-factly that God was in control. For example, Franz H. wrote to his parents in August 1914 about how God's will determined his fate: "The bullet that is destined for me will certainly hit me. Nothing can help that. It's in God's name!"[64] His feelings about this were not clearly expressed. He was simply resigned to the notion that he had no control, and that only God knew what the next day would bring. Franz H. was killed in combat in 1915.

Civilians also found solace in the idea that God was beside them, even if his will was mysterious, and it helped them process their emotions and mourn the deaths of fathers and husbands. Language used in *Sterbebilder* or *Totenzettel* ("Death Cards" or "Death Notes"), for example, reinforced beliefs that God had foreordained the fates of loved ones. Death Cards were widely distributed by families in mourning, and they often contained biblical quotes, prayers, and tributes to the dead. In the case of the parents and brothers of Franz Xaver Heudorfer, a thirty-eight-year-old Catholic soldier who was killed in action in February 1917, the Death Card gave them an opportunity to express their acceptance of God's will and ask the Creator to take care of their son's soul (Figure 2.4). The card included the tribute:

> Almighty, merciful God, who in your admirable providence (*anbetungswürdigen Vorsehung*) determines the moment of death for us, we ask you from our trusting

Figure 2.4 Sterbebild, Franz Xaver Heudorfer, von Schöneburg, fürs Vaterland gestorben am 7. Februar. 1917. Personal collection of the author.

and devoted hearts: look mercifully on the soul of this fallen soldier, accept that his death was suffered in the loyal fulfillment of his duty as a full penance, and lead [his soul] to eternal peace.[65]

Although it is difficult to ascertain the degree to which the card's inscription reflected the family's personal emotions, the tribute suggests that the family resigned themselves to God's "providence," and that they saw their son's dutiful sacrifice as deserving ultimate absolution. In this public display of piety, the family seemed to find comfort in the idea that God was in control and that their son's soul would be tended to in heaven.[66]

By giving up a sense of control to God, soldiers and civilians could relinquish the burden of responsibility, and subsequently alleviate the guilt and suffering triggered by death. This can be seen in the case of infantryman Ambrosius S., who wrote to his fiancée Elisabeth B. in April 1915 about a "terrifying battle" in which his battalion suffered "over 1,000 casualties." After a funeral for one of his comrades, he reflected on God's omniscience and omnipotence:

> In today's funeral sermon our brave fallen comrades were remembered. Our hut looks very neglected. God willing, it will not be turned into a pile of rubble and we'll be spared. Lord, your will, not mine, will make it happen. He alone knows what is best for me … Let us thank our dear God that I am still alive. Shared joy is doubled joy, shared suffering is half suffering.[67]

Ambrosius S. relinquished his sense of control over to God, imagining the Supreme Being as the sole determiner of his fate. If anyone got killed, pain and suffering could be diffused, allowing him to revel in the fact that he was still alive.

Fatalism could also be utilized by soldiers to cope with a variety of problems, including growing discontentment from the home front. Soldiers often grew impatient as their family complained about conditions at home, or when they expressed anxiety about when their husbands and fathers would return. In some of these cases, men brushed off their loved ones and washed their hands of responsibility by saying they could not do anything about the prolonged separation, because it was all in God's hands. For example, as early as late September 1914, Anton K.'s wife complained to him that there were not enough field hands on their farm, and their harvest was in jeopardy. He responded impatiently:

> From your letter I can tell that you're not doing well. Be satisfied and don't complain, because [at the front] we've got it ten times worse … The suffering caused by this war can't be described. If it's God's will, I will come home again. But if that is not the case, then so it is determined by our Lord God.[68]

He continued by telling her to complete the harvest as much as she could and "in the name of God, just don't starve."[69] Helpless to solve his family's economic crisis, Anton K. relinquished his patriarchal control. As the stress of separation put pressure on soldiers and civilians, a fatalistic outlook enabled them to relieve some of their anxiety, but it did not solve their nagging uncertainty about the upheaval caused by the war.

After months of attritional, industrialized combat, as letters started to betray growing despair, fatalism became as much of a burden as it was a comfort. One can see an evolution in the front soldiers' language, with letters moving from confidence to resignation and then to creeping apprehension or even doubt about God's omnipotence. For example, in July 1915 Max M. initially wrote in his diary with conviction that God intervened to keep him calm while under fire:

> On July 23, I stood at a trench post. About 100 paces from us the Frenchies hid with their damn snipers. Through the trench mirror I saw that one of them lined me up in his sights. It only took a second to throw myself into the dirt. Suddenly the ball whistled through the shooting platform and into the trench wall. All my limbs quivered (*zitterte*). I summoned a short prayer of thanks to the Lord who determined life and death. If they had got me this time, I would not have noticed, but my loved ones at home? There is a gracious God. Here in distress and danger one feels his controlling hand.[70]

Max M. described the act of prayer as a means of coping with his "quivering" nerves. However, as the war dragged on he became increasingly pessimistic about whether prayer would sustain him. Several months later on New Year's Eve, he lamented that though humans were dependent on God who determined their survival, "God's path" was frustratingly unclear, and the sheer magnitude of trauma and violence caused him to wonder about God's purpose.[71] God's "controlling hand" had become capricious rather than consoling, and, similar to many other soldiers, he struggled with chronic psychological stress in a world that seemed less and less comprehensible.

An evolution of feelings, from confidence in God's will to resigned fatalism and ultimately an erosion of religious belief altogether can be seen to unfold in a single individual's letters over time. This can be traced in the case of Ernst H., who volunteered in 1914 and kept a regular correspondence with his family through 1917, when he was captured and spent the rest of the war as a POW in France. Starting the war with a firm belief in God's support for the nation, he gradually became much more concerned with God's plans for his own individual fate. In his letters to his family in 1914 and early 1915, his language about God echoed what was found in army newspapers and popular media, as he expressed thanks to the Supreme Being for protecting the nation and, in his first Christmas during the war, prayed for a quick return home.[72] However, by the spring of 1915, his letters became starker, focusing on the brutal reality of combat. In one letter to his mother, he apologized for scaring her with graphic descriptions of artillery bombardments. He assured her that "thank God it's gotten better, and the bombs and shrapnel mostly crash above us without doing much harm."[73] But a few weeks later, he admitted that the war was psychologically stressful and that his initial toughness, and that of his comrades, started to erode: "The effect of artillery shells on the nerves are much worse [than infantry attacks], and many men who otherwise talk big suddenly appear in a different light when the bombs are falling."[74]

In the face of these traumatic experiences, Ernst H. found comfort in the idea that God alone determined whether he would live or die. When his grandmother expressed fear over his fate, especially after reading his letters detailing the horrors of combat, he told her that it was God's will that he fight in the trenches to protect the *Heimat* from the enemy. He asked her to pray for him, as he believed that her prayers improved the chances that God would hear them:

> There's so many things that preoccupy you, dear grandmother. You do not need to worry about me. Everything comes from God, and he will know what is good for us. And since you also pray a lot for me at home, he will also hear your prayers. At least you are healthy and, God willing, we can see each other later ... and if we don't see each other again in this world, then we'll meet in eternity.[75]

Ernst H.'s firm reliance on God seemed to peak in the summer of 1915. In subsequent letters to his family, he does not reflect on God's will and control over his fate, suggesting perhaps that his certainty dissipated as the war unfolded. By the time he was captured and interned as a POW in France in October 1917, he did not refer to God at all, but rather simply expressed hope for a quick return home, echoing the demoralized language often found in accounts by POWs, who often felt stigmatized and suffered a bruised sense of masculinity as a result of being captured.[76] Thus after several years of fighting and then finally the experience of becoming a POW, his carefully constructed language about God faded as he focused simply on the hope for survival.

Conclusion

Officially sanctioned religious language about nationalism, faith, and resilience echoed in letters and diaries of men and women in the wake of the "spirit of 1914." However, especially after first encounters with violence, letters home began to reveal much more complex relationships with religious beliefs. Traumatic violence produced powerful emotions, and preexisting mechanisms of beliefs and rituals that had once been so reassuring suddenly seemed less effective. The unstable psychological landscape in which many found themselves triggered diverse patterns of thinking and language about God. Some found fatalism to be consoling, while others found "God's hand" to be frustratingly mystifying. Communicating emotions through religious language gave some a bridge between home and combat fronts, while others felt isolated. Traditional rituals like Christmas might be reassuring in some cases, but even this cherished, familiar psychological haven could be stressful and alienating. There was no singular paradigm for spiritual-religious responses to initial encounters with trauma.

Within these diverse reactions to violence, however, a common pattern emerges. Nationalistic, often formulaic, rhetoric about God and nation gradually dissolved into greater reflection, and often anxiety, about religion's efficacy as a device for providing individual psychological relief. As will be seen in subsequent chapters, the struggle to diagnose, process, and heal the traumatic effects of modern war would lay the groundwork for more subjective religious concepts beyond the spectrum of strictly Judeo-Christian beliefs. But first, men and women would try to apply traditional religious beliefs to deal with the escalating psychological crisis that emerged out of the modern war experience. The effectiveness of religion as a tool for healing shattered nerves would be put to the test.

3

Processing Trauma: Nerves, Religious Language, and Coping with Violence

On October 1914, Georg G., who volunteered as a lieutenant at the outbreak of the war and fought mostly on the Eastern Front, reassured his wife that God gave him strength while under fire: "I was completely calm, had my cigar in my mouth and walked up and down the line of troops, exhorting my people to keep quiet and trust in God, who directs everything according to his will. During the shooting, more artillery opened up and we fired shrapnel and grenades at the enemy positions."[1] However, despite placing faith in God, the constant artillery barrages tormented his nerves: "In the end, the bombardments are terribly unnerving. You feel like helpless cattle."[2] While he was able to maintain control, and projected to his comrades a mask of discipline through faith, he could still confess to his wife the devastating psychological effects of combat. He even admitted to her that sometimes he needed more than God to take the edge off his nerves, which were tested not just by combat but also by oppressive officers: "The strong nervous tension that I feel requires appropriate measures, which are difficult to get without money. For example, in addition to good cognac and rum I often drink sparkling wine in order to get other thoughts in my mind and banish the troubling thoughts that come up when I deal with my difficult company CO."[3]

Georg G.'s letters to his wife illustrate how language about God and nerves became a cornerstone of letters and diaries, where soldiers and civilians ruminated on the unbearable psychological effects of total war. Military and medical authorities characterized total war as a "war of nerves."[4] As early as 1910, Kaiser Wilhelm II proclaimed to naval academy officers and cadets, "The next war and the next battle at sea will demand of you healthy nerves. It is through nerves that its outcome will be decided."[5] But as nerves broke down under the reality of industrialized violence, doctors were mobilized to combat an array of symptoms, diagnosed as "war hysteria" or "war neurosis," which appeared in front soldiers in the first months of the war. While military and medical authorities grappled with diagnosis and treatment, ordinary Germans used existing psychological and emotional tools, especially religious beliefs and rituals, to deal with nervous stress. This chapter explores the following question: How were the psychological and emotional effects of violence processed through the language of religious faith?

The language of nerves was the central prism through which the military and medical establishment evaluated the psychological resilience and mental fitness of soldiers. However, though this medicalized term "nerves" was ubiquitous in letters and diaries of soldiers and civilians, their methods of coping with, and treating, nervous breakdown was not expressed in medical terms. The central argument of this chapter is that ordinary Germans integrated the language of nerves with the language of religion in a complex, overlapping framework of thinking in which they applied their familiar and available cultural concepts to combat the psychological crisis triggered by modern war. Front soldiers and civilians relied on religious tools that included the concept of a transcendent, supernatural power generated through internal and external spiritual strength (acquired from the "Holy Spirit," the Christian concept of a channel between God and humans), rigorous prayer, the promise of salvation from the transient material world, and faith that forces behind their control or understanding would protect them and heal their frayed nerves. These concepts were constructed and applied in intricate, self-referential discourse between family members in their correspondence between home and combat fronts.

Historians like Elaine Showalter have persuasively argued that in order to heal psychological trauma, men had to find an outlet to express otherwise repressed or socially unacceptable "feminine" emotions.[6] Religion gave traumatized men that outlet, as it provided a language for venting feelings of anxiety, fear, love, and vulnerability. Soldiers and civilians began to express these emotions through the lens of religion in the early months of the war, as examined in the previous chapter, when rhetoric found in letters and diaries often reinforced prevailing traditional ideals about faith in God and "holding through." However, I would argue that as the war dragged on, religious language used to cope with psychological trauma became much more complex, based on immediate emotional needs that were often highly subjective. Further, beyond just providing a language for perseverance or resilience, religious faith also became a framework for conceptualizing psychological escape from violence. In particular, God's promise of eternal life gave soldiers and civilians an imagined space that helped remove them from this unbearable earthly reality.[7]

This chapter will examine the integration of language about religion and nerves through three major topics. First, it will explore how military authorities prescribed God as a countermeasure against nervous breakdown. At this level of discourse, the dual meaning of German terms like "*Geist*" (mind/spirit) and "*Seele*" (psyche/soul), was important, as these concepts, which had both medical and religious connotations, were employed in different ways by both elites and soldiers to articulate mental and spiritual resilience and collapse. Second, this chapter will closely analyze how the language of religion intersected with language about nerves in letters and diaries by soldiers and civilians. Families used their prewar religiosity to articulate the condition of their "nerves," thus often mixing modern and traditional language in self-diagnosis of mental health. In some cases, men and women would even assert that their religious rituals and belief systems were more effective tools for combating psychological pain than modern psychiatric treatment. Finally, this chapter will explore how religious language was employed to articulate psychological collapse, which was often conflated with spiritual collapse. Psychological trauma was for some a trigger that caused anxiety over whether God really was on their side, or whether God could actually help them, leading to complex forms of spiritual crisis.

The broad range of emotions mediated through religious language gives us a more complete picture, beyond the framework of medical categorization and diagnosis, of how individuals imagine and represent traumatic injuries.[8] In writing about their experiences in letters and diaries, men and women found a form of self-therapy in the language of religion, which helped them to stabilize and "regroup" emotionally and psychologically. Writing had a restorative function, helping individuals to externalize or capture their experiences, especially when these experiences were "handed over" to loved ones and the familiar cocoon provided by religious thinking.[9] However, the efficacy of religion as an antidote to trauma varied, as did the ways in which individuals applied religious therapy to heal their nerves.

God and Nerves: Official Prescriptions for Strong Mental Fitness

Doctors and medical authorities used the concept of "nerves" to both stigmatize and idealize front soldiers. "Steel nerves," characterized by discipline and self-sacrifice, were celebrated in the popular media as the cornerstone of the idealized warrior. In contrast, men who broke down with a diverse range of symptoms of mental trauma categorized as "war neurosis" or "war hysteria" were stigmatized as allegedly deficient in masculine character and unable to survive the test of combat.[10] By early 1915, the numbers of front soldiers who were suffering from symptoms of psychological injury continued to grow rapidly, and doctors noticed tics, tremors, paralysis, and other symptoms afflicting men with no visible wounds on their bodies. Debates raged in medical circles over whether men were fakers, "hysterics" with preexisting pathologies, or genuine victims of psychological injury.[11] By the end of the war, over 600,000 men in the regular and reserve armies had been diagnosed as suffering from a whole range of different nervous disorders that continued to bewilder medical authorities.[12]

As the war dragged on, and men desperately sought ways to cope with traumatic violence, some of the most popular media for soldiers, including army newspapers, offered prescriptions that emphasized spiritual cures for frayed nerves. The language used in army newspapers revealed how closely chaplains and military officers aligned mental health with religious well-being. Religious faith as a prophylaxis against psychological stress focused on the *Geist* of the front soldier. The term "*Geist*" ("mind" or "spirit") had a dual meaning, and it could be found in both medical and religious discourse, referring to "mental" or "spiritual" health, respectively. Similarly, the word "*Seele*," which was also frequently found in official rhetoric on soldiers' mental and spiritual health, had layered meanings, as it can mean "soul," "mind," or "psyche." Depending on its usage by both psychiatric experts and religious elites, *Seele* thus had different connotations, suggesting both the medicalized conception of the "psyche" and the more religious-spiritual notion of the "soul."

The widespread use of the term *Geist* by military authorities can be found in the army newspaper *Liller Kriegszeitung* in a 1915 article on "Mental/Spiritual Health" ("*Geistige Gesundheitspflege*"). The unnamed author begins with a reference to a speech by Field Marshal von Hindenburg in which the commander of the German army called upon men to apply the power of prayer to ensure future victories. The author then suggests that von Hindenburg's request "touches the deepest, holiest element of this war, that is the spirit (*Geist*), the inner content (*Gehalt*) of the people, who must really and truly win this war."[13] Each individual soldier's spirit or mind was part of the fabric of the collective spirit of the nation (*Volk*). Facing stress in this ongoing war, the success of the nation thus depended on each individual to conjure strength from their inner spirit, reach into their inner selves and remain resilient. The article concluded with a quote from Goethe to define this inner *Geist*: "The spirit that we are dealing with is of the highest form."[14]

Popular media geared for consumption by soldiers and civilians disseminated an idealized image of warriors who maintained spiritual strength, and in turn steel nerves. This can be seen especially in the case of fighter pilots, who were turned into god-like figures in newspapers and magazines, which fed a growing demand for images of hypermasculine heroes who displayed exceptional mental and spiritual powers that helped them transcend the dehumanizing, soul-crushing nature of modern industrialized warfare.[15] The nerves of one particular fighter pilot, Oswald Boelcke, were a major topic in popular media in 1915–16. He emerged as the leading ace on the Western Front, where he earned the coveted *Pour le Merité*, Germany's top medal for valor. Boelcke invented modern fighter tactics and was lionized in the press until he was killed in a mid-air collision in October 1916.[16] Shortly before his death, he was praised by the Protestant theologian and official war reporter from the German military headquarters Dr. Georg Wegener, whose articles appeared in the popular *Kölnischer Zeitung* and the trench newspaper, *Der Flieger* (*The Flier*). Wegener imagined Boelcke as a kind of spiritually superior, quasi-religious figure who embodied the physical and psychological characteristics of the ideal German warrior. Wegener praised and conflated Boelcke's physical prowess, psychological resilience, and spiritual fortitude as the foundation for his heroic accomplishments:

> He is an outstanding personality. He has trained his well-built body in gymnastics and athletics, so that he has great physical strength and skill. Before the war he even won awards in the Olympics … Spiritually, or better yet morally, he has trained with determination to keep his nerves calm, with his serious objectivity (*Sachlichkeit*) and his most perfect concentration on his task.[17]

Boelcke achieved his "objectivity" and technical skills, Wegener claimed, with superior spiritual and psychological traits. "Spiritual" training, though this was not precisely defined, was seen as essential for developing the skills needed to be a warrior.

While notions of "spiritual health" were celebrated by the military, by 1916–17, there seemed to be some anxiety about how long the soldier's spirit could hold through. Pastors frequently contributed to army newspapers with their prescriptions for how men under fire should deal with the psychological strain of the front experience. One of the most frequent columnists in army newspapers, the theologian Dr. Aufhauser, recommended faith in God as a vital psychological tool for coping with stress. If front soldiers let the Holy Spirit flow through them, Dr. Aufhauser wrote in June 1916, they could conquer their emotions as the war dragged on:

During the rush of the attack, the Holy Spirit exorcises everything. It eradicates all fear from soldiers' hearts, and it extinguishes in tongues of flame all that is weak, timid and hesitant. As fearless, unshaken men of action they arrive before the astonished enemy, announcing the victory of their master over death.[18]

Dr. Aufhauser reminded soldiers that in the traditional Christian sense, faith in God enabled them to conquer death and achieve salvation. But this cornerstone of Christian belief was now also grafted on to the environment of the trenches. Adopted as a kind of comrade in battle, the Holy Spirit became weaponized as an antidote against fear in the horrific conditions of the Western Front. In a subsequent article from 1917, Dr. Aufhauser reiterated that psychological strength derived from personal faith. He emphasized that soldiers could only harness the power of the Holy Spirit, and their own spiritual strength, if they maintained self-confidence and trust in themselves and in God, which he characterized as the key to victory. "Whatever terrible difficulties are encountered," Dr. Aufhauser wrote, "can be solved by faith in God, which generates faith in oneself."[19]

By 1917, front newspapers acknowledged that the gritty reality of war often overshadowed heroic ideals. The same trench newspaper, *Der Flieger*, which republished the lofty rhetoric about Boelcke, also published an article titled "Minus 30°" by an *Oberleutnant* Heydemarck, who flew reconnaissance aircraft, in which he described the stress of constant flights over the front. The "heroic pose" (*Heldenpose*) found in many accounts, he wrote, concealed the brutal reality of psychological and physical deprivation. The cold he experienced at high altitudes was particularly nerve-wracking, and Heydemarck used references to God and the Devil to capture the pain caused by flying:

> Lord God, once again, it's bitterly cold (*Hundekälte*) in this icy fuselage. Half an hour on the way to heaven—it's cruelly cold! From time to time, the wind blows in and out of the bomb hatch and hits me like a wild dog. Only Satan knows how he can get through my leather suit and the many layers. In any case, he can, and he gradually freezes my body to ice ... sometimes I have to take off my flying goggles and scratch off the ice. It's evil. Evil![20]

Heydemarck's account contrasts sharply with soldiers' narratives about finding God in the stress of war. Instead, he suggests that God has abandoned men to suffer. Heydemarck's memoir, titled *Doppeldecker "C666"* (*Biplane "C666"*), was released in 1916 by the popular right-wing nationalist August Scherl Publishers, who published periodicals like *Die Gartenlaube*, which had celebrated the outbreak of the war as a great opportunity for men to find a sense of meaning and the heroic ideal.[21] Considering the conservative publisher, the memoir is a bit of a paradox. Though it extolled the heroism of the ordinary front soldier, the book also offered a mildly dissonant tone. Heydemarck gave his titular airplane the fictitious serial number "C 666," the number associated with the Antichrist in the Book of Revelation, and he characterized the "evil" experience of combat as something inspired by Satan, suggesting Satan relished in wartime suffering, a topic that Heydemark did not gloss over.

If the destruction of war, and accompanying fear, was the work of the Devil, Christ's love was seen as the cure. In an April 1917 issue of the *Kriegszeitung der 4. Armee*, for example, a corporal named Heinrich M. contributed an essay on "The Strength of the Soul" (*Die Kraft der Seele*), in which he argued that the soul or psyche (*Seele*) could only survive the stress of war if it was built on the "strength of love" (*Die Kraft der Liebe*). Christian love, he wrote, provided a space that was a kind of refuge from the "torment that wracked the soul," and it "purified and clarified one's life, making them calm even if they knew they had to face death." Heinrich M. concluded that by purifying one's mind and conquering fear, "love makes us free."[22]

While Christian rhetoric was employed in army newspapers as a framework for healing stressed nerves, by 1917 this officially endorsed media also published articles that addressed psychological health from a spiritual perspective that did not strictly adhere to Judeo-Christian language. Articles about psychological resilience often referred to the "soul" and "miracles" of survival but not necessarily in the context of Christian imagery. This can be seen in an article in the *Liller Kriegszeitung* by an officer and company leader, von der Goltz, who reassured his men that it was natural for soldiers to experience strained nerves:

Comrades! We've survived heavy fighting, and our bodies still tremble with the last vibrations from tremendous stress. This isn't rank fear. It is the shocks (*Erschuetterungen*) to the nervous system, which strike our manly heart (*männlichen Herz*) against our will. We listen to the drum fire, which sets the vibrations in motion: they must tremble, because the law of nature commands it.[23]

Experiencing a nervous shock was thus nothing to cause shame, and it was expected that even men who possessed the most masculine character "must tremble" under shell fire. This company officer told his men that while nervous stress was natural, so was their power of resilience. "Weakness is a thorn in the side of man's body," von der Goltz exhorted, but "What a miracle is the human soul (*Menschenseele*)," which can withstand the terror of machine gun and artillery fire. He characterized the soldier's *Seele* ("soul" or "psyche") as his most important weapon of resistance against the enemy. In an age where war had become like a "business," he observed, where millions of men and countless factories churned out the fodder for war, the "soul" was the last bastion of spiritual strength in a material world. Von der Goltz sketched this image of spiritual strength with no mention of Judeo-Christian imagery. Instead, he characterized the resilience of the German infantryman as a modern miracle in its own right: "They say there are no longer any miracles. The miracle of our time is the soul of the German infantryman."[24]

As men sought definitions of the "soul" outside Judeo-Christian concepts, they began to explore the idea that it was at the moment of greatest fear that they discovered the soul's strength. This can be seen in the case of infantryman Bernt Hüfner, who published a poem in the *Kriegszeitung der 4. Armee* about how soldiers discovered their soul in combat. "Out there [at the front] you forget the petty worries," Hüfner wrote, "Out there you understand the terrifying power of your soul (*Seele*)." The nature of the soul was not concretely defined by Hüfner, but interestingly, counter to Christian conceptions of the soul as an entity separate from the body, Hüfner described the soul and the body as united. He imagined that when the soldier's nerves were at the breaking point, he would discover the essence of his soul:

> When the soul (*Seele*) joins the body,
> For the first time man feels like an effective force!
> And you see in the night of horror,
> When the nerves are stretched to the brink,
> When the senses are totally abandoned,
> Because death is combined with life!
> See in the terrible night of horror
> That all the gates of the soul are now open
> All paths of the soul are now free![25]

Without mentioning Judeo-Christian concepts, Hüfner maps out a prescription for front soldiers to overcome their nervous stress by embracing the horrors of the front to find their inner spiritual strength. The moment of greatest stress is thus idealized as a peak experience, when the soldier reaches a nirvana-like spiritual state where he can unify body and soul, let go of his senses, and become powerful and free. The stress of war thus presented an opportunity. By diving into the terrifying stress of combat men could liberate their soul, detach themselves from the burden of sensory perceptions, and transcend their body and their nerves. Transcending the body and overcoming one's nerves through spiritual beliefs and rituals, whether within or outside Judeo-Christian paradigms, would dominate many front soldiers' narratives of the war experience.

Nerves and God's Will in Letters and Diaries

While the language of "nerves" permeated the discourse of popular media controlled by military and religious elites, similar rhetoric also pervaded front soldiers' letters and diaries. However, in their letters home, soldiers' language for coping with nervous tension departed from the medical framework used by psychiatrists to diagnose and treat psychological trauma. Instead of applying terms like "neurosis" or "hysteria," men used religious language to measure their fear and nervous stress. For example, in a letter to his pregnant wife Dorle in November 1914, Friedrich B. described the horrifying experience of enduring British artillery fire at the Battle of Ypres. Friedrich B. opened up to his wife his feelings of terror:

> Oh, if only there were peace soon. We are all so war-weary, our bodies and nerves are so tense because of the constant stress and being in a permanent state of danger. Right now I just want to sit down on your bed, take your dear hand in mine and tell you about my recent experiences … I'm not ashamed to admit that right now tears are streaming down my face.[26]

As he continued his letter, he described the pain and stress caused by the bombardment in religious terms. He wrote about seeking "salvation" from the nerve-wracking artillery fire and believing God's hand determined his survival:

> Suddenly enemy bombs began to rain down on the village ... We didn't know how to save ourselves. The house we were in did not have a cellar and it offered no protection against the heavy artillery ... It was a terrible situation. I sat with about fifteen men in a room in the small cottage and we were cut-off from everything. Every moment we were being struck and there was no salvation. So we sat for three hours enduring the most fearful nervous tension (*Nervenspannung*) ... I look back—the field is sown with dead and wounded. The English have targeted us well. Death has kept a rich harvest. And I'm unhurt! That's no coincidence, that's the will of God, who was with me.[27]

Friedrich B.'s hope for divine intervention calmed his nerves and saved him from psychological collapse. He intimated that some of his comrades succumbed to nervous breakdown, but prayer helped him imagine an escape from the nightmare of war:

> God grant that Ypres, the main position of the British, can be taken without us. Our lieutenant, who leads the company, has suffered a nervous breakdown. A noncommissioned officer spent the day constantly crying—that's the reaction to all this. Hopefully we will have some rest for a while now. ... Now Dorle, we want to hope for the best, our collective prayers will be heard by God and we will celebrate around a [Christmas] tree in our little Biedermeier room.[28]

As he saw comrades break down, Friedrich B. relied on religious faith as a bulwark against nervous collapse. Faith, he imagined, made him immune to psychological stress. Friedrich B. was killed a few weeks after writing that last letter.

Religion provided a ready-made therapeutic path to men under stress. Soldiers confessed their psychological stress to their families, but reassured them that their faith in God would enable them to control their anxiety. Johannes W., a twenty-year-old Catholic who had just graduated from *Gymnasium* and volunteered in 1914 days after he had been hired as a teacher, reassured his parents that he had a reliable defense against the nightmarish scenes unfolding on the Western Front: prayer. He recounted, "The war is something so dreadful and terrible that one does not understand how a human being can endure the stress, privations and anxiety." However, one of his officers helped him get through these traumatic experiences by telling him that "God has protected me so far," and he agreed that this is what helped him survive too.[29] Johannes W. enlisted his parents to help him bolster his resilience by sending more prayers to the front:

> I think it will soon be time for you to send me the prayer book. It's just as important as my other things, because here one can only help oneself and one can only be helped through prayer. What else can one do if the terrifying shrapnel from a bomb

flies up and hits one lightly or hard. The only protection against this is prayer …
I'm glad I took a rosary with me. The day before yesterday I saw a soldier hanging
the rosary next to his sniper's platform, so that he always had it on hand like his
rifle. God will see us through.[30]

He pointed to his pious comrades' survival as evidence that prayer was the best
protection against enemy fire. It gave him a sense of control in an otherwise helpless
and hopeless environment filled with terror. Though he reassured his family that he
was shielded by God, he went missing in 1916 during the Battle of the Somme.

God also served as a source of comfort for women on the home front whose nerves
were shattered by the death of loved ones. Baroness Kunigunde von Richthofen, the
mother of Germany's most famous front soldier, Manfred von Richthofen, famously
known as the "Red Battle Flier" or the "Red Baron," whose exploits as Germany's most
successful fighter pilot were popularized in popular media and propaganda, recorded
in her diary the trauma of learning of her son's death in April 1918. After Manfred von
Richthofen went missing over enemy territory, rumors of his death swirled through
the press, and she had to endure several days of not knowing his exact fate. "They were
nerve-wracking hours," she recorded.[31] Before she received an official telegram from
the War Ministry, her friends brought her local newspapers that confirmed Manfred's
death. When she realized her son was lost, she wrote in her diary: "And I know that
I must prevail over my grief and find consolation in the Whole, the Holy, the Eternal."[32]
Tragically, her son's death was a kind of release from nervous tension, and she sought
comfort in imagining herself as part something larger, "the Whole," to ease her
isolation and despair. A telegram from the Empress Augusta Victoria reinforced this
in a personal note from one mother to another: "So often, at every news of a victory
by your son, I have trembled for his life, which he devoted to king and country. And
God has now indeed ordained that the pride of you and of all must conclude this hero's
career … The Lord be with you and yours in your great sadness."[33] In her reflections,
the Baroness, from a Protestant, Prussian background, did not expand in detail about
the content of her religious beliefs, but her rhetoric, filled with praise for "God and
fatherland," often suggested that her son's "immortality" and "eternal life" would be
achieved through both heaven and his memory as a hero for the nation.[34]

While the clinical term "nerves" was often referred to in letters and diaries, it was
interchangeable with other terms, which had both material and spiritual implications,
and often referred to their inner core of one's being. In discussing psychological
damage, men described the stress inflicted on their *Seele*. Doctors often used this term
to connote "psyche" or "mind," but in letters and diaries by front soldiers, *Seele* clearly
referred to the "soul" and it was mixed with Christian language that suggested these
men were trying to encapsulate the more ephemeral essence or spirit. For example,
WW wrote in his diary that when a few weeks after the outbreak of the war he was
quartered in a German home in Kassel and preparing to be sent to the front, his
landlady instructed the men that God would protect them. He wrote, "it was this
woman's advice in the home that provided for our bodily and spiritual well-being
… helping us maintain our true Christian essence, as we anticipated the effects that
the horrors of war would have on our souls."[35] Here WW idealized the essential role

of women on the home front in bolstering the spiritual health of soldiers. Echoing Wilhemian notions of women as more spiritual than men, WW's diary reinforces an image of women as preparing them emotionally for battle, helping them to prepare their "soul" for the horrors that await them in combat.

WW's diary also reveals his evolution from an idealistic volunteer to a brutalized veteran with frayed nerves. Before entering the trenches, his writing was filled with clichés about "heroic sacrifice," which was often conflated with Christian ideals of martyrdom and redemption. But once he experienced the horrifying reality of frontline violence, he became almost entirely focused on the task of survival. Under artillery fire, WW imagined God as a means of psychological escape, rather than a bulwark of idealized courage, who saved him from psychological breakdown. Here the language of "nerves" and God's salvation permeates his description of stress under artillery fire:

> Each time the battery fires four shots: they hit in close succession. Everyone scatters! From the left it comes closer. No spot of ground is spared. And we lie there and count ... now, now it's your turn, it will hit you ... another crash! Boom! A piercing scream! A bomb hits the trench: six are dead, torn to pieces. A whimper and a rattle ... then silence ... it's over. Our medical officer breaks down at the sight. Men with stronger nerves have taken the bodies away at night. You have to have strong nerves under the shell fire ... Shoom, boom! Crash! It's as if hell's been unleashed ... Now they will hit you, now, and you'll be completely still ... Nothing like this bears down on you at home, but you, dear ones, how you worry and grieve and ... God, God in heaven, if it must be, then give me a short death ... Oh, the mutilations (*Verstümmelungen*)! And then peace comes over me and beautiful images from other days pass by.[36]

WW coped with psychological pain by calling on God to release him from this stress through a quick death, and he comforted himself by imagining home and his life before the war. Thus, he conceived of God as an antidote to nervous collapse—not because God could give him the ability to remain courageous in battle, but because God has the power to remove him from his hellish experience, even if through death. WW finally escaped combat when he was wounded at the Battle of Langemarck, and he ultimately survived the war.

Prayer gave individuals a sense of self-control that allowed them to counteract strained nerves. This can be seen in the case of Berthold B., a twenty-year-old from Bietigheim-Bissingen in Baden Württemberg, who wrote to his parents in October 1914 that he "would thank God" when he was finally relieved from the "miserable nest" of his trench, where he and comrades suffered from hunger and diarrhea.[37] Several weeks later, Berthold B. wrote to his pastor, and he explained in greater detail how his belief in God helped ease the stress of life at the front. He wrote that once he returned to the front lines, he was pinned down under days of shell fire. "We were all trembling as the result of colossal nervous strain (*Nervenanstrengung*)," he told his pastor, "until I read your dear little leaflet and a part of your booklet, and during the night I prayed and slept more calmly than ever before at the front." Berthold B. wrote that he found solace because the pastor's words reminded him that while "man is an unspeakably mean and miserable creature," God provided a feeling of "stability." Even if the destructiveness of war caused despair at God's possible absence, he was convinced that God was still in control and had a plan for Germany's triumph: "God will impose a divine justice and he will give our weapons the ability to achieve final victory."[38] Berthold B.'s language to his pastor thus operated on different levels. He mixed rhetoric that was familiar in prevailing propaganda about God intervening to deliver the nation to victory. At the same time, he contemplated a more subjective, personal interpretation of God as a force who eased his pain and shielded him against trauma. In his last letters to his parents he focused on his own fate, as he confessed his fear of death and told them that he hoped to survive with God's help. Berthold B. was killed at the end of January 1915.

In addition to prayer, the certainty that they would earn God's eternal rewards, namely the promise of heaven, helped men at the front maintain resilience through unbearable experiences. This can be seen not only in the case of Christian soldiers but also men from Jewish backgrounds. German Jewish front soldiers used a similar language to their Christian counterparts as they found refuge in faith. For example, Moritz R., who volunteered in a Bavarian infantry regiment shortly after the outbreak of the war, corresponded with his friend *Fräulein* Pfaadt about the strain of life on the front. Writing in the frontline trenches "only 80 meters from the French," with shell fire flying over his head, he insisted that his patriotism buttressed him against stress: "I have successfully survived small and large battles in the Vosges and in the French Argonnes. The stresses [*Anstrengungen*] that I have to endure are great, but the thought of being able to defend the fatherland lets me get through the worst." But faith in the fatherland was only one component of his arsenal for resilience. He was also comforted by the conviction that his loyalty to his nation would be rewarded in the afterlife. On Rosh Hoshanah in September 1915, he told *Fräulein* Pfaadt that he hoped "the Most Merciful will inscribe us in the Book of Life," referring to the Talmudic tradition that during the Jewish New Year God opens up his list of those who will be allowed into heaven.[39] The promise of an afterlife helped calm his fears for the duration of the war until he returned home in 1918.

More than just an antidote to nervous stress, the ideal of heaven and God's promise of eternal life gave soldiers and civilians an imagined space that removed them psychologically from unbearable reality. This was reinforced by women on the home front who encouraged their husbands to take psychological refuge in God's will and the promise of heaven. When Paul K., at forty-two, a relatively older volunteer, wrote to his wife Elise during Christmas 1914 that he was struggling to endure the hardships of frontline duty, she reminded him that God was always present with him at the front, and he could imagine eternal life to assuage fear and loneliness.[40] While Paul's response is unknown, other front soldiers were not certain that they could transcend materiality through belief in God. Infantryman Karl W., writing to a friend at home, suspected that while he believed "the eternal" in humans still survived, modern war was quickly eroding his confidence in this central tenet of Christianity: "At the sight of the fallen, we think that the eternal and the best in man has not been destroyed. However, in my view of all culture and of Christianity, tearing the noble body through such machines of death contradicts it [Christianity] with such raw senseless power."[41] Karl W. found it difficult to separate the spiritual and the material. The "eternal and best" in man, presumably God's presence, was under threat as Europe's Christian culture tore itself apart. For many front soldiers, it was impossible to reconcile traumatic violence and suffering with their belief in God.

The promise of meeting again in the afterlife was extremely powerful to families stressed by separation. This can be seen in the case of a letter exchange of the Bavarian *Leutnant* von H. who wrote to his wife Gisela in the first weeks of the war. A pilot flying reconnaissance missions in one of the war's earliest aircraft types, the *Taube* (the "Dove"), he referred to himself as his wife's "falcon" (*der Falke*) and to his wife as "the falcon's bride" (*Falkenbraut*). Interestingly, he alternated between extreme pessimism about his fate and unbridled joy that he would be reunited with his "falcon's bride" after death. "You will not see me again," he wrote, "One hundred times I have stared at the dangers that threaten my plane, and still I calmy escaped into safety's grasp." But he was convinced that his luck would not hold out, and he concluded that death was imminent. Thus, their best hope was to be reunited in heaven. "Falcons," he wrote, could "fly and meet each other in God's heaven."[42] His letter closed with a poem in which he claimed to be ready to die, and he thanked God for the chance to "be your falcon." After his poem, he concluded, "Hear the wind roar, my falcon bride, listen to the organ in the immense dome play its song of eternal resurrection. Then you will know how I die. Our path knows no tears and no end. The sunlight finds us jubilant, silently trusting, as we go into eternity."[43] The letter offers his wife the consolation that though his death at the front is inevitable, they can look forward to eternal life together according to God's promise.

Soldiers' letters were punctuated with fears that psychological trauma might be inescapable, and thus simply something that had to be endured while on earth, despite their faith in God. Infantryman Ludwig W., from Württemberg, shared with his fiancée an experience in September 1914 under artillery fire that drove his comrades to the brink of collapse. Wounded and lying in a hospital bed, he dictated his letter. He recounted how men were so exhausted that they simply fell asleep while under fire. Nevertheless, despite their fatigue, men sang the popular Lutheran hymn, "A Mighty Fortress Is Our God" (*Ein feste Burg ist unser Gott*). But this only temporarily bolstered their morale, and he saw many comrades suffer nervous breakdown: "It was ugly to see how after many brave skirmishes their nerves could not withstand the pressure. Like little children they wept."[44] Ludwig W. walked a bit of a knife-edge. On one hand, he offered the language of resilience through religious faith, and on the other hand he admitted that he was on the verge of psychological breakdown.

By 1916, in the wake of horrific losses at the Somme and Verdun, many came to terms with unbearable psychological tension as an unavoidable aspect of their front experience. If soldiers could not conquer this stress, they hoped to at least endure and not be crippled psychologically. God may not be able to end the war, but he could at least help kill the pain. This can be seen in the case of Catholic infantrymen Joseph W., who experienced the Battle of the Somme. Toward the end of the fighting in October 1916, Joseph W. ruminated in his diary on how he could never have survived without God's intervention: "Whoever has been in the Battle of the Somme and happily escapes the hellfire can consider his life as a second one bestowed. And I too can't regard mine as anything but a gift from God who interceded through the Holy Mother Mary and my patron saint. Only they enabled me to stand firm and not despair."[45] He further reiterated that without God, he would have suffered a complete nervous collapse: "My head is feverish and my body trembles, all my nerves are highly tense. I think one would fall into despair if one did not believe in a higher power, and I would say that everyone here believes again, even if maybe afterwards they don't admit it."[46] Absent from Jospeh W.'s 1916 diary entries are references to heroic ideals or national sacrifice. Rather, his narrative is focused on his personal relationship with God as an anesthetic against nervous breakdown.

Not all soldiers believed God could save them from nervous collapse. Many imagined a savior-figure who gave them power to escape at least physical wounds, but they also recognized that God's ability to heal their psychological stress was limited. This can be seen in the case of noncommissioned officer (*Fahnenjunker*) AK, who volunteered shortly after the outbreak of the war. He wrote to an unknown loved one at home about how God intervened to save him from enemy fire:

> The shrapnel balls whizzed, bombs fell right into our area and covered us in a black smoke that almost suffocated us … There has never been such a hellish fire! We prayed out loud to God during this life-threatening danger. The Lord heard our plea and none of us were wounded. Thus, it is my firm conviction that this is a miracle of God. Oh, how I am grateful to the Lord for saving me! In position B, to the left of us, the trenches and shelters were turned into a heap of rubbish in a few moments … Unfortunately, our regiment lost 21 non-commissioned officers and 446 men. Ten officers were killed! What a pity about these young people! Thank God I'm fine, though my nerves are lightly damaged (*leicht abgegriffen*). Maybe I'll get leave in a few days.[47]

AK linked his escape from death directly to God's intervention. At the same time, he was not immune to psychological stress, and he reflected that although he escaped physical injury, he could not avoid strained nerves and needed furlough.

After several years of fighting, even army and trench newspapers, which had disseminated rhetoric about God as a foundation for resilience and calm nerves earlier in the war, began to publish articles by front soldiers that recognized the reality of nervous breakdown. Interestingly, while they still stressed the importance of faith in bolstering mental strength, some of these articles acknowledged that stressed-out front soldiers could not find all the answers in the Bible, and that instead of asking God to heal their nerves, they should instead focus exclusively on keeping their faith. The chaos of the war, one unnamed author in the *Kriegszeitung der 4. Armee* wrote, drove many men who were on the verge of nervous collapse to seek some prophecy about when the war would end. However, using the Bible to forecast the end of the war, and in turn to find some reassurance about salvaging one's nerves, was erroneous:

> As always in times of excitement and tension, in which the nerves are almost strained to collapse, so it also goes in the world war: it haunts many minds. And so many people want to know the future at any cost, be it out of sheer curiosity or out of nervous weakness. After all, it would give people pleasure to put their nose into

the darkness of the future, but this "pleasure" often leads to a slaying of the Bible. It is against this that one must object. The Bible is too good to be abused as an oracle, even if you hardly know what's going on.[48]

The article suggested that only "nervous" and "weak" men were desperate to know the future, and it stressed they should not over-rely on the Bible as a source of comfort that would reveal their fate. "The Bible is not a 'road map of world history,'" the author concluded, "it is about the most intimate experience in man—their relationship with God." While "nervous" men asked God when the war would end, men who were psychologically strong practiced self-control, and focused instead on unconditional faith. But despite official prescriptions for controlling one's nerves and relying on God, many men began to question their faith as they coped with nervous breakdown.

Collapsing Nerves and Collapsing Faith

While some front soldiers felt their faith was invigorated by nervous stress, or at least it remained intact, others described an erosion of faith. This could be difficult for men and women to admit. It was particularly difficult for individuals to concede that God could not always heal their shattered nerves. Acknowledging the reality of psychological trauma only intensified their conflicting feelings, and it placed them in an agonizing state where they had to recognize the limitations of their prewar spiritual arsenal. This can be seen in the case of Wilhelm S., mentioned briefly in the opening of this book's introduction. He called on his family to join him in asking God for protection, and he assured his wife Lisette and three daughters that they could maintain courage if they kept up their belief in God. Volunteering in 1914 at the age of thirty-nine, Wilhelm S. was older than most of his comrades. He was a plumber and proud member of the Social Democratic Party (SPD) who distributed SPD newspapers to other soldiers on the Eastern Front. He was critical of what he saw as the unfair treatment of men in the trenches, who faced danger, starvation, and neglect, but he saw his survival, and the end of the war, as in God's hands.[49] Faith in God, with the whole family praying for an end to the war, was essential for fighting despair both at home and at the front: "If you feel strong enough, I want to write you the full truth. Was twice in battle, but God had his protective arm over us. Just pray diligently (to comfort you, I'll do it for you too)."[50] However, only a few weeks later, he expressed worry that believing in God was inadequate:

> Just 50–60 km ahead of us a big decisive battle is under way, we hear the thunder of our heavy guns here. If it turns out to be good, we have hope that we may be withdrawn, but one can't know for certain. You just have to hope for the best that you do not lose courage and trust in God. You will wonder, you will think, that in times of need one recognizes God. This is not the case and I think you have already realized that for quite a while. This has been the case for some time, but I have not done it that way. Don't give my letters to everyone.[51]

Wilhelm S's confessional tone, and his worry about his wife sharing his letters, reveal a dramatic change from his earlier calls for family prayer and keeping the faith. He suggested to his wife that they were both struggling with the same fear, but it was too difficult to confess it. The painful, contradictory feelings that he conveyed, and his realization that there were limits to God's efficacy, exacerbated the psychological trauma of the front experience.

The familiar rhetoric about God being in control no longer provided comfort for Wilhelm S. On Christmas day 1914, he wrote to his wife that while he still believed that his fate was in God's hands, he was overcome with despair that so much time had passed and God had not intervened to stop the war. His sense of order and certainty began to crumble when he could not reconcile God's silence. He questioned why God would stand by and allow unbearable suffering:

> Who would have thought on the previous New Year's Eve that 1914 will bring so much pain and grief to all of us, and now we are back at the turn of the year…Will the war inflict further wounds on us? We do not know what is hidden in the dark lap of the future. We can only give it to the Almighty, remembering that beautiful song "What God does, is done well."[52]

Wilhelm S. felt ashamed of his anguish. He admitted to his wife that he suffered from doubt and was on the verge of emotional collapse: "My love, forgive my weakness. As I write this letter here, tears have started to flood … I have the confidence that I have a good wife and children at home, who pray for me. When I imagine this, then I regain courage and the future does not look so bleak. But sometimes the thoughts come and overwhelm me."[53] His embarrassment about being "weak" reflected masculine expectations that men maintain self-control.[54] Once his belief in God started to break down, so did his veneer of manhood and emotional self-discipline.

The language Wilhelm S. used to describe his emotional stress suggested a direct link between his nervous strain and his erosion of faith. He wrote to his wife in July 1915:

> We have put up with a lot the last few days. And who knows what we are facing? Indeed, I'd like to be able to endure the tremendous strain (*grossen Strapazen*), if only God allows me to tolerate it. I ask him daily many times about it … My legs hurt so much that I can barely stand. But almost everybody is like that. That is the only consolation.[55]

No longer entirely confident that God could explain or solve his suffering, Wilhelm S. instead took consolation in the fact that trauma is ubiquitous and he was not alone in his pain. Despite his ambivalence, he asked his wife to keep taking his children to church, so they could pray for him.[56] Wounded in 1916, he survived the war to be reunited with his family.

It is important to consider how individuals wrote to different audiences. In their letters to loved ones, men and women frequently put up a veneer of stoicism and faith in God. But they also revealed, often in a personal diary or when they wrote to another confidante (including themselves, in the case of a diary), that they were experiencing anxiety. This can be seen in the case of Antonia Helming, a middle-class Catholic matriarch from the Rhineland who encouraged her five sons to volunteer at the outbreak of the war. She was intensely proud of her sons' patriotism, and she encouraged them to maintain their courage when they wrote home about the stress of life at the front. However, though religious language helped them hint at the psychological impact of the war, Antonia Helming and her sons sometimes struggled to share their hidden emotions. In October 1915, her son Hans had difficulty conveying what he was experiencing:

> On the eve of departure, I went to confession and received the same evening the holy communion. So I was ready to fight and, if God wanted, to die ... Repeated counterattacks by the French were bloodily repulsed. I want to keep silent about details. It is too terrible. I have to tell myself that my nerves are taut as twine (*Nerven wie Bindfäden*).[57]

Her son's language here is interesting. He confided the horror of life at the front, but at the same holds back, telling her that the "details" are too gruesome to describe. He also suggests that he must "tell myself" that his nerves are strong, but his phrasing suggests that he suspected this was not actually true.

Antonia Helming transcribed her son's letter into her diary, where she also divulged her own emotional pain. Hans's diligence in taking communion and expressing faith in God reassured her, and she noted in her diary entries that faith was essential to assuring not just her son's salvation, but also his psychological resilience. She wrote in her diary that, just as it was for her son, taking the sacraments was the best cure for her anxieties:

> All Saints Day. I received the holy Sacraments. It's the best consolation for a heart full of worries (*sorgenvolles Herz*). I have recommended all my dear deceased and also my soldiers to the dear God ... My heart focuses on my dear dear children. God bless their life paths.[58]

In the case of Antonia Helming and her son, religious rituals enabled them to form a kind of symbiosis between the home front and combat front. Even if they were unable to entirely convey their traumatic experiences, they connected through shared religious faith to soothe their fragile nerves.

Perhaps the most interesting thing about Antonia Helming's letter exchange with her sons is that while they mixed a language of religion and "nerves" to describe stress, they explicitly expressed skepticism about psychiatry. For example, her son Hermann wrote about a Dr. Abbé who met with them just behind the lines and asked soldiers if they needed time on leave to recover from stress. Nobody volunteered that they had problems, Hermann wrote, because of the stigmatization that resulted when doctors singled them out and suggested they were weak. His comrades wanted to show they could "endure their post until the body or spirit can no longer permit it."[59] But he also suggested that this was just posturing. In reality, he admitted that men were concealing the fact they were on the verge of a nervous breakdown, and he told his mother not to let his brother volunteer: "Do not let Otto on any account even think about volunteering. The young guys appear to physically cope with the strain (*halten zwar körperlich die Strapazen gut aus*), but their nervous system is in a state of collapse (*ihr Nervensystem bricht zusammen*)."[60] Despite admitting that men were suffering from psychological breakdown, he was critical of the doctors, because they got offended if men did not maintain an image of steel nerves. At least outwardly, Hermann's mother assured him in a letter that faith in God was more reliable than doctors. She tried to console him with earnest promises that faith in God would keep him together and that the impending Christmas would bring all her children to her table where she could help them heal.[61]

Antonia Helming was fearful that the December 1915 Christmas reunion would be her last with her family. Indeed, her son Hans was killed near the end of 1917, and Otto was severely wounded that same year. In the wake of these disasters, her diary entries became much more sparse, but her faith continued to play a central role in how she coped with the trauma of the loss of her son. Her writing reveals how she oscillated between severe anxiety and some consolation that at least God intervened to save Otto after he was wounded in a shell-hole. But thoughts of the future without Hans caused her to feel like she was on the verge of a psychological breakdown:

> One thinks of the coming weeks with fear and trembling (*Angst und Zittern*) and it makes me so sad that Hans is no longer there. What else could he have done for the fatherland! Yet at the same time there arrives the thought again, "I should actually be thankful to God for the beautiful soldiers' death (*schönen Soldatentod*) that Hans found, and for the protection that he extended to Otto." If he [Hans] had been left helpless in the shell-hole, it would be inconceivable what a horrible fate would have befallen him.[62]

Helming identified an interesting tension between her raw emotions and what she thought she "should" feel. Almost overwhelmed by the stress caused by the death of her son, she tried to rely on familiar, idealistic rhetoric about a "beautiful soldiers' death" and gratitude about God's continued protection of her other son. But the rhetoric barely concealed her "fear and trembling." Her diary revealed how she was haunted by memories of her son. Prayer continued to help her soothe her anxieties and bring her closer to Hans, who she imagined still loved her even after death, albeit in a "transfigured" form, as she recorded in her diary a few months later: "My thoughts often rush forward to a hero's grave and I think of my dear Hans, who rests in France's earth … in prayer one feels so close to his transfigured love."[63]

Confidence in God's power eroded for many as their nerves broke down, but they were locked into a mental universe where they could not imagine any alternative to faith. Hans W., for example, went to war in 1915 certain that God would protect him, but his faith in God as a psychological bulwark broke down quickly in early 1916, when he suffered what he described as a nervous collapse. A Protestant from a middle-class background, he wrote to his mother shortly after mobilization that he prayed to God he would get to go to the front, and he invoked Luther's famous "Here I stand, I can do no other" (*Hier stehe ich, ich kann nicht anders*) to underline his desire to fight.[64] This certainty quickly broke down. The trenches were an "unholy space," he wrote a few months later, that was "abandoned by God."[65] Unending artillery fire and cowering in an underground bunker "wore away at my nerves," and he complained to his parents of chronic headaches and nightmares.[66] He no longer found comfort in God. Rather, he wrote that he could get through it physically only if he became psychologically "jaded."[67] During Christmas 1916, he told his parents that, though he had a chance to go on leave, he did not even want to come home, because he just wanted to be alone.[68] By 1917, Hans W. admitted that the idealism that fueled his desire for war had evaporated, and he wished that his teachers would have taught him "real values" rather than hollow ideals.[69] He intimated: "I am so indifferent to everything. I am as apathetic as never before … I alternate between anger, sadness and apathy again. I am angry and sad at the same time about the abundance of badness (*Schlechtigkeit*) that comes from the home front to the reserve trenches and then embitters us at the front."[70] He did not explain what this "badness" was, but one of his letters after the 1918 spring offensive in which he expressed hope that the war would bring an end to "militarism" was returned due to censorship.[71] In his last letters from the trenches he confided to his parents, "I've had enough of this war" ("*Ich habe den Krieg so satt*"). But, making clear he still believed in God despite it all, he told them that he prayed for peace.[72] Despite his apathy and increasing cynicism, he was unable to let go his belief in a Supreme Being.

In a number of these cases, a pattern can be found in which language about God and nerves evolves over the course of the war. In some instances, the same individuals who had started the war with religious ideals gradually began to narrate their inner lives and psychological damage without reference to God or spiritual language. This transformation can be seen in the case of Hans Wulf, who recounted his experiences from his days as a volunteer in August 1914 all the way through to November 1918 and beyond. Wulf was from a lower middle-class background in Kiel. He was training as an apprentice for a cheese manufacturer, and he was confirmed in the Protestant church. At the outbreak of the war he volunteered and became a corporal in an infantry regiment on the Western Front. In the first months, his diary and letters were filled with religious language that suggests he viewed God as the key to Germany's nationalist crusade as well as his own personal ability to cope with stress. In diary entries from August 1914, he repeatedly beseeched, "May God answer our prayers and make us victorious in this war," and he described the field services he went to as particularly poignant because he knew it "may be the last time that God forgives us our sins."[73]

As the army bogged down into stalemate and trench warfare, letter exchanges between Hans Wulf and his family reveal the importance of faith in how he maintained resilience and coped with increasing stress. His mother referred to God as a protector of the nation who also looked over her son: "May God continue to be with our just cause! We don't want to forget to ask him for help every day during this difficult time … I wish you health and strength that you can endure the stresses (*Strapazen*) of war, and may our dear God be with you through it."[74] Hans' letters to her showed similar rhetoric as he called on God to calm her and to bring peace.[75] He comforted his brother, also at the front, by saying, "I'm sure you will overcome all stresses (*Strapazen*) with help from God, who will look over you in this time of crisis."[76] As he survived the winter of 1914–15, enduring food shortages, constant fighting, and a minor wound and hospitalization, he thanked his mother for teaching him how to pray, which he said kept him calm in "the heat of battle," making him feel sorry for his comrades who "had to plead with the Lord later" when they realized too late that he was their best protection from harm. He characterized God as a shield who protected himself and his mother because they were faithful to him.[77]

But examining Wulf's letters and diary entries over the entire course of the war, a stark difference is apparent in his language from 1914–15 compared to his letters from 1916–18. In the latter part of the war, he omits mention of God or religion. Even rhetorical gestures like "God protect us," which were ubiquitous in his letters at the beginning of the war, are absent. Instead, his narrative is dominated by discussions of logistical problems, physical deprivation, isolation, and the unbearable desire to go home. Though he writes vaguely about the "internal" damage caused by the war, he makes no references to faith or a divine being. This is exemplified in a letter he wrote to his mother shortly after the war, in April 1919, where he reflected on how, "Internally, the destructive war rages on and hinders the development of our new fatherland, the unfolding of the full strength of our hard-working people and the resurgence of German trade." This internal damage, he elaborated, was inflicted on both Germany's economic infrastructure, as well as its "creative power," and he feared that German soldiers and civilians were too damaged to commit themselves to work and the future.[78] Perhaps what is most unusual is that Wulf's wartime letters and diary entries do not highlight a traumatic rupture, or schism, that would explain his change in language. Instead, this evolution between 1914 and 1919 can only be described as a gradual evaporation of religious language, and in turn the evaporation of God being used as a concept for measuring pain.

Conclusion

Religious language in letters and diaries by soldiers and civilians reveals the often hidden ways that individuals diagnosed psychological trauma outside the sphere of medicalized language about "nerves." These sources shed light on how religion was used for self-therapy as trauma victims achieved homeostasis and psychological restoration in the wake of violence. This self-therapy was often developed in conjunction with loved ones at home. Even if their experiences diverged, men and women on the combat and home fronts found in religion, with varying degrees of effectiveness, a space in which they could communicate about and heal trauma. Further, in contrast to doctors and military authorities who often stigmatized "hysterical" men, front soldiers found in God a figure who was empathetic with those who suffered from "weak nerves."

Letters and diaries also reveal how ordinary individuals attempted to manage their *Seele* and *Geist*. These terms were used by psychiatrists to refer to medicalized concepts of the psyche (*Seele*) or mind (*Geist*), but they were used by front soldiers and their loved ones to define the effects of the war on their "soul" (*Seele*) or "spirit" (*Geist*), often through Judeo-Christian language about the elements of their being that transcended their bodies and the material carnage of trench warfare. One of the challenges inherent in reconstructing the religiosity and self-therapy of traumatized men and women is that in contrast to discourse by medical experts or religious authorities, one rarely finds any systematic definitions of the "mind," "soul," or "spirit," or even carefully delineated definitions of "God" and "faith" in letters and diaries. Instead, these terms were often used self-referentially, pregnant with emotion, as soldiers and civilians assumed that their loved ones understood exactly what they were talking about. But even if ordinary people did not precisely define the meanings of the terms and concepts they used, the pervasiveness of religious language in their letters and diaries reveal the centrality of these concepts in processing the psychological effects of the war. Faith gave men and women a tremendous sense of agency as they struggled to cope with feelings of helplessness and isolation. However, as total war intensified, so did anxiety about God's presence. The application of religious faith to manage shattered nerves became increasingly difficult, and attempts at self-therapy fragmented into more and more complex, individualized strategies used to heal trauma. As the next chapter will explore it was not only nerves, but also faith, that would be brutalized by the front experience.

4

"Where Is God?" The Brutalization of Faith in the Front Experience

Corporal (*Gefreiter*) Emil Z. wrote letters home to his parents in which he expressed more and more skepticism about pastors and officers whom he blamed for the war. In 1914, his letters echoed conventional nationalist rhetoric and Christian concepts that he relied on to reinforce resilience and courage, as well as duty to his fatherland. But by December 1915, he had become sick of the whole hierarchy of authority. Company commanders who stayed behind the lines and never faced bullets but strutted around with their iron crosses drew his resentment. He also described pastors' piety sardonically: "The chaplains preach in unctuous tones: 'The *Heimat* thanks you all.'" Emil Z. insisted that he was not the only one who had grown disillusioned: "I'm tired of getting excited about the German cause. Mind you, I express what's on many peoples' minds. Recent times have totally shown this."[1]

However, while he had become disillusioned with traditional authority and the values that motivated him to volunteer, Emil Z. still found God in the trenches. In a letter to his sister, he invoked Psalm 23 ("The Lord is my shepherd; I shall not want"), and he revealed how much he still depended on faith in God to cope with stress.[2] But these beliefs had become largely detached from religious institutions and leaders, whose support for the war tainted them in Emil Z.'s eyes. On a cold night in January 1917, he wrote again to his sister from the trenches:

> Today I am on watch and it's a nice opportunity to write. Everything is peaceful. Only the quiet breathing of my comrades betray that there is a bit of life here still. Sometimes there is a sigh, maybe a difficult dream, or a yearning for mother and home. How everything revolves and turns on these trusted words and yet they're so far away: home and peace. But at some point the great master and Lord must speak the power of the word and a new spring will follow the winter. Stay healthy and do not despair. In faithful love, your brother Emil.[3]

Emile Z. still imagined God's power as the ultimate authority, but by 1917 his connection to the "great master" bypassed conventional rituals and secular authorities. The Supreme Being was in his mind now a source of hope for ending the war and bringing him home, rather than a lens through which he articulated nationalist sentiment, conformity, or obedience.

The religious responses of men and women to trauma are difficult to classify. These very human emotional reactions do not fall into tidy compartments, and they often overlap with different contradictory impulses. Like Emil Z., many became disillusioned with the war or traditional authority figures but still "found" God in their families, experiences, or in the sheer fact of their survival. Others expressed growing skepticism about the existence of an all-powerful being. Those who became skeptical as a result of their experiences rarely fit into clear categorization, as they seldom self-identified as atheists or agnostics. Instead, their expressions of doubt were through the lens of intense emotions, rather than a carefully constructed system of thought, where they struggled for words to describe their unfolding psychological and spiritual metamorphosis.

The central argument of this chapter is that the trauma of the front experience damaged not only bodies and minds but it also wounded faith. Damage inflicted on individual belief systems was perhaps the most difficult form of trauma to process, as individuals struggled to find language and concepts that articulated how the war altered the way they perceived themselves, communicated with God, and constructed spiritual realities.[4] Trauma inflicted on religious beliefs took on considerable emotional power, challenging the core assumptions that defined many of these individuals' lives. Focusing primarily on case studies of soldiers traumatized by combat, this chapter reveals how men tried to convey the intimate spiritual effects of the front experience. However, their struggle with faith was not experienced in isolation. German front soldiers still sought out emotional support from their wives and mothers, who they depended on for empathy and commiseration. At the same time, even if they sought support, some men found it extremely stressful or frustrating to convey their inner turmoil to a home front universe whose belief systems seemed static to them.

Using a series of case studies, this chapter will explore first how believers articulated the traumatization of faith. Then it will examine two divergent responses to this trauma, including examples of "finding" God and "losing" God. Establishing categories, however, might be too clear-cut for the complex and varied religious responses to trauma, as within these categories one finds a broad spectrum of perceptions, behaviors, and experiences. Further, the loss of faith was usually gradual, subdued and marked by silence rather than shock. This has also been found in studies of British soldiers, as diaries by chaplains reveal that men reported an incremental breakdown of confidence in God's plan, mixed with doubt over the righteousness of killing.[5] For those who found their faith revitalized, this was also a rather complex and heterogeneous process. Men and women often described it in terms that were highly personalized, developing subjective relationships with God, or newly constructed beliefs, which will be explored in greater depth in subsequent chapters.

One of the factors that caused so much stress to front soldiers' religious beliefs was the extreme, seemingly unbridgeable dichotomy between the brutality of the trenches and the individual's image of God and themselves. Perhaps the most traumatic experience from a religious point of view occurred when soldiers feared that the war, or even worse, their own actions in it, transgressed their conceptions of a moral universe. Scholars from diverse fields who deal with "moral injury" suffered by veterans, in particular from the Vietnam War and more recently from the wars in Afghanistan and Iraq, shed light on this complex form of trauma, which has substantial religious implications. "Moral injury" results from a break between moral beliefs and actions that are perceived to transgress those moral values. It can lead to feelings of betrayal, either by governments whose administration of war is deemed immoral, or a sense of betrayal within one's self for the "sin" of individual transgressions against moral norms.[6] This was a central trauma for many men in the trenches who struggled with fundamental questions about who was to blame for the disintegration of moral norms, responsibility over their role in this catastrophe, and anxiety over whether God still existed.

Traumatized Faith: Searching for God at the Front

The collision between belief and the reality of modern war was deeply traumatizing. Letters and diaries of men at the front reveal their difficulties reconciling senseless destruction with their prewar beliefs in a loving and just Supreme Being. For many, traumatic experiences led to powerful emotions including anger, pain, and disillusionment, which they expressed by blaming humanity, military and religious authorities, or God for their emotional distress. The diverse ways in which men expressed their emotions can be most effectively illuminated through a variety of case studies. Though letters and diaries reveal some cases of a shock or rupture, erosion of faith was rarely triggered by a decisive "schism" or singular traumatic experience. More often it was the result of grinding brutalization and an inability to process the war experience through the lens of religious belief. Many men began to rely primarily on their relationships with their families to help them process the psychological effects of combat, especially as they lost faith in military and religious authorities, even if their connections with loved ones at home became strained.

Maximilian J.

Maximilian J., twenty years old when the war broke out, volunteered with a Baden-Württemberg reserve unit and saw extensive combat on the Western Front. His spiritual beliefs were shaken by the mass slaughter he witnessed during some of the most horrific battles, including the Somme, Ypres, and the Spring 1918 Offensive, Germany's last-gasp attempt to win the war. During the course of his war service, his letters home changed substantially. When he entered the trenches in 1916, he processed his emotions almost exclusively through the lens of his religious beliefs. He wrote extensively about humankind's immorality, as revealed in the brutality he encountered at the front, and his feeling that the war signaled God's judgment and the end of the world. However, by the last months of the war, his focus on God's role faded from his narratives, and he became more obsessed with how the war transformed him psychologically. His narrative changed focus from the collapsed moral structures of God's universe to the collapse of his own nerves. By the end of the war, he no longer tried to interpret the meaning of trauma through his prewar religious prism, but instead expressed "faith" in comradeship and his own resilience in the face of brutalization.

Maximilian J.'s letters to a close school friend, Kurt B., survive in the Special Collection on the World Wars Archive at the Württemberg Regional Library in Stuttgart. Though his archive file does not reveal whether he was Catholic or Protestant, his letters offer a glimpse into the impact of the war on his spiritual universe. In the summer of 1916, following the Battle of Somme, he first began to suspect that humans had abandoned God, as evidenced by pervasive cruelty and hatred. When he witnessed the mistreatment of POWs, he wondered if human compassion had been totally replaced by inhumanity:

> The fighting here at the front is currently very cruel and murderous. Mankind speaks of the treatment of prisoners, and whether there have been instances in which men get caught up in hate, cowardice and insanity and the conquerors kill or murder the conquered ... But where is humanity today? We can only find revenge, greed and annihilation in the world's nations, not least among our comrades. After the arrival of peace, there will be a long period of unrest afterwards. I ask, "Where is God! And where do people seek God?" Nowhere! Every human being has made himself his own idol (*Götze*). He only loves and glorifies himself.[7]

Shocked by the brutalization of prisoners of war, Maximilian J. feared that humans, engulfed in the hatred and violence of war, had replaced God with power and greed. Individuals had thus been corrupted by the cruelty unleashed by governments who ignored God's laws.

The Battle of the Somme was a turning point for Maximilian J. Writing in September 1916, during peak losses for German forces who experienced in total over 400,000 killed and wounded over the course of battle, he reached a kind of emotional nadir. He believed industrialized warfare made it impossible for men to maintain their humanity. Prewar values of self-sacrifice and heroism collapsed in this environment, replaced by brutality and dehumanization. In a letter to Kurt B., he wrote:

> The Somme, the Somme! Yes, this word is unmentionable for us ... whoever has done his duty there has performed inhuman acts. Let's not talk about this further. I'd prefer to fight a heroic battle (*Heldenkampf*) than to fight against weapons that you cannot see, which make it impossible to fight heroically. It's a mass struggle (*Massenkampf*), which is not worth it for individuals.[8]

Maximilian J. also confessed to his friend that what he experienced at the Somme shattered him psychologically, haunting him with traumatic images and memories. When Kurt B. suggested that he take a short leave to calm his nerves after extensive combat, Maximilian J. replied:

> Dear Kurt, You'll realize that when terrors (*Schrecken*) are sent through your limbs once, or shall we say multiple times, a short rest has little use in helping one regain command over one's nerves, especially when deeply buried experiences want to unearth themselves again. Thus, I'm not able to fulfill your wish.[9]

Maximilian J.'s metaphorical writing, in which he describes his traumatic memories as something buried in the "earth" of his psyche, reflected his awareness of the long-term psychological damage inflicted by the front experience.

Maximilian J.'s psychological trauma fueled his increasing cynicism about humankind's relationship with God. He saw the war as the harbinger of the apocalypse, with God watching man and testing his behavior in this crisis. The war proved that humans were ultimately hypocrites who put up only an image of morality: "I despise the German man. Outwardly he gives the impression of leading a good life ... Phooey! He is like dead weight crawling along with the poisonous slithering of the hypocritical."[10] He was convinced that his comrades were living in a kind of daze, unaware that God was watching and judging. Enduring the Third Battle of Ypres in 1917, which saw over 200,000 German casualties, he wrote to his friend that he believed the world was on the brink of collapse, which he interpreted through the Christian lens of the Last Judgment, when Jesus returns to earth to judge humankind during the apocalypse:

> We're hearing strong artillery fire coming from Ypres. What is about to happen in the next bit of time is gruesome. The entire front is being hammered and one can't be sure where exactly the great battle is going to take place. I would like to say, whoever is a Christian should not fail to consider these times from a Christian standpoint. Are we not at the gates of the Last Judgment? Whoever does not have a numb spirit (*tauben Geist*) should pay attention to these times in which we live. It is important to think through what our Lord God has to say in this world and what he wants to say through the signs of the time![11]

Maximilian J.'s letters offer an interesting glimpse into his spiritual imagination. Behind the visible world, in his mind, there existed a spiritual universe that could only be perceived by those who had not yet become entirely jaded. Further, he believed that his comrades were being scrutinized as to whether they could recognize that the war was God's test of their moral constitution. But he was pessimistic and believed that his fellow Christians would fail this test. Shortly after this letter, he wrote another to his friend in which he lamented that Germans did not deserve peace because they were not remorseful for their cruelty. He concluded, "We are all sinful and not worthy of God's mercy!"[12]

As the war dragged into its last year, Maximilian J. still believed in God, but he fell into deeper despair about the "criminal war" and humankind's future, and whether believing in God was sufficient to ensure his survival and salvation. Interestingly, instead of analyzing this through the lens of Christian ideals about spiritual renewal, his narratives by early 1918 moved away from religious language. In increasingly despondent letters, he focused on pain, and speculated on how he had changed psychologically: "Patiently I'll wait in position at the front for the next few days, because I am curious about how the warrior's game will affect my heartstrings and emotions. I would like to suffer more pain. To become iron in feeling but firm and noble in the heart."[13] Conscious of the war's brutalizing effects, he became his own psychologist. He saw himself as a kind of experiment in the effects of brutality, as he welcomed physical pain and turned it into spiritual strength.

Maximilian J. had the opportunity to explore pain even more intimately when he was wounded a few months later in the Spring Offensive of 1918. By this stage, he was still denouncing what he described as a "criminal war," but the religious rhetoric that dominated his 1916 letters had largely disappeared.[14] Instead of turning to God, he focused on the emotional support that he drew from his friendship with Kurt:

> You can be sure that love based on friendship (*freundschaftlichen Liebe*) is strong. And I cannot lose you as a friend—you possess such sympathetic attitude, which I love ... Keep going Kurt, but still seek to improve more and more and try to become a completely noble man; this is my heart's desire for you. Do not let the world and your comrades fill you to despair. The world is very bad now!!! We are getting worse every day!!![15]

Maximilian J.'s mechanisms for coping with psychological and emotional pain had dramatically shifted. By 1918, he no longer tried to uncover God's purpose for the war and the potential for humans to withstand the Last Judgment. Instead, he ruminated on how the war had changed his emotions and how it had both brutalized and ennobled him. In the last months of fighting, his letters suggested that his friendship with Kurt was at least as reliable, and comprehensible and real, as his previous belief systems.

Heinrich G.

The collision between prewar beliefs and frontline brutality was so traumatic that it could trigger a transformation in thinking. However, this transformation was often subtle, gradual, and characterized more by silence than a systematic shift from one paradigm of thinking to another. In many of these cases, men who began their war experience with intense reflections on the nature and will of God gradually gave up trying to understand their environment through this prism. This narrative arc can be found in the case of noncommissioned officer (*Unteroffizier*) Heinrich G. His archive file contains no background on him, but only a collection of his correspondence to his family from 1914-18. His letters from the front reveal an interesting existential evolution. In the first weeks of the war, he relied on his belief in Jesus as humankind's savior and a provider of hope and meaning. But by the end of 1914, as the war dragged on, his letters began to change dramatically in tone. He became obsessed with fears about death, and faith in God ceased to be the central prism or even a topic of discussion through which he interpreted his experiences.

Mobilized shortly after the outbreak of the war, Heinrich G. wrote a flood of letters to his father in which he expressed worry about whether there was any kind of spiritual truth in the wake of escalating violence. In December 1914, he wrote about standing by the grave of a friend and not being able to comprehend the senseless death all around him.[16] That first Christmas at the front made him reflect on what he called the "mysticism and mysterious joy" that the holiday once brought him, but he wrote that he could no longer connect to the "joyfulness and laughter that is true to children's hearts, the pure child's soul!" Instead, he was overwhelmed with what he described as "thoughts about the 'how' and 'where' of existence, about pain and anxieties felt by our faithful parents! Now the game of life remains unresolved."[17]

In the midst of this existential crisis provoked by experiences with mass death and the stress of separation, Heinrich G. expressed a longing for answers that would help him make sense of this increasingly chaotic world. He relied on his belief in Jesus Christ, who gave him a framework for thinking about how a broken world could be saved, but, by the end of 1914, he suspected that the world had reached a level of sinfulness that made it nearly irredeemable. Power, jealousy, and greed, he told his father, had overshadowed all that was good, and blocked humans from recognizing "the creator of all true humanity: Christ."[18] "Germany," he wrote, "could become a God-blessed land and spread the word of the Redeemer and all that is beautiful," but only if it did not fall into the same trap of sin that engulfed the rest of humanity.[19]

While Heinrich G.'s writings just before Christmas in 1914 concentrated on Jesus as the Redeemer of the world and his personal savior who gave him hope and meaning, his narrative underwent a startling transformation over the next year. He did not identify a decisive moment nor did he express that he had abandoned his belief in God. Instead, God and Jesus Christ vanished from his writing. His letters focused on the fear of death, but he processed this fear through narratives about spirituality that no longer incorporated Christian iconography. For example, in November, writing to his father shortly after fighting at Arras, he described a vision of death, a kind of supernatural landscape written in a dream-like, self-referential language between father and son:

> In my mind I see an old graveyard shimmering in magical leaves that fall over our beautiful crypt, in front of which you request and receive your first birthday wish, a spirit, who arrives in the form of a deeply internal voice, and who plays an accordion that reverberates beautifully in the fall wind! For your whole life as a man you imagine this grave, and you imagine me![20]

The conclusion of Heinrich G.'s letter is difficult to decipher, as he wrote incoherently about being surrounded by "soil rich with death," and the "all-consuming thought world" that invaded his dreams with haunting images.[21] His abandonment of traditional religious language in favor of this self-referential, almost impenetrable style, suggests he was struggling with traumatic images that scarred his psyche, which he could not describe or comprehend. Unable to modify prewar beliefs to explain the front experience, and powerless to adjust his circumstances to fit into his belief systems, he occupied a fragile, liminal psychological zone.

By Christmas 1915, the tone of Heinrich G.'s writing altered dramatically once again. His letters home became shorter and more infrequent, and instead of lengthy reflections on the spiritual or psychological effects of the war, whether through a Christian lens or more subjective language, he focused exclusively on the physical stress of life at the front. In a letter just before Christmas, he told his father that war weariness had become overwhelming, and he could not believe that the war had dragged on for so long.[22] His letters in 1916 were filled with descriptions about unending artillery fire, the inability to sleep, and the loss of friends. For the duration of the war, his correspondence home became more intermittent, with the last one written in September 1918. Food shortages, conflicts with superiors, taking refuge in comradeship, and other practical issues dominated his narratives. Further, these were even written in a notably different handwriting style, perhaps reflecting the profound changes he had experienced. Religious language that had dominated his letters at the beginning of the war had evaporated entirely. He did not describe any kind of break or crisis. The topic of religion was met with only silence.

Heinrich Gontermann

Soldiers and civilians often shared their crises of faith. However, though they shared intimate feelings of spiritual breakdown, a sense of helplessness often took hold, almost symbiotically, as loved ones on the home front sensed a crisis but struggled to heal spiritual wounds. This sense of helplessness or failure might cause civilians, going through their own spiritual crisis, to be wracked with guilt that they could not help their soldiers rediscover God and maintain prewar beliefs. This can be seen in the case of fighter pilot Heinrich Gontermann, a famous figure who was celebrated in propaganda for his heroism in aerial combat. He was awarded the *Pour le Mérite*, Germany's highest medal, and his visage and exploits were circulated in popular postcards and newspaper stories in the summer and fall of 1917 (Figure 4.1) Gontermann was featured, for example, in the *Berliner Illustrirte Zeitung* as a heroic figure who embodied masculine characteristics, including self-sacrifice, discipline, and emotional control.[23]

Gontermann's letters were published shortly after the war in a volume edited and annotated by his maternal grandfather, Lutheran pastor Leonhard Müller, who characterized his beloved grandson as a model youth whose faith should be emulated by the next generation. Though it was edited by his family, the volume is still revealing on a number of levels. The agony felt by Gontermann's grandfather is on full display, as the old man struggled to assimilate his faith in a benevolent God with the trauma of Heinrich's senseless death while testing a new aircraft type in October 1917. The grandfather selected and published letters that reinforced the image of his grandson's piety, yet despite its edited content, the volume also hints at Heinrich's building anxiety and unfolding psychological collapse. While he struggled to explain his deteriorating condition to his parents, Heinrich Gontermann's comrades detected the young ace was experiencing a gradual nervous breakdown as he struggled to come to terms with the meaning of pain and suffering in the context of his religious faith.

Heinrich's grandfather introduced the letters by emphasizing that his grandson possessed faith in God, strong nerves, and masculine discipline. These traits were acquired in their hometown of Siegen, in Westphalia, "For here dwells a people who had healthy nerves and strong sinew, genuinely German blood that the Romans found hard to break in the decades before Christ's birth."[24] Describing their community as one based on "fear of God, integrity, and diligent work," the grandfather emphasized that "this was the atmosphere in which our Heinrich Gontermann was raised." In moving style, the old pastor walked the reader through his grandson's postwar, still-preserved childhood room, describing his pictures, hobbies, books, and musical instruments, recalling that he was a "sensitive boy" who loved his parents and God.[25]

Figure 4.1 "Leutnant Gontermann," from the popular Sanke postcard series, No. 527, 1918. From the author's personal collection.

Shortly after he volunteered at age eighteen and went to the front as an artillery officer, Gontermann began writing home regularly. At this early stage of the war, he connected his faith in God with soldierly ideals of strong nerves and manly discipline. Experiencing artillery bombardments and trench warfare as an infantry officer in 1915–16, he wrote to his parents that he believed the war was a test of his faith, manhood, and national loyalty. He felt certain that his German "spirit" (*Geist*) and his own nerves would withstand this challenge.[26] He reassured his family that his religious convictions would sustain him through war, and he told his mother that he befriended a pastor at the front. Gontermann also predicted that a "good angel" protected him.[27]

Enthralled by the aerial combats unfolding over the demolished landscape of the Western Front, Gontermann wanted to further test his resolve, and he volunteered for training as a reconnaissance pilot. While undergoing pilot training in March 1916, he wrote a letter to his parents about how his life was pushed to the limit, but he was careful to nourish his soul:

Once again, one has the feeling that one is standing with scissors in hand in front of the thread on which life hangs. A twitching with the hand—and the thread is cut through, when it would otherwise not be severed. Thus one has his life in hand up there. A wonderful feeling for anyone who has courage! Hellish for anyone who is afraid. My body is in my hand, the soul is in God's hand! That gives one courage. It's one of my ideals to understand this more clearly.[28]

Gontermann understood these spiritual feelings as a precarious balancing act between his body and soul, in which the former was preserved as long as he gave the latter to God. He bragged to his parents that because he understood this, he was blessed with strong nerves. While many of his friends broke down from "nervous shock" while training to fly, he claimed to be able to conquer his fear.[29] Though he admitted to suffering from nausea and susceptibility to colds, he characterized himself as psychologically intact because his faith gave him resilience. His grandfather, commenting on the letters, expressed great pride and approval. Upon news that Heinrich graduated to become a single-seat fighter pilot, the grandfather was confident that Heinrich's "calm nerves as enemy bullets swirl around him," combined with Jesus Christ's promise of protection to true believers, would see his grandson through combat.[30]

Gontermann joined a new squadron as a fighter pilot in January 1917. The psychological and physical stress of open cockpit aerial combat started to take its toll. Pilots risked being burned alive (they did not acquire parachutes until 1918), and many carried pistols to give them an alternative to such an agonizing death. German pilots regularly flew three two-hour missions every day and encountered increasingly frequent dogfights over the Western Front.[31] Gontermann's letters reflect his escalating anxiety in this environment, and he grew even more obsessed with how his soul would survive such stress. He wrote to his parents that in order to survive, he had to surrender concern for his bodily well-being, even if this meant ignoring physical pain so he could focus exclusively on his spiritual health. In a letter to his father in February 1917, Gontermann wrote:

There are people who can withdraw into the consciousness of the soul for hours of deep inner contemplation, and then they know what it's like after death when they no longer have a body with its physical senses. At the front one can achieve—also in the Christian sense—such unbelievable experiences. Whoever recognizes this is strongly attracted to the realm of those who are transformed, where the soul has the full knowledge of God, and he becomes wary and repulsed by everything earthly, which is ungodly. These are the only happy people—those who have lost all desire for earthly things. I have also experienced hours of this kind of happiness; and always feel that this should be my main goal.[32]

Bifurcating the body and soul, Gontermann espouses a traditional Christian perspective. But what is most interesting here is that he tries to apply this thinking to surviving trauma. By abandoning "earthly things" and retreating entirely into his spiritual self, he believes he can endure the extraordinary stress of daily combat.[33]

Gontermann experienced great success and national fame in the summer of 1917, shooting down over twenty enemy aircraft and earning Germany's highest award for valor. But this outward success barely concealed internal turmoil. He confided to his parents that several comrades had been sent home after suffering "nervous collapse" (*Nervenzusammenbruchs*).[34] While he wrote to his parents about the psychological problems experienced by his comrades, reassuring them that he was "spiritually" intact, he shared with a girlfriend that he was not immune to psychological stress. These letters to an unnamed woman, which his grandfather—who called her Heinrich's "motherly friend"—discovered later, had a more pessimistic tone. Gontermann wrote to his female friend about a terrifying experience when an incendiary bullet from a French aircraft grazed his head, shattered his flying goggles and injured his eye. When Gontermann's plane caught fire, he thought he would perish. He revealed: "But it's just too difficult to describe, and I could only produce a distorted picture of what happened. I've never before experienced something so horrifying. Please don't write anything home about this."[35]

His grandfather interjected his commentary on Heinrich's letters, expressing dismay that his grandson did not feel comfortable sharing this traumatic experience with his immediate family. But the grandfather once again interpreted Heinrich's experience as evidence that Heinrich's piety paid off and God had intervened:

> We can understand that at that time he wanted to hide the experience away from the parents, so their worries would not pile up. It was evidently an extraordinary double example of God's protection, a double one. Twice his young life hung by a thread, from the shot that shattered goggles covering his eyes, as well as when the incendiary bullet ricocheted off his coat button, then ignited, and burned so fiercely that he thought his young life was over.[36]

While he may have concealed some of the details of his terrifying experiences, Gontermann did intimate to his parents that he was depressed from losing so many friends. And perhaps most strikingly, his rhetoric about God protecting him also gradually disappeared from his letters. His previous conviction that spiritual fitness would counterbalance physical hardship began to wane as his writing shifted more toward rumination on the brutality and human toll of the war.[37] His grandfather even conceded that by August 1917, Gontermann's family recognized the war had "gnawed away at his physical and psychological strength," but they struggled with how to help him reclaim his balance.[38] Indeed, his grandfather does not mention that they specifically tried to reach out to Heinrich about his psychological decline.

Gontermann's gradual psychological breakdown also made an impression on his comrades, including one of his closest friends in *Jagdstaffel 15* (Fighter Squadron 15), which Gontermann commanded in the summer of 1917. Fellow ace Ernst Udet, who greatly admired Gontermann's skill and character, later recalled in his memoir his friend's exceptional piety: "He exudes great calm. His broad farmer's face rarely exhibits the least bit of emotion. He is a profound believer."[39] However, Gontermann's facade of emotional self-control concealed inner turmoil, and Udet commented on the mental strain and gradual breakdown suffered by his friend. Udet was shocked after one particular combat sortie by what he described as the disintegration of Gontermann's nerves: "For the first time I see him immediately following a fight. His face is pale and damp with perspiration. The rigid calm he always radiates is gone. I see before me a man whose nerves have been completely wrought up."[40] Gontermann's deterioration and increased despair was alarming. After returning from another combat mission, Udet was philosophical about the hits he absorbed to his aircraft after each fight, which he shrugged off with a joke, but he recalled that his friend was deeply "upset" by each bullet hole, certain that his time was up. To demonstrate his fear, Gontermann picked up a handful of pebbles and dropped them on a leaf, mimicking the randomness of bullets: "'You see, Udet, that's the way it is,' he says while he is doing this, 'the bullets fall from the hand of God'—he points at the leaf, 'they come closer and closer. Sooner or later they will hit us. They will hit us for certain.'" Udet was at a loss of words, feeling his comrade was on the verge of collapse: "He is wrought up deep down inside. I feel strange in his presence, and my desire to get away from him gets ever stronger."[41]

By September 1917, a month before his death, Gontermann was on the verge of a total collapse. For several weeks he did not write to his parents—an aberration considering he wrote several times a week since entering the war. When he picked up his pen again, the optimism found in his earlier letters about spiritual health ensuring his survival had evaporated, and he dwelled instead on the loss of friends. He wrote about how he spent much of that month confined to bed with stomach ailments brought on by stress. Nevertheless, despite the physical and psychological breakdown, Gontermann was convinced that love and compassion were still achievable: "If a man has the strong urge to goodness, then he can pretty much achieve what he wants. There is no internal inhibition to progress. This urge is partly in-born, but largely triggered externally by the greatness of love, which is the guiding star of all goodness."[42] In his letters from October 1917, he was despondent about the recent deaths of friends and fellow aces Kurt Wolff and Werner Voss. But in his last letter, written on October 28, 1917, to his unnamed female friend, he tried to find solace in his hope that love would bind him to those he cared about and lift him out of his despair:

> I have different places in Germany where a strong light shines for me. Everywhere there are tender thoughts of love, which I keep in quiet hours and which always bring me invisible help. All those who know what love is are spiritually connected through God. Those who receive that little piece of love, which enables them to function, really feel and experience life.[43]

His letter to the young woman remained unfinished. On October 29, he took flight in a new type of fighter aircraft, a Fokker triplane, that had recently arrived at his squadron. Shortly after takeoff, the top wing collapsed and was torn away from the aircraft, causing it to plunge to the ground. Gontermann died a few hours later from severe head injuries.

In the wake of Gontermann's death, his family wrestled with the puzzling existential question: why did such a faithful young man full of love and devotion to an all-powerful God still face such a horrible fate? The family's faith, though it remained intact, was traumatized by their inability to resolve this dilemma, and the grandfather felt a sense of guilt that he was unable to help Heinrich, and that his grandson could only share his deepest thoughts with a woman outside the family. The grandfather concluded the volume with numerous letters and testimonies from Gontermann's friends about his character, loyalty, comradeship, and skills as a pilot. Several of these testimonies praised Gontermann's piety, and they reflected on the enigma of God's will. Gontermann's friend and fellow pilot, Hans Hermann von Budde, quoted from a letter in which Gontermann insisted that even if God's plan is unknowable, "we must believe and we must pray no matter what,"[44] and he included a description of the funeral and the eulogy in which passages from the New Testament were read, including Matthew 5:6: "Blessed are those who hunger and thirst after righteousness, for they shall be filled."[45] While ending the volume with reassurance and affirmation of God's divine will, the unknowable "why" permeated the grandfather's commentary, as Gontermann's family and friends struggled to reconcile their unwavering faith with senseless death.[46]

Edwin Halle

For many men, prewar religious beliefs seemed static and increasingly disconnected from the front environment. As soldiers grew estranged from rhetoric about God and nationalism that may have been appealing at the beginning of the war, they also became resentful of religious authorities who still conformed to and disseminated those increasingly irrelevant ideals. This can be seen in the case of Edwin Halle, an infantryman from Saarbrücken who was nineteen years old when the war broke out. Halle was Jewish and a noncommissioned officer, and his war diary is preserved at the Leo Baeck Institute archive in New York. The diary includes detailed reflections on experiences with both Christian and Jewish services conducted at the front. Though a self-professed believer in God, Halle was skeptical about most clergy. He continued to seek God as a refuge and source of comfort, but his traumatic experiences fueled his skepticism toward religious leaders' rhetoric, especially their endorsement of the heroic ideal and the necessity of killing. Antisemitism from officers further fueled his alienation from traditional authority, especially Christian leaders and military authorities, who he conflated as out of touch with the reality of the front experience. He gradually realized that men could only rely on themselves to find spiritual comfort, and as the war dragged on, he struggled with the question of God's purpose.

Halle's diary gives a fascinating glimpse into how men experienced the alternating Catholic, Protestant, and Jewish frontline services, sometimes in the same places of worship. Halle reflected on sermons by Protestant and Catholic clergy. After months of combat experience, he became critical of Christian leaders' call for resilience, as well as the blessings they bestowed on military machinery. Clergy, he argued, had no right to tell men who had seen the worst of human cruelty what to believe anymore:

> One Evangelical clergyman and a Catholic priest delivered a sermon; they asked us not to lose faith in God. It's a bitter travesty (*bittere Hohn*) if clerics, who may well know the basics about frontline beliefs, also simultaneously bless murderous instruments like cannons and other weapons while their mouths speak of charity

and state the fifth commandment, "Thou shalt not kill," yet in the same breath they urge us not to lose faith in God ... those of us who are at that moment "bidding farewell" in defense of the fatherland, and who are killing enemies that have done nothing to him.[47]

According to Halle, the hypocrisy of preaching God's commandments while blessing weapons of war seemed particularly egregious. This contradiction also caused widespread cynicism in his unit, he claimed in his diary. He observed that the mood of men at the front was dominated by gallow's humor and he quipped that he would have preferred to spend the day walking around with a girl on his arm rather than go to church.[48]

Halle's criticism of Christian leaders also reflected a general frustration with authority, and with the antisemitism he faced from officers. He praised the genuine comradeship between himself and other noncommissioned officers, but he suffered harassment from an antisemitic officer in his artillery battery, who kept "picking fights with Jews." Halle wrote that he was as loyal and patriotic as his comrades and did everything he could for the fatherland despite the prejudice from officers. But when he failed to give a proper salute and greeting to one of the bigoted officers, he was arrested for insubordination.[49] He was torn because he knew God would want him to control his anger, but his diary gave him an outlet to explain how he really felt:

> I am certainly a patriot in heart and soul and so far have done everything in my power to serve the fatherland. I learned that I wanted to get ahead! But when one is treated like this, one loses the desire to be a fully devoted soldier. If one's honor is cut away, then one's life is, in moral terms, killed off! And so this is my accusation: If from now on I cannot do everything that is required of me, then it is the fault of the man who at the moment runs our artillery battery and hates me for no reason—just because I am a Jew! God forgive me! But I had to vent my heart. There is a threshold where even the best person loses his temper![50]

Halle tried to follow with "heart and soul" the expectations of self-sacrifice and emotional control, as dictated by national ideals, masculine norms, and religious beliefs, but encounters with antisemitism pushed him over the edge. In addition to the trauma of combat he had to cope with hatred, and the pressure he felt from God to control his anger seemed impractical in this stressful environment.

Despite his alienation from officers and Christian leaders who came to the front line, he still drew emotional strength from his faith. However, he struggled to understand God's purpose for letting the war drag on. Reflecting on biblical passages that gave him a sense of hope, Halle used his diary to ponder over how the war had brutalized him:

> I sat on a wall for a while, brooding and looking dreamily into the distance. One year has now passed since the beginning of this killing. How many more days will it take for the fury of war to extinguish its torch and not burn the beautiful

landscapes like this one here? What awaits us at the end of these horrors? Hundreds of thousands have already lost their lives; and thousands more will die. Life-long invalids—what will become of them when there will once again be peace? There are too many of these questions about which you can wrack your brain in vain. But fundamentally: what's the sense in worrying? .... Psalm 46 comes to my mind: "God is our confidence and strength, a help who is always with us in times of troubles..." There on the horizon shines the red ball of the setting sun. Like fire, it burns you in the soul. There remains the consolation: After rain follows sunshine. After a fierce fight, peace will come. The front experience is gradually turning me into a serious person![51]

Halle struggled with the same question that tormented so many of his colleagues: how could an all-powerful, loving God permit such carnage? Unable to find an answer, he took some "consolation" in the Book of Psalms. Perplexed, he still found a ray of optimism that the war would eventually end, while recognizing that it had transformed him into a more "serious person."

Though Halle struggled with the existential questions posed by his front experience, and he had been alienated by many of the religious leaders he encountered, he was deeply moved by a particular rabbi he met at a service given in a Catholic church on the Western Front on Rosh Hoshanah in September 1915. Rabbi Leo Baeck stood out as a genuine man who possessed both combat experience and religious wisdom. Baeck, a chaplain in the German army, would later emerge as one of the German Jewish community's leading lights. Fighting to protect Jews after Hitler came to power, Baeck was deported to the Theresienstadt concentration camp. He survived, settled in London after the war, and chaired the World Union of Progressive Judaism. At a Rosh Hoshanah service at the front in 1915, Baeck made a tremendous impact on Halle: "Devoutly, like hardly anywhere else in a temple, we all followed the rabbi's preaching, as he spoke the words, 'It is repentance, prayer, and goodness that gives people peace!' ... There was no one among us for whom these words did not reflect our soul, who all had, in this last year of war, probably repented in his own way."[52]

Rabbi Baeck's optimism that faith would provide comfort touched Halle deeply. In particular, the rabbi's emphasis on finding individual peace resonated. Despite Halle's cynicism about religious leaders' hollowness or hypocrisy, Baeck's words struck home, as he believed men at the front were still seeking personal fulfillment through individual repentance and reflection. In his diary entry, he wrote that Baeck had rejuvenated his comrades, both Christians and Jews, with his sincerity. Baeck's appearance in the "*Feldgrau*" (field-gray) uniform of a frontline soldier—he even carried a rifle by his side when he gave the sermon—also clearly made a connection. Men who had become skeptical, Halle argued, "learned to pray again" after hearing Baeck: "All followed the words of the young speaker in *Feldgrau* who, with his rifle beside him, announced the words of God from a small prayer book. As Rabbi Dr. Baeck also implored in his prayer for the blessing of our *Heimat* and the loved ones who were so far away, tears rolled down the eyes of otherwise hardened men."[53]

Though spiritually rejuvenated by Baeck's earnestness, Halle could not escape emotions of fear and despair that still paralyzed him in the front line. He was on the verge of psychological collapse. Just two days after meeting Rabbi Baeck, Halle recounted in his diary the terror of constant shell fire, shrapnel whistling through the air, and the fear of impending death. "This eternal trench warfare wears down the nerves," he wrote desperately in the last diary entries.[54]

Halle's diary in the archival file only continues through 1915. But at the end of the diary transcription, he included a page of reflection that was clearly added after 1933, when he typed-up his original diary. He wrote in this postscript that he hoped his diary was more than just a narrative description of events but rather a "mirror into my soul."[55] His cynicism toward authority had only intensified since the end of the war. He railed against the hollowness of militarism, blasting generals who called themselves "heroes" while front soldiers got killed. The false cult of heroism, he wrote, had only worsened after 1933. Thus, he said it was "like a kick in my behind" when he received from the Nazi regime the medal widely nicknamed the "Hindenburg Cross" (*Frontkämpferkreuz*), which was given to all world war veterans in 1934. When some Nazis suggested excluding Jews, socialists, and other racial and political "outsiders," the army published an ordinance stipulating that any veterans who served could not be denied the medal.[56] Halle sardonically noted the irony of a Jewish veteran getting the medal from Hitler, and he felt he did not really deserve it, since he was merely the beneficiary of the "good fortune" of not getting killed while so many of his comrades were less lucky. Tearing down lofty ideals of heroism, he reflected that the war taught him about his own individual ability to withstand stress.[57]

In his postwar supplement to his diary, Halle also included a poem that he originally wrote while in France in 1915. Here he returned to his frustration with what he saw as human beings who had largely abandoned God's prescription for a moral life. The poem highlighted the contradictions between God's laws and the cruelty of humankind, with lines that included:

Why does man have to go to war,
When nobody wins in the end?

… Why doesn't anybody issue a proclamation:
"Thou shalt not make bombs
Or any other dangerous things!"
After all, "Do not kill!" is a commandment![58]

Placing this wartime poem into his postscript to the diary, Halle was clearly still pondering his disillusionment with humanity. The poem distilled his resentment of those who ignored basic Judeo-Christian precepts when they prosecuted the war. Halle learned to distrust authorities and realized he had to develop an individual relationship with God for spiritual comfort, but in his isolation he found it difficult to explain the meaning of the war. Biographical data in his archive file is scarce, but he eluded Nazi persecution and emigrated to Argentina where he lived until 1967.

Finding God in the Carnage of the Trenches

Edwin Halle's estrangement from militaristic religious leaders who celebrated the heroic ideal was widely felt. Such disillusionment with organized religion was traumatic for many front soldiers, as it weakened their ties to institutions and traditional heroic or masculine ideals that had provided psychological resilience for many at the outbreak of the war. At the same time, men often still retained a sense of belief in a Supreme Being, no matter how bewildering the world seemed. Hope for reunification with loved ones in an afterlife, and the promise of salvation, remained powerful antidotes to an unbearable front experience.

While many struggled at the front with the apparent disparity between institutionalized religion and the brutality of war, men in the trenches wrote about how traumatic stress led them to "find" God. For some, the war experience reinforced, or helped them reignite, prewar belief systems about God's role in their lives, but others discovered for the first time a belief in a higher power. Such revelations came even in the middle of the war, years after the exuberance of the "spirit of 1914" had worn off. This can be seen in the case of infantryman Karl B., who wrote home from the Carpathians in August 1916. His unit had just been in the front lines at Verdun before being transferred to the Eastern Front, where he reflected on the carnage he had just witnessed. He wrote:

> At Verdun in France, with hands folded over our chests we looked up into the sky, and prayed during the shell fire, drum-fire as they call it, going day and night without sleep, and on July 13 after the enemy attack all who were still healthy and alive prayed and thanked God. However, many comrades were still down and wounded and later died because the French fired poison gas bombs. There was even one comrade, who did not believe in God so much, who said to me that here at Verdun I have again believed in God and learned to pray.[59]

It is also interesting to note what is absent from Karl B's writing: he did not reflect on theological dilemmas that tormented other soldiers, and he did not engage in debates over the significance or sincerity of pious pronouncements by religious leaders. Instead, he described prayer and belief in visceral terms, as an antidote to the horrifying violence that consumed him.

Stress and deprivation in the trenches led front soldiers to reflect on what made their lives worthwhile beyond the transient material world. Men described in their letters and diaries how they underwent an inner transformation, which was often the result of rumination on what was most significant in their life—usually love for their families. Despite the experiential gap between combat and home fronts, many still drew life-affirming emotional sustenance from memories of home and loved ones. Men often expressed the emotional power of these memories through gratitude to God, who they saw as a kind of last remaining thread that kept them connected to their families and *Heimat*. This can be found in the case of Georg G., a lieutenant mentioned in the previous chapter who emphasized how God kept him psychologically calm under fire.

His letters to his wife were filled with intense longing for her. He even characterized the war as an ultimately positive experience, because it reminded him of how much he loved her and God. His descriptions of both forms of love were very similar, and the theme running through his letters was that the war gave him the chance to realize just how much he valued his wife and his faith. In the first few months of the war he wrote to his wife from the trenches about how he would dream of her and talk to her in his mind:

> I have often turned on the lights and for a long time, without you realizing, looked at you for a long time to read into your eyes. I fell asleep while thinking that you were only meant for me alone. You know that with me one's essence is much more important than one's words, and it's in my inward nature (*Innerlichkeit*) that I can be certain about our marriage. If I should return home again, I will consider it to be a gift from God and will set up my life in a strictly Christian sense. I'm sure that you'll support me in this.[60]

Separation from his wife made Georg G. feel even greater love for her, and it bolstered his commitment to a Christian life. Survival, he emphasized, would result in his total devotion to God. This commitment to Christian beliefs was not new for Georg G., but he wrote that the experience of family separation made him realize that he had been too lackadaisical in his faith. He told his wife that while some men discovered God as a result of stress, he always knew that God was with him and this gave him a sense of "inner harmony" that helped counterbalance the chaos that surrounded him.[61]

Though he was outwardly optimistic and believed God wanted him to survive, by early 1915 Georg G. confessed to his wife that he was inwardly nervous. After describing a terrible cold and his inability to sleep or eat, he wrote, "I've recently noticed that in my dreams I have become very nervous, but that's got to be temporary."[62] His letters in early 1915 suggested that the war had profoundly changed him. He told her of a "vivid dream," in which he had been wounded and returned home, but he felt no joy on homecoming, and in his dream his wife and kids did not recognize him. He recounted that the captain in his unit was blown apart by artillery fire, and that "it's better that nobody at home will see his shattered body. The war is a terrible thing."[63] His last letters contained far fewer references to faith and God than his correspondence in the first months of the war, and Georg G. was killed in combat in May 1915.

In the turbulent and stressful atmosphere of the front, pervasive evil sometimes fortified the conviction that the alternative, goodness, must also exist. The search for goodness led some to find God. This can be seen in the case of correspondence between nineteen-year-old *Leutnant* Otto von R. and his friend, Leutnant Mundschick. In a June 1916 letter to his sister, Otto von R. included a letter from his comrade Mundschick, a theology student who had just been killed in fighting against the British. Mundschick wrestled with a fundamental theological question that seemed to trouble him and his friend Otto von R.: How does one continue to believe in God in the face of so much violence? Mundschick surmised that a world without God was simply unthinkable. It was impossible, he insisted, to imagine a conscience without God, and that without the "inner feeling of God," we would have no concept of good and evil, and subsequently no sense of responsibility or fear of judgment.[64] Mundschick went on to ask his friend how he could even wonder why God allows so much misery. The answer to him was obvious: "War improves humanity. It teaches people to pray again."[65] The war, he surmised, was God's test of true believers. Mundschick pointed to biblical precedents, and he noted that Germans who were Christians had God's protection, and the promise of everlasting life, while "the blacks and the Turks and other pagan peoples (*Heidenvolk*) had no hope of salvation."[66]

Otto von R. was not as convinced of God's presence or aims. Writing to his sister about Mundschick's theological musings, Otto von R. clearly agreed with his friend's interpretation that God intended the war as a kind of test of piety.[67] However, he also expressed to his family skepticism about whether wars would really "improve" humanity. Unlike his idealistic, theology-minded friend, von R.'s letters from the trenches were filled with sober, graphic accounts of artillery battles and subsequent human and material destruction. For example, after a four-day artillery battle that "rattled my skull until I couldn't hear anymore," he concluded, "There will be nothing left of even the strongest nerves, if the [artillery] fire continues as it did yesterday."[68] It could not be God who was responsible for so much carnage, even to test his believers, von R. concluded. Instead of God's plan, he saw the war as proof that "the Devil is on the loose."[69] This statement preceded his description of another artillery battle followed by a mass charge by French soldiers, hand-to-hand combat in the trenches, and then a gas attack.[70] This letter exchange with his sister in which von R. obsessed over God's will evaporated over time. Meditations on religion were absent from his letters in the last year of his life before he died in Flanders in 1917.

The home and combat fronts both tried to prop up each other's crumbling faith. Women tried to bolster men's resolve by insisting that God still existed despite all the carnage. For example, nineteen-year-old Friedel H. wrote daily to her fiancé, Hellmuth B., filling letters with proclamations of faith. She told him that the fact of his survival was proof of God's benevolence. In October 1916, Friedel wrote that the war helped her rediscover God's power through the act of prayer, which she was convinced helped protect her fiancé. Prayer also gave her a sense of control: "May the good Lord God keep you healthy. I fall to my knees to ask him to preserve your life. I could give up everything, but not you. I give all my hopes to our dear father in heaven."[71] She believed that her tenacity and devotion could activate God's protective hands, as though the Supreme Being was an extension of her own willpower.

Men at the front also found themselves trying to convince skeptical civilians that God really still held power. An interesting example of this can be found in the case of a 1915 letter exchange between the sergeant (*Vizefeldwebel*) August S. and his friend Ernst, whose letters can be found in the federal archive in Freiburg. Ernst was still at home, not yet called up for service, and he complained to August S. that the war had eroded German society's piety and loyalty to God. When his neighbor, a young widow whose husband had just been killed at the front, attempted suicide by jumping into a river, Ernst castigated her for "laughing at the first commandment" and "idolizing" herself, in violation of God's will.[72] The stress of the war made civilians on the home front forget God's laws, Ernst complained, fueling a selfish world driven by egotism.

While his friend complained about moral and spiritual breakdown on the home front, August S. asserted that the combat experience had actually rejuvenated his spiritual life. The war, despite its brutality and chaos, made an awesome impression on him, convincing him that even if it was incomprehensible, there must be a powerful being in command of it all. He wrote that when he had doubts, angels comforted him and helped him "make sense of it all." In a letter to his friend, August S. included a poem that he wrote: "From near the mighty bank of the river I look out over the land/and look out in the night at our benevolent God's mighty power in humble amazement ... Do you know that even in the thick of battle, your Lord God is here, your God in heaven?"[73] Similar to other front soldiers, August S. struggled with the meaning of the war and its terrible effects but nevertheless believed vaguely that God was still present. He was in awe of the "benevolent God's" power and omnipresence.

Families at home anxiously asked their men at the front if their faith was still intact. One sergeant (*Feldwebel*) named Rudolf H. responded to inquiries from his concerned pastor and family who worried that he was vulnerable to losing faith in God. He wrote to his pastor in November 1917 and expressed understanding that many at home might assume that brutalization, and this was the term he used, would damage his faith and lead to religious skepticism:

> In this dull life a human being is brutalized (*verroht*). He becomes more serious when he sees the misery of a battlefield. Death also plays with him and it's imprinted on his face. In these 3½ years [at the front], he only knows about life at home through hearsay, but no one can get a clear picture of what is actually going on. Hence the view that the man standing at the front hears nothing but the roar of the guns, and must be brutalized, thus he no longer recognizes God.[74]

There were substantial misconceptions between combat and home fronts, according to Rudolf H. While civilians equated brutalization with loss of faith, he assured his pastor that the opposite was true. Rejecting the assumption that frontline soldiers were descending into atheism, he wrote: "What a rich misconception: external appearance hiding inner pain. The frontline soldier actually knows there is a God. On him he builds all trust. Crisis and danger to his life puts this pressure on him. Only a small percentage deviate from this rule."[75] He protested the image of front soldiers hiding their psychological breakdown behind a fragile exterior of self-control. In reality, he argued, despite all the stress and violence, most men maintained their faith in a higher being.

This need to reassure the home front was expressed by many men who saw themselves on a bit of a spiritual tightrope. Aware that mass death and senseless slaughter might damage their belief in a benevolent, all-powerful God, some men made a conscious, concerted effort to believe in God's plan despite the horrors that surrounded them. Infantryman SL, for example, wrote home in 1917 that he still felt God had a hand "even in the smallest things," but one had to be exceptional to recognize it:

Human nature is such that you have to stop from time to time to take stock of things if you don't want to fall into the same condition as the broad masses. It's better, of course, to walk in the presence of God and to take his guidance in everything, even the smallest things. Then everything becomes easy. Even the greatest sacrifice can be endured joyfully.[76]

SL's reference to "the broad masses" contained a political edge, as he complained that the population was being negatively influenced by the social democratic movement, which had staged strikes and organized public protests against the war a few months before he wrote his letter. Social Democrats, he lamented, had made it shameful to be proud of the fatherland, and they attacked Christian beliefs: "Look at how much monstrous damage social democracy has inflicted with its inflammatory press, and how they try to de-Christianize (*entchristlicht*) everything. Many of them have only scorn and ridicule for religious things."[77] Portraying Christianity as the victim of left-wing politics, SL saw himself as a crusader not just for finding God in everyday life at the front, but also as a defender against aggression from growing antiwar movements. He concluded that in remaining loyal to his belief that God was still on Germany's side, he was fighting for a "higher justice."[78]

When the war experience triggered disillusionment with humanity or despair with civilization, men compartmentalized and took refuge in their Christian beliefs as if they were a kind of shell that made them immune to the shattering violence that surrounded them. As seen in case studies so far, many found this refuge gradually and subjectively, as they grew skeptical of officers, chaplains, and religious leaders. It is interesting to highlight one case study of an individual with a theological background who was aware that faith in religious and military authorities had eroded, and that these representatives of Christianity had their work cut out for them. Siegfried E., a chaplain who served on the Western and Eastern Fronts in 1915–18, kept a detailed diary in which he concluded that the war proved Christianity triumphed where science and reason failed, but the emotional and psychological stress of modern war often distracted men from finding God's power and presence. He began his studies as a Protestant theologian before the war, and he survived the cataclysm of Verdun and carnage on the Russian Front in 1917–18. When he first reached the front in France in 1915, he began to characterize the war as an affront to Christian faith, which threatened to damage men's souls. He argued that "despite all the outward cultural progress and intellectual and moral development, the life of the soul (*Seelenleben*) has moved backwards and downwards."[79] The war, he believed, was the main culprit in this degradation of the soul. Embodying modernity in its most powerful form, the war experience unleashed emotions that completely absorbed front soldiers and distracted them from religious rituals, beliefs, and traditions: "The war has placed its bloody fingers on the great festering wound of the national body, and brought the unbelievers, who are tempted by a culture of one-sidedness, a modern religion of feeling (*Gefühlsreligion*) without God and church, in front of a court martial for sentencing."[80] Siegfried E. thus saw religion in competition with the war experience, which distracted men from their spiritual center. He feared that even if the nation were victorious over its political enemies, Germany could still be defeated if individuals gave in to what he described as moral degradation, which was caused by men's emotions being so focused on the struggle for survival that they forgot their inner moral compass and devotion to God.[81] Pornography and other salacious reading, he complained, not to mention the sexual temptations of military-regulated brothels just behind the lines, further distracted front soldiers and made it difficult to win over their attention.[82]

By the spring of 1916, Siegfried E. was assigned to a unit stationed near Verdun, and the escalating killing that he witnessed there seemed to have a profound effect on him. He struggled to help another pastor who succumbed to "nervous shock" (*Nervenschock*) after surviving a prolonged battle under artillery fire.[83] He was disillusioned to see traumatized officers screaming at each other, and he concluded that "the troops are totally finished" (*Die Mannschaften sind kaputt*).[84] His encounters with comrades who were breaking down, however, did not erode his Christian convictions. He regularly led prayers at burial services, and he hoped that his words were effective in helping men find their path to faith in Jesus. While tending to wounded soldiers in hospital, he was reassured when one turned to him and said, "Here you learn to believe in God."[85] These religious experiences, he wrote, were more profound than any other, including national loyalties, as Christ's promise of redemption transcended battle lines. A statue of Jesus on a road behind the lines made him reflect: "Between the two enemy positions on the road to Forges there is a crucifix. One arm points to the Germans, the other to the French trenches. It's as if he wanted to stretch his outspread arms to both parties. I died for you both. Find yourselves in me."[86]

Siegfried E. was optimistic about what he called the "triumph of Christianity," but he understood that men were becoming disillusioned with authority figures, including officers and religious leaders like himself. He believed that theologians, including chaplains, had to detach from their official image of authority, which was too inflexible and aloof, and embrace what he described as an "artistic, poetic and intuitive" role that was open-minded and responsive to the practical problems faced by front soldiers.[87] As a pastor who was sensitive and compassionate to traumatized men, he saw himself as an agent for helping revitalize religious belief, so that "so many sorrows and sins have not been able to destroy the indestructible power of Christianity!" He also expressed a feeling of spiritual rejuvenation that he found in his love for his new wife, Gertrud and, in 1917, the birth of his baby boy, Erich.[88]

Perhaps voicing a perspective popular among pastors, Siegfried E. was convinced that where science fell short in healing the psychological wounds of war, Christian faith would be much more successful. In one of his diary entries, he wrote skeptically about one particular "statistician by profession" he read who claimed that outbreaks of nervousness could be reduced through scientific analysis.[89] Instead, he saw his role as a chaplain who helped men find God as much more effective than medicine in combating the pain of life at the front. In the summer of 1918, he continued to express doubts about the experts behind the lines who were out of touch with the spiritual and psychological needs of front soldiers. However, in the last days of the war, he became more pessimistic about the potential reach of pastors like himself and whether they could bring men to Christ. This pessimism reached a crescendo when defeat seemed certain, and the nation's disaster mirrored his own sense of collapse:

Germany staggers. The war is lost! ... Why have two million died? It's too much for me once again. I am falling apart. I let myself drift. I escape into Gertrud's love. I have to forget everything, not to completely despair. My soul is encased in ice. I cannot process it anymore. We humans are so vain![90]

The entire war seemed completely futile to Siegfried E., and he hesitated to speculate on what it all meant. His diary entries in the weeks after the defeat suggest he was frightened by the spread of socialist revolution, which seemed to dash his hopes that the war, even if destructive, would result in the revitalization of Christian faith.[91] After the war, he rose through the ranks of the Protestant hierarchy in Magdeburg, committing himself to Christian education during the Weimar Republic. Shortly after Hitler came to power, he joined the German Christian church, which embraced the National Socialists. He died in Freiburg in 1984.

Losing God

Fewer letters and diaries suggest an outright loss of faith. But while many men and women who may have been disillusioned with the war or traditional authority figures still "found" God, some expressed growing skepticism about whether an all-powerful, omniscient, and loving Supreme Being existed at all. Skepticism about God rarely fit into clear categorization. Examining available files of letters and diaries, it is rare for individuals to identify themselves as atheists or agnostics, though as the next chapter reveals, contemporary psychologists argued that individuals who were nonbelievers often concealed this fact. Instead, expressions of doubt were often through a lens of intense emotional despair, where individuals struggled for words to describe their unfolding psychological and spiritual metamorphosis. Skepticism was expressed as more of a feeling than a carefully constructed system of thought.

While a number of front soldiers, as explored earlier, withdrew from the imploding material world into a more subjective spiritual haven in order to survive, others had a very different reaction to physical and psychological stress. The pressure of their environment made them feel cut off from spiritual concerns, or made them suspect that the "spiritual" refuge preached by chaplains and pastors was false, designed to distract them from the "real" world. This can be seen in the memoir of Artur Boer, who transcribed his wartime diary into prose in the 1920s. Boer was an engineer for the Prussian State Railway before 1914, and he was recruited after the outbreak of the war. Surviving over three years of combat, the loss of friends, and several wounds, he was exhausted and jaded by 1918. During the Spring Offensive in March of that year, he wrote about the hunger that men at the front had to endure, which drove them to steal food off the dead and wounded. When burying fallen comrades, there was often no time to bring in a chaplain, so "our officers held forth with trembling voice and a funeral service that no minister could approach." The officers, who knew their fellow comrades and spoke from the heart, were so "simple and eloquent," making him wonder "why would we even have to walk such a long way to hear a chaplain."[92] When they did finally march behind the lines to hear a burial service led by a chaplain, Boer was dubious:

> The chaplain arrived and began to speak. We weren't in a Sunday mood and listened to his words with indifference. But soon he began to spout a phrase that almost made us laugh: "We do not live by bread alone." We couldn't believe our ears, but it was true: they had attempted to console us with the help of a chaplain because there was no food to be had on that occasion![93]

The chaplain's attempt to remind them of their Christian spiritual ideals—"We do not live by bread alone" (a reference to Jesus's teaching from the Gospel of Matthew 4:4)—rang hollow to Boer. By this stage of the war, spiritual consolation seemed inhumane when men faced starvation. Boer could relate more to his comrades who shared the front experience than the chaplains in the reserve trenches, whose rhetoric now seemed to be a grim joke. Boer survived the war, but, ruined by postwar inflation, he emigrated to Sweden in 1920.

Especially after the unending carnage in 1916, some front soldiers began to question the existence of God. Infantryman Hans F., for example, finding no comfort or possible end to the war, asked whether there was an all-powerful, benevolent Creator. In 1916, he wrote:

> Certainly no sign of an imminent peace. And we've had enough of this life to the point of despair. How often do you ask yourself: is it possible that there is still a Lord God (*Herrgott*)? Won't Germany see that life cannot continue this way? We've reached that point here already. Potatoes have gone out, bread and meat portions are getting smaller. Even coffee and cocoa are no longer enough ... When one hears the comrades longing for a crust of bread, the last remnant of love for the fatherland disappears.[94]

At the beginning of the war, love for the fatherland was often equated with love of God, conflating religious faith and nationalism. However, in the case of Hans F., with the erosion of faith in the nation, faith in God also broke down. When authority figures could no longer provide the physical sustenance (food) or emotional comfort (God) needed to survive, men fell into isolation and cynicism.

The breakdown of religious faith could be triggered by the fundamental question of God's silence in the wake of so much pain. Rudolf G., for example, struggled with this after several years of fighting on the Eastern and Western Fronts. When the war broke out, he had just started architecture school in Kassel, but he interrupted his studies and volunteered in August 1914. A year later, he was profoundly changed by his experience. Writing to his parents before Christmas in 1915, he tried to describe the brutality of war, and he wrestled with God's role in allowing it: "Today in Kraljevo, on the way back from the former Serbia, with every glance one sees misfortune and deep distress. Lord God, you wanted this. One becomes hard and raw against everything that is brought on by hunger and hardships."[95] It is difficult to discern if his interesting remark—"Lord God, you wanted this"—was accusatory or sarcastic, suggesting that God wanted all this brutality, and that he wanted men to become numb to it.

Rudolf G. was wounded in 1917 and while in a field hospital he reflected further on the effects of the war by writing a memoir focusing on how the front had changed him. Brutality seemed to replace any sense of something transcendent or redeeming. He recorded words from his girlfriend, Betti E., who tried to cheer him up: "My dear Betti E. wrote to me: 'The war also has some good consequences, people would be bettered by the suffering and terrifying experiences.'" But Rudolf G. rejected this optimism and wrote in his memoir that he believed that one could find the opposite response, that people would be psychologically brutalized and realize there was nothing to believe in but their own suffering.[96] After recovering from his wounds he returned to the front and was wounded again in September 1918 and spent the rest of the war in a British POW camp, where his left leg was amputated. He returned home in January 1919, but he had become a morphine addict and struggled with numerous surgeries and ongoing pain.[97]

On the home front, some civilians were experiencing a similar erosion of faith. Feelings of isolation, loss, and resentment toward authority figures plagued women and children as they waited in suspense for word from their loved ones. A rather interesting case of disillusionment on the home front can be seen through the eyes of a young Marlene Dietrich. Looking back on her career as one of the world's most famous actresses, she completed her memoir in the late 1980s toward the end of her life. It is highly suspect in its reinvention of her past, and it must be taken as a retrospective construction of the meaning of her own experiences and perceptions. Nevertheless, the candid descriptions of her crisis of faith during her adolescence and teenage years at the Auguste-Viktoria Girls' School in Berlin provide a useful glimpse into the war's psychological effects on a young woman.

After Marlene Dietrich's biological father died in 1907, her mother married *Leutnant* Eduard von Losch in 1914, whom she would call her father during the war. Marlene recounted the fear and isolation she felt, waiting every day with "terrible and insufferable anxiety," as she and her mother braced themselves for news from the Western Front.[98] In an almost stream-of-consciousness style that revealed how difficult it was to find the language to describe her feelings even decades later, Dietrich intimated her disillusionment with humanity, religion, and God as a result of the trauma of loss. The war fueled growing moral confusion, and it made her suspect that religious beliefs were nothing more than the inventions of parents and pastors:

> Good and evil, these poorly defined concepts, have a clearly etched meaning in the world of children. They are like a primal law: unchangeable, always explainable, inexorable and mighty. Outside the world of children, on the other hand, good and evil seem to be changeable, deceptive and invented arbitrarily.[99]

Looking back on her life, Dietrich identified the war as the trigger for her realization that religion was a construct. She described this as the moment in which her cynicism with the world took hold. As the war forced her to grow up quickly, she became frustrated with authority figures who expected children to be "only the passive witnesses of history's upheavals," and she started to question adults who made her sing patriotic songs while the killing dragged on. "Because men were slaughtering each other and making a mockery of human and divine laws," she could not imagine singing nationalistic songs about God punishing England or being on Germany's side.[100]

Dietrich's skepticism intensified in the wake of her stepfather's death in 1916. As the pain of loss and apparent hypocrisy of teachers and pastors become unbearably acute, she asked whether or not God really was "with us," as the propaganda promised. Her thinking was full of uncertainty and contradiction. She did not totally abandon the idea that God existed, and she wrestled with the notion that perhaps God could return after the war. But she could not imagine why God allowed the world to descend into such destruction. Dietrich tried to recapture her childhood thoughts in a kind of free associative, rhetorical style, imagining retrospectively what went on in her head while she sat in a classroom as a little girl:

> God is with us, don't you know that? God, do You know that You are with us? Us the Germans? How do You choose what side You are on? Do you support the best ones? The best pupils? Are You only on one side? Then You cannot be God, or can You? You let the just and the unjust come to You. Are we the just? We are victors. Doesn't that mean that we are the just? Don't ask questions. Do your homework. Attend to your daily chores. And, finally, don't forget music.[101]

Dietrich's frustration with authority figures who squashed critical thinking and touted God as selective in his national leanings is on full display. By the last year of the war, fearful that her cousin Hans would not survive, she said that she secretly prayed to God for the Americans to defeat Germany and end the war. But she suspected this was useless: "I had already prayed for a long time. I didn't believe, admittedly, that God heard me or that he wanted to hear me, for even more strongly than before, I was convinced that He really wasn't at all interested in humans."[102]

Conclusion

Marlene Dietrich's almost stream-of-consciousness attempt to recreate, many years later, the disintegration of her religious beliefs suggests an awareness of the contradictory emotions that erupted in response to the trauma of loss, including loss of values as well as loss of loved ones. Why did individuals go in different directions, oscillating between belief and skepticism? It is difficult to ascertain why certain individuals "found" God while others struggled with religious and existential questions. Details of social and religious backgrounds, and complete narratives of wartime experiences, are often incomplete in archival files. Available letters and diaries typically provide only a relatively brief snapshot of time, or, despite intimations of religious crisis, they only hint at the deeper nature of their psychological and emotional breakdown. But whether men and women "found" or "lost" God, one can detect a process in which they constructed more personalized, subjective existential, and religious explanations for trauma.

Religious responses to trauma fell across a broad spectrum. The wide range of religious feelings, ranging from revitalization to skepticism, are difficult to categorize, and they were expressed more as emotional responses to trauma than as dogmatic or carefully delineated revaluations of theology. Damaged or fragmented prewar beliefs were not necessarily replaced by new systems of thought. Rather, trauma inflicted on religious beliefs often created a kind of void, or silence, which could make individuals feel cut off from prewar structures, even if they continued to reach out to family for reassurance. Anxieties over moral injury were particularly difficult to express, as front soldiers only hinted at their suspicions that they, or their society, had violated God's laws. As will be seen in the next chapter, psychologists theorized that many men concealed their unfolding religious crisis because, though they often tried, they did not feel like they could articulate it, or did not feel like people at home would understand.

5

Diagnosing Religious Beliefs: Contemporary Scientific and Popular Debates over the Spiritual-Psychological Effects of the War

By the middle of the war, the damage inflicted by mass violence on the religious faith of soldiers and civilians became a topic of academic research. For example, the University of Kiel's Institute of Psychology funded language instructor Georg Willers, who had volunteered for duty in 1914 but returned to teaching two years later after being wounded, to undertake what he described as an "investigation into the psychology of religion." In 1917, Willers sent a call out through various front newspapers as well as civilian newspapers for participants in his study to share their perspectives on the impact of the war on religious beliefs. In his call, he expressed empathy for men and women who were experiencing a religious crisis, which he characterized as a natural outcome of total war. Interestingly, he conflated combat veterans and civilians, calling them both "comrades," a community who shared similar psychological damage:

> All of the comrades who have had religious or other experiences under the influence of war-time events (battles, loss of relatives, economic hardship) are of interest to our religious-psychological examination (in connection with the Psychology Seminar at the University of Kiel), which strives to reach as many people as possible, and kindly asks you to send in your observations. If you are looking to reveal your inner religious life, you do not need to disclose your name and address, but your age, gender, educational background and profession are of interest. As a former wounded war veteran, the undersigned kindly asks comrades in the trenches and in the air, and especially doctors and nurses, for their contributions.[1]

Though he did not seem to complete or publish the results of this intriguing study, Willers's attempt to gather data reveals an awareness of the collective trauma inflicted by the war. His call for responses also included a preliminary thesis: "The tremendous events of this time have shaken our hearts and souls to the core. The inner religious life (*religiöses Innenleben*) has been profoundly damaged. Conceptions of God, prayer life and faith, whether they have been reinforced or eroded, have been fundamentally changed."[2]

Willers was exceptional in trying to explore the religious impact of total war on both soldiers and civilians.[3] As will be seen in this chapter, most contemporary studies of religious wounds inflicted by the war privileged the voices of men on the combat front. The focus here is on nonreligious specialists from diverse academic and professional backgrounds who investigated the impact of the war on the religious beliefs of front soldiers. Though Sigmund Freud, Magnus Hirschfeld, and other leading psychoanalysts published famous investigations of the psychological effects of the war, including on sexuality and religion,[4] this chapter turns instead to a number of thinkers who are lesser known but who were pioneers during the war in collecting data on how religious beliefs and trauma interacted. How did contemporary specialists in trauma and religion, including psychiatrists and cultural critics, interpret the impact of the war on religious faith?

The scholars examined here, including Paul Plaut, Walter Ludwig, E. Schiche, Paul Göhre, and Erich Everth, came from varied backgrounds in psychology and philosophy. But they saw themselves as a discrete group who often referred to each other's work. All of these specialists had combat experience, which made them feel uniquely positioned to theorize on soldiers' spiritual and religious values. Their combat experience often gave them a conviction that their subjective experiences enhanced their investigation of the war's effects on the religious beliefs of front soldiers, who they felt were misunderstood by civilians who had never seen combat. These theorists often portrayed themselves as advocates for veterans, and they were critical of what they saw as the oversimplistic and stigmatizing "war hysteria" diagnosis for traumatic neurosis. At the same time, their status as front veterans also tended to bias their approaches, as their studies were almost entirely focused on the narratives of soldiers, who they described as a group that was distinct from communities on the home front. According to these specialists, combat soldiers were fundamentally different from civilians because they had undergone a much more powerful spiritual and psychological transformation that required careful study and exploration.

The central argument of this chapter is that, compared to religious authorities, contemporary scientists developed a more multilayered, subjective approach to the religious impact of the war. Using surveys of soldiers, as well as their own combat experiences, secular specialists in psychological trauma explored broadly the individual religious beliefs and emotional experiences of front soldiers. Psychiatrists postulated that theorists had to move beyond what they saw as an increasingly stale debate over whether or not the war stimulated or eroded religious faith. Instead, they asserted that the actual impact of the war on religious belief was much too complicated to categorize into the bifurcated battle between advocates and critics of religion, neither of whom could claim victory. Psychiatrists characterized soldiers' beliefs as too ever-changing and elusive to pin down, and they saw front soldiers as occupiers of a kind of liminal state, oscillating between belief and cynicism, piety and irreverence, the rational and irrational, seriousness and humor as men navigated through the extremes between intense and banal spiritual and material worlds. Instead of fitting into any particular spiritual or religious category, men survived these extremes by striking a balance between sometimes contradictory, dissonant or taboo beliefs, behaviors, and attitudes. Traumatized by violence, and disillusioned to varying degrees with existing religious structures, front soldiers experimented with language and thinking remote from Judeo-Christian paradigms, and outside the rhetoric of militarized, nationalized religiosity. Psychiatrists made the case that as a result of their encounters with inexplicable suffering, traumatized men entered a new space that made them search for ways of thinking that were more tangible, experience-based, meaningful or "real" in the extraordinary, surreal, and self-contained world of the trenches.

Studies of the psychology of religion in war reached beyond psychiatric and academic circles. By 1916-18, popular periodicals also began to publish articles on the subjective, complex world of front soldiers' spirituality and religiosity. This chapter first looks at one of the most systematic studies of the psychological impact of the of war, including on religious belief, which was undertaken by the Institute for Applied Psychology (Institut für angewandte Psychologie und psychologische Sammelforschung) outside Potsdam. It then turns to similar studies on religion and psychology published in mainstream media, which tried to introduce to a lay audience the intricacies of front soldiers' psyches, including the distinct ways in which they conceptualized religion and spirituality, and the transformative psychological effects of the front experience.

Paul Plaut: Scientificizing Religious Beliefs and the Psychological Effects of War

During the course of the war, the German government funded studies on the psychological effects of combat, primarily in order to evaluate and optimize the mental fitness of frontline soldiers. One of the most interesting studies of soldiers' psyches was undertaken by the Institute for Applied Psychology and Psychological Collection Research, which was originally founded before the war by Dr. Louis William Stern and Dr. Otto Lipmann. Stern and Lipmann were psychologists, and Stern participated in the founding of the German Society for Psychology (Deutsche Gesellschaft für Psychologie). Since 1908, both served as editors of one of the leading journals in their field, the *Journal of Applied Psychology and Psychological Collective Research* (*Zeitschrift für angewandte Psychologie und psychologische Sammelforschung*). In 1912 Stern, who worked with Sigmund Freud just before the war, invented the "intelligence quotient" (IQ) to test and measure intellectual ability. Stern and Lipmann led the Institute for Applied Psychology beginning in 1916. Even before, in 1914-15, they gained a reputation for collecting data through mass surveys of soldiers that focused on military psychology. Later on, similar studies were sponsored by the War Ministry as the army sought methods to test the psychological health of recruits as well as the impact of combat experience.[5]

Stern and Lipmann's institute developed a major survey that, in addition to assessing the personality and performance of front soldiers, also investigated diverse aspects of their experiences, including responses to violence, feelings of comradeship, and the impact of the war on their religious beliefs. They developed a field of study that Stern called "psychotechnics." It was used to diagnose the psychological aptitude of soldiers, and potentially civilians, and to measure their occupational suitability.[6] The initial survey project encountered a number of problems, as the War Ministry restricted their questions due to the military's fear that the survey could expose and publicize the war's psychological wounds and thus lower morale.[7] However, another researcher working for Stern and Lipmann, Paul Plaut, was able to conduct interviews with soldiers and publish his results just after the war in an essay titled, "Psychography of the Warrior," which appeared in the *Journal for Applied Psychology*.[8] Paul Plaut was not a trained psychologist, but he was a veteran with combat experience. From a German Jewish family in Berlin, the twenty-year-old Plaut volunteered for war in 1915. He saw combat as a corporal (*Gefreiter*) at Langemarck and Verdun and other battles while fighting with Reserve Infantry Regiment 237. Awarded the Iron Cross second class, he was promoted to noncommissioned officer (*Unteroffizier*).[9]

Plaut's "Psychography of the Warrior" was based on data collected during the war but it was not published until 1920. It offered a glimpse into conflicting and complex experiences with disillusionment, isolation, and psychological stress. As historian Julia Barbara Köhne argues, Plaut's work contradicted the widely held assumption that men felt unified through comradeship, patriotism, and nationalism, and instead he emphasized the divisive, fragmented, and brutalizing effects of wartime violence.[10] Perhaps most interestingly, Plaut's work was iconoclastic because he criticized the idea that the war caused a "renewal" or "revitalization" of religious faith. He was interested in what he called the "soul life" (*Seelenleben*) of men at the front, but he did not see the war experience as one that stimulated traditional religious beliefs. Instead, in his eyes, the war triggered basic instincts toward survival, which affected the human psyche in complex ways.

One of the sections of Plaut's "Psychography of the Warrior" deals with "Faith and Superstition," which he approached from his perspective as a scientist investigating the "psychotechnics" of front soldiers. However, he found it to be a "difficult task" to tackle religion from a scientific point of view. "Religion is a separate psychology in its own right," Plaut wrote, as it resists reason based on evidence and instead embraces dogma. To illustrate his apprehension, Plaut pointed to Nietzsche's *On the Genealogy of Morals* (1887), summarizing Nietzsche's argument that "morality is the main obstacle to all honest psychology."[11] The psychology of religion, Plaut observed, also required a lot of myth-busting, because there were so many assumptions about the effects of war on religious beliefs that were inaccurate. For example, it was widely accepted that religious sentiments intensified because front soldiers were in constant danger and threatened with death. "It was taken for granted," he wrote, "that there were a thousand prayers before and during battle, and that the stronger the artillery fire became, the nearer that hour of death approached, the more fervent were the prayers."[12] Plaut conceded, based on his personal experience, "I have witnessed moments when many men cried like animals being led to the slaughterhouse, as if they wanted to outrun the roaring of the grenades with the 'Lord's Prayer.'"[13] Further, he wrote about how he witnessed comrades at the front who, even if they were not particularly religious, or even atheists, would attend field services and "in the hour of their death, try to find a bridge to what they had previously constantly denied."[14] However, Plaut argued that the image of increased piety at the front was a misleading narrative promoted by the churches and the military. He believed that in reality there was what he called an "underground" to soldiers' belief systems and experiences that was much more complex, and which eluded the self-serving narrative of elites.[15]

In measuring the "depths of religious experience of the frontline soldier," Plaut found the anecdotes reported by religious and military leaders, who rarely interacted with actual men in the front lines, to be essentially useless. He relied instead on interviews with soldiers who had fought in the trenches, but even these sources were problematic, he admitted, because men concealed their personal beliefs and many did not actually like to talk about religion. The "real religiosity" and "innermost conviction" of men in the trenches was ultimately almost too subjective for analysis.[16] Plaut made a distinction between the outward displays of religiosity, including rhetoric and participation in rituals, and what he saw as the more important subtle evidence of religious belief:

> Much more valuable are the individual signs (*Einzelerscheinungen*), expressions of simple soldiers, who generally do not like to talk about religion and religiosity, because in the immediacy with which they face things, they recognize the absurdity (*Widersinn*) that lies in ecclesiastically-inspired enthusiasm for war.[17]

Soldiers were not only skeptical of religious enthusiasm generated by institutions and leaders, but they were also cynical about whether or not religious faith was really helpful in warding off danger. According to Plaut, front soldiers were quite practical. They would ask skeptically "what can one get" from religious rituals or beliefs, and when they evaded death, they were simply happy to still be alive, and less willing to attribute it to supernatural intervention or an elaborate religious belief than to everyday, unpredictable circumstances.[18] Plaut gives an example from an interview with a soldier:

> If, in spite of it all, people still feel happy when they leave this hell, it's just because they have escaped hell. They return from the battlefield and are saved ... Soldiers in war have a childlike philosophy about the small and big things. They never think very far ahead. They don't look around themselves much, and they don't think very far into the future. They live rough from hand to mouth and today they are content to be able to live a little while longer.[19]

Preoccupied with survival, front soldiers were focused on day-to-day conditions, jaded to complex philosophical or religious explanations for existence. Plaut thus suggests that any attempt, either by elites or individuals trying to reconstruct their frontline experiences, to ascribe larger meaning to events ultimately imposed false consciousness. If men engaged in religious rituals, like attending church services or giving the sign of the cross, it was often a gesture of "habit," which did not actually reflect deeper feelings. While they might outwardly display religious behavior in the face of danger, inwardly, soldiers were often spiritually numb, as in the case of one veteran Plaut interviewed: "I had absolutely no feeling at all. I was frozen inwardly."[20]

Plaut did not try to determine whether front soldiers were believers or atheists. Categorization did not interest him. Men could be simultaneously religious and cynical. Plaut realized this when he tried to interpret contradictory statements from soldiers, where there was a dramatic difference between surface image and inner reality, including one who reported, "Personally, I did not experience any religious emotions on the outside, but inside I underwent the strongest moral shake-up and strengthening (*die stärkste moralische Erschütterung und Kräftigung*)." Because of the difficulty in uncovering what men actually thought, Plaut warned against those who would argue that religious faith had eroded entirely at the front: "It is useless to pile up examples of a negative religious kind (*negativreligiöser Art*) in order to attempt a counterpoint against the opinions put forth by theologians. Because of the scope and depth of the psychological experience of the war, this is out of the question." At the same time, advocates for religion could not be confident that religious convictions made men stronger, as they often claimed: "The efficiency of the soldier cannot be attributed to the strength of religious feeling. It could also be due to a complete break from it."[21]

Plaut also made the case that if there was either spiritual breakdown or renewal, it might not be experienced or articulated through the prism of traditional religious beliefs or language. Soldiers resented pastors who tried to speak for them and claim authority in explaining the spiritual effects of the war, especially if soldiers felt condescended to or criticized. As one soldier intimated:

> The little fest in the church was very serious and dignified, but the pastor should not have spoken so much about how we should repent. It's not like that with us. We don't just crawl around and bow down as poor sinners, pastor! We walk proudly and upright, because we want to fight for truth, justice and freedom in the trenches.[22]

Men at the front felt misunderstood and alienated from civilians and prewar experiences and ways of thinking. If some men were strengthened or motivated by religion, it had to be acknowledged that, sometimes in the cases of those same individuals, men could also be invigorated by psychological factors that had nothing to do with religion.

Plaut emphasized that front soldiers existed in a kind of ambiguous state between different forces. The spiritual condition of soldiers was constantly changing as they oscillated between enthusiasm and paralysis, faith and skepticism, joy and despair. As one volunteer wrote to Plaut, sacred texts and cynical humor both made sense, "Over time, we front soldiers have become a strange sort of people (*komische Sorte von Menschen*). Sometimes we're frivolous (*leichtsinnig*) and sometimes pious. The New Testament often lies right beside *Simplizissimus*."[23] Plaut tried to describe what he saw as a "middle ground" or "balance" that men occupied, a kind of new plane of existence unique to the front. He wrote:

> Now we get closer to the whole problem, because we get a glimpse into the middle ground (*Mittellage*); it will be shown over and over again that one's whole psychological development (*seelische Entwicklung*) in war balances between the initial heightened feeling of happiness during the period of mobilization and the

increasingly clearer feeling that the war is an eerie fall into some kind of dark thing (*unheimlichen Sturz in irgendein dunkles Etwas*).[24]

Plaut tried to explain this "fall into some kind of dark thing" in scientific terms by pointing to biological theories about excitement and paralysis as symbiotic, with organisms finding a balance between the two stimuli. As front soldiers were pushed from one extreme state to the other, Plaut argued, they had to find a middle state where they could survive. This was also the case with soldiers' spiritual lives, where men had to find some kind of balance between the extremes of faith and cynicism, so they were neither captive to officially sanctioned religious piety nor were they completely engulfed in that "dark thing."

As men occupied this middle ground between experiential extremes, Plaut argued, they became convinced that it was most spiritually healthy to find your own way. Soldiers grew skeptical of dogma and any other religious pressures, and they started to believe what made the most sense for them in this extraordinary environment. Ironically, Plaut characterized these subjective "religious feelings" as the result of men becoming more "objective" about their beliefs. That is, they became less susceptible to "dogma," and they simply acted and thought as they pleased:

> The religious feelings of the majority of these soldiers have also become more objective: people become more sober, no longer running to church spontaneously during leave behind the front as they once did before. Criticism of dogma became very strong, but even more so they became critical of how religious dogma had been colored by political agendas. Since church attendance was considered part of their military service, people were forced to be comfortable with it, but when there was "no order" and they were not "commanded" to go, they stayed at home and exercised their right, as in peacetime, to be able to believe what appeared good to them (*glauben zu können, was ihnen gut schien*).[25]

The reach of church services and dogma was thus ultimately limited, according to Plaut, and front soldiers were disaffected by compulsory rituals and the politicization of religion. Instead, men grew more intuitive, grabbing on to what made sense based on their experiences and environment.

Plaut argued that even if the war did not generate a substantial return to traditional religious beliefs or rituals, it did arouse interest in what he called "deeper" reflection. This was often not related to orthodox religious traditions: "As for the revival of religious consciousness that was predicted by theologians, this has been disputed strongly by many. The world-view (*Weltanschauung*) has certainly become a different and deeper one, and certainly less related to church (*unkirchlicher*)."[26] This "different" worldview included superstitious beliefs, some familiar and others created in the environment of the trenches, which Plaut considered to be just as, if not more, important to the front soldier's worldview as religious orthodoxy. He argued that when one's emotions were peaked by traumatic experiences, and other belief systems did not help to contain fear and anxiety, superstition offered a "release." A kind of "middle ground" between the "purely sensible" (*rein Sinnliche*) and that which was "purely supernatural" (*rein

Übersinnliche), superstition was a natural outgrowth of the individual's yearning for a "favorable solution to such affective states."²⁷ In some ways, superstition was similar to faith, Plaut argued, but the former was "less dogmatic" and thus more appealing to men under stress. While faith and superstition had the same goal, "hope for self-preservation and further survival," superstition was "more impulsive," and it actually gave men more hope than orthodox religion.²⁸

Whether it was superstition or any other system of thought, Plaut ultimately saw all these as mechanisms for easing nervous stress. In his analysis, he conflated orthodox, traditional religious beliefs with popular beliefs and superstitions as having ultimately the same function. Thus a wide array of protective devices, including "lucky clovers, lucky pens, blessed coins, amulets," had the same potency as crucifixes, consecrated saint medals, or Bible passages sewn into the hem of clothing. Any coincidence of a soldier surviving while carrying one of these devices was cited as proof of their efficacy, reinforcing their psychological dependence on such mechanisms for personal insurance.²⁹ Plaut deduced that superstitious beliefs were even more popular and "normalized" than they were before the war. He cited interviews and letters with front soldiers, including the following from a student he corresponded with, who described superstition as a haven into which someone could insulate themselves:

> Whoever has a bit of imagination (*ein bißchen Phantasie*) and maybe also possesses a bit of nervousness (*Nervosität*) probably also cocoons himself with some superstition (*der umspinnt sich wohl auch mit etwas Aberglauben*). I'm so used to it—I always make up little oracles for all sorts of more or less important questions about the future. Right now, there's only one question: will I get hit?—If only it wasn't the 13th! That number has something malicious about it.³⁰

The soldier then went on to describe the vicious circle of rationalization and overthinking about the "malicious" number thirteen, until something terrible happened on the fourteenth of the month, making him believe fourteen was actually the cursed number he should fear. The irrational effects of trench warfare on the psyche were thus clearly evident, and, where men otherwise had little agency, such thinking was extremely common. At the same time, while faith could help assuage frayed nerves, men could also became so obsessed with elaborate belief systems that it could inflict even further psychological distress.³¹

Fear and the Psychology of Religion

Plaut's layered, intricate analysis of soldiers' psyches is significant on a number of levels. He suggested that the extraordinary front experience created a space in which men were more preoccupied with powerful emotions, especially fear, than with the validity of particular dogmas. Their visceral responses to fear profoundly changed them, and this emotion shaped their thinking more than any other factor. The different mechanisms used by men to cope with fear was a central theme in the Institute for

Applied Psychology's research on the psychological effects of the war, and this topic became the focus of studies by other psychologists at the institute.

Walter Ludwig on Fear, Death, and Religious Belief

One of the most extensive studies of the psychological effects of the war was sponsored by the institute and undertaken by Walter Ludwig, who published his 1919 University of Tübingen PhD dissertation, "On the Psychology of Fear in the War" (*Beiträge zur Psychologie der Furcht im Kriege*). Excerpts from his thesis were published in the same 1920 edition of the *Journal for Applied Psychology* in which Plaut's essay appeared. Ludwig was an infantry officer who served on the Western Front, where he saw combat at the Somme and Ypres and was wounded three times.[32] His data were collected during the war, and it included surveys and essays written by over 200 Württemberg officers as they convalesced in a hospital for disabled soldiers. Unfortunately, Ludwig did not collect data on the prewar religious background, lengths of service, or age of those interviewed.[33] Further, because they were all officers, the survey is biased in terms of social class.

Despite its shortcomings as a study that is not necessarily representative of the social backgrounds of men at the front, Ludwig's work offers intriguing analysis of the subjective psychological experiences of this sample of soldiers. The officers were asked to write an essay titled "Observations from the field regarding what the soldier thinks in the moment of greatest danger in order to overcome the fear of death."[34] Similar to the problem with Plaut's work, the military was reluctant to publish a candid study of the psychological stress generated by the front experience, but by the time Ludwig completed his investigation, the new postwar social-political atmosphere allowed him to release his findings. The officers surveyed provided extraordinarily blunt descriptions of the effects of enduring trench warfare, and they illuminated how heavy artillery bombardments and machine-gun fire tested their psychological and emotional coping mechanisms, including their religious beliefs.

The central psychological experience of the war, according to Ludwig, concerned the fear of death. This emotional experience was ubiquitous in responses to his survey. The task of psychologists then was to uncover how men overcame this fear, and he theorized that there were at least three primary ways in which soldiers worked through it: (1) by devaluing life (and thus becoming desensitized); (2) through fatalism and; (3) through religious belief. The different ways in which men employed these psychological mechanisms depended on their experiences at the front. But fatalism, which could also be combined with religious beliefs, "was one of the strongest counterweights to the fear of death," and it appeared to different degrees in most of the surveys. Ludwig quoted from a number of responses to show how closely fatalism grew out of desensitization and giving up a sense of agency to cope with a horrifying reality:

> The constant hovering between fear and hope, especially when it is tied to the imagination of total annihilation and one's own powerlessness, leads to the fundamental mood of fatalism. The impressions are often so strong or of such a lasting impact that the will to life is crushed and gives rise to a dull indifference

and resignation: "Gradually, one surrenders to destiny, which cannot be changed." "No one can escape death, I won't run, a corporal in my company often says, when we as a [medical] evacuation unit (*Trägertruppe*) reached the most dangerous positions." "The soldier becomes used to a certain fatalism, and at the moment of danger he thinks: when you're gone, you're gone."[35]

Over time, as men survived countless artillery attacks, aerial bombardments, and other experiences in which they had to passively endure life-threatening peril, they grew increasingly numb. Even when they were rotated into the reserve trenches, men continued to remain desensitized and did not regain their previous exuberance, as they steeled themselves for a return to the brutalizing environment.[36]

Fatalism was often accompanied by what Ludwig called a "strong religious coloring," as fatalistic beliefs were conflated with Christian conceptions of God. Ludwig pointed to several other studies, including an essay by socially progressive Lutheran pastor Paul Göhre, whose work will be further explored below, to argue that while some evidence of revived religiosity can be found, and "the force of experience can indeed urge man towards God," this was "undoubtedly overstated" by theologians and military authorities. Based on the data he accumulated, Ludwig concluded that "there are not a few people who are very brave without any religious expression and who let their actions and sufferings be determined by motives that have little or nothing to do with religion."[37] One respondent to Ludwig's study summarized the coping mechanisms used by comrades in his unit, highlighting the varied techniques men at the front employed to counteract stress:

> As if by chance, my eyes fall on a soldier aged around 25; he is writing to his family back home; he keeps looking at a photo beside him (probably his wife); he seems to have quite forgotten the danger. … Over there sits an older man who is turning gray; he has a book on his lap, the New Testament, and is eagerly reading it. Another cracks jokes, which might make people laugh out loud if they were in a different situation. Another man is crying; he's in a pretty bad way. Over there two men are conversing with each other; they're already happy that they might get decorated once the whole mess is over.[38]

Religion was not special, but rather it was just another lens through which men dealt with their emotions. To reinforce his argument, Ludwig included in his essay a chart listing the diverse emotions and frequency with which they appeared in surveys. While "religious stirrings" (*religiöse Regungen*) were mentioned most often by the officers who replied to Ludwig's questions, he listed a plethora of other emotions that men used as tools to ward off fear. These included indifference, humor, memories of home (*Heimat*), hope, feelings of duty and loyalty, "social emotions" (which included comradeship), "fighting emotions" (*Kampfemotionen*), feelings of activity and passivity, narcotics, memories of past life, and other emotions or behaviors.[39] Interestingly, patriotism was one of the least mentioned mechanisms for maintaining one's nerves. The psychological tools men used to cope with fear were subjective, based on their application of various emotions, which each individual possessed to a different degree.

Ludwig tried to take a scientific approach to the different expressions of religiosity, linking particular religious feelings to specific experiences. He asked front soldiers: how often do you invoke religious thoughts, and in exactly what way did you find these beliefs and rituals to be helpful? Punctuating his analysis with quotes from surveys, Ludwig tried to quantify the diverse applications of religious thinking:

> Religious thought can move in different directions. One time it appears while praying for divine help; this was expressed between 9 and 14 times. "Religious feelings are awakened by a brief prayer." "Marching down the street—suddenly some 15 cm artillery shells hit directly in front of us on the street. As fast as an arrow, everyone throws himself on the ground and then just as quickly gets up and continues to march. There—a buzz, and one almost grazed my head. 'Lord help you,' the mouth says it mechanically; only afterwards was there reflection and earnestness about it." "When last year seven days of artillery fire raged at the Somme, religion strengthened me. I saw many comrades who once had rejected religion now pull out their prayer books." "When entering a battle, I always performed a prayer with the hope that God and my guardian angel will protect me from the worst."—Belief in providence and confidence in divine assistance is invoked 11 up to 19 times. "Under extreme danger and tension—suddenly an unimaginable power comes over me; there is a force, a higher being, who guides our destinies and watches over us." ... "I realized that there were many of my comrades in the same position who thought like me: whether I already wandered in the dark valley, I feared no evil. Thy rod and thy staff comfort me."[40]

From this Ludwig deduced that the expression of religious beliefs and rituals did not necessarily reflect a deep or elaborate system of thought, but rather they were an automatic, emotional, and visceral response to extreme vulnerability, invoked even by men who before the war did not consider themselves religious.[41]

Ludwig argued that the most powerful mechanism offered by religion for coping with fear was the belief in an afterlife. By imagining a tranquil afterlife, men were psychologically able to escape the nightmarish environment of the trenches. One soldier reported in a survey, "I was afraid of being hit, but not afraid of the thought of death." When he thought about his past life and imagined the next, he found "a sense of balance." This was not a new phenomenon, and Ludwig cited prewar studies of how in the moment when an individual faced peril and death, their mind rushed with thoughts of an afterlife that made everything else seem trivial and surmountable.[42] But for men in the trenches, Ludwig argued, this feeling was even more intense. One front soldier reported on how thoughts of life after death affected him: "The soldier thinks of another life in a world after death. He also thinks of all that he has already done for the fatherland, which makes him realize that in the other world he could not feel so bad."[43] The thought of an "other world" thus made the front soldier feel like his life was fulfilled and complete.

Religious beliefs, Ludwig concluded, were ultimately only a surface layer that concealed deeper psychological foundations. It was actually the preexisting "psychic strength of the personality," and their willpower, that determined resilience. Every individual had a breaking point, according to Ludwig, which even the most religious-minded soldier could not control. Religion only provided a language through which one processed inherent natural instincts or emotions and in turn helped them "restore and strengthen the ego, which is in a state of shock under threat."[44] Religious beliefs themselves, Ludwig argued, were not decisive in determining whether men could survive psychologically.

E. Schiche: Premonitions of Death

The fear of death was not always most acute in the front line. It was often when men got a break from the adrenaline rush in the trenches that they had time to dwell on their past and anticipate future experiences. Brooding behind the lines, waiting for their next rotation into the trenches, men could become obsessed with premonitions of death. This period of rumination between the fighting was the focus of a study by E. Schiche, one of the psychologists who worked with the Institute for Applied Psychology and published in the 1920 special issue of the *Journal for Applied Psychology*. In his essay "On Premonitions of Death at the Front and their Effects" ("*Über Todesahnungen im Felde und ihre Wirkung*"), Schiche stressed that there was no uniform psychological reaction to fear, and that the mental state of frontline soldiers was always fluctuating, depending on conditions and their own background. Similar to Ludwig, he argued that factors separate from religious belief, including one's inner character and willpower, ultimately determined one's ability to overcome fear. What makes Schiche distinct and interesting is that he interpreted the emotion of fear as something that was potentially positive. Fear could ideally be weaponized if individuals came to terms with it, and he suggested that religious prescriptions for coping with fear actually stood in the way of front soldiers' abilities to confront their emotions and become more effective warriors.

Methodologically speaking, Schiche found it difficult to identify and track diverse and elusive religious responses to fear. He argued that one had to be embedded for a substantial time within a unit of soldiers to understand their frame of mind before and after combat operations. The magnitude of impending danger was a decisive factor in understanding how they coped, and "the general mood often changed significantly in short periods of time," depending on a variety of factors.[45] In the front lines, where danger was greatest and one's fate was most unpredictable, one often had little time to dwell on fear. It was only when one had time to think, often while removed from that immediate danger, that men began to consider "what they would lose if they lost their lives."[46] Contemplating past or impending danger threw their emotions into turmoil, causing long-term psychological and even physical damage. He found that fear placed so much stress on the nervous system that men's bodies also suffered physiological deterioration.[47]

One of the functions of religion, according to Schiche, was to counteract the suicidal thoughts that permeated the front experience but were rarely openly discussed. He referred to Freudian models to emphasize how the drive to self-destruction overwhelmed front soldiers, as they consciously or unconsciously struggled with thoughts of suicide to escape anxiety.[48] Belief in religion (which Schiche referred to as "superstition," an all-encompassing term he applied to orthodox religion and popular beliefs) was partly a "side effect" of these instincts, used to psychologically self-medicate and sublimate these tendencies. Humor in the front lines, often macabre or irreverent, had the same function as religion, as it helped men to cope. Like religion, frontline humor was self-referential or simply impenetrable to anyone outside this experience. It could be used to deflect thinking about impending death, neutralize suicidal thoughts, or help men come to terms with the certainty that their life would end by looking at it from a kind of out-of-body, flippant, or even contemptuous point of view.[49]

Schiche was also interested in studying fear responses on a deeper level, which he believed had so far been overlooked by scientists. He tried to discern the psyches of men who did not display outward signs of emotions, but rather bottled up their feelings and controlled physical and emotional manifestations of fear. Some were obsessed with what he called "dark forebodings," but pretended not to be. Schiche argued that soldiers only subtly let on, with "accidental messages," that they were terrified of imminent death. He called for scientists to find "cases where someone has dark forebodings but lets as little of it as possible show."[50] These provided insight, Schiche noted, beyond just the trenches, as he observed that this was a universal way in which soldiers and civilians repressed their emotions. They hoped that if their comrades or family did not pick up these cues, the danger, and in turn their fear, would ultimately evaporate. He linked this to "the superstitious notion that if you anticipate a disaster you will bring about its fulfillment," and he also pointed to the popular assumption that if you mention impending danger you risk jinxing an otherwise stable and safe moment.[51] This notion gave individuals the feeling of agency in determining their survival, as they could imagine that they wielded some sort of supernatural power, controlling their fate by managing their emotions, thinking and behavior.

Hiding emotions was not necessarily a detrimental response to fear. In fact, Schiche claimed, if men could control their emotions, or even embrace their anticipation of danger and fear of death, they could become better warriors. Schiche thus suggested that the front soldier did not need to escape fear through religion, whether orthodox beliefs or superstition. Rather, he needed to accept the heightened senses that came with anticipating death. This would sharpen his senses and increase his chances of survival. Schiche argued that this could not be built on religious beliefs that insulated soldiers from fear but ultimately made them obsess over "depressive forebodings" and the death experience. Instead, it was more optimal for a front soldier to have an unshielded, practical, and healthy understanding of how violence altered his physical and psychological health. Schiche described this as a process by which men would accept how the front environment changed their senses, allowing themselves to become so immersed in their stressful environment that their heightened anxieties and the rush that came with panic seemed normal to them. Echoing Nietzsche's famous "that which does not kill me makes me stronger" axiom from *Twilight of the Gods*, Schiche prescribed that men eagerly seek out danger, learn how it affects them, and conquer their fears. However, he warned men who were able to do this would grow isolated from the world outside the front universe. Their loved ones at home, though wrestling with loss and mourning themselves, did not have the same heightened sensory experiences that came with daily confrontations with death and thus they could not understand what their husbands and fathers endured.[52]

Men who could internalize and befriend their fear of death were rare. More often, Schiche argued, front soldiers became numb and apathetic. "Premonitions of death," he observed, "have a detrimental effect on those who become preoccupied by them because it drains their ability to focus on avoiding danger and concentrate their senses as intensely as they can to protect themselves on the front." In these circumstances, the individual just "gives up in critical situations" or he perseveres "in a state of resigned indifference," making him more vulnerable.[53] Whether religious or not, some men grew apathetic and lethargic, brutalized by the stress of life at the front, while others became emboldened and even psychologically strengthened. The determining factor was not their level of religious belief, he argued, but the individual agency or willpower that they exerted to either confront and control their fate, or to capitulate and resign themselves to imminent death. These complex ways in which men coped with brutalization might be too hidden from psychologists and religious leaders. Veterans did, however, try to illuminate the multilayered psychological effects of the front experience for a mass audience.

Die Tat and Popular Studies on Religion, Psychology, and War

Critics who examined the effects of the war on religious beliefs from a variety of disciplines were not confined to academic circles. Cultural critics, journalists, and theorists from diverse backgrounds, many of them with combat experience, debated the psychological effects of the war and shared their findings in the mass media with a lay audience. They disseminated their findings in publications that were popular on the home front as well as in army and trench newspapers. Though they offered diverse theories on the religious effects of the war, there was consensus that the trench experience triggered seismic spiritual-psychological ramifications from which German soldiers and civilians might never recover.

Popular authors writing on the religious impact of the war tended to privilege soldiers' narratives and the combat experience. Editors of periodicals invited writers who had served at the combat front to share their perspectives on the spiritual effects of the war for civilian consumption. One of the most popular publications in Germany that disseminated numerous articles on trauma and spirituality was *Die Tat—Eine sozial-religiöse Monatschrift für deutsche Kultur* (*The Deed—A Social-Religious Monthly for German Culture*), which was published by Eugen Diederichs in Jena. The journal was originally founded in 1909 as an organ of the Monist League, which was directed by two adherents of Nietzschean philosophy, August and Ernst Horneffer, who expressed their interest in breaking down the boundaries between the body and the mind, exploring all phenomena as a single substance.[54] When the journal went bankrupt, Diedrichs bought it in 1912, and during the war it was absorbed by a right-wing, nationalist publishing house then eventually purchased by neoconservative publisher J. F. Lehmann.[55]

As the profits earned by the Eugen Diedrichs publishing house increased during the war, they were able to fund various nationalistic journals, including *Die Tat*, which, despite their conservative-nationalistic leanings, also published work by authors from diverse social and political backgrounds, including some rather eclectic perspectives. Thus, in addition to pamphlets (*Flugschriften*) for its "war series" by right-wing voices, *Die Tat* listed works by Karl Bittel, a left-wing historian who at the end of the war would join the soldiers' and workers' revolutionary councils and in 1919 became a member of the German Communist Party. At the same time, even while Diedrichs coordinated a range of different perspectives on a particular social issue for his "special topic" editions, his goal was to promote the voices of conservative writers who concentrated on Germany's aim of cultural "renewal."[56] The popularity of *Die Tat* grew during the course of the war with loyal reading groups who organized a "*Tat* war fund" to provide free subscriptions for men serving at the front.[57] The periodical reached out to men in the trenches by publishing articles by combat veterans, including Erich Everth and Paul Göhre, who shared their perspectives on the psychological and spiritual impact of the war.

Erich Everth's *On the Soul of the Soldier at the Front*

One of the most interesting writers for *Die Tat* was Erich Everth, whose *On the Soul of the Soldier at the Front—Observations of a War Veteran* (*Von der Seele des Soldaten im Felde—Bemerkungen eines Kriegsteilnehmers*) was published as "*Tat-Flugschriften* 10" (*Tat* Pamphlet Number 10) in 1916. Before the war, Everth studied art history, psychology, and philosophy at the University of Jena, where he earned his PhD in philosophy. In his thirties, when the war broke out, he served and saw combat on the Eastern Front and then in 1915 began work as a journalist at army headquarters, where he found time to write his forty-five-page booklet for *Die Tat*. *On the Soul of Soldiers at the Front* became one of the journal's most popular special publications, with 20,000 copies sold and continuous printings after its first appearance at the end of 1915.[58] His work was also influential for professional psychiatrists like Walter Ludwig, who used data compiled by Everth to support his arguments about the psychological effects of combat.

Everth's study of the "*Seele*" (soul or psyche) of front soldiers is remarkable for its restraint. Instead of glorifying men at the front with familiar nationalistic rhetoric found in most wartime publications, Everth described soldiers as ordinary men coping with practical realities, as well as their own subjective encounters with psychological stress, which had both positive and negative effects. Shortly after the booklet was published, Hermann Hesse, who would build a distinguished career as one of Germany's most famous writers, and most committed anti-war voices, wrote a review for the *Neue Zürcher Zeitung* in which he praised Everth for showing that even in the catastrophic violence of the war, individual soldiers could find positive psychological experiences that were the basis for some optimism for the future.[59]

Everth began his study by criticizing civilians who tried to categorize and interpret the front experience, which he argued they could never really understand. It was natural for home front supporters and loved ones to try to comfort men with "cozy or even cheerful, delicate admiring words for our warriors," but these efforts ultimately sterilized the complex psychological effects of combat.⁶⁰ The impact of the war on what he called the "soul" (*Seele*) of front soldiers was most misunderstood. The "essence" (*Wesen*) of men at the front was too difficult to capture, as soldiers processed "a wide range of emotional experiences" through the prism of their diverse backgrounds and worldviews. Thus, there was no homogeneous "psyche" or common denominator that could be identified. Everth also criticized prominent psychiatrists like Otto Binswanger, famous for once counting Friedrich Nietzsche as one of his patients, for mischaracterizing and overgeneralizing the front experience. Following a lecture in which Binswanger claimed to be able to explain the psychology of front soldiers, Everth observed, "Binswanger from the University of Jena did not speak of the actual front in his lecture on the psychological effects of the war because he had never stood in the line of battle with me." ⁶¹

The psychological effects of the war could thus only be interpreted by front soldiers, Everth argued, whose testimonies offered the most authentic glimpse into the reality of the front experience. Letters home, he emphasized, gave loved ones a more intimate account of the war's impact on the soul than any psychologist or journalist could provide.⁶² As an experienced front veteran himself, Everth proclaimed he could provide "the truth and the facts," which he characterized as the primary aim of his book. What people at home did not understand was that going to the front was like crossing over into "another world," both physically and psychologically. The experience was "so strong that you actually feel infinitely different from the usual bourgeois life. To a certain extent you also voluntarily and deliberately detach yourself from your relatives in order to prepare for any possibilities." This feeling of detachment, he argued, was to some degree alleviated by "Christian humility and submission, which creates a psychologically favorable attitude towards suffering of all kinds." This did not mean that soldiers had to be particularly pious or dogmatic in their religious beliefs, but Christian ideals of self-sacrifice enabled men to rationalize and endure their own suffering.⁶³ As observed by Ludwig and Plaut, Everth also noticed that front soldiers were bolstered by other psychological mechanisms, including humor, which civilians at home did not at all understand. Though war correspondents tried to shed light on or even replicate the humor used by front soldiers, they simply did not get the grim and serious subtext behind soldiers' jokes, which were a device for simultaneously acknowledging and insulating themselves against the surreality of traumatic violence.

Despite their descent into "another world," Everth warned against putting front soldiers on some kind of pillar as a unique group who had special insight into human nature or spiritual matters. Civilians' tendency to idealize front soldiers was altogether repulsive to Everth, who argued that these men should not be sentimentalized, idealized, or romanticized. Instead, men who experienced combat were "ordinary people" trying to adjust to an exceptional environment, which placed them between the extremes of terror and banality. Men survived by occupying what he described as a kind of "middle position" between these poles. Burdened by "extreme emotional contradictions" that oscillated between fear of death and stultifying monotony, men gradually began to experience a change in their "consciousness of reality" (*Wirklichkeitsbewusstsein*).

They could not anticipate whether death would hit them next, so they had to "become numb," which enabled them to repress their nervousness. On the surface, they seemed indifferent to terror, but when they returned home their repressed fears came to the surface and their emotions boiled over.[64]

It was in this psychological state where religion was most potent but also the most fragile. On the one hand, in an ever-fluctuating, surreal world, Everth argued, familiar religious beliefs gave one a sense of rootedness or continuity: "This longing for certainty explains in part the pull to religion that affects most people. When so much becomes uncertain, the more you look for a reality that remains unchanged above."[65] Compared to all the unreal scenes of mass death and material carnage, religion actually seemed reasonable. On the other hand, Everth argued that this did not mean there was a revitalization of religion, as some religious leaders claimed. In fact, he observed, "it remains relatively unimportant whether one's position on religion became positive or negative due to the war; in any case, it just becomes different."[66] Those differences tend to get oversimplified, Everth claimed, by religious authorities who automatically repeated the cliché, "Crisis teaches one to pray." Everth characterized this as a "childish observation." In reality, men with different psychological constitutions react to stress in different ways, with some falling back on faith in God as a protector, and others abandoning this belief in the face of unprecedented pressure. Some found a sense of order in their conviction that God had saved them, others found nothing but meaninglessness and chaos. Everth discovered that the most complicated impact of the war was that even men who believed in God, and maintained that belief in the wake of violence, still often "experienced at least a deep horror about the existence of the abyss and a partly changed psyche that leads to a greater sense of seriousness in their later lives."[67] The subjective ways in which men at the front relied on religion thus could not be oversimplified.

Everth portrayed most bursts of religious feelings as temporary and superficial. He argued that men processed trauma through the prism of religious language because this was the only spiritual language they knew, and "they cannot cope with such experiences in any other way." He concluded that men who might have experienced this invigorating spiritual rush would see it evaporate shortly after the end of the war, when they were removed from the extreme environment of the trenches that triggered desperate religious emotions. Further, he was critical of religious leaders who tried to claim victory, and he argued that whatever religious sparks emerged from the war experience could not be categorized as a coherent movement: "I just want to warn against marking all religious feelings, without differentiation, as a win for culture or religion."[68]

As a combat veteran, Everth claimed he was uniquely qualified to make a general interpretation of the religious effects of the war. But in the last few pages of his study, he shifted from his general analysis to a more personal assessment of the war's effects on his own religious beliefs. He conceded that his own religious beliefs had eroded, partly because the war experience shook his assumptions, but also because he was disillusioned with religious leaders' zeal for war. Interestingly, he observed that while the war had some positive psychological effects, including finding strength in controlling turbulent emotions, his own religiosity imploded:

> The religious effects that I experienced were negative, and this was all the more noticeable because the other effects were actually valuable. The war changed many things. It made everything amplified, created "polar" extremes, meaning that it made things not only very distinct, but in many situations it made them opposed to each other. This was also the case with religion. In addition to reinforcing lower and certainly higher forms of religiosity, there was also a weakening and destruction of religious belief. War shakes religious consciousness more than a terrible earthquake. It doesn't take an earthquake to first learn that nature follows its own laws regarding human activity and human life. That's acceptable and many of us have long since adapted to this emotionally. But the fact that people who have been committed externally and internally to the doctrines of Jesus for over a millennium have been enthusiastic about this war, so that we have been forced to accept it, is deeply depressing for some.[69]

Everth's "spiritual" rebirth was not necessarily through the prism of "religion," but rather it was part of a more subjective path of self-enlightenment. Attempting to articulate the emotional and psychological impact of the war outside religious language, Everth ruminated on how the war heightened his emotions and illuminated his ability to cope with extreme experiences. This led to his revelation that "nature" takes its course independently of religious laws and beliefs. Believers vainly attempted to explain it all in the context of religion, and authorities odiously supported the war and forced that enthusiasm on to increasingly disenchanted front soldiers. Humans, he suggested, could survive without religion.

The front experience uncovered a secret that Everth believed had been concealed by religious authorities: not only could one survive without religion, but one could actually thrive. Everth characterized this realization as liberating, and he pointed to famous historical figures to show that a successful life, and military victory, could be achieved without religion:

> Thus it is not true that religion alone is needed to stand firm. How many times has it been said that in the end there can only be religion, especially regarding morals. That is false ... I have not experienced any external religious sensations, but I have experienced the strongest moral shock (*Erschütterung*) and strengthening. Undoubtedly, "morality cannot replace religion," that is, morality is not religiosity and has no claim to replace religion; but outside of religion it is something completely independent and great and it is in some ways just as powerful in certain people as piety is in others.[70]

In the trenches, Everth realized that he could maintain resilience without ascribing it to religion, and though he did not clearly define it, he felt a sense of morality outside the framework of religious belief. It was not something inferior to religion, or the result of his "lack" of religious sensations, but rather it was what he described as a "new consciousness" exposed by the traumatic shock of the war experience.[71]

Despite this realization, Everth was empathetic toward both believers and the disillusioned. He could understand those who lost their religious beliefs, as well as those who still clung to faith. "The [front] experience," he wrote, "is emotionally powerful enough to kill the last remnants of religiosity in some people," especially when they tried to explain how God could let the carnage continue. At the same time, he was sympathetic to those who continued to explain the "tensions of life" through a religious lens, though he placed himself in the category of those who could not reconcile religion with the "gigantic irrationality and the horror" that surrounded life at the front. He also understood why men continued to hold on to religious beliefs: the promise of not dying in vain was emotionally too important for many men, and they simply could not abandon this way of thinking.[72]

What kind of spirituality existed outside religion? For individuals like Everth who did not experience religious "sensations," a subjective spiritual life had to be constructed in the intense environment of the trenches. This "self-developed spiritual world," however, did not have to be an elaborate "system of philosophical metaphysics" that replaced religion nor did it have to be rooted in fundamental cynicism. Rather, "one only needed to keep a hold (*man braucht nur einen Halt*)." He did not expand on this, but only suggested that the fight against fear, by any means, was the basis for a moral or spiritual foundation.[73] When men faced certain annihilation, to find any form of hope to cling to, rooted in any moral, religious, or spiritual feeling, was an "act of bravery." To live "without fear of falling" gave him a sense of dignity, mental strength, and a "spiritual home for which one fights."[74]

Perhaps most interestingly, in describing this internal battle, Everth's language was detached from the prevailing rhetoric about nationalism, duty, or masculinity. Though this 1916 study *On the Soul of the Soldier at the Front* does not make any explicit political statements, Everth was also undergoing, in addition to his spiritual revelations, a political transformation. By the end of the war, he abandoned his conservative views and embraced democracy, and in 1926 he transitioned from journalism to become an art history professor at the University of Leipzig. In February 1933, a few weeks after Hitler became chancellor, Everth organized a demonstration in Berlin attended by left-wing intellectuals including Käthe Kollwitz and Heinrich Mann, who affirmed the freedom of the press against encroaching dictatorship. The demonstration was broken up by SA Stormtroopers. By April 1933, he intensified his criticism of the new National Socialist regime, and he was pushed out of his professorship. He succumbed to illness and died in Leipzig in June 1934.[75]

Paul Göhre: Finding a "New Religion" in the Trenches

Erich Everth was not the only socially and politically iconoclastic voice published by the conservative journal *Die Tat*. Another combat veteran who published in *Die Tat*'s series of *Flugschriften* was Paul Göhre who, like Everth, was also cited by psychologists like Walter Ludwig for his insightful perspective on war and religious faith. Göhre was an intriguing figure. A socially progressive former Lutheran pastor trained in theology and economics at Universities of Leipzig and Berlin, he joined the Social Democratic Party in 1900, which led to the church hierarchy pushing him out of his job as a pastor in 1906. Disappointed with being removed from his clerical career, he published a memoir, *How a Pastor Became a Social Democrat*, in which he called for social reforms as a way to ease social class divisions, and he promoted equal voting rights.[76] Shortly after the war broke out, at the age of fifty-one, he volunteered to fight on the Russian front, where he saw combat. He published articles about his experiences in mass media for front soldiers, including one article titled "War and the Sexes" in the front newspaper *Der Flieger* (*The Flier*).[77] The conservative editors of *Die Tat* published his booklet, *Front and Homeland—The Religious, Political and Sexual Effects of the Trenches* (*Front und Heimat—Religiöses, Politisches, Sexuelles aus dem Schützengraben*) in 1917 as volume 22 of their *Tat-Flugschriften* series on the social and psychological effects of the war. *Front and Homeland* was a collection of three essays, including "The Psychology of Religion in the Trenches," "Front and Politics," and "War and the Sexes," which were originally released in other fora in 1916 before being published collectively as a *Tat-Flugschriften* in late 1917.[78]

Having once been a member of the religious establishment who turned into a left-wing activist and then became a combat veteran, Göhre provides an exceptional take on the psychology of religion. He is particularly interesting because, similar to Everth, he respected what he described as the heroic character of front soldiers, while at the same time he was critical of lofty idealism from civilian and military elites on the home front. In his preface, Göhre stated, "My goal is to engage the psychological facts of the war based on the most sober, personally experienced reality. To my knowledge, not much has been produced about the war from this perspective." The only exception, he noted, was Everth's *On the Soul of the Soldier at the Front*, which he expressly admired.[79] In order for religion to appeal to front soldiers, Göhre proposed what he characterized as a more "realistic" and practical religiosity. He called for idealism and abstract spirituality to be replaced by belief in what is self-evident, including comradeship, and he recommended a more intense appreciation of the value of human life as the basis for spiritual strength.

The first chapter of *Front and Homeland*, "The Psychology of Religion in the Trenches" (*Religionspsychologisches aus dem Schützengraben*), began with an assessment of religion in Germany just before the war. He emphasized that before 1914 there was a broad spectrum of beliefs, which included not only Catholic, Protestant, and Jewish traditions, but also movements that challenged prevailing Judeo-Christian cultures, including monism (the belief that the universe is a single entity, with body and mind united), atheism, free religious movements, and socialist movements that appropriated and applied Jesus's message to political revolution. Whatever doctrines these movements followed, all of these, even atheism, he argued, should be categorized as "God religion," as they were ultimately attempts to reject, understand, or get closer to divine power.[80]

Göhre's central argument was that religion was not the main prism through which men at the front processed their emotions. He conceded that his observations on religion were based on his own experiences, which were ultimately subjective and not necessarily representative: "I know that some have had experiences that are very similar, but also some that are very contrary to mine."[81] At the same time, he attempted to give his work some scientific basis by pointing to a body of evidence that he considered statistically significant, albeit biased in favor of a particular group that was from a background similar to his own. Göhre based his observations on interviews with men who were relatively older (thirty-nine to forty-five years old) of various ranks in a Saxon infantry reserve battalion (*Sächsisches Landsturm-Ersatz-Bataillon*) that he was attached to, which served mainly on the Eastern Front. Within this group of mostly Protestant, older men, Göhre noted that there was "one of those pious old patriarchal types" who prayed constantly and called on God for protection before each battle. However, this religious individual was the exception. Otherwise, there was almost no talk of religion at the front or behind the lines in the reserve trenches. He wrote:

> When we crouched in the dugout with no sleep, we naturally talked about thoughts of home, confessed family worries, complained about the difficulties of the moment, made comradely jokes. But the topic of religion was never touched, not even from a distance. Not even with the news of a newly wounded comrade, or even one that had been killed. Sometimes letters from home were read out loud: I never heard a word of religious admonition or consolation from them either.[82]

The absence of discussion about religion is one of the key revelations in Göhre's study, which emphasized that men processed the trauma of the war through other forms of language, thinking, and psychological mechanisms.

If this group of front soldiers he interviewed were largely indifferent to religion, they were also not very susceptible to attempts by religious authorities to spark their interest. Chaplains in the front lines, Göhre observed, made virtually no impact: "We never saw a field chaplain who awakened any dormant religious feelings, and we never really experienced a field service." When they did hear a sermon given behind the lines, it was not very inspiring, and Göhre claimed that men were interested only if the pastor or priest discussed "more general questions, or ethics, not theology." Perhaps most surprisingly, contradicting claims by theologians and many front soldiers who insisted on the old cliché that "crisis teaches you to pray," Göhre contended that "while under fire and in the danger zone, never, neither during the day nor night, did I hear any of my people [in my unit] say anything about God or offer a prayer, let alone express any thoughts about eternity."[83]

Instead of turning to religious rituals and beliefs for comfort men turned to what Göhre described as more secular means of coping with stress. The most common refuge in which men found psychological reassurance was in the experience of comradeship. Göhre recounted that this hit him when he spent some time recovering from an illness in a field hospital, which was set up temporarily in a synagogue. He walked up and down the rows of men from his unit and was struck by how they found consolation:

> Those among them who were wounded regularly called for help, but they always only called out for comrades for this help, never God. I made this same observation in a field hospital … Here too not a word was spoken that was remotely related to a mood for prayer (*Gebetstimmung*) or religious beliefs. People cried and whined, one helped and comforted them in a totally human way (*ganz menschlich*): but any consciousness about God (*Gottbewusstsein*) never broke through.[84]

Göhre added that even though the language of God did not appear in the field hospital, this did not mean that there was not any spiritual dimension to their suffering. "The dirt, blood, waste, exhaustion," he wrote, "all of this certainly depressed men's souls." However, he did not hear men deal with their psychological pain, or their "depressed souls," through Judeo-Christian language or thinking.[85]

While the first part of *Front and Homeland* was a kind of anthropological study of religiosity in his own unit, Göhre shifted to a more subjective analysis of what he admitted he knew best: his own psychology and belief system. Göhre was always conscientious of his personal biases, but he suspected that his own perceptions and experiences were not exceptional. Characterizing himself as a once strong believer, Göhre described a falling out with religion just before the outbreak of the war. "In my prime, between twenty and thirty years old," Göhre wrote, "I was the most passionate religious enthusiast and ascetic. At the time I practically remained silent in a dedicated life of prayer." Göhre claimed that he believed he could only live a "completely full and honestly lived religion" if he "shared my lot with the masses," so he became a Social Democrat and even briefly worked in a factory, where he preached the gospel. However, this experience sent him spiraling into disillusionment:

> My preoccupation with politics, economic problems and other challenges of our times brought about a profound change in me: my religious enthusiasm has been subdued. I no longer dare to lead a life of prayer, and for me the thought of an eternal life is not only problematic, but I've become fundamentally indifferent to it.[86]

Thus just before the war Göhre had become jaded, but he wrote that he still retained a "belief in a final, eternal, omnipotent, divine power, though I am neither able, nor do I dare to, imagine her." This gendering of God as female is startling. Göhre did not explain his reason for referring to God as feminine. Whether or not such gender-twisting was an attempt to distance his thinking from the Judeo-Christian patriarchal Supreme Being is unclear. But he had lost interest in trying to understand God's will, and, reiterating his use of the feminine in reference to the Creator, he confessed that he had given up "any controllable connection with her." Nevertheless, he was content: "I went off to the front with this simple but ultimately happy religion."[87]

This belief in God, feminine or otherwise, was shattered when Göhre came under fire. Combat was a turning point for him, and he tried to describe the psychological effects of violence and how it further eroded his religious beliefs.

> When I first came under fire, what did I experience? My whole person was torn apart like a thunderclap. It shuddered through me: now it's about your life and death. In a flash I thought of my wife and children, and then suddenly, almost against my will, a second-long wish: prayer! But then an echo immediately followed: no, it's senseless. And from then on I was absolutely calm and unshaken inside (*innerlich unerschüttert gewesen*).[88]

Göhre provided an interesting revelation that contradicts many of the assumptions held by religious authorities. Though he had an impulse toward prayer, likely the effect of prewar socialization for coping with stress, Göhre quickly sensed that prayer was "senseless," and when he let go of that impulse, he felt profound relief. Less distracted by what he characterized as useless dependence on a Supreme Being, he felt "fulfilled" by focusing on the tangible reality that he was responsible for helping the men in his unit.

The experience he described above was almost instinctual, an involuntary, lightning-fast response to extreme stress. But even when he had time to process the experience after he was out of the fire zone, he did not return to praying. In fact, he said that his religious feelings in the wake of combat were "meager" (*dürftig*)—no revelations came to him later as he dwelled on his experience. After reflecting on the impact of combat, "I never thought of praying again, either in these or later battles. It just seemed impossible to me to relate these struggles to divinity (*Gottheit*) in any way." Conversing with other men in his unit, he concluded that his own perceptions were not unique: "I was, like most of my comrades, not godless, but very distant from God."[89]

While recognizing the subjectivity of his own experience, Göhre also thought that he was on to something more universal. Though he acknowledged that many still believed in God to different degrees, he also argued that the war laid bare a certain truth for many men, especially Protestant but even some Catholic front soldiers (he did not analyze the experiences of Jewish veterans): many had become indifferent to the religious institutions and their archaic rituals, which seemed increasingly irrelevant in this modern, industrialized environment. This development had been fomenting before 1914, but the war highlighted "for the masses" the gulf between "on the one hand, a Christian religion handed down from the most narrow, ancient world view, versus the new so-called modern world-view, which is driven exclusively by science." The war, Göhre argued, exposed the obsolescence of Christian traditions that had governed their thoughts and behaviors their whole lives, pushing them to "throw the traditional religion overboard." As a result of their front experience, men did not "exit the Church," he argued, but rather they simply became "indifferent" to it because it no longer seemed authentic in the much more real world of modern war. Those who were religious before the war struggled more to detach themselves from religious institutions, while the less religious deduced more quickly that religion is not compatible with the modern world.[90]

The war may have triggered widespread skepticism about "archaic" religious institutions and traditions, according to Göhre. But what next? Even if men "detached" from their Church institutions, their post-detachment religiosity fell along a broad spectrum. Some men "broke down into a religious void," while others "went in search of a new religion." Others continued to theoretically adhere to their traditional church. Some became indifferent to the church's beliefs and practices, while some "remained loyal and close." The latter, Göhre argued, were mostly Catholic soldiers, for whom traditional Catholic rituals, more tangible than Protestant beliefs, still held some meaning at the front. This trend did not reflect a seismic change from prewar patterns of religiosity. Instead, the war reinforced an already existing pattern: "Our army looks just as religious as our people (*Volk*) did before the war, and the pattern was this: half were religious, half were indifferent or even hostile to religion. And between both those halves existed a not so small group of people looking for new religion."[91]

Unfortunately, Göhre did not explore in-depth the nature of "new religion" that he mentioned, but he did analyze what he saw as a liminal space occupied by traumatized men. Similar to Schiche's interpretation, he argued that men had to find a means to "tame war and all its horrors, and master his experiences spiritually." This required soldiers to find new spiritual and psychological tools to survive. War was not ennobling and did not teach you to pray. Rather, Göhre argued, it taught one to adjust to a brutalizing, animal-like reality:

> The circumstances [in war] under which everyone exists do not promote religion, but rather inhibits religion. In any case, these conditions all contribute to the fact that one's whole inner life is infinitely simplified. Everything psychological is "reduced to the most basic level"; a purely animal existence quickly takes over. Eating and drinking, starving and thirsting, freezing and sweating, waking and sleeping—these are all the essential questions at the front.[92]

Any form of "spirituality" could thus only be generated in this base context of survival. But once the front soldier "surrenders" to the banal and brutalizing environment, it "makes the soul calm and relaxed." Men grew to realize that there was really no mental space for familiar, traditional spiritual exploration.[93] In fact, the pressure that religious authorities placed on men to remain pious and loyal to traditional beliefs and practices could actually be dangerous, as it made men feel stressed, depressed, and anxious about whether they were in accordance with God's will. Instead, men had to practice common sense, "not speculate on what is going on in heaven."[94]

It was only when men stopped dwelling on unknowable questions about the afterlife and focused on the day to day of survival that they found peace of mind. At this point, Göhre observed, they began to discover spiritual fulfillment in the tangible experience of comradeship. This was a kind of "religion" based on nurturing others and helping humans to survive. The need for comradeship was reinforced by the front soldier's "fading" relationship with his family, and the subsequent evaporation of the relevance of traditional religious and social structures. Whatever their prewar religious background, men found in comradeship a shared experience and an awareness of the profound value of human life.[95] Göhre saw this new awareness as the only real "spiritual" revolution of the war. This was a kind of fulfillment of a prewar prediction he made in his book *The Unknown God* (*Der unbekannte Gott*), written in 1913 but first published in 1919 when he thought it would resonate in "the new, confused time after the world war." Göhre theorized:

> The modern man is a factual person. Basically, only what is real is of value to him. But what is real to him is what is perceptible, or essentially perceivable, through experience and conclusive proof. He rejects anything above it in a cool, determined and completely definitive way … The real is at the same time the necessary. He

moves beyond questions about in what way the real exists. [*Über Fragen etwa der Art, inwiefern das Wirkliche ist, ist er hinaus*].⁹⁶

Göhre argued that the war confirmed this theory of "the modern man." Mass death brought about an awareness of a new reality to the broad masses. The world is what one can see, and one does not need to interrogate the "why" of visible reality. The quicker men came to terms with this, the better chance they had to survive.

Conclusion

Wartime psychologists suspected that religious beliefs were too hidden and complex to reconstruct. They theorized that many front soldiers were not as religious as authorities or loved ones assumed and that men concealed or distorted the psychological and emotional impact of the war in letters home. Powerful emotions, especially fear, placed men in a liminal state that was difficult for them to define or articulate. But even if their religious beliefs remained elusive, specialists found evidence of a spiritual shift. Prewar religious beliefs and rituals, they argued, seemed less useful as front soldiers sought new ways to think about spirituality. In fact, as Plaut and others argued, front soldiers had undergone a powerful spiritual and psychological metamorphosis that fundamentally separated them from civilians. Traumatized men occupied a fragile zone between their prewar spiritual selves and "something else," a space in which they oscillated between emotional extremes and, to avoid falling into what Paul Plaut called that "dark thing," they hungered for more tangible, practical, and visible means for achieving psychological balance.

These psychologists and critics who specialized in the spiritual lives of front soldiers are important because they reveal how, even during the war, there was a push to move beyond the limited debate over whether or not the war reinforced or eroded religious beliefs. Instead, trauma produced emotions that propelled men beyond this dichotomy constructed by religious authorities. Worries about salvation, the afterlife, and other familiar Christian concerns evaporated in the trenches. Instead, many soldiers sought new, more immediate forms of spiritual sustenance and they found solace in irreverence, cynicism, and humor as useful tools to cope with psychological stress. As Paul Göhre observed, men turned to their subjective experiences in the trenches, developing alternatives to what he called "God religion," finding new "religion" based on more tangible realities, including sense experiences like human interactions, especially the bonds of comradeship, to achieve psychological balance. In their yearning for alternative means for coping with trauma, men would experiment with a broader array of beliefs and rituals, and even invent some of their own, which will be the focus of the next two chapters.

6

Alternative Beliefs in the Trenches: Superstitions, Gods and Monsters, and Religious Humor

As men and women tried to explain the irrational, brutalizing effects of the war, they often experimented with existing belief systems, or even invented new ones, to explain their fate in the chaotic atmosphere of frontline and home front experiences with death and destruction. Superstitions, numerology, talismans, techniques for communicating with the dead and other devices and rituals, sometimes loosely connected to "official" religion and sometimes rooted in popular or folk beliefs, permeated the combat and home fronts. Letters, diaries, memoirs, and front newspapers offer a glimpse into these "alternative" belief systems, which have recently been called attention to by historians studying the diverse forms of popular and religious culture expressed in war.[1] This is one of the most exciting sites of inquiry, as it involves the complex, often messy beliefs that exist beyond the control of official religious systems and authorities. At the same time, this can also be frustrating, as popular belief touches on mindsets and emotions that are difficult to reconstruct or interpret, especially when these beliefs are more ad hoc than systematic. Sources like letters between home and the trenches offer a glimpse into this layer of religiosity, but they also highlight just how little we can know about the meaning of belief systems that are often self-referential, encoded in the intimate language between individuals who share common experiences.[2]

Despite these challenges, this chapter attempts to shed light on a wide range of what is called "*Aberglaube*" in German (meaning alternative beliefs, often translated as "superstition"), as well as pagan iconography, popular and folk beliefs, and irreverent religious humor, all of which fall under the blanket of non-"official" spiritual thinking. Such beliefs do not necessarily exist separate from the structures of orthodox Judeo-Christian systems of thought. Rather, there was commonly a hybridization of orthodox and "alternative" belief systems. This chapter explores these diverse popular beliefs with a focus on how traumatic wartime experiences influenced the way individuals utilized these ways of thinking. What alternative beliefs did men and women embrace? How did traumatic experiences trigger the impulse to experiment with spirituality and religion? What was the function of these alternative beliefs? Though the focus of this chapter is on front soldiers, it also demonstrates how the utilization or application of superstitions was a symbiotic venture, with men and women on the two fronts sharing prescriptions for warding off danger and coping with psychological stress.

In the previous chapter, we saw psychologists and other specialists argue that men tried to achieve a spiritual "middle ground," a kind of homeostasis between the extremes of frontline violence and the banality of daily life in the trenches. Letters, diaries, and soldiers' media indeed reveal how alternative beliefs were a major part of the psychological toolbox used by soldiers and civilians to achieve this. However, the central argument of this chapter is that alternative beliefs were not just a kind of opiate for stress. They were also an attempt to find new psychological devices to help match the surreal world of the trenches. As men tried to adjust behavior and beliefs to survive the fluctuating experiences and states of mind, they not only relied on available superstitions, but they also experimented with new systems of thought from the images and paraphernalia found in the turbulent environments that surrounded them. The erosion, or at least apparent irrelevance, of old structures, assumptions, and belief systems yielded space for experimentation, as front soldiers "played with" hybrid beliefs and alternative explanations to suit their extraordinary circumstances and help give them a sense of power in an otherwise powerless universe. Fresh from combat and haunted by traumatic memories, front soldiers dabbled with images and beliefs that interlaced Judeo-Christian, pagan and popular beliefs in a mental and physical laboratory where they concocted "systems" that worked for them. By expanding their cultural toolbox to include non-Judeo-Christian iconography, especially invoking Norse mythology including goddesses and Valkyrie, they were also able to branch out beyond male-centered deities, even in a playful way, to bring an element of the feminine into the otherwise all-male combat experience.

While popular beliefs functioned as useful coping mechanisms, there were also anxieties and tensions surrounding the practice of superstitions. Tensions emerged between military authorities, civilians, and front soldiers over whether or not popular beliefs really served to ease psychological trauma. By the middle of the war, soldiers' media, especially the army newspapers, began to publish critical articles about civilians who burdened their loved ones in the trenches with omens, superstitions, and folk beliefs, which were blamed for distracting men from maintaining their psychological balance and concentration. It was feared that men might become overly obsessed with popular beliefs, or even be taken advantage of by charlatans who sought to exploit the vulnerable emotions of front soldiers. This attempt by the military to clamp down on the oversaturation of popular beliefs was not a battle over reason or over orthodoxy, as dictated by Protestant, Catholic, and Jewish authorities, but rather it reflected military authorities' anxieties about psychological resilience and mental fitness. There was greater concern over the emotions, rather than the doctrines, of men who were trying to survive the front experience.

In looking at a broad spectrum of alternative beliefs or popular beliefs and their significance, it is important to not just analyze the content and function of these beliefs but also to examine how they reflect front soldiers' attitudes toward religion and prevailing culture. One way in which soldiers "played with" religion was through humor about both "official" and popular beliefs, which alternated between irreverence, the macabre, and satire as a platform for conveying more serious fears, resentments, and disillusionment. Gently poking fun at, or experimenting with, religion reveals an important development after several years of total war, in which the relevance and power of officially prescribed beliefs started to erode. Patrick Houlihan observes that the interactions between orthodox and alternative beliefs could be imagined "as a model of concentric circles, with official organized religion at the center of the model. Thus, popular religion has both centripetal and centrifugal tendencies related to established institutions and practices."[3] While this model helps explain the complex interplay between orthodox and popular religious beliefs, I would argue that traditional belief systems became less centralized in the consciousness of front soldiers. Soldiers were in some cases detached from a particular center, operating in their own universe, which is one of the reasons their beliefs are so difficult to reconstruct. As will be seen in this and the next chapter, the war inspired the invention of new visual and narrative language, and it stimulated the imagination to play with the material and psychological landscape in ways that could not be explained entirely as outgrowths of religion, or of hypermodernity. Instead, the war produced "something else."

Superstitions

When looking at alternative spiritual belief systems, the most prominent examples of ideas outside the strictly Judeo-Christian model of thinking can be found in the myriad superstitions practiced at the front. The term "superstition" is rather loaded and was broadly used by Christian leaders in the medieval and early modern periods to categorize, and often denounce, any beliefs outside prescribed church traditions. Though superstitions were seen by church leaders over the centuries as invalid or a threat, those in power often had to tolerate or allow "official" beliefs to coexist with popular and folk beliefs. Thus, the term "popular religion" encompasses a wide range of beliefs that are more or less loosely related to officially well-known, locally well-known, or otherwise widely accepted beliefs.[4] In many ways, the German word for superstition, *Aberglaube* ("alternative beliefs"), is a more all-encompassing term for the broad spectrum of rituals and thinking that gained even more traction in the stress of modern war.

In the trenches, men engaged in a number of rituals using talismans, omens, signs, numerology, fortune-telling, and a plethora of other practices that were centuries old, sometimes linked to but often outside conventional church beliefs. The pagan, that is non-Christian, elements of Catholic religious culture enabled many soldiers and civilians to see themselves as Christians while at the same time they engaged a wide range of superstitious practices, or operated in a gray area between official and popular religion.[5] One Catholic military chaplain, Karl Egger, noted that during the war it was sometimes almost impossible to separate the boundaries between "faith" and "superstition."[6] Beyond the question of boundaries between orthodox and popular beliefs, these customs and rituals also reveal the persistence of popular and folk beliefs that are preserved, often by working class or rural communities, into the modern industrial age.[7]

Popular beliefs functioned in a twofold way that may seem paradoxical. They allowed both passivity, as individuals could adhere to a ready-made set of rules and fatalistically await the results, and they also gave people a sense of an active role in trying to manage or control their destiny. As Jay Winter observed, "Superstition described a world in which men were both powerless and all-powerful: in which they could do nothing to alter their destiny, and could survive by touching a rabbit's foot."[8] As humans struggled to comprehend or control the horrifying conditions that surrounded them, they relied on preexisting superstitions and improvised or invented their own belief systems, which provided both a sense of structure and allowed individuals to assert some kind of agency.

The proliferation of superstitions, including popular and folk beliefs in wartime, drew considerable attention from contemporary scholars who studied these phenomena. Specialists in folklore, religious culture, and other fields saw the war as a kind of laboratory for studying how humans adopted popular beliefs to fit their environments.[9] For example, Hanns Bächtold, a professor of folklore in Basel, undertook extensive studies of superstition during the war. His work culminated in a ten-volume study published in Switzerland between 1927 and 1942 titled the *Dictionary of German Superstition* (*Handwörterbuch des deutschen Aberglaubens*). In October 1916, he gave a lecture titled "German Soldiers' Practices and Soldiers' Superstitions" for the Union of German Associations of Folklore (*Der Verband deutscher Vereine für Volkskunde*), which held a conference at the University of Frankfurt that focused on soldiers' language, rituals, and superstitions. In his lecture, Bächtold argued that war had a greater impact on the emotional and psychological life of individuals than any other event, and it caused men and women to focus on or revaluate their religious beliefs. In particular, he observed, the stress endured by otherwise rational and ordinary men in the trenches made them more susceptible to preposterous superstitious beliefs.[10]

Bächtold categorized and outlined a wide range of alternative beliefs that were popular at the front. His source base included interviews with German, French, and Italian soldiers who were interned as prisoners of war in Switzerland.[11] The most commonly reported superstitions included a wide range of omens, signs, prophecies, as well as rituals and practices used to ward off threats, many of which had roots in centuries-long popular beliefs, and were popular and well-known especially to soldiers from rural backgrounds who were immersed in the wonder and cycles of natural phenomena.[12] Blood-red sky, for example, was believed to be a harbinger of more violence. Many soldiers were preoccupied with numerology, which they used obsessively to try to calculate when the war would end, to predict when they would be cursed (the number thirteen was widely considered ominous), or if they would be lucky.[13] The number of matches it took to light a cigarette suddenly took on vital significance, as more than two matches prophesized bad luck. Adding material like chalk or straw to food and drink was believed to bolster physical and psychological strength.[14] Superstitions surrounding the skill of shooting were particularly elaborate, especially when linked to numerology and other beliefs, so that the number of bullets used, precise rituals for cleaning the weapon (including using a piece of clothing that once belonged to a dead person), a talisman hidden in one's uniform to aid one's aim, and other devices were used to ensure success. In turn, complicated rituals were employed to prevent being struck by an enemy bullet. For example, if one put a knife with a black handle in the left pocket, with the tip pointing downward, it would make it impossible for the enemy to hit you.[15]

Scholarly and mass media interest in the paranormal, that is, phenomena that are supposedly beyond the realm of scientific explanation, also exploded during the war.[16] Headlines about paranormal activity, especially ghost sightings, sometimes even displaced news about the front. In 1916, for example, news of ghosts haunting the farm of a widow, Rosine Kleinknecht, in the small town of Großerlach in Württemberg dominated local and national newspapers. The widow, whose husband was killed on the Western Front in November 1915, reported animals mysteriously set free, logs dancing around on their own, and a possessed and malevolent black goat. Testimonies from the family and neighbors, including a teenage boy who claimed to be a medium to the spirit world, suggested ghosts and poltergeists were at work. In addition to capturing newspaper headlines, stories from "the haunting of Großerlach" were collected by professors at the University of Tübingen, and these became a topic of debate into the postwar period in scientific periodicals like the *Journal of Parapsychology* (*Zeitschrift für Parapsychologie*).[17] Though investigators could find no evidence of paranormal phenomena, popular media continued to publish, in headlines side by side with stories about the critical battles at the Somme and Verdun, stories about further ghost sightings, and poltergeist activity. The widow was accused in the press of being unfaithful to her husband and making it all up to cover or deflect from her adultery. However, local eyewitnesses claimed, despite accusations of charlatanism and mass hysteria, that the hauntings and supernatural activity were authentic. The farm was abandoned and ultimately destroyed by neighbors.[18]

Popular publications by self-appointed experts on superstition, paranormal activity, and other phenomena filled bookstores and magazine stands. One of the most successful entrepreneurs of what he proclaimed as "the new mysticism" was the writer Bruno Grabinski, who published a flood of books on prophecies, omens, alternative beliefs, clairvoyance, spiritualism, and ghosts during and after the war. Grabinski considered Christianity to be just one step toward what he called an "unfinished mystical awareness," and he argued that the war experience made clear to a wider population that there was another spiritual world beyond Christianity that promised what he described as "true Enlightenment."[19] While Grabinski believed that there was a broad spectrum of paranormal phenomena that required further study, he argued that the war triggered a particular fascination in spirits and ghosts, as so many people were desperate to contact dead loved ones.[20] Seeing ghosts of the dead, he observed, had "always been part of nature," but awareness of their presence, and interactions between ghosts and humans, intensified in wartime because modern society was not entirely satisfied with existing religious or psychological explanations for these phenomena. Christianity had powerful appeal as it taught that the souls of humans exist eternally, but humans still yearned to understand the relationship between, and they wanted more direct contact with, the "soul" (*Seele*), "spirit" (*Geist*), and body.[21]

Grabinski organized his study with careful categorization of a variety of supernatural phenomena. Using reports from media coverage of paranormal events, as well as testimony by religious leaders and ordinary people, as the backbone of his evidence, he differentiated between "unconscious powers," "psychic power," and "mysteries of the life of the soul," some of which could be explained by science, while other phenomena remained "mystical." He categorized further paranormal events that included mental telepathy, telekinesis, and mediation between material and spirit worlds. Grabinski focused his attention on categorization of these phenomena, but his main conclusion was that there was still a plethora of knowledge about the spiritual and supernatural universe that psychologists, theologians, and laypersons did not yet comprehend.[22]

While popular writers theorized on categories of supernatural activities, as well as the boundaries between orthodox and alternative beliefs, soldiers and their families put these beliefs into practice. Letters and diaries reveal the widespread application of a broad range of beliefs and rituals, and approval from authorities seemed irrelevant to ordinary people. They were most concerned with the efficacy of various beliefs and their function in helping them through extreme stress. Correspondence between home and combat fronts reveal that popular or folk beliefs were most often embraced by families as a means of coping with pain and suffering, or as an antidote to ward off danger. This can be seen in the case of Minna F., who made an interesting request of her husband, who was serving on the Russian front, in a letter written in July 1915:

> My dear, good husband and good-hearted father! Today I found out from an old woman that there's protection for you. I should always wear a few hairs from you. Please be so good and cut some from you and send them to me in a letter ... [The hairs] however must be from below your stomach: you know, of course, from your genitals. [The hairs] must be approximately half a measure long. If I had already known that when you were here, it would have been better. Please cut some and send them to me.[23]

Minna F's request for a physical connection to her husband gave her a sense of control where she could imagine that she had a hand in protecting him from harm. Her belief in the efficacy of her husband's pubic hair and an old woman's superstitions did not preclude her from following more orthodox religious practices. A few months before the above letter, she told her husband about an inspiring church service where the pastor's sermon about Psalm 90 gave her hope and moved the entire congregation to tears.[24]

As the war dragged on, alternative beliefs became more prominent in letters and diaries of soldiers at the front. In some cases, superstitions or popular beliefs even supplanted orthodox religious beliefs and practices, especially as the latter seemed less relevant or ineffective. For example, in the war diary of Heinz T., a lieutenant who served on both the Eastern and Western Fronts during all four years of the war, one can see a marked change between 1914 and 1918. In the early stages of the war, Christian rituals and beliefs were at the center of his thinking and practice, but by the latter part of the war, references to Christianity eroded and instead alternative beliefs became the focus of his spiritual narrative, For example, in Christmas 1915, the nineteen-year old recorded field worship services as moving experiences that helped bolster him spiritually.[25] In subsequent years, however, reflections on Christian religious beliefs do not appear in his diary. By the last year of the war, his diary recounts instead how pervasive superstitious habits had become at the front, even if men did not necessarily believe in them. Several days after the end of the war, when he was demobilized and about to be loaded onto a truck with comrades to return to Germany, he paused and worried about the date, which was December 13: "I've always had an aversion, even though I'm not actually superstitious myself, against the number 13, and once again it looks like such a date should be an omen for a not very smooth homecoming. But the first day went by satisfactorily."[26] Though he denied believing in superstitions, Heinz T.'s thinking was clearly influenced by fears of breaking familiar supernatural rules, especially at the fragile moment when he survived the war and tried to get back home. Heinz T. did make it home and his diary also contains his reflections on visiting the Verdun battlefield and memorials in 1932, where he meditated on the memory of comradeship, albeit with no reflection on the supernatural, Judeo-Christian or otherwise.[27]

Whether men believed in the supernatural or not, superstitious beliefs produced anxiety. Numerology was particularly fear-inducing, and the notion that thirteen was an unlucky number, a belief that can be traced to Judeo-Christian, pre-Christian, and pagan traditions, was widespread. Paul Plaut, in his study on the psychology of men at the front discussed in the previous chapter, included the case of a soldier who was so frightened that he would be killed on the thirteenth of the month that he believed he could only avoid harm by sacrificing exactly thirteen flies as a way to "appease the gods."[28] The fighter pilot Lothar von Richthofen, who fought in the shadow of his famous brother Manfred, was deeply aware of numerological and other supernatural phenomena, even if he was a skeptic. Lothar was shot down and wounded three times during the war, and each time it was on the thirteenth of the month: on May 13, 1917, March 13, 1918, and August 13, 1918. After the war, looking back on this coincidence, he wrote that the first two times he did not think about it: "Many times [at the front] one did not know one day from another, so I had not thought at all that the thirteenth would really be my unlucky day."[29] But in the last months of the war, whenever the thirteenth rolled around, his friends would joke with him and discourage him from flying. On the morning of August 13, 1918, he took to the air, despite thinking, "Today is the 13th—your unlucky day—the day on which you've been wounded twice."[30] Indeed, he was shot down and wounded again. In an afterword to his brother Manfred's bestselling memoir, written just after the war, Lothar also recalled the myriad talismans, amulets, and superstitions held by pilots, including the fear of being photographed, especially just before taking off for a sortie. Reflecting on the death of ace Oswald Boelcke, Lothar wrote, "Getting photographed at the front just before take-off brings misfortune. This happened to Boelcke who was once photographed before take-off. He did not return from this flight."[31]

Superstitious beliefs drew plenty of attention in soldiers' media, especially the army and trench newspapers. Writers from different backgrounds, whether clergy, journalists, or soldiers, were ambivalent about the usefulness of alternative beliefs, sometimes affirming them as natural and harmless, but in other instances they warned men about the anxiety that could be generated, and the potential for charlatans to take advantage of them. This ambivalence was often conveyed through humorous and entertaining anecdotes. One anonymous front soldier writing for the trench newspaper

Der Flieger (*The Flier*) observed in a May 1918 article that before the war, amulets and talismans were a normal part of everyday life. Bits of hair, cloth, notes, and other trinkets alleged to have supernatural potency, "with and without clerical consecration," were a familiar part of family rituals, and when the war broke out, such devices "were much sought-after and gifted items." He further asserted that "it was widely believed by many that these items had magical powers."[32] Despite the omnipresence of "magical" devices and widespread belief in their efficacy, the anonymous soldier writing for *Der Flieger* was not entirely convinced. "I cannot claim," he wrote, "that these things give anyone strength through magic means." Nevertheless, he understood that they were psychologically vital to those who used them, and he told a humorous story to illustrate how people could still believe against all reason. Shortly after his friend received a talisman from a fiancée, he was wounded in an attack in Belgium, and brought to Cologne for hospitalization. Believing that the talisman, a small tin charm (*Blechmark*), saved him from death, he showed it to his doctor. The charm was covered in inscriptions in a foreign language, which the doctor could read. When the wounded soldiers asked the doctor to decipher it, the doctor replied: "It's an old Indian script, and in German it means, 'There is no protection against death!'"[33] Thus, with a dose of humor, the trench newspaper could acknowledge the psychological power of superstition, while also reminding men that these beliefs were irrational. At the same time, the joke also recognizes what was at stake, and how the fear of death made men susceptible to believing anything that bolstered their resilience.

Even if superstitions were pervasive and normalized, authority figures found their widespread use to be a bit problematic. In 1915, the *Kriegszeitung der 4. Armee* published a series of articles on alternative beliefs, including one by a specialist in the history of superstitions, Edmund Scheibener, who produced studies on the topic before the war. Scheibener argued that alternative beliefs had deep historical roots "in Teutonism (*Germanentum*) and antiquity," and thus it was reasonable for modern soldiers to share these same patterns of thought. Scheibener began with an anecdote about one of the most popular devices given to soldiers, the "letter from heaven" (*Himmelsbrief*), which was a note or message that was alleged to be written by God and filled with power to protect the bearer, as long as they adhered to God's will. These were popular items in Catholic and Protestant communities, sold in market places, and passed down through families for generations. Scheibener narrates the story of a soldier who keeps a *Himmelsbrief* that protected his father in 1870. His mother insisted she "won't rest until I take it with me," because it would shield him from bullets.[34] These "letters from heaven" were popular. Minna F., mentioned earlier for her letter requesting a sample of pubic hair from her husband to give to an old woman who promised protection, also told her husband to keep his "letter from God" close to him, "As long as you carry God with you, nothing will happen to you … carry the letters from our dear God with you at all times and don't lose them."[35] Scheibener argued that this kind of thinking was quite understandable. It was no different from the story from the *Song of the Nibelungs* (*Nibelungenlied*) of Siegfried bathing in the blood of a defeated dragon or Jason receiving an ointment from Medea to protect them from harm. Scheibener, a Protestant, noted that Martin Luther "was familiar with all of these alternative beliefs" (*Aberglaube*), some of which were tolerated by Protestant clergy after the Reformation. However, Scheibener was worried about charlatans exploiting stressed soldiers and their families. He warned that many were willing dupes when fear of death was involved, and thus war was an optimal time for con-artists to take advantage of families under stress.³⁶

In addition to essays by scholarly experts, army newspapers also did in-depth coverage of soldiers who embraced alternative beliefs, trying to understand why superstitions were so popular at the front. The *Kriegszeitung der 4. Armee* published an article titled, "Accident, Idea, Superstition," which detailed conversations with wounded soldiers in field hospitals who shared their stories in which they tried to clarify that their close experiences with death and miraculous survival were not coincidences, but rather the outcome of supernatural forces beyond their understanding. The wounded men did not pretend to understand these forces, but they were convinced that their survival could not be explained rationally. Without judgment, the article recorded these front narratives, concluding that these were instinctive responses to the chaos of war.³⁷

By 1918, the tone of army newspaper articles about alternative beliefs changed dramatically. Editors replaced their sympathetic treatment of superstition with a much more skeptical view, and even front soldiers themselves reported that these beliefs could ultimately be destructive. Ernst Oehrlein, a corporal and front soldier who wrote numerous articles for both the *Kriegszeitung der 4. Armee* and the *Liller Kriegszeitung*, published an article on "Soldiers and Superstition" in August 1918, in which he expressed bewilderment that men could believe in things that were obviously bunk. "Soldiers are not and cannot be a bunch of old ladies," Oehrlein wrote, "But this fact does not prevent them from holding on to their superstitions." Oehrlein argued that there were so many examples of superstition and "Hocus Pocus" in everyday life, including figurines of the Virgin Mary, four-leaf clovers, lucky coins, and locks of hair given by wives to protect their soldiers, that many did not even think about it.

To some degree, Oehrlein observed, such trinkets were benign, but "superstitious beliefs could also do harm," and he blamed civilians for whipping up hysteria.³⁸ He used an anecdote based on personal experience to show that even the best intentions from the home front could actually be harmful. If men put too much stock in these beliefs, or if they were burdened by loved ones from home with premonitions and warnings, superstitions could distract them psychologically, weakening their ability to focus on the real and immediate dangers that surrounded them. He related an experience in which a comrade received a letter from his wife who said she had a "terrible premonition" and that she recommended he immediately go on leave before he got killed. Oehrlein accompanied his friend through a town under heavy fire, and with bullets flying over their heads, his friend showed him the letter, which he said had shaken him deeply. As they slowly made their way through the town, an enemy aircraft dove through the clouds and dropped a bomb which seriously wounded his friend, who died shortly thereafter. Oehrlein lamented:

> I wondered whether my comrade would have had the same fate if he had not received the letter. I don't think so. His thoughts were so pre-occupied with the content of that letter that he didn't hear the whistle of the bomb. If he had jumped

into a nearby shell-hole, he would have survived. But at this moment he wasn't thinking about his own security. This case shows those at home what kinds of things they should never write about, and how a letter from home weighs heavy, and its contents can pre-occupy a soldier's thoughts.[39]

This conclusion to Oehrlein's narrative castigates loved ones on the home front who may not have a clue about the psychological fragility of men in the trenches. Even if his comrade's wife had good intentions, the fearful premonition that she shared placed such psychological pressure on her husband that he could not focus on the basic techniques he had learned to survive.

In the last year of the war, other front newspapers took a critical approach to the proliferation of alternative beliefs, including one particular strand of fascination with the supernatural that gained currency, and fueled anxiety: spiritualism. Spiritualism, which encompassed a wide range of beliefs and practices rooted in religion, folklore, and psychical research, gained widespread popularity before, during, and especially after the war.[40] Spiritualism was widely condemned by Catholic and Protestant authorities, but nevertheless it found adherents among many who continued to embrace Christian beliefs. Acting as a conduit between the physical and spiritual realms, spiritualists claimed they could put someone in the earthbound realm in touch with the soul of a being in the spiritual realm, usually in the setting of a séance.[41] Those who were desperate and emotionally vulnerable went to mediums and clairvoyants who promised to put them in touch with their dead loved ones.

Front soldiers writing for trench newspapers set their sights on these mediums who promised communication with the spirits of the dead. An infantryman named F. Schiefer, writing for *Der Eigenbrödler* (*The Loner*),[42] one of the trench newspapers that were more abrasive and dissonant than the more official army newspapers, used humor to warn front soldiers, and chide civilians, about the dangers of charlatans who took advantage of their emotional distress over the loss of friends. In his essay "The Ghostly Hand" (*Die Geisterhand*), Schiefer tells the story of a group of soldiers briefly on leave a few kilometers behind the front in Belgium. Looking for adventure and relief from the worries of the front, Schiefer, who describes himself and his friends as "practical and well-educated guys," finds companionship with "Madame M.," the wife of a Belgian officer. She invites him to join in a "spiritualist meeting" in a special room in her apartment, where he found several civilians and a handful of other comrades waiting eagerly to take part in a séance. "I have to admit," Schiefer wrote, "that I didn't take the table rapping, ghostly knocking, or invisible writing hands very seriously." But instead of exposing his skepticism, "I let on total objectivity, even belief in it all, in order to reach my goal of winning over this beautiful woman."[43] He quickly realized how Madame M. tricked her guests by fake knocking and tapping with devices under the table, but he could not believe that his comrades were taken in by this. The séance culminated with a "ghostly hand" that materialized in the middle of the group, which Schiefer could discern was done by Madame M. with a trick through a hole in the table. With lighting effects and well-timed screams, the experience had a terrifying effect on the gullible audience. After Madame M. called on participants to lay money on the table to help bring out more spirits, Schiefer decided at the last minute to block

Madame M.'s next trick, revealing the ruse to everyone else at the table. In the end, his friends joked that it was all benign good fun, but Schiefer expressed shock that his comrades could be so easily bamboozled.⁴⁴

The story of "the Ghostly Hand" echoed another popular theme found in the trench newspapers. With a dose of humor, it warned men about being tempted by "foreign women," in this case a charming and exotic Belgian lady, who were often portrayed as malicious characters who reveled in taking advantage of innocent German soldiers.⁴⁵ Further, the author suggested that though he is at first enchanted by the tempting Belgian woman, he makes the right choice and chooses to help his otherwise duped comrades, prioritizing loyalty above carnal instincts. On one hand, the story portrayed German soldiers as usually rational and even-headed, but it also suggested some anxiety that the stress of combat lowered their guard and made them susceptible to irrationality.

Hybridization of Judeo-Christian, Pagan, and Subjective Religious Imagery

In the indescribable world of the trenches, men had to generate an original language to narrate the bizarre conditions that surrounded them. They often used language that employed a hybrid of Christian imagery and more subjective beliefs drawn from their war experience. This process in which men mixed traditional religious icons with images that were particular to the front environment gives a unique glimpse into how humans generate religious and spiritual beliefs. In their writings, one finds front soldiers trying to make sense of the extreme conditions in which they lived, navigating through a horrifying environment with a psychological toolbox of various rituals, devices, and beliefs that might help them adjust or stabilize themselves. These are also some of the most curious and difficult to understand belief systems, full of improvisation and sometimes failures to make sense of the surreal front experience.

The language men used to describe the spiritual effects of the war often mixed scenes of barbed wire, mud, shell holes, and trenches with their conceptions of God. For example, in an article for a July 1917 edition of the *Liller Kriegszeitung*, a soldier named Corporal (*Gefreiter*) Rust ruminated in almost stream of consciousness style on the nature of the soul (*Seele*). Rust speculated that this was a natural question for men who were traumatized by the loss of friends in a war of material carnage. Standing over the graves of fallen comrades, many asked, "What is the soul? Was it God's breath that comes out of the earth? A flower that grows out of the grave?" These explanations seemed to fall short, according to Rust, who made the case that one could touch the soul through electricity: "Do you know electricity? It brings an end to life, but it also re-generates a life that has been killed. Perhaps the entangled wire in front of your trench position is loaded with it. Try putting a bar on it, and sparks will fly all over. Tell me, is that your soul? … Is it a star that, in its downfall, actually rises to become a new planet?"⁴⁶ In the other-worldly environment of the trenches, these basic spiritual questions appeared mysterious. Metaphors about "God's breath" seemed less tangible than the trench experience, where visible phenomena, like sparks off barbed wire, seemed more real as men sought some evidence of a spiritual universe.

The search for religious metaphors that made sense in the front environment triggered a hybridization of Judeo-Christian and pagan imagery. This can be found in the war diary of fighter pilot Rudolf Stark, which was edited and enhanced for publication in 1932. Stark relied on Nordic mythology, with a touch of Christian iconography, to find emotional comfort in the face of loneliness and isolation. For example, when the famous fighter pilot Manfred von Richthofen, who was constructed by the popular media as a kind of invulnerable hero, was shot down in April 1918, Stark put his grief in these terms:

> Richthofen dead! We whisper the dread tidings softly to one another; our laughter dies away in the mess. The hammers are silent in the workshops, the engine that was just being given its trial stands still. A gloomy silence broods over all.
>
> A great one has gone from us. In the midst of his successes after a record number of victories, he found a swift and happy death when leading his Staffel [squadron].
>
> Oh God of Battles, you can often let men die happy deaths!
>
> Clouds bank up—huge white pillars.
>
> Two ravens, birds of Odin, fly aloft and vanish in the high, blue vault.[47]

Trying to come to terms with the capricious "god of battles," Stark evoked images of the Norse god Odin sending his raven messenger, and men hoping for a "happy death" to release them from mortal suffering. Explicit Judeo-Christian ideals were absent in passages like this, but an interesting decision was made by either Stark or his publisher in the 1932 edition. Throughout the narrative, after every description of a comrade's loss, a cross was printed in the text between paragraphs. Since these crosses were inserted after the mention of any death, they appear to be an explicitly Christian gesture rather than a coincidental symbol between sections of the book.[48]

Such stylized writing and imagery found in postwar memoirs was of course less prevalent in wartime letters and diaries. Nevertheless, narratives written while under fire also mingled diverse religious iconography. Perhaps most interestingly, some letters and diaries reveal how men could invent new beliefs that made sense and provided comfort. An example of this can be found in the case of Karl Außerhofer, whose diary includes imagery generated out of both Catholic traditions and trench-saturated beliefs. Außerhofer wrote about how he conjured images of his dead comrades as protectors, fusing Christian notions of spiritual intercession with ideals of comradeship and pain at the loss of friends. A Catholic farmer originally from Tyrol, Außerhofer emphasized the importance of Catholic ritual and belief in God as an all-powerful protector. Außerhofer described in his diary the experience of going to mass and how he felt bolstered by attending church services with other men. He also believed the war was God's will, designed to test men's faith, and he was optimistic that his piety would give him courage.[49]

However, after a year of combat, Außerhofer's language for describing traumatic experiences changed. As he succumbed to despair at the intense violence and the loss of close friends, his language became more subjective and shaped by the universe of the trenches rather than his Christian background. It was at this stage that he recounted how his dead friends were still with him, guarding him against bullets and shells. He described in his diary how his friends intervened from heaven to protect him from enemy fire:

> It roared all night with cannons and explosions. I dreamed that a 42er [artillery gun] has exploded in an Italian camp and as I woke up, I realized I shit my pants … Today I got word from home that my [friend] Fritz had died, and this causes me much pain. When I was home last he ran everywhere after me like a puppy dog. He was already a little sickly then, but now he can now look down from heaven and protect me from the enemy bullets as my guardian angel. I already have three such angels above that pray for me to come home healthy.[50]

Außerhofer found psychological strength by imagining that his dead friends could shield him from harm. These were not saints or angels from biblical myths but rather figures of dead front comrades. As the war continued, Außerhofer continued to express these kinds of beliefs, writing diary entries about how his dead friends intervened on his behalf.[51] He stopped explicitly referring to Catholic rituals or worship services, which had taken such a prominent place in his diary in the first months of fighting. Instead, he seemed to borrow Christian iconography and reconfigure it to be more relevant within the most important experience he found in the trenches, namely comradeship. Außerhofer survived the war, became a German citizen, and lived in Germany until 1965.

Examples of traditional religious imagery morphing into more self-constructed, subjective imagery are extremely difficult to interpret. They are often bizarre, and self-referential writing that occasionally crops up in letters and diaries is almost impenetrable. This can be found in a letter exchange between a sergeant (*Vizefeldwebel*) named August S., a frontline infantryman who was analyzed in Chapter 3 for his complaints about the erosion of piety, and his friend Ernst R. on the home front. The almost indecipherable imagery and rhetoric that they used highlights the extremes in subjectivity of language about spiritual beliefs and practices. Ernst R. was not drafted and mobilized until 1917, but his letters to his friend August at the front in the preceding two years were filled with anxiety about death, God's will, and their fate in the war. In August 1915, Ernst self-penned a poem that echoed the religious ideals that were prevalent in the early part of the war, before he was sent to the front. He wrote:

> I had to be silent even when there were harsh words.
> But there was a good angel who helped me see reason:
> You know that we are not allowed to be defeated?
> Your Kaiser—your Kaiser must win!!—
> Do you also remember that even in the swarm of battle
> Your Lord God (*Herrgott*) is Lord, he's your God in heaven?[52]

At this stage of the war, Ernst R. saw a clear hierarchy and meaning to the world. God's will and commandments strictly governed his life. When a neighbor and war widow committed suicide after receiving news of her husband's death at the front, Ernst R. criticized her unforgivingly: "This is what happens when people mock the first commandment and idolize themselves."[53]

However, as the war dragged on, the spiritual and religious content of letters between Ernst R. and August S. shifted dramatically. In 1916, writing from the front, August became more anxious and desperate as news about the deaths of schoolfriends began to overwhelm him.[54] He told Ernst that he still prayed for peace, but he felt his courage was "sinking" as he struggled to maintain confidence in God.[55] Over the course of the next year, his letters became quite remarkable, a kind of stream of consciousness with imagery and ideas that were increasingly divorced from his earlier Christian rhetoric. After the battle of the Somme in the summer of 1916, he wrote of the "bad omens" that clouded over him when he did not hear from August S. for several months.[56] Mysteriously, Ernst R. named himself "the white raven" (*Der weissen Rabe*), a term that he used when he signed his letters and which he also used on the return address of his envelopes. It is unclear if this was a childhood reference between himself and August, or if Ernst constructed this character as a kind of alter ego or persona as he coped with stress. Even more curious, he wrote about this character in the third person. By 1917, "the white raven's" writings had become more rambling and nearly incomprehensible, at least to outside readers:

> He [the white raven] had even promised to deliver the Easter bunny, who as of now lives so far away. He baked and sizzled "something"—everything from last Easter's reserves—with real butter, real eggs and not "overdone," as they say here, if they want to be smart!! But have pity and charity—just a little bit, no? Indeed, what else did Schopenhauer and Nietzsche live for?! Thus it happened that the white raven could not send a proper Easter greeting.[57]

With cryptic and obscure references to Nietzsche, Schopenhauer and the Easter bunny, Ernst's language was a far cry from his 1915 letters. August's replies to these later letters from Ernst are not preserved, but the writings of another friend, Heinrich S., are in his file, and they shed some light on the thinking of these three comrades after several years of war. While recovering at home from wounds inflicted at the front in November 1917, Heinrich S. wrote to August S., and his cynicism about old ideals and values was palpable: "All those examples of good and moral characters, full of thoughts, feelings, and wishes, that one found in the library and in stories is really just for school children. Oh well, let's leave them behind."[58] August S. was killed in May 1918.

Gods, Monsters, and Pagan Icons at War

Experimenting with spiritual and supernatural imagery, men began to explore different forms of mythology further away from the Judeo-Christian framework. Much of this imagery came from the imaginations of middle-class men who, seeped in classical literature, brought the cultural capital from their educations into the trenches with them. Gods and monsters proliferated in front soldiers' media, especially in army and trench newspapers, where ancient pagan deities and other supernatural phenomena seemed better suited to characterizing the awesome horror of modern war. This was often done in a playful and humorous spirit, but sometimes it had a darker edge. The supernatural imagination also could serve as a coping mechanism that allowed men to sterilize or escape from their immediate reality. Further, it could function as a tool for asserting agency, as men could imagine themselves as larger than life, wielding control over the seemingly supernatural field of battle. Through such imagery, men could neutralize the unnerving effects of war machinery, but they could also amplify it into something exponentially more terrifying.

Much of the imagery that toyed with gods and monsters was light and geared toward entertainment, especially in army and trench newspapers. For example, the *Liller Kriegszeitung* utilized a stable of artists who specialized in elaborate illustrations, often with comedic or amusing tones. In one full-page drawing from a 1916 issue, "The Ruler of the Seas," an ocean titan wearing a union-jack loincloth was used to personify British naval power. Depicted as subhuman, primitive, and oafish, the cartoon shows him first unable to spear swarming German U-boats with his trident, and then he is stymied by Zeppelins flying over him while he's preoccupied with the submarines (Figure 6.1).[59] The drawing suggests that newer German technology and military ingenuity easily vanquishes the primeval, oafish British guardian of the seas. The nature of modern warfare begged for such fantasy-laden imagery to represent it. The philologist and army volunteer Carl Wilhelm Marschner published a poem, "The German Terror," that spun images of dragons and monsters to describe German military technology. Zeppelins were "brave dragons" that floated in the clouds, submarines were monsters who dwelled on the seabed, and heavy artillery shook the earth with volcanic, primordial power.[60]

One of the most frequent contributors to the pages of soldiers' newspapers was the artist Otto Josef Olbertz, a twenty-five-year old who served in the front lines and constructed intricate images of demons and monsters, sometimes humorful and sometimes harrowing. In one that mixes whimsy with the macabre, he drew two anthropomorphic sea monsters, apparently in charge of cleaning up the ocean floor, who look at a sunken ship in despair. Unable to manage their custodial duties as they are overwhelmed with piles of new victims of the German navy, they complain: "All this damn up-keep."[61] In another illustration, drawn while he was stationed at Lille, Olbertz depicted a wild scene full of demons in a dark underworld, with "England's witches' cauldron" as the centerpiece. Wearing John Bull-style bowler hats, the demons torture whimpering, desperate figures who symbolize "the little nations" thrown into the cauldron by the bullying monsters of Hades.[62] Thus the British Empire is portrayed as a hellish landscape where cackling imps exploit their European neighbors.

While demons and monsters often served as propaganda devices or to poke fun and entertain, they were also employed as a language to help convey the trauma of modern war. By 1918, even official army newspapers like the *Liller Kriegszeitung* published dark images that emphasized the terror of trench warfare. In the edition that appeared a week after the start of the March 1918 offensive, the German army's

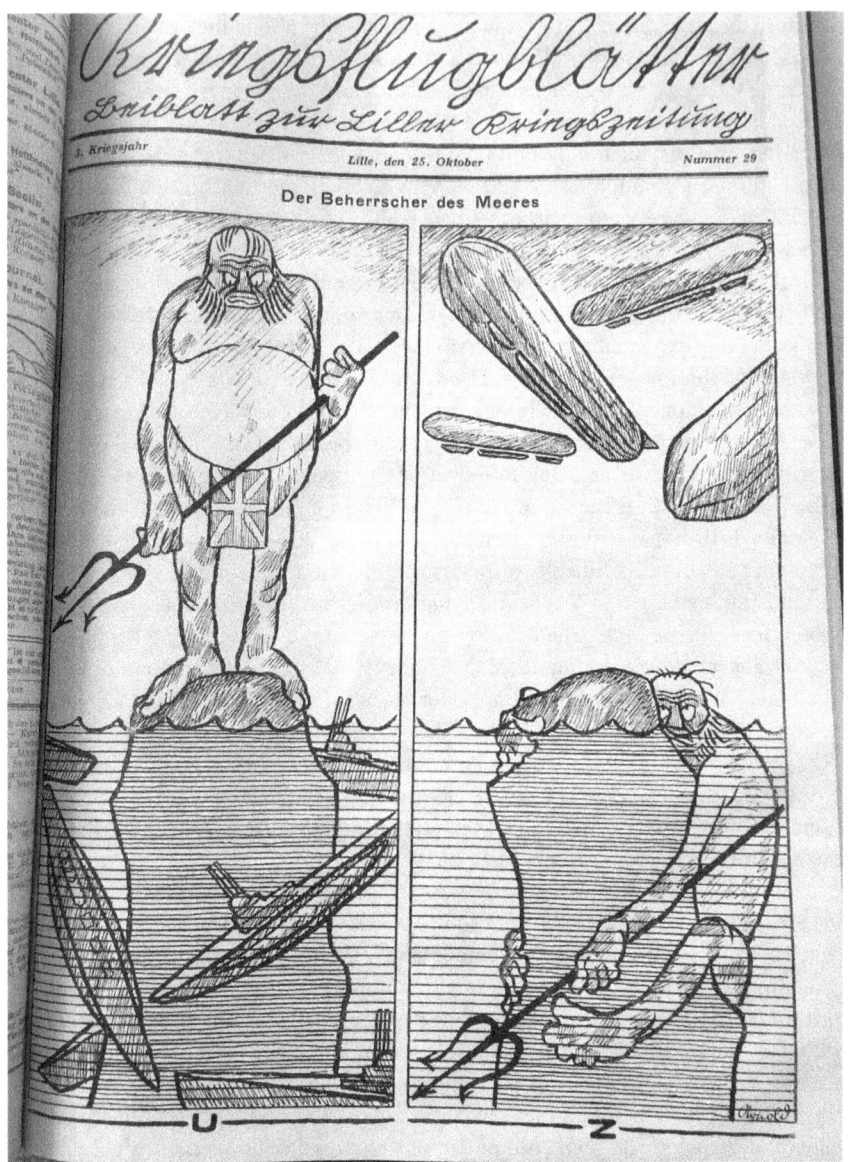

Figure 6.1 Arnold (artist), "Der Beherrscher des Meeres," *Liller Kriegszeitung*, No. 29, October 25, 1916, PH/23/200, *Source*: BArch-MA.

Figure 6.2 E. George, "Trommelfeuer," *Liller Kriegszeitung*, No. 82, April 1, 1918, PH/23/202, *Source*: BArch-MA.

last push to capture Paris and win the war before American forces could play a decisive role, the army newspaper published an image of a gigantic skeleton creature with bat wings striding across the crater-filled battlefield, wielding a cannon-like weapon while artillery explodes around him (Figure 6.2).[63] Titled "Drum Fire" (*Trommelfeuer*), this evocative image conveyed the horrifying world of the trenches, without any of the redeeming allusions to heroism or glory that pervaded army newspaper images in previous years.

In poetry and narratives found in front newspapers, soldiers also described demons and ghosts slugging it out in No Man's Land alongside desperate front fighters, creating an image of a supernatural landscape that tested the nerves and willpower of mortals. In a poem titled "Attack" (*Sturm*), corporal (*Gefreiter*) Gustav Schoedon recounted the "death and destruction" of the artillery, which "smashes man and animal and house." In the chaos of fog and violence, evil spirits emerge:

The earth shakes—
The bullets hiss, the bombs crash.
As ghosts from hell (*Hoellengeister*) ride through the middle of the battle,
My blood coagulates, my heart stops,
It seems to me as if the earth wants to open itself up,
And before me my brothers stagger and fall:
"Lord God, keep my will under control."[64]

Trench warfare thus descends into a nightmare of supernatural darkness, as if the trauma is so extraordinary that earth collapses on itself and is taken over by the underworld. Fearful that he will break down under the strain, Schoedon relies on prayer and God's guidance to calm his nerves against ghostly warriors. The poem ends with Schoedon standing watch, maintaining control over his own fears, and looking over his exhausted, sleeping comrades.[65]

Supernatural or pagan imagery in war was not just confined to imagined scenarios. Men often tried to unleash their imaginations into the tangible world. They named their war machines after gods, or applied symbols on aircraft and tanks that had spiritual or mythological significance. For example, a unit of German crews who went into combat named their A7V tanks after various gods and mythological figures, including "Wotan" (Odin, the chief of the Norse gods), "Mephisto" (the devil's agent in folklore and in Goethe's *Faust*), "Cyklops" (the one-eyed giant encountered by Odysseus), "Herkules" (the famous Greek hero), and others.[66] It is difficult to ascertain the intentions behind much of this iconography, which likely ranged from playful to serious, reflecting self-referential jokes or more personal gestures. But the names seemed to reinforce the feeling that these steel titans had come from another world.

German pilots were particularly prolific, even more so than their French and British counterparts, in adorning their aircraft with brilliant art, names, icons, and symbols, which often had obscure meanings but seemed to answer contradictory emotions and impulses. For example, the fighter pilot Josef Jacobs painted an image of a fire-breathing winged humanoid with horns on the side of his all-black Fokker triplane. (see Figure 6.3) The significance of this symbol is ambiguous and difficult to pin down.

Alternative Beliefs in the Trenches 153

Figure 6.3 "Leutnant Josef Jacobs, Führer der Jagdstaffel 7 (48 Luftsiege), Flandern 1914/18" (Lieutenant Josef Jacobs, Leader of Fighter Squadron 7 (48 aerial victories), Flanders 1914–18). This is a postcard made by Jacobs after the Second World War, depicting himself standing next to his black Fokker triplane in 1918 on the left, and then a photo of him on the right, likely in the 1950s. In the lower center is a rendering of the "devil's head" image that was painted on the side of his aircraft. His autograph also appears on the card, "Jacobs—nicknamed Köbes." From the author's personal collection.

In a May 1918 combat report, he described it as a "devil's head" (*Teufelskopf*).[67] His wife recalled after the war that it was a "the god of the north wind" from Norse mythology.[68] To complicate it further, in the 1960s and 1970s he told interviewers that it was a "fire-spitting devil" that represented himself, painted on his plane by mechanics as an affectionate joke after he lost his temper and yelled at a fellow pilot.[69] Adding another interesting layer to his psychological landscape, Jacobs, from a Catholic background and a small town on the Rhine, also carried a rosary in a small leather pouch, given to him by his mother, as a kind of talisman.[70] An enigmatic figure, Jacobs seemed to dabble with a whole range of iconography and beliefs to bolster his spirits and stay alive. Wounded several times, he escaped many close brushes with death, including one of the first successful parachute escapes and an episode in which he shot off his own propeller and crashed into a pile of cow manure.[71] He eventually shot down forty-eight aircraft and survived the war. His postwar life was as full of as many contradictions and lucky escapes as his wartime exploits. An ardent nationalist who fought communist uprisings in the Baltic states in 1919, he also nursed an ongoing business feud with

Hermann Göring, which culminated in 1933, when he refused to join the Nazi Party and was actually arrested and briefly put into custody. When Göring attempted to seize Jacobs' assets, Jacobs had to escape the head of the Gestapo's wrath by fleeing with his bobsled company to Holland, where he lived in hiding with the help of some old friends during the course of the war. Jacobs returned to Germany after 1945 and died in 1978. He was buried in Munich wearing his *Pour le Mérite* medal, which he earned for valor in 1918.[72]

Pilots amplified the supernatural feeling of aerial combat by likening it to familiar mythological stories. Aerial fighting, in open cockpits with intense sensory intake of wind, smoke, and fire, reminded their crews of war gods and ancient battles. For example, pilots in *Schlasta 27* (Battle Squadron 27), flying Halberstadt CL.II aircraft laden with grenades and machine guns to strafe and bomb ground troops, painted the name "Brünhilde" on the fuselage of one of their aircraft, which was featured in propaganda photos for magazines and in the popular postcard series produced by W. Sanke in 1918.[73] (Figure 6.4) Other aircraft in that squadron included Freja, goddess of love, beauty, and war. In Norse mythology, Brünhilde was one of the Valkyrie, immortal female warriors who flew into battle to choose who would live and who would die. In the Germanic tradition, Brünhilde was also warrior queen and key figure in the *Song of the Nibelungs* (*Nibelungenlied*), and she was a central character and one of the Valkyrie in Wagner's popular opera, *Ring of the Nibelungen*

Figure 6.4 "Startbereite Schlachtstaffel—Die Flugzeuge sind mit Maschinengewehren, Signalpatronen und Handgranaten ausgerüstet" (Ready to Start Battle Squadron—The aircraft are armed with machine guns, signal flares and hand grenades), "Brünhilde," from the popular Sanke postcard series, No. 1071, 1918. From the author's personal collection.

(*Der Ring des Nibelungens*, 1876), which is likely the source for the young men flying these planes.[74] Anthropomorphizing their aircraft as "Brünhilde," these ground-attack specialists equated their task in the skies with that of the warrior goddess, who selected those to be killed in battle. Playing with this kind of iconography thus also allowed them to bring an element of the feminine, albeit through female icons who possessed "masculine" warrior spirit, to frontline combat.

The most common markings on war machines, especially aircraft, tended to be a wide range of symbols drawn from diverse traditions that included folk culture and pagan iconography. The meanings of these symbols for individual pilots are challenging to interpret, as they rarely explained their significance, but the pervasiveness of such a wide range of iconography is remarkable. For example, a pilot in *Jagdstaffel 5* (Fighter squadron 5) painted on his plane a triangle with an eye in the middle, which is recognizable as the "Eye of Providence," or God's eye looking over humanity, a symbol found with minor variations in Jewish, Christian, Hindu, and Freemason iconography. Pentagrams were one of the most common symbols painted on aircraft, with variations in shape and additional symbols inscribed into them. Its roots are in ancient Greek culture, where it referred to the creation of the earth, but it was also used by early Christians as a symbol of the five wounds of Christ as well as a variety of modern religious movements, including freemasonry.[75] The *Hakenkreuz* (swastika) was also widely used by German pilots, as well as their French and American counterparts. It had diverse meanings in Western and Eastern cultures, but was most often used in the First World War as a symbol of good luck. For example, the German Jewish pilot Fritz Beckhardt painted a large white *Hakenkreuz* on the fuselage of his all-black fighter aircraft in 1918, a photo of which is featured on the cover of a book published about Jewish pilots by the National Association of Jewish Front Veterans (*Reichsbund jüdischer Frontsoldaten* or RjF) in 1924.[76] Finally, the six-pointed star, sometimes known as the "Star of David" was also widely used. Its meaning was interpreted in different ways, and it could generate confusion even among squadron mates. For example, when the German Jewish fighter pilot Willy Rosenstein joined his new fighter squadron (*Jagdstaffel 40*) in July 1918, after he had been bullied with antisemitic comments by fellow pilot Hermann Göring in his previous squadron, he felt particularly welcome because one of his new comrades, Adolf Auer, had a Star of David symbol painted on the side of his fighter aircraft. Thinking this was a fellow Jewish pilot, Rosenstein suggested a "special toast of comradeship," but Auer, who was Christian, was slightly embarrassed and intimated that he had no idea it was a Jewish symbol. He thought it was just "an emblem from his favorite beer brewer" from his home town.[77] The honest mistake resulted in a long-lasting squadron joke that cemented a lifelong friendship between Rosenstein and Auer. Their paths crossed multiple times even after Rosenstein was exiled to South Africa in the wake of the 1935 Nuremberg Laws. In 1945, Auer faced a de-Nazification inquiry, where Rosenstein provided testimony that his old friend had been a good comrade to him.[78]

Humor and Religious Imagery

Religious imagery, whether it was traditional Judeo-Christian iconography, popular and folk culture, or more subjective spiritualities could also be employed to evoke humor about war. Like other rhetoric that used spiritual or supernatural references, this kind of humor often served as a coping mechanism to help men survive the unbearable. At the same time, similar to experimentation with the supernatural, humor enabled men to explore, in a largely safe framework, new attitudes about spirituality that included irreverence, ambiguity, or frustration with prevailing assumptions.

Many saw humor itself as an instrument from God to help one survive psychologically. This idea was emphasized by linguist and folklorist Paul Orlamuender, who in 1908 published a book on *Vernacular and Folk Humor: Contributions to Folklore Studies (Volksmund und Volkshumor: Beiträge zur Volkskunde)*.[79] Writing for an army newspaper in late June 1918, as the German army struggled to keep its gains after the opening of the spring offensive, Orlamuender described humor as a spiritually powerful tool for coping with stress: "Humor is a gift from God ... humor heals many wounds like a gentle balm. If you have humor, then you have the spirit of God within you."[80] Soldiers' media consistently prescribed humor as a necessary device for healing wounds. Especially by 1917–18, humor was ubiquitous in army and trench newspapers, but it was not always as reverent as Orlamuender's essay suggests, as men often poked gentle fun at authority, including religious traditions and iconography.

Humor tinged with religion was often directed at the enemy. In particular, British, French, and Russian authority figures were depicted as in league with Satan, bolstering the notion of the war as a crusade between the forces of good and evil. This can be seen in a September 1918 edition of the army newspaper *Kriegszeitung der 4. Armee*, which published "An Open Letter from the Devil to his Business Partner John Bull." The satirical letter was a response to a July 1918 article from the conservative American periodical *National Review*, excerpts of which were published by the *Kriegszeitung* to kick off their satirical response. The *National Review* editors described "the German" as "a repellent beast ... who is in some ways the Devil in the shadows."[81] In response, the editors of the *Kriegszeitung* turned the accusation on its head to suggest that Satan was actually on the side of the Allies. In the article, Satan expresses approval and admiration for John Bull's skill at agitating for war, subjugating the world, and getting people to believe in lies. Satan even complains that when he goes to visit earth, he is actually a bit bored as he has nothing to do—John Bull has already perpetrated all the necessary evil.[82]

Humor that used religious iconography could also be mildly irreverent about German military culture, lampooning authority and the image of the front soldier. In some of these cases, religious humor might also raise themes about the psychological stress of life at the front, including soldiers' feelings of helplessness, fatalism, and futility. For example, in one army newspaper, a series of cartoons and text about a beleaguered soldier named Hiasl, written by corporal Joseph Mauder, pokes affectionate fun at the "front hog" (*Frontschwein*), a widely used term for front soldiers, who seems to have no control over his destiny. First Hiasl is told by an angel that because he has done a good job at the front, he gets a leave pass to visit heaven. Bemused at this stroke of luck, since he does not have any particular knowledge of the Bible or the conviction that he has been a good and moral person, Hiasl enjoys the creature comforts of paradise, where there is no stress and meals with comrades are never-ending. Suddenly he is given another pass and sent for a quick visit to hell, "to greet comrades from the alpine corps who are stuck there." Hell does not seem much different from heaven, as his hosts in the underworld treat him to beer and introduce him to old comrades. Eventually, he meets the devil, who, like a power-hungry company officer, insists on being addressed as "*Herr* Teufel" ("Mr. Devil"), suggesting that the petty tyranny of everyday life in hell is not vastly different from the military discipline that governs Hiasl's life on earth.[83] For a "front hog" like Hiasl, distinguishing between heaven and hell seems the least of his problems. Securing food, avoiding the wrath of officers, and enjoying comradeship seems to be more important than worrying over which afterlife awaits him.

Soldiers' humor about religion was just irreverent enough to be entertaining without crossing the line to be too offensive. One of the main themes found in this kind of humor was that religious icons and traditions had to make concessions for the reality of war. This kind of humor poked fun at ordinary men who tried to follow the prescriptions of Christian leaders for moral behavior while still surviving in the day-to-day stress of life at the front. For example, a humorous poem by journalist and soldier Georg Querl for the trench newspaper *Der Flieger* recounts a Bavarian pilot who is enamored of his girlfriend, Maria Schmidt. The pilot is killed and goes to heaven where he encounters a grumpy St. Peter. Heaven's gatekeeper refuses the Bavarian entrance because the pilot has no halo, which is required as a ticket to God's kingdom. The pilot pleads that in the chaos of war, with so much destruction that engulfed his airplane as it crashed, there was no time to get a halo, and that he should be allowed in heaven anyway.[84]

Even St. Peter had to cope with the trauma of modern warfare, and macabre humor was often fueled by images of him dealing with the carnage with mass death. In one cartoon from the 1916 Christmas edition of the *Kriegszeitung der 4. Armee*, St. Peter gives an angel advice about how to survive in the trenches (Figure 6.5). The cartoon depicts the angel descending from heaven to bring a Christmas tree to the crater-filled Western Front, but just before he begins his journey to the trenches, St. Peter reminds him, "Take this gas mask to put in front of your face, then you can go down to earth."[85] Thus even God's messengers must gear up for the horrors of the trenches, as modern war consumes both mortals and heaven's elite. Religious figures visiting the trenches were a frequent topic of humor, creating incongruous images, like baby Jesus in the middle of a shell-hole-filled No Man's Land, with artillery flying through the starry sky (Figure 6.6).

Trench newspapers were less stringently censored, and they offered ribald humor that bordered on the bizarre.[86] An example of this can be seen in the trench newspaper *Die Scheuner Kriegszeitung,* produced for the First Hannover Infantry (1. *Hannoversche Landstrum*), which was handwritten and relatively crude compared to the more official army newspapers. The newspaper's Christmas edition included a drawing titled "And Peace on Earth…," which depicted an image of a Russian officer as "Niko-laus," a play on St. Nicholas, Tsar Nicholas II, and the word "lice" (*Laus*), who delivers a Christmas

Figure 6.5 Cartoon of St. Peter giving a gas mask to an angel, *Kriegszeitung der 4. Armee*, No. 209, Weihnachten 1916, PH/5/II, *Source*: BArch-MA.

tree decorated with hanged German soldiers as ornaments.[87] On one hand, the image reinforced prevailing nationalist rhetoric that attacked the demonized enemy. At the same time, it also gives an unwavering image of pervasive fear and violence as it starkly contrasts the Christmas season's "peace on earth" rhetoric with wartime brutality. Trench newspapers like the *Scheuner Kriegszeitung* also included macabre humor about coping with mass death. One 1916 issue contained a death notice for a dog, Lotte, with a cartoon depicting the poor canine under rifle fire. Its meaning is obscure.

Figure 6.6 Drawing of baby Jesus in No Man's Land, *Kriegszeitung der 4. Armee,* No. 312, December 24, 1917, PH/5/II, *Source*: BArch-MA.

Perhaps it satirized ubiquitous death notices and pious rhetoric, striking a bitter note that mimicked death notices for humans. Or it can be seen as a poignant message about four-legged comrades who are otherwise overlooked by "the mournful ones who are left behind."[88] Either way, tackling the serious ritual of mourning suggested a kind of grim irreverence about the pervasiveness of mass death. Such impudence was typical in trench newspapers, which did not shy away from gallows humor, with horrifying imagery that played with religious tradition. The trench newspaper *Der Drahtverhau*

(*The Wire Shack*) published an image of a skeleton wearing a steel helmet and playing a fiddle, engulfed in the flames, with a poem telling readers that death gleefully plays his "cruel song," which ends with a cold grave and the fires of hell. A far cry from army newspaper narratives that espoused hope for heaven's rewards as a psychological escape from carnage, such imagery warned that there was only one destiny that awaited a world drenched in killing.[89]

Conclusion

"Alternative" beliefs were an ad hoc solution to a chaotic world. They were not necessarily a conscious, or systematic, protest against traditional belief systems. Rather, they emerged out of desperate conditions in which men manufactured impromptu psychological weapons that seemed suited to increasingly surreal material and psychological landscapes. Traumatized imaginations crafted innovative visual and narrative languages to describe, and exert some agency over, the bizarre world of the trenches. Though the adaptation of popular beliefs rarely signaled a concerted protest against "official" religious ideologies, they did mark an increasing irreverence toward the status quo, especially in cases of humor that helped men cope with not only trauma, but also the breakdown of traditional structures and beliefs that seemed remote or ineffectual.

"Superstitions" and popular beliefs could be just as frustrating as the traditional Judeo-Christian belief systems that did not always seem to work. But the improvisational process of generating hybrid or newly constructed beliefs were important for both men and women who tried desperately to communicate stories and share the meaning of experiences, or even feelings of meaninglessness that seemed to overwhelm them in the irrational, inexplicable environment of total war. Popular beliefs, superstitions, and paganism, including imagery derived from classical mythology and Norse iconography, were of course not "new." But what is extraordinary is the degree to which men dabbled with devices, symbols, and rituals to cope with or escape from trauma, narrate bizarre and fantastical experiences, or even just to amuse themselves in the drudgery of life at the front. Visualizing themselves, or their war technology, as gods and monsters, allowed men to at least briefly conceptualize an environment where they transcended the banality and helplessness of modern war. As we will see in the next chapter, this experimentation could also lay the groundwork for constructing religious belief systems that were original. Fiddling with the religious toolbox gave way to inventing beliefs that were drawn entirely from the experiential landscape of the front and almost totally detached from preexisting systems of thought.

7

Spiritual Subjectivities: Constructing New Beliefs Out of Total War

One morning in the summer of 1917, the fighter pilot Adolf *Ritter* (Knight) von Tutschek was feeling exceptionally low after being shot down. He had narrowly escaped death when he was attacked by British aircraft and lost control of his plane at 2,000 feet. Plummeting to the ground, he just barely recovered seconds before crashing. He wrote in his war diary, which was published and became a best seller in 1918, that after the plunge to earth he stood in stunned disbelief next to his shattered aircraft, a nervous wreck "with my knees shaking." He confided, "to be shot down and to lose control of my aircraft, it was so embarrassing." Later that day, after returning to base to be assigned to another plane for a sortie, he wrote: "it took some effort to get back into my plane" because he was so shaken up. But this fear was quickly rectified: "When I shot down a British [Sopwith] triplane that same afternoon, I was once again entirely the Lord of my nerves" (*war ich wieder ganz Herr meiner Nerven*).[1]

Von Tutschek's 1918 war diary, which is filled with language about his feelings of immortality after shooting down enemy aircraft, and references to airplanes as "rescuing angels,"[2] offers a glimpse into some of the unique religious language men used to describe their own psyches, nervous tension, and traumatic experiences. If many relied on preexisting popular religion, folk culture, and superstitions, the focus of the previous chapter, to help ease anxieties and explain the terrifying, chaotic front experience, there is also evidence that individuals could take "alternative" religion to another level. Beyond utilizing preexisting popular and traditional belief systems, some constructed subjective language and beliefs that were almost entirely original. Men processed and narrated sublime war experiences in diverse ways, but for many of them there was a common denominator in that they were seeking new concepts to help them define and communicate their experiences outside the paradigms established by traditional religious authorities.

The central argument of this chapter is that the subjective language and beliefs that grew out of the front experience enabled men and women to narrate emotions and psychological phenomena, especially the feeling of being transformed by the front experience, where preexisting belief systems seemed inadequate or irrelevant. Subjective language and beliefs filled a space left by the disintegration or incongruity of prewar systems of thought. Exploring these individualized, elusive, and complex approaches to spirituality offers a glimpse into the genesis of religious beliefs and language, which were often constructed spontaneously in frantic and desperate circumstances, under extreme psychological stress. This chapter tries to uncover metaphysical worlds and imaginings that are difficult to pin down, largely because historical subjects themselves often struggled to articulate their ideas. These were not carefully defined belief systems, but rather idiosyncratic, intuitive responses to traumatic violence that were in a constant state of flux.

Three major sites of subjective spiritual experiences produced by front experience will be the focus of this chapter. These include ideas about spiritual "rebirth," the concept of "comradeship" as a sacred experience, and the deification or worship of technology and violence. First, exploring concepts of spiritual rebirth, we see how men, who are the focus of this chapter, but in some instances also women at home, simultaneously echoed but also turned away from a strictly Christian framework of thinking. In many of these cases, individuals described how their core being was shaken and transformed by traumatic experiences. This triggered a search for psychological revitalization to restore their sense of balance, especially after a period of individual stress and cultural distortion, an evolutionary process that has been analyzed by anthropologist Anthony Wallace in his classic work on how individuals and societies try to construct "a more satisfying culture," especially in the wake of trauma.[3] For some, including the famous writer Ernst Toller, this could lead to a sense of spiritual renewal or enlightenment inspired by left-wing activism and conceptions of humanism.

Second, perhaps the most powerful "spiritual" experience identified by men across the political spectrum was the feeling of comradeship. Many described comradeship in reverential tones, as a sacred bond that provided emotional needs, including love and compassion, for traumatized men. The reverence for the bonds of comradeship, which some explicitly stated was the most profound spiritual connection in their lives, reveals the impact of the front environment in shaping the psychological universe of front soldiers.[4] This is not to say that ideals of comradeship necessarily replaced prewar religion, but for many it became the central spiritual experience through which they processed trauma and narrated resilience, especially in postwar memoirs. Through the lens of comradeship we also see how the crisis of faith could dovetail with other existential crises, including, for example, the crisis of masculinity, where men would seek ways to construct being "tough," resilient or heroic outside preexisting paradigms. The crisis of masculinity in some ways mirrors the crisis of religious beliefs. Similar to how men reevaluated hegemonic masculine norms, developing more subjective, flexible, or complex ideals of manhood that fit the trench experience,[5] they also moved away from dominant religious ideals to generate their own perceptions that made sense in the world of the trenches.

Finally, this chapter examines how men came to worship the storm that engulfed them. The seemingly supernatural power of technology and weaponry led some to suspect that a new spiritual paradigm was being produced by the war. Experiences with technology, extraordinary violence, and bonds of friendship did not just influence religious perceptions. These experiences and objects gradually became the "religion." Humans described the melding of minds, bodies, and spirits into technology, producing what they described as a "new man" who could harness and control technology and violence.[6] Much of the historical scholarship that has been explored so far focuses on how belief systems helped victims of war to cope with, explain, or escape the unbearable. However, new spiritual paradigms were also constructed by individuals who were enamored of their roles as perpetrators of violence. The act of killing produced complex psychological effects that included the rationalization and worship of violence as a spiritually satisfying event.[7] The sense of power that killing gave soldiers, most famously individuals like Ernst Jünger, whose philosophical reflections on the "inner experience" of war were celebrated in right-wing circles,[8] pushed them to reevaluate their values and construct whole new worldviews based on their experience, and infatuation, with violence.[9] As this chapter will demonstrate, those postwar ruminations on the spiritual effects of killing can also be found in wartime writings of individuals who, feeling an inner spiritual transformation, often tried to express in their letters and diaries how the war had transformed them fundamentally.

Spiritual "Rebirth" and Subjective Belief Systems

Christian-infused language about spiritual renewal and salvation enabled some men to reconfigure despair and isolation into a positive experience. The tendency to turn suffering into something meaningful and spiritually invigorating was a familiar element in how Christians approached physical hardship, and this generation had been taught before the war that conquering fear and pain through faith gave their lives meaning and emulated Christ's suffering.[10] They were thus inclined to not only survive but also to find some sort of redemption or revitalization through adversity, a kind of triumph over pain. At the same time, while language about spiritual "rebirth" and "redemption" had a familiar Christian context, some started to experiment with notions of "rebirth" outside a strictly Christian framework. Instead of being reborn through pain, individuals conceptualized renewal through other experiences or frameworks of thinking.

An example of spiritual renewal imagined largely in a Christian framework can be found in the case of Theodor K., a businessman from Stuttgart who volunteered shortly after the outbreak of the war. Compared to other men in 1914, Theodor K. did not anticipate the war was going to be an "adventure," or an invigorating nationalistic experience, and he reassured his wife that he would not go "blindly" into battle seeking an iron cross.[11] Instead, he saw the war as a test of his Christian faith, which gave him a sense of resilience against stress.[12] More than just perseverance, Theodor K.'s faith also provided him a language to both withstand pain and find spiritual renewal. In a letter to his wife just before Christmas, he described the war experience as regenerative:

> I do not want to complain, because this time should become a time of moral regeneration for me, even if I do not survive it. It should at the very least allow me preparation and purification for life in the judgment of God, which we hope for as Christians. I am in good spirits and cheerful about the dangers that threaten me.[13]

Faith gave Theodor K. the resilience to endure pain, but it also enabled him to psychologically transcend the material world, purified and transformed.

The appeal of Judeo-Christian ideals about rebirth, however, eroded for many as the reality of industrialized slaughter became overwhelming. Christian leaders who called on their flock to find rebirth or resilience in pain started to draw skepticism. Based on their own experiences, front soldiers sometimes decided that God would be empathetic and forgive them if they were not courageous or if they could not maintain strong nerves. This can be seen in the case of Hans F., whose archival file unfortunately does not provide any biographical background. However, his diary entry on All Soul's Day (November 2) 1915 reveals his emotions about pervasive death and how this affected his religiosity. He expressed belief that God would forgive him for breaking down, and he mocked the rhetoric of religious leaders who called on men to be resilient:

> All Souls' Day mood! But my mood is not shaped by thoughts of the dead, the fallen comrades—no, it is despair, which is aroused by the most horrific conditions that surround us …. If you pray at home for the poor souls, then we stand here in the marsh for 12 hours without interruption, trying to make a ditch from 7 o'clock in the evening. After an hour we are soaked. Our feet have become cold, everything is stuck to dirt. Well, I think our Lord will forgive us if we lose patience in such an hour—but [they say] "You have come here as a battering ram. You are destined to defy the enemy here in the most vulnerable place and to impose the same respect as you would in yours … Show your trust in God worthily."[14]

At the end of this entry, he sardonically quotes the chaplains who call on him to show an iron will out of respect for God. Disillusioned with masculine ideals of toughness and sacrifice, he distinguished those official pronouncements from his actual belief in a God who sympathized with stressed, traumatized men.

"Trauma" stemmed from not only physical and psychological suffering, but also from the realization that preexisting beliefs did not work. In turn, "rebirth" came to be defined as a break away from prewar beliefs. As men became disillusioned with religious leaders who prescribed rebirth through pain, they sought concepts of rebirth and spiritual transformation that were detached from familiar religious thinking or even constructed in total opposition to militaristic and religious values. This reevaluation of values could become the basis for a quasi-religious personal transformation and reawakening, or what some individuals characterized as a spiritual enlightenment. Such a concept of spiritual rebirth was a central part of the writer Ernst Toller's war experience, which he narrated in his postwar memoirs. Originally from a German Jewish family, Toller volunteered shortly after the outbreak of the war, which he initially hoped would be a path to integration. He fought at Verdun, where he was decorated for bravery. There he suffered a nervous breakdown and he was diagnosed with "war neurosis," which led to his discharge from the military.[15] His war experience radicalized him politically. He joined the independent socialists and he was involved in the brief establishment of the failed Munich Soviet republic in 1919. Toller's subsequent plays and writings, before he went into exile in 1933 and committed suicide in 1939, focused on the psychological trauma unleashed by the war and the brutality of militarism and nationalism.[16]

Toller characterized his "nervous breakdown" as a spiritual transformation. His narrative in which he described the particular experiences that led to his reawakening is interesting because he struggled to find a language that reflected his spiritual metamorphosis. While inflected with some familiar Judeo-Christian religious rhetoric, his account emphasized how trauma triggered new spiritual sensibilities, a kind of alternative religion based on anti-war values. This might stem from the fact that while he was raised as a believer in a Jewish household, he struggled with the concept of God even before the war. In his postwar autobiography, Toller recalled his Jewish upbringing in Posen in East Prussia but emphasized that he doubted God's existence from an early age when he "killed the Lord God dead."[17] As he began university, he nurtured his spiritual torment after he immersed himself in Nietzsche and Dostoyevsky.[18] When he volunteered in August 1914, caught up in the fervent patriotism that swept the nation, he wrote that he still possessed some residual faith. However, the horrifying violence of the war brutalized him, and he was shocked by images of corpses, comrades killed, and power-hungry officers.[19] He described this trauma as a kind of assault on not only his senses but also any remaining faith in God, as in the instance when he had to helplessly listen to the dying screams of a comrade in No Man's Land:

> One night we heard a cry, the cry of one in excruciating pain; then all was quiet again. Someone in his death agony [in No Man's Land], we thought. But an hour later the cry came again. It never ceased the whole night. Nor the following night. Naked and inarticulate, the cry persisted. We could not tell whether it came from the throat of German or Frenchman. It existed in its own right, an agonized indictment of heaven and earth. We thrust our fingers into our ears to stop its moan; but it was no good: the cry cut like a drill into our heads, dragging minutes into hours, hours into years. We withered and grew old between those cries.[20]

His helplessness drove him to the brink, and while Toller "prayed desperately" for the wounded man's death, God's silence compounded the trauma.[21]

After reaching a state of emotional numbness, he described himself as in a vulnerable psychological space, and his next experience triggered a turning point and revelation. While digging a trench, he unearthed a dead body, and it struck him that he could not tell whether it was a dead German or a Frenchman. When he realized that national distinctions ultimately did not matter, he characterized this moment as a profound spiritual awakening:

> All these corpses had been men; all these corpses had breathed as I breathed; had had a father, a mother, a woman whom they loved, a piece of land which was theirs, faces which expressed their joys and their sufferings, eyes which had known the light of day and the color of the sky. At that moment of realizing I knew that I had been blind because I had wished not to see; it was only then that I realized, at last, that all these dead men, Frenchmen and Germans, were brothers, and I was the brother of them all.[22]

Echoing Saul's revelation on the road to Damascus, Toller constructed a narrative of religious conversion. However, despite the allusion, it is not a Christian conversion experience, but rather one that sparks his commitment to declare war against militarism and nationalism. He envisioned society going through a spiritual transformation based instead on an awareness of the essential value of humanity. When he was diagnosed with a mental breakdown shortly thereafter, he identified this as the central, seismic experience of rebirth and revitalization that changed his life.

A psychological and spiritual trajectory similar to Toller's can also be found in narratives by civilians on the home front. The trauma of losing loved ones sparked a similar conversion experience, or in some cases, a discovery of new values. The artist Käthe Kollwitz recorded this evolution in her letters and diaries, where she traced how she was initially swept up by the spirit of nationalism at the outbreak of the war until the death of her son shattered her conformity to these ideals. From a middle-class background, her grandfather, Julius Rupp, was a Lutheran pastor in East Prussia who founded an independent Protestant movement, the Free Protestant Congregation, which emphasized freedom from state control. Her humanism was derived from this religious background as well as from her experiences living in a working-class district in Berlin, where her husband, a doctor, treated the most vulnerable in society. Focusing her expressionist art on the suffering of working-class women and children, she became sympathetic to socialist ideals and wrote that she "was powerfully moved by the fate of the proletariat and everything connected with its way of life."[23] However, when her eighteen-year old son Peter enthusiastically volunteered at the outbreak of the war, she supported him, though she confided in her diary her pessimism and fears about the "insanity" of war.[24]

After Peter was killed in October 1914, Kollwitz spiraled into depression. Committing herself fully to pacifism, she wrote in her diary, often speaking to her dead son, that she had to break away completely from the nationalist ideals that drove Peter to war, though she feared her anti-war stance might betray her son's memory: "Is it a breach of faith with you, Peter, if I can now see only madness in the war? Peter, you died believing."[25] Kollwitz turned Peter's room into a kind of shrine. She set up a Christmas tree behind his bed, read his letters with friends, and tried to commune with the memory of her dead son.[26] Desperate to save her surviving son, Hans, from suffering a similar fate, she implored him to reject "the nationalist spirit [which] in its present forms leads to blind alleys." Regretting her conformity at the outbreak of the war, Kollwitz argued that it was a mistake in August 1914 to believe "the idea of internationalism must be put aside right now." The reality of the war, she wrote, revealed how crucial it was to instead embrace Social Democracy. But she described a fundamental revaluation of values that transcended socialism. It was a kind of spiritual awakening about a "new creation," which she had "faith" in: "It seems to me that behind all the convulsions the world is undergoing, a new creation is already in the making. And the beloved millions who have died have shed their blood to raise humanity higher than humanity has been. That is my politics, my boy. It comes from faith."[27] Though she did not precisely define the basis of this "faith," she was hopeful the "convulsion" of war would alter the world and redeem the death of her son and his generation.

Kollwitz and Toller's humanistic awakening is echoed especially in accounts by those who embraced left-wing activism by the end of the war. This was a path in which men and women started as prewar soul searchers who patriotically volunteered and then were psychologically shattered and transformed to embrace new humanist values. A similar narrative, with even more detailed reflection on the new spiritual mindset of the front soldier, can be found in the case of Karl Bröger. In 1914, Bröger enthusiastically volunteered and published lyrical poetry celebrating the heroism and sacrifice of ordinary Germans. In September 1917, at a crucial moment in his life when he said he was transitioning from a lyrical poet to a social democratic revolutionary, he published the essay, "Encounters with God—A Chapter on War Piety," for the left-leaning *Neue Hamburger Zeitung*.[28] After the war, Bröger contributed essays for Social Democratic Party journals, joined the SPD's *Reichsbanner* paramilitary organization, and was imprisoned by the Nazis in a concentration camp in 1933.[29]

Bröger's "Encounters with God" is a fascinating exploration of the spiritual and psychological worldview of a front soldier. He tried to define what still made sense spiritually to men who had experienced so much violence and killing. Echoing Paul Göhre's theories, discussed in Chapter 5, on the spiritual and psychological condition of front soldiers (which had appeared shortly before Bröger's piece), Bröger argued that men experienced a revelation that led them to develop a kind of new "religion" based on what their senses told them was true. Their new focus on tangible, immediate realities of human suffering did not so much lead to a new theological paradigm, but rather it was a visceral longing for something more real than what was found in Christian traditions:

> The soldier at the front has no drive towards theology. And why should he? His life out there follows different laws, and it acquires buoyancy and balance from sources of power that draw only the smallest influx from knowledge about God. So does the front soldier have no piety? Doesn't he see God? First of all, the soldier believes in life at the front. The more consciousness he has about the danger of losing this dear life, the more heat and fervor he brings to belief in life.[30]

The front soldier's beliefs thus became entirely driven by his deep knowledge of the value of life and its counterpart. Only the horrors that surrounded him still seemed real:

> Have you ever looked a soldier directly in the eye? Then you have also seen at the bottom of those big, staring eyes that a star is shining, which is nothing but the reflection of a deep, expansive yearning for life ... A flood of desolate, terrible, horrible images has flowed through these eyes. These eyes drank all the misery, all the pain of the world. They are always an open door to death, which they could not shut off, even if they wanted to. Will such eyes still see God?[31]

His last question here—"will such eyes still see God?"—is left ambiguous, as he suggests that in the trauma of the front experience, God seems remote compared to the overwhelming sensory reality that floods his mind and body.

The sensory overload that he experienced pushed Bröger to rethink the nature or definition of God. Like Ernst Toller, he traced this revaluation of values to a particular turning point. This decisive moment led him to first become aware of the essential value of human life, which wiped out his nationalism and militarism, and required a new "religion" that brought into focus the centrality of humanity. He recounted a few years later that this critical moment was his reaction to the mutilated body of a French soldier: "I looked at the dead man with the feeling of a brother and now I feel the shivers of pain, devotion and awe that moved me then." This experience triggered a kind of rebirth and what he described as a "salvation" (*Erlösung*) that washed away his prewar values and sense of self:

> If it is proof of an encounter with God that the world appears to you in a new light, then I am certain that I have encountered a supreme power at the shot-up train station in Lautersingen … I suddenly feel an inner solution, a redemption. My war enthusiasm was a lie. I was no longer a hero, no longer a bearer of incredible power. I only saw the victim, and not the hero, and the victim seems to me to be the meaning of this war, which is beyond all comprehension.[32]

Bröger described himself as in a transitional state. Seeing the world "in a new light," he found God, but not in the sense he had been raised to believe. "God" was not the same entity that had been given to him by authorities who lied about war and heroism. This was revealed by the hypocrisy of authority figures, as the war exposed how the world ignored God's laws:

> The piety of the soldier in the field cannot be reduced to a category. The tablets with the commandments from Mount Sinai do not apply to the firing zone of Krupp cannons. Of the ten commandments, the fifth [thou shalt not kill] has been cancelled out, and thus all are. Either you keep all ten commandments or none at all.

Bröger concluded that God had to be found by individuals on their own. As the war experience shattered prewar belief in authorities and their ideals, he reveled in rebuilding moral and spiritual beliefs that were more relevant to the front experience and more consistent with his interpretation of God's will.

Bröger found his new subjective relationship with God to be liberating. He wrote of his euphoria in finding his soul independent from what he called the "formula" of religion: "In spite of the brutality and horrors of war, a total sense of happiness is awakened as I long for the completeness (*Vollkommenheit*) of life. It is a victory of the soul over every formula."[33] Searching for his own path, Bröger outlined what he called a "new piety." By the middle of the war, he began to embrace socialism, which appealed to him because it demanded "solidarity with others." However, aware of the possible contradiction, he admitted, "But wasn't that duty also just another formula?" Religion and socialism both fell short, he argued, because they imposed a structure and set of rules on the individual that did not fully address what he characterized as the "inner self." "What is a God," he asked, "who only approaches you from the outside?"[34] He thus theorized that the individual soldier had to take the initiative, without conforming to external ideologies, to find his own soul. Religion and nationalism, in emphasizing difference, had effectively blocked the individual's ability to connect with humanity and in turn their soul:

My piety as a soldier was the striving to recognize life everywhere, to look for people in humans, animals in animals and then to bear witness to the common foundations of all feelings ... If you look at your God as black-white-red or blue-white-red, you separate him from the soul, which is without limits.[35]

Any notion of God thus had to be detached from the prewar ideologies, and nationalism, which had severed the self from common humanity. However, he confessed that he was uncertain how to do this. By 1917 he felt he was no closer to knowing God: "I did not know what God was before, nor did I experience him during the war."[36]

Despite not being any closer to knowing God, Bröger still reflected on the nature of the Creator. He claimed to have no interest in trying to explain God or clarify his personal experience: "It is not my concern to spread a scientifically sound explanation of my relationship with God and the world." Nevertheless, he concluded his essay with a reflection on how the war had transformed his thinking. He suspected that God could not be defined or categorized because he was not an external entity with a personality, as had been taught before the war. "God is not an automaton," he concluded, "that always makes the same move with the same goal or direction."[37] Rather, the war experience instead taught him that God was a subjective feeling that was generated by humans through their gestures of humanity. To express this feeling of God, he concluded with a poem, written to the Supreme Being, in which he suggested that the divine cannot be categorized or explained.[38] Bröger came close to contacting an elusive "God," perhaps finding it inside himself, or in fleeting gestures that reminded him of the good in humanity, before being confronted again with God's silence.

While some like Bröger still latched on to some elusive, subjective concept of God, men also described their spiritual condition, and ways to overcome fear and pain, without any reference to Judeo-Christian language or thinking. Much of this kind of rhetoric was expressed through Nietzschean concepts. For example, Konrad S., drafted in 1916 while studying to become a businessman, was captured by French troops in fighting near Reims in September 1918 and taken to a prisoner-of-war (POW) camp. From there he wrote a letter to his parents, where he detailed the terrifying experience of being pinned down under artillery and machine gun fire and captured, and then the subsequent conditions in the POW camp where food shortages and disease made him fear for his survival. He concluded, "Sometimes I can't believe that a person can still keep going even with such chronic bad food. But people often do superhuman (*übermenschliches*) things—this is something that we experienced plenty of times during this war." Adopting Nietzsche's language about "superhuman" instincts that allow one to transcend physical and psychological deprivation, Konrad S. was able to articulate what humans were actually capable of under extreme stress without falling back on Judeo-Christian rhetoric.

Nietzsche's observations about the psychological and spiritual effects of war were a source of inspiration for many front soldiers. For example, Ernst Emmerich, an eighteen-year-old lieutenant from a Protestant background who volunteered in 1914, wrote to his parents about how he would apply different philosophical theories he had learned before the war to the reality he encountered in the trenches. The broad spectrum of experiences, ranging from terror to banality to chaos and even humor reflected Nietzsche's often multi-layered or even contradictory axioms and celebration of irrationality. The war seemed to reinforce and affirm "that I'm pretty much in agreement with Goethe, and with Nietzsche for whom all the contradictions could lead to madness." The physical deprivations and psychological stress that he experienced drove Emmerich to the edge of madness, and he speculated that the only way to avoid collapse was to find that which was sacred within oneself, a total affirmation of the subjectivity of belief in the insanity of war: "We know where to look for the sacred, to which man's need for veneration turns; everyone carries that within themselves ... We don't need to go crazy, we carry our gods (*unsere Götter*) around within ourselves."[39] In subsequent letters, Emmerich also seemed to adopt Nietzsche's famous axiom, "That which does not kill us makes us stronger." While fighting on the Russian front, he wrote "So it's good times out here again [in the Ukraine], just like it was terrible in the Carpathians. Conditions are always extreme, there's never a middle-ground—one just has to find a way to deal with stress."[40] Enduring another year of war, Emmerich was killed in August 1916.

Nietzsche's ideas were so popular that they were even circulated in the army newspapers, signaling the military's willingness to weaponize Nietzschean philosophy for its front soldiers. A February 1915 edition of the *Liller Kriegszeitung* published an article titled "Friedrich Nietzsche: On War." This was an excerpt from Nietzsche's *Human, All Too Human*, aphorism 477, which he published in 1878 and reflected on his experience as a medical orderly in the Franco-Prussian War, where he treated wounded soldiers and witnessed the effects of combat. The excerpt suggested that "war is indispensable" and consistent with man's natural instincts, and Nietzsche argues that even if civilization condemns it, war brings out the brutal, essential drives that the soul desires. War triggers "that inarticulate, earthquake-like shuddering of the soul" that offers a brief glimpse into "existence itself."[41] The trauma of war, Nietzsche suggests, may not be trauma at all, but rather the fundamental building blocks of culture, the soul and human existence. Violence is thus not something to fear or shy away from, but rather an experience to be embraced. To emphasize this, the *Liller Kriegszeitung* added an excerpt from Nietzsche's *Thus Spoke Zarathustra*, which encouraged readers to conquer any inner reservations and throw themselves wholeheartedly into battle: "Man is something that should be overcome. So live your life of obedience and war! What is long life! Which warrior wants to be spared! I won't spare you, I love you from the ground up, my brother in war!—Thus Spoke Zarathustra."[42]

It is difficult to reconstruct how readers would have responded to Nietzsche's complex and often ambiguous writings on war and suffering. But men were clearly searching for ways to confront pain outside Christian paradigms of thinking, and they embraced Nietzschean thinking that welcomed suffering as an experience that made one stronger. For example, the pilot Hans Müller, who flew with a frontline fighter squadron and shot down twelve aircraft in the spring and summer of 1918, reflected on pain with a quote from Friedrich Schiller, which Müller handwrote on a mass-produced postcard of himself in fur coat and uniform labeled, "Our successful fighter pilot, lieutenant Hans Müller." The quote was personally added by Müller, possibly sent to a friend or admirer, shortly after he survived being shot down over No Man's Land and escaped back to German lines: "Whoever fears nothing is no less powerful than he who fears everything!"⁴³ Müller does not offer any interpretation of this quote, which might suggest that there is essentially no difference between those who can overcome their fears and those who cannot. But his inscription reveals that he was meditating on how the war had transformed front fighters like himself and made them capable of getting used to violence, fear, and pain, in a way that may have seemed impossible before the war.

Comradeship: A New Religion

The most tangible and real experience discovered by many at the front was relationships with other human beings. The experience of comradeship facilitated friendship and affection, social relations, and mutual support that were key to maintaining resilience and mental health. For many, comradeship also developed into a sacred, transcendent experience that supplemented, or even replaced, prewar religious rituals and beliefs. The experience of comradeship became one of the most important legacies of the war. It was a cornerstone of German ideals of masculinity, celebrated after the war as a central part of the front experience, which for some redeemed the brutality and horror of the trenches. As historian Thomas Kühne has demonstrated, "comradeship" was largely constructed, especially by right-wing groups in veterans' postwar memoirs, to articulate their vision of war as a unifying experience that transcended socioeconomic boundaries, cemented male bonds, and provided the emotional and psychological foundation for men to continue fighting. "Comradeship" would also become the basis for National Socialist memories of the "front community" (*Frontgemeinschaft*) and, in turn the "national community" (*Volksgemeinschaft*), which excluded Jews, socialists, and other groups deemed racial and social outsiders.⁴⁴

While "comradeship" was constructed and contested in the intensely fragmented sociopolitical landscape of Weimar Germany, it was also a crucial site of male identity during the war itself. It was ubiquitous in letters, diaries, and front newspapers produced by soldiers, though a bit more complex than postwar memoirs, or wartime propaganda, would suggest. The masculine ideal, disseminated in popular media and military, medical and political discourse, was closely linked to the image of the disciplined, emotionally controlled "good comrade" who subsumed his individual desires and emotions as he sacrificed himself for the nation. However, this hegemonic image of comradeship was unstable, or at least flexible, as ordinary front soldiers, traumatized by the front experience, often embraced "effeminate" emotions of compassion and even love for their fellow comrades in order to survival the emotional and physical stress of combat.⁴⁵ These emotions were a central part of the homosocial bonds celebrated by "male associations" (*Männerbünde*) that were so popular in early twentieth-century Germany.⁴⁶

But beyond its significance as a foundation of German masculine identity, comradeship was also characterized as a spiritual experience, a psychological haven, and even a path to eternal life that often seemed more real than prewar traditional religious belief systems. The letters and diaries of front soldiers reveal the spiritual and psychological strength they found in comradeship. The enthusiasm and passion about these friendships that they injected into their writing was exceptional. This can be seen in the case of Alfred S., who wrote from the front to his mother a few weeks into the war about the importance of friendship at the front. He began one of his letters affirming his belief in an all-powerful if mysterious God who, "despite all the misery" must still be "wise and prudent." But the bulk of his letter is dedicated to telling her about what he called the "good side" of the war. He told her that the war caused a "revaluation" (*Umwertung*) of a lot of things, including "sins" like smoking and drinking. It also sparked his discovery of comradeship, which he cemented in his now favorite pastime, playing the popular card game Skat:

> Playing Skat! It's not totally the devil's invention. While waiting endlessly in the trenches, it saved our guys from mental collapse (*seelischen Zusammenbruch*); the Skat brothers were the quietest defenders and never suffered from monotony. Berliners! There is nothing more blessed by God (*Gottgesegneteres*) than a genuine Berliner in the company; he always keeps good spirits and courage with his casual demeanor (*Schnodderigkeit*).[47]

God's purpose for the war was impenetrable, but playing Skat with his friends gave Alfred S. the psychological foundation that he needed to endure the front experience. His unpretentious Berliner comrade, in particular, was a "blessing" who gave him as much spiritual comfort as he could expect from any forms of happiness provided by God before the war.

The revaluation of values did not necessarily entail disillusionment or abandonment of prewar structures, but rather a revelation about what tools in their immediate environment were most important when it came to enduring trauma. The experience of comradeship served this function. If "God" and other Judeo-Christian spiritual concepts seemed abstract, comradeship was discernable. Carl Degelow, for example, published in 1920 a memoir in which he characterized comradeship as the most important spiritual experience at the front. Degelow was a fighter pilot with *Jagdstaffel 40* (Fighter Squadron 40), which he led until the end of the war, during which time he amassed thirty confirmed aerial victories and was the last recipient of the *Pour Le Merité* medal, awarded on November 9, 1918. His memoir, *With the White Stag through Thick and Thin*, which referred to the emblem of a stag painted on the side of his fighter plane, contained reflections on what he called the *Seelenleben* ("mental life") of pilots, which he defined in medical terms, making observations on the stressful effects of flying on the mind and body.[48] But he also dedicated a chapter to "The Spirit (*Geist*) of the German Pilot," which made no mention of God or Christian iconography. Instead, he suggested a kind of new "religion" learned at the front that would provide resilience and spiritual comfort. The central tenet of the "spirit" of the pilot was the willingness to die for comrades. He described the ultimate comrade as his friend Willy Rosenstein, a Jewish pilot mentioned in the previous chapter who had transferred from Hermann Göring's squadron to *Jagdstaffel 40* after experiencing antisemitism. Rosenstein was a kind of savior-figure, according to Degelow, the most valuable member of the squadron because he flew protection cover over the other pilots and was willing to sacrifice his own life for his comrades. For Rosenstein's spirit of sacrifice, Degelow described him affectionately as a "saint": "[Rosenstein] was our 'patron saint,' performing for us the essential duty of keeping our squadron formation free of enemies, as he flew last and highest in our formation."[49] In the last weeks of the war, when German fighter pilots were strained and at their breaking point due to losses as well as shortages of fuel and aircraft, Degelow found in feelings of comradeship a sense of renewal and restoration. He wrote in the conclusion to this chapter:

> In the evening after a hard fight, if fighter pilots sit around comfortably like members of a large family, you saw a few hotheads who were rattled after a bad landing, but you also saw a lot of deep-thinking (*Gemütstiefe*) people, who won us over. From such a genuine spirit that grows out of the soul of life in the squadron there emerged a slogan: Comradeship in the air—comradeship on the earth.[50]

Here the squadron mates generated their own spiritual strength from within. Rather than anticipate external inspiration from Christian-based spiritual concepts, Degelow saw the birth of a unique spirit, a "soul of life." These concluding words to this chapter about comradeship "in the air and on earth" ring as a kind of benediction, with the concept of comradeship taking on a sacred power, delivered as a blessing to his fellow soldiers. The sacredness of this concept, and the memory of the war experience, was reinforced in one edition of the volume personally signed by Degelow to a veteran friend of his: "In old comradeship (*In alter Kameradschaft*)—C. Degelow, March 1934."[51]

The spiritual power of comradeship could also re-spark diminished prewar faith. For infantryman Samuel Jacobs, an orthodox Jew from lower Saxony, the experience of comradeship had a familial dimension that reminded him of the feelings of love that were almost obliterated by the war. He described how these feelings restored and reinvigorated his love for God. In 1920 he compiled a collection of letters he sent to his parents between 1914 and 1918 into an unpublished memoir, *Thoughts and Memories from the World War*.[52] He began with an overview of his burst of patriotism in August 1914 and the Kaiser's call for unity. He conveyed his sincere feeling that antisemitic prejudice would be put aside in the common cause to save the fatherland, and he expressed hope that through "individual achievements" he and other Jews could prove their loyalty and patriotism.[53] However, by 1916, his letters were dominated by analysis of the traumatic effects of combat. Antisemitic experiences, whether with individuals in his unit or from the notorious "Jew Count" imposed by the military, are notably absent from his narrative. Instead, he tried to detail the brutality and carnage of the front experience. "It was here that my nerves became openly strained," he wrote of the Battle of Ypres, "So terrifying were the explosions ... I don't want to go on further about the war's events."[54] To cope with trauma, he relied on comradeship, which more than providing emotional support, also made him feel spiritually fulfilled. He wrote about the close friendships that made him feel accepted, which helped him to maintain a sense of psychological stability.[55] Comradeship meant "caring for one another, covering for one another ... [Our regimental commander] actually cared for us the way a father does for his children and he had a nickname and an affectionate word for each of us."[56] Love of comrades reminded him that, "G-d is with me and therefore I am not afraid. Our faith in G-d has strengthened us, warmed our hearts, against the heavy pain of the last year."[57]

One of the most interesting ways in which comradeship was depicted as a kind of religious experience can be found in articles for front newspapers in which soldiers described comradeship as a path to eternal life. This was sometimes inflected with Christian rhetoric, and in other cases it was devoid of Christian language. Often, such language could echo Christian terminology about "the spirit" and everlasting life, without actually alluding directly to Christian precepts. For example, a 1917 article for the trench newspaper *Der Flieger* (*The Flier*) suggested that the path to eternity could be transmitted from the dead to the living through the spirit of heroism and sacrifice. Referring to the famous aces like Boelcke and Immelmann who were killed the year before, the author noted that the comradeship of old aces was passed on to the next generation, and "the spirit of the dead lived on in the [new] fighter pilots."[58]

Rhetoric about eternal life through comradeship also fused overtly Christian language with trench imagery. The trench newspaper *Der Kamerad*, for example, which was relatively crudely typed, with cartoons and also handwritten poems, contained pieces by soldiers who melded traditional Christian ideas with frontline experiences. In a 1918 issue, front soldier Richard Volker wrote a poem, "Comrades," that blended the spiritual power of comradeship with expectations of Christ's return. As he comforts a dying friend, he lays him to rest with words about eternal life with his comrades: "Let's sleep until the Lord God awakens us/ Shoulder to shoulder in a line: We comrades!"[59] Volker hoped that he could be buried with his comrades to meet God after the resurrection. Such imagery merges the traditional Christian belief about the afterlife with his idealization of friendship bonds found in the front experience.

Eternal life through comradeship could also be imagined outside the Christian paradigm. Another poem that appeared in *Der Kamerad* in 1918 mourned the death of fighter pilot Manfred von Richthofen, "the brave hero and great warrior" who was killed in April. Completely devoid of Judeo-Christian rhetoric, this poem instead placed von Richthofen in the context of pagan mythology and the memory of his warrior prowess. The author celebrated von Richthofen's entrance into Valhalla, where the Viking god Odin welcomed warriors who had died heroically in combat. According to the poem: "With other heroes he is united in Valhalla … Whether or not he is not dead, his spirit still lives on and he calls on his people (*das Volk*) to continue great deeds."[60] The poem suggested that von Richthofen was dependent on the German people to ensure his eternal life through the memory of heroism and comradeship. The connection between the dead hero and his comrades who preserved his spirit stood outside the influence of a Judeo-Christian God.

The God of War and Creation of a "New Man"

War was such a profound, all-pervasive experience that it seemed to take on enormous spiritual power. As technology and weaponry threatened to overwhelm the individual, many saw industrialized war as heralding a new spiritual epoch. In this new paradigm, men feared that the mind or spirit was threatened with total destruction unless it modified itself to adapt to technology. These kinds of anxieties were certainly brewing before the war.[61] But the trench experience intensified this problem for millions of individuals. Some men tried to solve the crisis by acclimatizing themselves psychologically and spiritually to technology and war. They often described how they could subsume their minds and bodies into the technology, imagining themselves becoming one with their weapons. Further, front soldiers prescribed a "rebirth" of their relationship with technology, which included imagining supernatural capabilities that enabled them to gain superiority over, or least control of, the devastating machinery of war. Finally, many came to terms with war and technology by turning war machines, and their experiences with these machines, into objects of worship. This "worship" of war was politically charged, as front soldiers who aligned with the political left lamented what they saw as an inescapable slide into spirit-crushing adulation of war, while men who embraced right-wing politics often celebrated the idea that war had become their new god.

The worship of war as a kind of all-powerful entity that would replace all other forms of culture can be found in the writings of volunteers from the outbreak. In August 1914, one freshly recruited young sculptor and artist from Berlin named Kauer wrote to his circle of fellow artists about his vision for the war, which he anticipated would "bury all the pitiful kitsch with which we have tortured ourselves and the world."[62] Kauer had embraced Futurism, a movement emerging just before the war that celebrated speed, technology, and industrial power, and now he saw in those first days "one of the greatest works of art: German mobilization!" The war, he wrote, would replace all art, religion, philosophy, and laws. The experience of confronting death, he anticipated, would so consume the soul that it would eclipse all previous ideas and experiences.[63]

Not all soldiers were so optimistic about war becoming a kind of new god. The editor of one of the more dissident trench newspapers, *Der Flieger* (*The Flier*), Kurt Tucholsky, who would go on to become one of Germany's most famous writers after the war, used poetry to explore the psychological destruction unleashed by violence. He lamented the ways in which war and technology had become an object of worship that destroyed everything else that was sacred. Tucholsky was from a German Jewish family in Berlin and he was an editor for the Social Democratic Party's newspaper, *Vorwärts*, before he was drafted in 1915. After experiencing combat on the Eastern Front, he become an editor for *Der Flieger* in 1916 while he served as a clerk for an artillery-observation flying school. A longtime critic of militarism, he wrote poetry and prose during the war that attacked military leaders and the establishment for stubbornly continuing the war. Writing under the pseudonym "Theobald Tiger" for *Die Weltbühne* (*The World Stage*), a periodical focusing on art and culture that narrowly avoided censorship, Tucholsky published the poem "August First" on the fourth anniversary of the war in 1918. In this poem, he took Psalm 90, "A Prayer of Moses the Man of God," and replaced every instance of the word "God" with "War," starting with "Lord War (*Herr Krieg*), you are our refuge now and forever."[64] He then constructed "War," rather than "God," as the ultimate creator of the universe: "Before the mountains were brought forth and the lands and the world created, you, war, were from everlasting to everlasting." Elevated to the status of the Creator, war thus deserved prayer and reverence: "And may WAR, our God, be friendly and bless the work of our hands; yes, the work of our hands may he bless!"[65] Although a sardonic, satirical critique of his society's worship of war, Tucholsky's poem also suggests that the war experience had become so spiritually profound that it could be comparable to a religion. War, he feared, had replaced God in cultural importance, becoming a kind of eternal, monstrous event that overshadowed all other belief systems.

To counteract fears of bodies and spirits being crushed under the overwhelming power of war, some predicted a "new man" with enormous spiritual and psychological strength would have to be created. The image of a "new man" completely reborn and acquiring supernatural powers became widespread in postwar memoirs, especially from the political right,[66] but it was also a recurring theme in wartime soldiers' media, including periodicals produced by left-wing editors. The "new man" can be found, for example, in the trench newspaper edited by Tucholsky, *Der Flieger*, which dedicated a number of articles on the spiritual and psychological impact of modern technology. One writer for this trench newspaper concluded that in the face of stress, the war produced an unprecedented steel-nerved warrior, a "new man" and a "new race" (*ein neues Geschlecht*), who uses "only cold concentration and complete obliviousness to death" to reach peak performance and command of his weapons. This "new race" displayed "new miracles of courage," as they conquered their nerves and became jaded to pain and death. With help from comrades, they could "laugh" at death in their barracks and fortify themselves for the next day's stress.[67]

This "new man" had to acquire a level of spiritual strength greater than the material power of war. Especially after the arrival of American troops by 1918 and their overwhelming numerical superiority in aircraft, tanks, fuel, and other weaponry, hard-pressed German troops imagined themselves as spiritually, if not materially, superior. In July 1918, after the last-gasp March offensive had come to a grinding halt and Germans found themselves on the defensive, one anonymous author for the army newspaper *Liller Kriegszeitung* wrote an essay titled "Machines and the Mind (or Spirit)" ("*Maschine und Geist*"), in which he reflected on how German soldiers could vanquish the Allies' overwhelming numerical superiority. The author theorized that while the Allies now had greater numbers of troops, tanks, and aircraft, the German soldier's *Geist* was superior and resilient and would ultimately conquer the enemy's material dominance. The author began by arguing that the war signaled a distinct break from man's relationship to military technology during ancient times through the nineteenth century, when humans were in control of the weapons that were tools for mankind's quest for power. Now, the war marked a transition to a stage in which, "The machine, previously in the service of human culture, is now used to destroy humanity … Now almost all science and technology are used to destroy life."[68] He placed the blame for this primarily on the British, who arrogantly and "without conscience" imposed their materialistic values on the world. British materialism was antithetical to German culture, which emphasized spiritual values.[69] German soldiers used their spiritual superiority to transcend the "huge quantities of hand grenades, artillery, tanks, poison gas, etc. that Woodrow Wilson wanted to release against the German army." The war proved that "it is not the masses, not power and not the machine, but the mind/spirit [*Geist*]" that brings victory."[70] In this section, the author conjured one of the most striking images from the essay, when he characterized German soldiers as ethereal beings who were superior to machines:

> From those days of artillery drum fire in Champagne in 1915, when German heroes emerge out of the trenches like ghosts to throw themselves against the enemy (*als die deutschen Helden wie Geister aus Gräben sich dem Feinde entgegenwerfen*), until these last days, when death threatened us from the air, it was always the singular heroic spirit that made us Germans certain, even if we were inferior in numbers of troops and in quantity of machines of destruction.[71]

Comparing men to "ghosts" climbing out of the trenches, the author constructed an image of German soldiers as consisting more of spirit than matter, which allowed them to rise above the base material world of trench warfare. He concluded with the conviction that, "From this war humanity derives this fundamental realization: we cannot be ignored forever and that no machine kills the spirit. Thus the spiritual life (*Geistesleben*) is victorious over death. By trusting in this we arm ourselves against the coming days."[72]

The "new man" maintained spiritual superiority by embracing war as his new religion, worshiping it as a monstrous but beautiful, liberating experience. This kind of language can be found in the diary of Rudolf Stark, for example, the fighter pilot mentioned in the previous chapter for his mixture of pagan and Judeo-Christian imagery. In his diary from the last months of the apocalypse, he depicted war itself as a kind of god, with front soldiers coming to terms with their own destruction by fearing, respecting, and loving this deity. Biographical background, in particular his political orientation, is obscure. But Stark's wartime diary, edited and published in 1932, is interesting for its descriptions of redemption from death, notions of transcendence beyond the material world, and a sense of spiritual belonging in the war. In his preface, he wrote:

> War will be eternal and stronger than any religion.
> Every war has a purpose. Sometimes this is clear enough for everyone to understand it, but often it is quite obscure. The limits of necessity are blurred, and so no one can grasp the purpose of the war.
> But Death lost his terrors for us, because he became commonplace and natural. Our fear of Death vanished because we learnt to despise him ...
> And we loved those combats above all else. Because we loved them wholeheartedly, the war became a thing of beauty for us. A set of values was created for us, and we knew nothing else save war. Therefore we found a home in the war.[73]

Though this ability to conquer death often echoed Christian ideology, Stark's narrative remained outside the paradigm of Judeo-Christian language. Instead of a Judeo-Christian God, Stark found meaning, belonging and redemption in the war experience itself. Interestingly, Stark avoided delineating any dogma or concrete ideology. He surrenders any hope of understanding the "purpose" or will of this new religion's god. Rather, the "beauty" of war was self-evident, in itself a justification for its existence.

In turning the war into a kind of religion, front soldiers often described the tools of combat in reverent language, as though their machines possessed supernatural powers. One of the most striking elements of Stark's diary is his portrayal of war machinery as beautiful objects that transcended the cold, material world. Stark described the aircraft he flew with great awe. Portraying flying as an act of communion, he saw himself as a pilot in an observation plane whose life force melded with his machine: "The observer puts his trust in the pilot's flying skill, the pilot in the observer's watchfulness. A single stream of blood flows through the machine from the pilot to the observer and back again."[74] When he graduated to become a fighter pilot in a single-seater aircraft, his worship of machines became even more intense. The newly arrived Fokker D.VII fighter, which frontline pilots revered as the most outstanding airplane of the war (the type was considered so exceptional that it was even specifically named in the Treaty of Versailles to be handed over to the Allies), seemed like creatures from another world when they arrived at the squadron: "Our machines are already on their trucks—two to a truck with their bare struts pointing upward and outward, they look like antediluvian monsters."[75] Stark's "antediluvian" reference evokes a murky ancient world where mysterious behemoths walked the earth. The extraordinary powers he assigned to his machines, as animate objects from something beyond the modern world, spilled over into the way Stark saw himself as a deity. Motivating his comrades and preparing his aircraft for combat, Stark reflected, "In short I rage around like a war god (*Kriegsgott*)."[76]

This language in which men referred to themselves as gods of war permeated letters, diaries, and memoirs. They recast themselves with supernatural abilities that allowed them to meld into their technology, unifying their bodies and minds with their war machines. This can be seen in the writings of *Kapitänleutnant* Edgar von Spiegel von und zu Peckelsheim, who had served in the imperial German navy since 1903. He was promoted to captain of a U-Boat in 1914, and he led his men through extensive combat until his ship was severely damaged in battle with British surface ships in 1917, when he was captured, spending the remainder of the war in a POW camp. Just before his capture, von Spiegel published his war diary, *U-Boat 202—The Diary of a German Submarine*, which became one of Germany's most popular sellers, and even a best seller in the United States after the war. The diary was edited and stylized for a popular audience, but its language is still revealing, casting a glimpse into how he perceived his body and psyche under the pressure of naval combat. Von Spiegel imagined himself as a being whose own flesh and mind merged into his machinery, creating a single body. Narrating an attack on a British freighter, von Spiegel wrote: "Oh, and that delightful sensation of the power of the U-boat's grip! The splendid co-operation of the boat and her crew, of inert machinery and energetic men! The blending together in a single harmonious body of the steel and nerves and spirit of a thousand inanimate things with the whole human element."[77] Imagining the "steel" of his ship intertwined with the "nerves" of his body, von Spiegel constructed himself as a kind of hybrid between organic matter and machine.

This human–machine hybrid was capable of extraordinary acts. Von Spiegel described the marvel of modern technology with references to ancient deities. After torpedoing a freighter, he narrated what he saw through the periscope: "Then a frightful explosion followed, and we were all thrown against one another by the concussion, and then, like Vulcan, huge and majestic, a column of water two hundred meters high and fifty meters broad, terrible in its beauty and power, shot up to the heavens."[78] After a prolonged, twenty-hour combat with French destroyers, he was amazed that he survived unscathed. He attributed this to the supernatural abilities of his ship and crew who, when "the portals of the underworld" opened, were able to escape what he described as Neptune's wrath and certain death.[79]

Von Spiegel's language does not reveal any kind of systematic belief system. Instead, he threw around playful metaphors that mixed iconography from different mythological traditions using ancient images to narrate modern war. But the language that he employed did hint at a kind of "religion" based on worship of technology. It is perhaps not an accident that references to Greek and Roman gods permeate von Spiegel's diary, since, like the ancient Greeks, he anthropomorphized the ships and weapons that he deified. Immersed in the environment of modern war technology, one can see the construction of religion unfold in how he and his crew narrated their belief systems. For example, the ship's mate who was in charge of the bow torpedo tube compartment, Schweckerle, "loved [his torpedoes] as if they were his children, and he was oiling, greasing, and testing them the whole day long, and his affection for his carefully tended treasures knew no bounds."[80] Schwekerle was so worshipful of his torpedoes, which he named "Brisk" and "Quick Devil," that von Spiegel called him a "torpedo-soul," who "mourned each of his charges which he had to give up." The torpedo specialist's mood was totally interlaced with his technical marvels, and if the weapons ran badly or missed their targets, "he went about broken-hearted for several days eating nothing at all."[81] So dependent on their technology for survival, combatants developed intense emotional relationships with their god-like weapons and connected with them spiritually and psychologically.

Von Spiegel's narrative is generally lighthearted in its description of the bonds between men and their machines. But one of the themes he evokes, the psychological and emotional connection between humans and technology, had a darker element to it. Some men developed such a symbiotic relationship with their weapons that their mental health depended on the success of their melding mind, body, and machine. The measure of "success," and in turn their psychological balance, was the ultimate object of their performance, the act of killing. For example, the fighter pilot *Ritter* von Tutschek, mentioned at the opening of this chapter for his war diary entry where he described himself as "the Lord of my nerves," discovered that his nervous tension built up so unbearably between missions that he only found release when he shot down the enemy. He described himself as caught in a vicious cycle in which he oscillated between the extremes of stress and calm, with high performance and the killing of his opponent restoring a sense psychological equilibrium until, like an addiction, anticipation for another fight made him a nervous wreck again. Von Tutschek's narrative echoes the letters and diaries closely analyzed by Klaus Theweleit in his well-known study of language used by front and *Freikorps* veterans to describe killing, where Theweleit interprets their accounts through a psychoanalytical lens that links the fascination with or addiction to violence to sexual release.[82] Interestingly, von Tutschek's drives did not seem to be unconscious. He was quite aware of his psychological dependency on violence. In the last lines of the war diary, completed a few weeks before he was killed in March 1918, he reflected on his exhaustion after years of fighting and the difficulty of climbing into his bullet-ridden plane to face another fight. He concluded by acknowledging the vicious cycle that enveloped him: "To overcome the horror I felt once again and to calm my nerves, the next day I shot down a French observation balloon for number 25 [victory]."[83] Thus the act of killing became the antidote for the nervous stress brought on by the act of killing.

To some front soldiers, the act of killing was something to relish, rather than a source of shame. A new religion had to be invented to treat killing not as a sin, but as the ultimate experience. This search for a new language and belief system can be seen perhaps most famously in the postwar writings of Ernst Jünger, one of the most well-known and prolific survivors of the trenches, who was obsessed with the "inner experience" of war and his capacity for withstanding extreme stress and danger.[84] He developed a language that mixed different mythological metaphors to reflect on how men replaced the old gods with the worship of war, as in one passage from *Copse 125*:

> Hence man has no choice but to become a bit of nature, subjected to its inscrutable decrees and used as a thing of blood and sinew, tooth and claw. Tomorrow, perhaps, men of two civilized countries will meet in battle on this strip of land; and the proof that it must happen is that it does. For otherwise we should have stopped it long ago, as we have stopped sacrificing to Wotan, torturing on the rack, burning witches, or grasping red-hot iron to invoke the decision of God … The blood shall circle in [the land] fresh and earthy as the sap of a wooden spring and beat with as manly a pulse as in the veins of our forefathers who made a saint of the Messiah. Rather than be weak and timorous, let us be hard and merciless on ourselves and on others.[85]

Here Jünger makes his case that war is a kind of eternal experience that men desire. He rejected the notion that its brutalizing effects would remind men of their sinful nature and cause them to repent and return to Christian faith. Instead, he saw the war experience as valuable and deserving of worship in itself.

Jünger's postwar writings were a self-conscious attempt to reconstruct himself as a "superhuman" figure who transcended the brutality of the trenches. As historian Benjamin Ziemann has observed, Jünger's postwar reflections were a stylized literary treatment of the psychological effects of war, which were in contrast to his more reserved wartime diaries that focused on everyday mechanisms of survival.[86] During the war, he made almost no mention in his letters home of religion or spiritual experiences. He had been raised in a family of atheists (he converted to Catholicism in 1998, a few months before he died).[87] But in his famous narratives like *Storm of Steel* (1920) and *War as Inner Experience* (1922), he constructed the front soldier as a "new man" and "new race" who conquers the dehumanization of industrialized slaughter and turns war, and himself, into an object of worship. *Copse 125*, mentioned above, was a stylized postwar reconstruction of his war diaries published in 1925. He started it with a description of front fighters as a new "healthy race" whose "experiences have separated us too far from ordinary life."[88] He relished in the artillery fire that heralded this otherworldly experience: "Then a thundering salute was fired to a new age and a new race of men; blood flowed in streams and a hundred towns went up in smoke."[89]

The new race of men, according to Jünger, drew spiritual power from their encounters with violence, the masculine warrior ideal, and the experience of comradeship. Filling the gap left by failed old religions, comradeship revitalized men and gave them meaning again: "[War] educates one in the comradeship of men, and sets in their right place again values that were half forgotten … One is conscious again of the blood in one's veins, of fate and future rolled into one."[90] Reinvigorated by comradeship, the front fighter also found a quasi-religious experience in his encounters with violence. No longer victims of mass slaughter, men found in their masculine character and the act of killing something god-like: "Sport and the kill have a meaning of their own in these surroundings," Jünger wrote, "We are offering sacrifice to some invisible God of manhood."[91] Jünger's portrayal of the front experience as spiritually rejuvenating was a counterpoint to liberal-progressive politics in the Weimar Republic, and his work would be celebrated by Nazi ideologues looking for philosophical justifications for their memory of the war and cult of the fallen soldiers.[92]

The myth of a "new man" did not go uncontested, even in narratives by some of Germany's most famous heroes. During the war, there was perhaps no more famous "new man," celebrated in the mainstream press for possessing almost superhuman spiritual character and mental skills, than Germany's most famous fighter pilot, Manfred von Richthofen. While recuperating from a head wound in July 1917, von Richthofen completed a memoir, *The Red Battle Flier* (*Der Rote Kampfflieger*), which became Germany's best seller, selling more than half a million copies when it was released just before the end of that year.[93] Richthofen's memoir reinforced his heroic image with its portrayal of war as an adventure and combat as the ultimate sport. However, the adulation he received in the months after its publication seemed to embarrass him, and he set out to dismantle his own idealized image. Shortly after the book came out, von Richthofen began a revised version. He wrote a few additional chapters, but did not finish it before he was killed in April 1918. These additions would be included in a version published in 1920 as *A Hero's Life* (*Ein Heldenleben*). In these passages, von Richthofen reflected that he was no longer the same person as he was when he published the original. He lamented that he had once been arrogant, and he asserted, "I no longer possess such an insolent spirit." The real possibility that death "will catch up with me one day" had brutalized him:

> I am in terrible spirits after every aerial combat. But that no doubt is a long-term effect of my head wound. When I set foot on the ground at my aerodrome after I return from a flight, I go to my quarters and do not want to see anyone or hear anything. I think about the war as it really is, not as the people at home imagine it, with a cheer and a Hoorah! It is very serious, very grim.[94]

At about the same time he wrote that, he visited his family home for the last time in January 1918. His mother recorded in her diary that her usually gregarious and charming son had changed dramatically. "He was serious—very serious—and quiet," she wrote, "I found Manfred very changed, anyhow … He was taciturn, aloof, almost

unapproachable; every one of his words seemed to come from an unknown distance …
I think he has seen death too often." The Baroness was most frightened when Manfred
suggested it would be the last time he would see her and that plans for the future were
pointless. She tried to console him with praise for his heroism and sacrifice, assuring
him, "Already now your name is immortal," but her son, "said nothing, only a small
melancholy smile passed over his mouth."[95]

Conclusion

Constructing notions of spiritual transformation and revitalization, and discovering spiritual sustenance in comradeship and the power of human relationships, were an attempt to salvage some sort of meaningfulness in an otherwise incomprehensible environment. The invention of such imaginative worlds, especially the creative psychological and spiritual affinity men developed with technology, reveals the nimble, flexible capabilities of human minds under pressure to conceive a tolerable reality. Further, these subjective notions of spiritual renewal or rebirth, often inflected with politicized concepts that fell across a broad spectrum, suggest a kind of desperate struggle to reconfigure one's sense of self and reclaim a sense of psychological balance out of the shattering effects of the war experience.

But rather than reclaiming homeostasis, many front fighters found themselves wracked with new psychological problems. Constructing themselves, and their weapons, as supernatural beings with extraordinary powers might provide some sense of agency over an environment that made them feel powerless. Adolf von Tutschek's discovery that "I am the Lord of my nerves" was the supreme assertion of self-reliance. At the same time, narratives that professed worship of violence and killing were often tinged with obsession and rage, hinting at deep-seated psychological injury. German soldiers' narratives echo the altered psychological states analyzed by American psychiatrist Jonathan Shay in his treatment of Vietnam veterans who were so profoundly traumatized by a sense of moral injury that resulted in "berserker" rages. Shay found that as men became enamored of and even addicted to violence, they broke their connection to humanity and became detached from their prewar community. Vietnam veterans studied by Shay occupied a kind of exceptional state of being that was simultaneously beast-like and brutal, but also god-like, above human restraint.[96] Similarly, German soldiers were also fascinated by their seemingly god-like powers discovered in the act of killing, which both severed them from their prewar life and elevated them above it. Instead of imploding, many relished in and glorified their newfound penchant for violence, even if, as in the case of von Richthofen just before his death, hesitation and doubt lurked just beneath the surface. Embodying an ultimate form of "lived religion," front soldiers made themselves into their own gods and metamorphosed their bodies and machines into rituals and props that were just as profound as those found in their prewar *cultus*.

Epilogue: Defeat, Revolution, and Aftermath

Samuel Jacobs, the German Jewish veteran analyzed in the last chapter who had such a powerful experience with comradeship, survived the war with shattered nerves but a persistent faith in God. While on leave in October 1918, civilians asked him if the war was winnable, and he replied that it was in God's hands and they should be proud of their front fighters.[1] Despite his fatalistic faith in God's will, he was profoundly shocked by rising antisemitism from right-wing groups who scapegoated Jews for defeat and revolution. In the months after the defeat, he added a summary of thoughts to his collection of wartime letters, which he hoped would help his grandchildren understand his war experience. Eager to counter widespread accusations that Jews were responsible for a "stab-in-the-back" and responsible for defeat, he emphasized that he was "a loyal German warrior, bearing the suffering I had to carry around with me every day due to the destruction of my nerves, and now I am filled with the pain brought on by the decline of our German fatherland."[2]

For Jacobs, the war did not really end. The trauma of defeat added to his nervous collapse suffered in the trenches, and when the revolution broke out in November, he reached a low point and described his lingering psychological wounds: "My nerves were totally destroyed. Wild dreams disturb my rest at night."[3] Jacobs was subsequently treated in a military psychiatric hospital shortly after the war. Still, despite the psychological trauma he suffered, he asserted that his belief in God was unshaken. He indicated that he now had to derive strength from God to fight against what would become the National Socialist memory of the war, in which Jews were excluded from the front community as racial outsiders and *Reichsfeinde* ("enemies of the nation"). Jacobs included with his collection of letters a list of comrades with whom he believed he had cemented an eternal friendship and a promise that he would be true to his "holy duty" to remain devoted to God and the fatherland.[4]

From diverse backgrounds, many ordinary Germans, like Samuel Jacobs, were psychologically traumatized by the war but retained their belief in God. This was the lens through which they now processed Germany's collapse. This epilogue examines how some of the individual men and women whose religious lives have been examined in previous chapters perceived defeat and revolution. It takes the original goal of this book, to analyze how religion shaped narratives of trauma and how trauma influenced religious beliefs, into the immediate postwar period. How was the trauma of defeat and revolution processed through the prism of religion? While some Germans broke away from or modified prewar spiritual and religious thinking, as seen in previous chapters, the trauma of defeat and revolution reveals that many had not "demobilized" their religious beliefs. The same thinking about God as a protector and provider of emotional stability was applied to postwar conditions, including the trauma of defeat, revolution, economic crisis, and social leveling. However, in contrast to 1914, 1918 saw more widespread uncertainty about whether God would help individuals and the nation through this next catastrophe after four years of carnage. Prescribed coping mechanisms seemed less reassuring, and the traumatic effects of the war seemed to overwhelm prewar language, beliefs, and rituals.

In addition to mourning and coping with spiritual and psychological devastation, Germans also struggled with the religious implications of a lost war. If God was "on our side" and gave Germans the psychological strength to win, how did one explain 1918? Scapegoating, political upheaval, and street violence that erupted in the wake of defeat were seen by many through the lens of their religious beliefs, as ordinary men and women attempted to explain the nation's crisis, as well as their own individual trauma.[5] The central emotion felt across the social and political spectrum was the feeling of betrayal, which included accusations of moral or spiritual treachery and breakdown. This epilogue will not explore in depth the impact of the war on religious institutions, or the myriad postwar religious movements that sprang up or were fueled in the wake of the total war experience. Instead, it will examine individuals and their families to illuminate how the impact of the war on ordinary Germans created conditions where many who felt a sense of betrayal in the wake of defeat searched for spiritual or psychological meaning out of postwar violence. First, this epilogue examines how religious beliefs and language shaped perceptions and narratives, especially in letters and diaries, about defeat and revolution. Second, several case studies offer a glimpse into the religious crisis that many families experienced while coping with the traumatic memory of the war. Men and women often tried to conceal the profound religious doubts and confusion triggered by the war, even if they maintained a veneer of loyalty to prewar patterns of faith in God, the heroic image, and the value of sacrifice.

Defeat and Revolution through the Lens of Religious Language

Germany's defeat in 1918 was a lightning rod for the political right, which fueled the "stab-in-the-back" legend to falsely blame socialists, Jews, and other alleged "November criminals" on the home front for betraying soldiers by sparking the revolution and causing defeat.[6] The memory of defeat, and the scapegoating of "national enemies" for Germany's catastrophe, became one of the main sources of political division in the crisis-plagued Weimar Republic. While the politicization of defeat and subsequent fracture lines in Germany's first democracy have been widely analyzed, less attention has been given to the religious dimension of 1918. Just as the outbreak of the war was widely seen as a trigger for religious renewal, defeat was perceived by many as a symptom of religious crisis. The meaning and cause of this crisis was interpreted in two distinct ways. First, some conflated religious crisis with the "stab-in-the-back," as "enemies" were blamed for betraying not only the nation but also religious faith. Interestingly, this accusation of betrayal went both ways as the home and combat fronts both blamed each other for losing faith in God and thus weakening the nation. Second, some perceived that Germany was suffering a kind of spiritual collapse that preceded the defeat and ran deeper than politics.

Many Germans, especially those who had been caught up in and still believed in the "spirit of 1914" and God's alliance with the nation, could not process the trauma of defeat. This can be seen in the case of infantryman turned fighter pilot Rudolf Berthold, analyzed in Chapter 2 as an example of mobilizing front soldiers who believed Germany was enjoying a religious revitalization. He had embraced ideals that conflated God and the nation, faith, and the warrior ideal, but he found his world in shambles in November 1918. Berthold's views on religion had not substantially changed. His diary traces his exuberance about a renewal of faith in God and the fatherland at the outbreak of the war, and this confidence in God helped bolster his nerves through 1918, after extensive combat and several injuries.

Arriving home in January 1919, Berthold was intensely bitter about what he perceived as the home front's denial of its failure to remain true to beleaguered but faithful, hard-fighting front soldiers. While he imagined that soldiers still universally believed in "victory under God," he felt that the home front had collapsed but would not admit it. He recorded the way he thought civilians rationalized defeat: "Without saying 'it's my fault' because of my inner weakness, because of my constant cry for peace, and because my godlessness brought about this breakdown. Oh no—they [the home front] claimed to patiently endure four years—only the [combat] front, the army, has failed in their opinion."[7] In addition to the "godlessness" he found on the home front, Berthold was also perturbed by what he saw as immoral, disloyal women, who had become independent and "impure," making the *Heimat* an alien and unwelcoming world for the supposedly psychologically and spiritually intact front veterans. Berthold recounted indignantly: "women forgot us [front soldiers] and with their constant complaints and whining they lost their faith in us." He thus conflated the erosion of faith in God with the erosion of patriarchy.[8] Shortly before he was killed in street fighting against communists in Harburg in 1920, Berthold lamented what he saw as Germany's humiliating crisis at home, and he expressed the wish that he could be back at the front with his comrades who had kept their "inner strength" while the home front disintegrated.[9]

The "stab-in-the-back" legend also had a spiritual and religious dimension for one individual who would become Germany's most famous front veteran. In his narrative from *Mein Kampf* about the cause of defeat, Adolf Hitler claimed that the "Jewish and Marxist" betrayal of the nation was able to take hold because of "an ethical and moral poisoning" on the home front.[10] Aiming his antisemitic attack on alleged Jewish war profiteers, he suggested that materialism had replaced religious conviction: "In proportion as economic life grew to be the dominant mistress of the state, money became the god of whom all had to serve and to whom each man had to bow down. More and more, the gods of heaven were put into the corner as obsolete and outmoded, and in their stead incense was burned to the idol Mammon."[11] Like Berthold, Hitler believed that soldiers had remained spiritually intact while the home front had been become morally corrupted, turning to new hollow "idols."

While veterans blamed civilians for losing faith in both God and the nation's warriors, civilians developed their own narrative about spiritual betrayal to explain defeat. It was not the home front, many argued, but rather the combat front that had lost its moral compass. Morality organizations that had been waging a war against what they saw as the creeping immorality of sexual promiscuity, alcoholism, and the general erosion of middle-class values of discipline and self-sacrifice blamed front soldiers for failing to adhere to the Christian values that they believed were so essential to victory. Conservative groups like the White Cross Association for Moral Order (*Der Sittlichkeitsbund vom Weißen Kreuz*) organized a conference in Freiburg in 1923 on the legacy of defeat and Germany's moral condition. Mary Young-Rißmann, a Catholic activist, delivered a speech there in which she compared Germany's collapse to the fall of Israel. The main cause of the disaster, she claimed, was the failure of the common soldier to maintain Christian values: "Though the Germans won the battles, they lost the war through sexual offense and alcohol addiction ... the German giant was not defeated militarily, but it was internally, morally ruined, with God's unbroken sword passed over to the hand of the enemy."[12] In contrast, she argued, civilians maintained their faith in God, self-discipline, and willingness to sacrifice, though their willpower was weakened when they learned that front soldiers were giving in to self-gratification.[13] From Young-Rißmann's perspective, women at home did a better job remaining loyal to God and the nation than did the morally corrupt front soldier.

Just as many soldiers and civilians had approached wartime violence through the prism of religion, they also saw God's hand determining the course of political violence in the context of defeat and revolution. The chaotic transition from the imperial order to the nation's first democratic government seemed incomprehensible to many returning soldiers and civilians, who saw themselves as caught up in another violent world that, similar to the front experience, they could not control. In January 1919, a representative for the Protestant congregation in Bietigheim produced a pamphlet in which he advised churchgoers on how they should make sense of the revolutionary violence that had engulfed Germany since November: "It was an uncanny experience in the November days [1918]. How powerless we were as we trembled under God's mighty hand."[14] Like during the wartime period, the trauma of revolution made some believers feel a loss of agency, as though events were too turbulent and inexplicable. Fatalistic language about "God's hand" thus rolled over from the trenches to the postwar period.

Similar to how many returning veterans did not demobilize psychologically,[15] many on the home front were unable to demobilize their religious beliefs. Those who still saw the war as sanctioned by God to vanquish the nation's enemies abroad now called on the Supreme Being to help defeat the enemy at home. Middle-class Germans on the political right often saw themselves as vanguards in a moral crusade against what they perceived as the threat of godless left-wing revolutionaries who aimed to destroy the spiritual fabric of the nation. For Antonia Helming, the Catholic matriarch discussed in Chapter 3 who lost one of her sons, the same rhetoric about maintaining strong nerves in the war against enemies of God and the nation remained essentially intact after 1918. Though the death of her son Hans traumatized her, she found comfort in the belief that he was merely "spiritually transformed" as he went to heaven, and that his "transfigured love" still lived through her.[16] Her belief in Germany's righteous war, now waged against internal enemies who allegedly threatened the conservative cultural and political order that she cherished, carried over into the revolution. A few days after the Kaiser abdicated and the armistice finally ended the war, she wrote a prayer in her diary: "God grant that this delusion of Bolshevism, which already seems to be ebbing away in Russia, will pass like an epidemic and that the people of Europe, as long as stability and reason and historical insight are still available, will join in peace and control the epidemic."[17]

Calling on God to help stop what she saw as the plague of left-wing radicalism, Helming compared Germany's plight to that of God's chosen people from the Bible. She portrayed the revolutionaries as a gang of lazy parasites who persecuted Germany just as the pharaoh enslaved the Jewish people in ancient Israel: "'Oh come, oh come, Emanuel, let your poor Israel free.' Oh, God, free our country from its external enemies, but also free us of the immature fellows who don't want to work, but who earn a lot of money and incomprehensibly rule the city and country as soldiers or workers councils. Free us from the Bolshevik gang in Berlin."[18] Comparing Germany's plight to that of Israel suggests a striking level of cognitive dissonance considering how the political right accused Jews of betraying the nation. She also speculated in her diary that she thought socialists, out to corrupt the nation's moral fiber, were infiltrating all aspects of life, even her own church, where she believed revolutionaries were secretly plotting with members of her parish.[19] But she saw some ray of hope. When communist leaders Rosa Luxemburg and Karl Liebknecht were murdered by *Freikorps* paramilitary soldiers in January 1919, she celebrated it as proof that God was still protecting Germany and she recorded, "God has helped us, God still helps, and God will continue to help further."[20]

Extreme right-wing movements that emerged in the immediate wake of defeat capitalized on middle-class desires for order, both spiritual and political, to counteract what they saw as postwar chaos. Retaliating against left-wing revolution and redeeming the memory of wartime sacrifice was turned into a sacred, religious quest by a number of right-wing groups, most famously the National Socialist movement. However, the Nazis' interpretation of the war experience as a sacred event had its roots in prewar movements that sanctified violence and racism. One of the most famous organizations that synthesized visions of spiritual-religious revitalization with the war experience, and which would become a springboard for political radicalism, was the Thule Society. Cofounded by the artist Walter Nauhaus, a wounded combat veteran, in August 1918, the Thule Society had links to prewar movements but was born out of the war experience. Nauhaus and his colleagues were influenced by arisophy, a nineteenth-century movement obsessed with reviving pre-Christian German rituals, language, and beliefs, including Odin-worship (*Wotanism*) as a means of revitalizing society.[21] Arisophists were pan-Germanists who espoused *völkisch*-nationalism, eugenics, and eliminationist antisemitism. Influencing Nazi ideologues including SS chief Heinrich Himmler, arisophists imagined Aryan Germans to be a supernatural, racially superior blend of humans and angels.[22]

When the war broke out, arisophists interpreted it as proof that their prediction of a new order was imminent. They characterized the war as a kind of cosmic struggle between their conceptions of good and evil, with quasi-religious visions of elite Aryan soldiers triumphing over what they saw as a base, materialistic modern culture represented by the Allies.[23] When it was founded in 1918, the Thule Society melded many of these nineteenth-century ideas from arisophy and other sects to envision a new world that would emerge out of the ashes of the existing society in decay.[24] They characterized war and defeat as a kind of apocalypse that could only be survived by the spiritually invigorated veterans of the trenches. Veterans who joined the Thule Society scorned the civilian world as spiritually hollow, waiting to be redeemed by veterans who brought the spirit of comradeship into the dying world.[25]

Defeat, revolution, and the memory of the war thus became intertwined with notions of spiritual degradation and the struggle for revitalization. In the wake of defeat, the Thule Society celebrated never-ending war as essential to Germany's spiritual survival. They founded newspapers in Munich to disseminate their hatred of Jews, communists, and the new Weimar Republic, and they interpreted the battles between socialists and reactionaries as evidence of an apocalyptic racial war that would usher in either the end of the world or the triumph of German culture over Judaism, which they saw as the cause of the nation's collapse and left-wing revolution, manifested in the short-lived 1919 Bavarian Soviet Republic.[26] As historians Eric Kurlander and Richard Evans have demonstrated, the Thule Society was an ideological precursor to Nazism. Many participants in Thule Society meetings, including Anton Drexler, Hans Frank, and Rudolf Hess, went on to found the DAP (*Deutsche Arbeiterpartei*), which gave a platform to Hitler and the nascent National Socialist German Workers' Party (NSDAP, *Nationalsozialistische deutsche Arbeiterpartei*).[27] Much of the symbolism and rituals, especially used in commemoration for the fallen of the war, that were sanctified by the Thule Society would find continuity in Nazi ceremonies, which generated a cult of memory that claimed to resurrect and redeem the spirit of the war dead.[28]

Trauma, Postwar Memory, and Individual Crises of Faith

While interwar political movements employed religious language to try to manage and control collective memory, subjective experiences with religious trauma, which are the focus of this book, were much more elusive and complex. The traumatic memory of the war haunted families and surviving veterans. Especially for men and women who still tried to maintain an image of faithfulness unchanged since the beginning of the war, their memories of the war experience trapped them in a kind of liminal state, caught between the world of prewar beliefs and the damage that the war experience inflicted on their psyches. Traumatic memories of lost loved ones, or memories of the violence they inflicted, shattered their certainty that a benevolent God governed an ordered world. How does one reconcile so much loss with belief in God's benevolence? Further, families of returning soldiers were ill-equipped to deal with religious crises of men traumatized by what they had seen and what they had done, including the act of killing, in the war.

For some, the lost war confirmed suspicions that religious institutions and leaders, who had embraced the rhetoric of heroism and sacrifice since 1914, were a fraud. Those who faithfully followed the rules and did what their pastors and priests beckoned often felt swindled. For example, in August 1918, a few days after the British breakthrough at Amiens on the Western Front, which General Erich Ludendorff called "The Black Day of the German Army," infantryman Otto W. wrote to his wife Luisle about his despair that the war was lost. Out of food, sick of "Ersatz" (substitute) rations, and exhausted from the fighting, he told her not to bother sending care packages, as he speculated that things were worse on the home front and she probably needed it more than he did. He told her about going to a church service, but the experience only reinforced his bitterness:

> The service was in the small parade ground, and we had to wait a long time for the pastor to come. He then preached that same old song. "Now you're in the final fight, now you have to stand firm and endure until victory." But you notice that the soldiers have finally had enough of it ... Those guys [the pastors] are just stupid.[29]

Otto W. saw the pastors as nothing but liars. He concluded his letter to his wife by saying, "Almost everything is a hopeless sham (*heilloser Schwindel*) from A–Z like the world has never seen."[30]

Survivors of the war struggled to reconcile their prewar selves and beliefs with the traumatic memories that made the postwar world alien and inexplicable. Men and women might tenaciously hold on to prewar religious beliefs, but they felt lost. For example, the Catholic matriarch mentioned earlier, Antonia Helming, projected an image of total confidence that her faith would see her through Germany's crisis. However, inwardly, her confidence in God's divine plan was deeply rattled by the painful, unshakable memories of the war. Despite her conviction that God was still "on our side," now in the war against left-wing revolutionaries she labeled "national enemies," Helming confided in her diary that she was still deeply traumatized by her son's death and the memory of the war. She ruminated about how God could allow this to happen to a faithful follower. Christmas 1918 struck her hard with the painful realization that though her son died a "peaceful heroic death," she would never see him again.[31] Then a kind of tipping point came when her husband died on Christmas Eve 1919. She wrote in her diary: "Life softly fled away from him. We've lost everything. He said throughout his entire illness: 'It was God's will.' We want to find courage to believe this and to say, 'God wanted it,' but it's hard for us to accept."[32] Even as she confided in her diary that she no longer gained comfort from God's will, she wrote a letter to a family friend, a father whose son survived the trenches but died shortly after he returned home. She tried to console them with thoughts of God's divine hand watching over everyone, and she encouraged the father to merge his individual sadness with the collective mourning of the nation:

> God has taken your dear son out of this miserable life to reward him for the most faithful fulfillment of duty, for brave perseverance during the hardest wartime stress, for humble modesty in the bleak days after the war. May this thought

comfort you. My husband always said during his illness when we expressed hope that he would recover: "We want to put everything in the hands of God!" A higher power watches over us and he guides our destiny.[33]

Helming balanced between two worlds. Outwardly, to her friends, she continued to embrace the same rhetoric that remained constant through the war, defeat, and revolution. But inwardly she strained to find the comfort in God that she prescribed. Under the shadow of the war, families struggled to resolve this tension.

Images and memories of the dead haunted veterans returning from the war. Such images included not only memories of dead comrades who inflicted a sense of guilt on men who survived. Veterans also struggled with guilt triggered by memories of killing. Despite the act of killing being officially sanctioned by many religious leaders at the outbreak of the war, some pious front veterans could not escape the guilt they felt from contravening God's commandment against taking human life. This can be seen in the case of the decorated war hero Friedrich Röth, who committed suicide in December 1918. Röth's narrative and the motive for his suicide was fiercely contested by his family, who later suggested that journalists, old comrades and later the National Socialist regime tried to cover up the cause of his depression by characterizing it as an act that stemmed from his deep despair over Germany's defeat and "decline" into left-wing revolution. However, Röth's family insisted that he actually suffered deep despair over the loss of comrades as well as moral injury, as he could not reconcile the act of killing with his religious beliefs.

Röth, the son of a factory owner, was raised in a conservative Protestant family in Nuremberg. He began the war as a volunteer in an artillery regiment before he was seriously injured in 1915. After he recovered, he volunteered for flying school and was transferred to a Bavarian flying squadron (*Jagdstaffel 23b*) in late 1917, and then took over as commander of *Jagdstaffel 16b* in the spring of 1918, where he won considerable attention from the media as one of Germany's newest heroes (Figure 8.1). After the war, Röth's comrades described him as an exceptional soul, both deeply religious and patriotic. His fellow pilot Max Goßner wrote that Röth was not a braggart, nor did he possess a brutal fighting nature. Rather, he was a sensitive, empathetic man, and "a religious idealist in the fullest sense."[34]

As a fighter pilot, Röth distinguished himself by specializing in shooting down observation balloons, which were used to spot artillery and control fire on enemy trenches. He shot down twenty in the last year of the war, making him Germany's most successful "balloon buster," which resulted in the award of the *Pour le Mérite*, Germany's highest award for bravery. Shooting down balloons appealed to him because, due to his poor eyesight, these were optimal targets, and, since balloon observers were able to parachute from their hanging baskets before the balloons were set on fire, this combat activity rarely resulted in death.[35] Decades later, Röth's close friend and fellow pilot Theodor Rumpel told a historian that Röth was always relieved and happy if the observer in a balloon was able to escape with his parachute, but that if he had to shoot down an enemy aircraft and the pilot was killed, Röth was closed off and brooded.[36] Trying to preserve human life as much as he could in these circumstances was an important factor for Röth. In a letter to his senior officers who recommended him for a Military Order of Max Joseph, he also expressed his hope that by shooting down observation balloons that directed artillery, he was saving lives the lives of men in the trenches.³⁷

By the end of the war, Röth suffered from multiple physical injuries as well as psychological problems. On December 31, 1918, a few weeks after Germany's defeat, he shot himself in his Nuremberg apartment. Because they considered suicide a sin and shameful, his deeply religious family buried him unmarked in another family's plot in Nuremberg's St. Johannis cemetery. His suicide was controversial and traumatic for more than just his family, as the media tried to explain to the public why a war hero, who had been lionized in newspapers and popular postcards as a model of heroism and

Figure 8.1 "Unser erfolgreicher Kampfflieger—Leutnant Röth" ("Our successful battle flier, Leutnant Röth") from the popular Sanke postcard series, No. 647, 1918. Personal collection of the author.

masculinity, would take his own life. The *Fränkischer Kurier* reported a few days after his suicide that Röth returned home from the war a profoundly changed man: "On November 17 he returned to his hometown of Nuremberg, appearing healthy on the outside, but he was struggling with his nerves. He thus needed a well-deserved rest and relaxation after such unprecedented activities and stress."[38] This suggestion that Röth suffered from mental illness was reiterated in his military file, which recorded that he "committed suicide due to a total nervous breakdown."[39] However, other newspapers reported that Röth's breakdown was not triggered by the war. The conservative *Münchener Neueste Nachrichten* added a political dimension to the narrative of Röth's suicide and reported that "Röth shot himself because he was suffering from melancholy (*Schwermut*) due to the political revolution ... and he believed that he could not survive the misery and humiliation of Germany."[40] The editor suggested that Röth "is not the only one who has been driven to this step because of deep feelings for the fatherland."[41] Anticipating that their readers were also in despair over Germany's "misery and humiliation," the editors called on those who shared Röth's depression to avoid this same fate.

After the National Socialists came to power in 1933, they used Röth's suicide to reinforce this narrative that defeat sparked psychological and spiritual crisis, which they characterized as understandable for a deeply patriotic front fighter. Journalist Oskar Döbeli, writing in July 1933 for the *Münchener Neueste Nachrichten*, which had been recently coordinated under the Nazis, described Röth's heroic exploits in detail before launching into an explanation of the fighter pilot's suicide. Döbeli claimed that Röth's central trauma was the experience of defeat and being forced to turn his squadron's aircraft over to the revolutionary soldiers' councils, who humiliated and "treated him terribly" in the days after the war. The trauma of national collapse was the background for Döbeli's dramatized version of Röth's suicide:

> Röth, who had achieved incredible things with faith in Germany's future, saw his fatherland hopelessly crushed to the ground. He could not overcome this pain. A shot rang out through his quiet apartment in Nuremberg on Sulzbacher Strasse. A hero had ended his life after happily withstanding the dangers of the war ... However, we will remain faithful to his memory in the newly emerged *Reich*.[42]

Röth was thus turned into a national martyr by Nazi propagandists, who constructed his personal crisis as the spiritual collapse of a hero who could endure combat but not the pain of defeat and revolution. In turn, Röth's sacred memory was maintained for the next generation and its national resurgence.

The National Socialist narrative of Röth's suicide, however, was contested decades later by his family. Röth's younger sister, Hedwig, in interviews with Bruno Schmäling in Germany in the 1970s, was eager to set the record straight on her brother's actual motives for taking his own life. She intimated that when her brother returned home from the war, he was profoundly changed, and the family was not able to cope with or understand his crisis. Hedwig Röth claimed that her brother was not traumatized by defeat, but rather his psyche was haunted by the deaths of friends and the horror of what he had seen over the Western Front. His suicide so shocked his deeply religious parents, who condemned his "sinful" act, that they removed and destroyed all of his possessions from their house. Hedwig, whose love for her brother had not wavered, deeply regretted her parents' attempt to wipe away his memory. She also repudiated how the press and later the Nazis tried to rewrite the narrative of her brother's suicide.[43] It is not certain whether Hedwig Röth tried to describe what she sensed about her brother's psychological breakdown to her family or to journalists in 1919, but the conservative journalists and Nazi ideologues who controlled his narrative could not accept that a war hero who earned medals and praise for his heroism and comradeship could be psychologically traumatized by combat, the presumably ideal masculine experience. Outside his family, the religious dimension of his personal crisis was ignored. Instead of moral injury, Röth's narrative was rewritten as a tragic symptom of national injury.

The Nazis cultivated an image of their movement as "redeeming" the dead of 1914–18, who had been allegedly betrayed by defeat and revolution.[44] With its cult of violence, emphasis on ritual, rhetoric about "redemption" and "salvation" for the memory of the front generation, and racial ideology that emphasized belief over evidence, Nazism could, as a number of historians have observed, be described as a "secular religion."[45] To what degree did this "religion" appeal to actual veterans? The Nazi Party's cult-like obsession with the sacred memory of the front experience, especially the spirit of comradeship, resonated with many survivors of the trenches. As historian Alon Confino has pointed out, Nazi ideology's "liturgy of death for the national community" would find accommodation and continuity with traditional notions of redemption and salvation.[46] This is reflected in interwar memoirs by right-wing veterans like Claus Bergen, an artist who joined a submarine crew in 1917 and used his experiences to produce a series of popular paintings that idealized militarized masculinity and life in the imperial German navy. In his preface to a postwar collection of U-boat stories, Bergen expressed his admiration for the "the bravest [who] lay united in death in their steel coffins on the ocean bed," and he reminisced on the memory of comradeship that gave them eternal life. "That spirit of comradeship and faith is still alive," he wrote, "I hope that it may, in many distant places, sow a seed of conviction that unity and loyalty produce a strength that is inevitable and leads surely to success."[47] Bergen found fulfillment of this belief in comradeship in the Nazi Party, which he joined in 1922, which brought him considerable success after 1933 as an artist endorsed and exhibited by the regime at the House of German Art in Munich.

It would be inaccurate and overgeneralized to suggest that Nazism replaced a void left by the spiritual devastation of 1914–18. In actuality, for right-wing veterans, Nazism built on already existing structures that gave ex-soldiers, and many younger men who had missed but longed to belong to the "front community," a sense of hope that the movement shared and would preserve their spiritual goals, which were often expressed in Christian language. For Great War veteran Heinrich T., for example, Nazi propaganda matched his notions of "salvation" and the spiritual meaning of comradeship, with Hitler as the redeemer who saved the nation and the memory of the front experience. A businessman from Kiel who served in the infantry as a lieutenant for three years, Heinrich T. recorded at the end of his war diary that he felt betrayed by socialists and Jews whom he blamed for defeat and revolution.[48] In 1933 he transcribed his diary and added a twenty-page narrative about his return to France to visit the old battlefields. He wrote that the emotions he felt at the cemeteries in France moved him so greatly that he decided to join the National Socialist Party.[49] Standing at graves of German soldiers, he envisioned Hitler as a savior figure: "I'm watching over the graves of our comrades. But today we know that everything has meaning, even Germany's difficult fate, and we see that shining over the simple, black wooden crosses is the word of the *Führer* for our new Germany: 'And you did not fall in vain.'"[50] Heinrich T. saw Hitler as a redeemer of the dead. If defeat and revolution were Germany's fate, it was all part of a larger plan in which Hitler would save the nation and the memory of the fallen. At the outbreak of the next war, Heinrich T. rejoined the army, and he was killed fighting in Russia in 1942.

The Nazis were not the only political movement to appeal to audiences' desires for renewal and redemption. Many also saw the chance for a kind of spiritual revitalization through the antiwar movements and activism in left-wing politics. Käthe Kollwitz, the artist mentioned in the previous chapter who was left psychologically traumatized by the death of her son, Peter, immersed herself in the production of art dedicated to human rights. Her work included posters for antiwar activists in the German Communist Party, and one of her most famous pieces was a sculpture of parents in mourning, "The Grieving Parents," which were representations of herself and her husband, for the Vladslo German war cemetery in Belgium.[51] Her art was a form of personal therapy for her to work through her traumatic memories, which she described in her diary in 1920:

> I want to show death. Death swings the lash of famine—people, men, women and children, bowed low, screaming and groaning, file past him.
>
> While I drew, and wept along with the terrified children I was drawing, I really felt the burden I am bearing. I felt that I have no right to withdraw from the responsibility of being an advocate. It is my duty to voice the sufferings of men, the never-ending sufferings heaped mountain-high … Tranquility and relief have come to me only when I was engaged on one thing: the big memorial for Peter. Then I had peace and was with him.[52]

Her art work, more than religion, helped Kollwitz to heal from the trauma of war. In many ways, her art had become like a religion, in that it provided her a path for comfort and self-therapy. From a family of Protestant pastors and theologians, Kollwitz still believed in God, but she was angry at the Creator and could not understand the meaning of her son's sacrifice or the fate that God had imposed on her family. After an Easter service in Berlin, she wrote in her diary that she could relate most to Jesus's words on the cross: "My God, why hast Thou forsaken me?"[53]

Estranged from her prewar faith, Kollwitz turned her focus to finding spiritual sustenance through humanism. She hoped that there was a chance for reform and recovery through a socialist movement, which she at first believed was the most effective means of creating a society based on humanist ideals. A few weeks after the war, she was deeply moved at a Freedom Celebration by the "divinely beautiful" performance of Beethoven's Ninth Symphony, which she felt synthesized humanism, socialist ideals, and the realization that one could only commune with the Creator when one found joy in life: "Yes, in the Ninth there is socialism in its purest form. That is humanity, glowing darkly like a rose, its deepest chalice drenched with sunlight. Divine rejoicing in existence. How I was moved when the chorus sang: '*Feelest* thou thy Maker, world!' "[54] However, she lamented, the left's "splitting up into parties who hate one another like poison" made this an "impossibility." Further, she was pessimistic about any lasting positive spiritual renewal to come out of the war: "Our losses in the material realm would ignite in all the brighter inner life. But what is most depressing is that there is so little evidence of this inner life."[55]

Kollwitz felt isolated and lost. She began a 1921 diary entry thus: "Low. Low. Touching Bottom."[56] Preferring inner withdrawal, she wrote: "I am contracting into myself. Complaining does not help, praying does not help either—*it is so.*"[57] Disillusioned with faith and politics, Kollwitz was left struggling in the postwar world, committed to humanism and fighting against war through her art, but fearful that these goals could never be translated into reality. Her diary during the interwar years is filled with anxiety about the world's failure to overcome its divisions and avoid another catastrophe, and she was pessimistic about whether any political movement or religion could save the world. She suffered from grinding depression and further personal loss when her grandson, also named Peter, was killed in the Second World War. In one of her last diary entries before her death in April 1945, she concluded with a quote from Goethe, whose work she greatly admired: "But let us stop worrying our particular religions like a dog its bone. *I have gone beyond purely sensual truth.*"[58]

Conclusion

By the end of the war, religious language still framed how many Germans narrated trauma. However, memories of mass death, moral injury, and encounters with traumatic violence had eroded certainties about God's role as a companion and protector. Prewar Judeo-Christian religious beliefs had been destabilized, decentered, or fused with more subjective belief systems shaped by the experience of total war. Individuals experienced this destabilization of 1914 religiosity in different ways and to varied degrees. The varieties of religiosity sometimes overlapped and blurred, and at any given moment were in a state of flux, and thus defy categorization. But the religious imaginations of front soldiers encompassed a broad spectrum that included reaffirming traditional Judeo-Christian roots, detaching from prewar assumptions to different degrees, reinventing or hybridizing existing beliefs, finding pragmatic and humanist-oriented spiritual support, and inventing new avenues of belief influenced by preoccupation with death, violence, and technologies of destruction.

Why did some engage in more religious experimentation while others found spiritual sustenance in preexisting sources of belief? Why did some find in violence an object of worship while others became dispirited in the face of brutalization? This is difficult to determine. In many cases, only fragments of their social and cultural backgrounds are available with the letters and diaries in archival files. But in some instances, the line between their backgrounds and their religiosity is more readily apparent, as in the case of Ernst Jünger, who was raised in an areligious household. Jünger made virtually no references to religion in his wartime letters, and he constructed narratives after the war in which he found spiritual nourishment from violence and the front experience. In other cases, some experimented with multilayered, often obscure imagery that reflected prewar beliefs modified or intertwined with wartime experiences and emotions that seemed to better fit their immediate experiences and emotions. In the case of fighter pilot Josef Jacobs, his dabbling with pagan or demonic iconography, which after the war he suggested was a reflection of himself, on the fuselage of his aircraft is all the more intriguing in light of his Catholic background. His penchant for carrying rosary beads with him on every flight in an aircraft with a demonic image on the fuselage highlights the hybridization of prewar beliefs with imagery that made sense and fulfilled complex and contradictory psychological needs in wartime conditions.

Even if precise cultural backgrounds are lacking, narratives of trauma reveal that front experiences were seismic events that for many triggered a schism between prewar and wartime life. Letters by both soldiers and civilians suggest that encounters with violence and loss precipitated gradual or sudden spiritual disorientation, revaluation, or silence. In this study, which focuses on narratives by front soldiers, it might appear that religious transformations were more dramatic for men than women, and that religiosity on the home front was more static. However, available letters and diaries suggest that the range of religious feelings experienced by both soldiers and civilians were diverse. This impression that religious experiences may have been more dramatic on the combat front might be caused by a practical problem found in archival files, which tended to contain primarily the soldiers' side of the correspondence preserved and donated by family members decades after the war, while the replies from women and children to these husbands, fathers, and sons were in many cases lost in the destruction of the trenches.

At the same time, letters and diaries by women that are preserved suggest that their experiences run the same spectrum as men, and scholarship on letter exchanges between families should inspire more research on mutual reinforcement, or breakdown, of religious beliefs within families.[1] Further, like their counterparts on the combat front, women also concealed complex layers of religious feelings, as in the case of the matriarch Antonia Helming who hid her feelings of despair, which she confided in her diary, while bolstering up a facade of indefatigable stoicism in her letters to her fighting sons. Nevertheless, while we can sometimes find the symbiotic ways in which emotions were shared through religious language between families, the often one-sided collections of correspondence in archives can frustrate attempts to compare degrees of religious trauma between combat and home fronts.

As with so many other varieties of total war experience, religion was a site of trauma. By looking at religion through the lens of trauma studies, we can move forward the conversation about religious history and war past the question of whether or not the war eroded or reinforced religious beliefs. Instead, religious beliefs and rituals were altered in complicated ways. This was recognized by contemporary psychologists, especially those who had combat experience, who argued that religious responses to the war were more complex than the bifurcated debate over a strengthening versus weakening of religious beliefs. Front soldiers, psychologists argued, often concealed their actual beliefs, making it difficult to fit them into clean categories. But they did afford a glimpse into the ways in which their psyches were adapting and metamorphosing different beliefs and rituals drawn from more reliable experiential realities, especially their human relationships and affinity for comradeship, which for many seemed more relevant and immediately efficacious than prewar beliefs.

German soldiers' responses to trauma raise the question of whether or not there was a particularly German religious response to the psychological effects of war. This is not to suggest a kind of religious *Sonderweg* ("special path") in German history, in which disillusionment with religion created a kind of void that would be filled with the "secular religion" of Nazism. Indeed, Germany's experience with religious trauma is comparable to patterns found in other societies. For example, while some historians have argued that religious rhetoric in Germany was exceptional in its nationalistic fervor,[2] the gradual breakdown of nationalistic language in ordinary soldiers' letters, and increased fragmentation or erosion of beliefs, can be found in the case of British and French soldiers and civilians. Letters and diaries from both sides of No Man's Land suggest that men and women became critical of nationalist religious rhetoric and developed more personalized relationships with God as industrialized slaughter unfolded.[3] One common theme that can be found across national lines includes the spiritual effects of brutalization, which became a central feature of memoirs. British veterans like Siegfried Sassoon, Robert Graves, and T. E. Lawrence, haunted by their traumatic experiences and feelings of moral injury, and French veterans like Henri Barbusse, tried to capture the inner effects of violence and were obsessed by the war's brutalizing spiritual and psychological effects.[4] Their memoirs tended to focus on war as a desensitizing experience that hollowed them out spiritually. Though their counterparts can be found most famously in the work of German veterans like Erich Maria Remarque,[5] other German ex-soldiers like Ernst Jünger who portrayed war as a spiritually invigorating, quasi-religious experience that deserves worship and eternal glorification found traction in Germany's crisis-ridden atmosphere of defeat and escalating political resentment. In contrast to British and French memoirs, the intense politicization of memory in the wake of defeat, which also shaped religious language, is exceptional in German narratives that fall into competing postwar genres in which war is either condemned as spiritually destructive or celebrated as revitalizing by the political left and right.[6]

Despite the damage inflicted on religious beliefs, religion was still a vital language and conceptual framework for narrating and healing trauma. Outside the sphere of medical and state systems for defining and treating "war neurosis," religion was the central prism and language through which individuals diagnosed mental trauma and practiced self-therapy. Thus religious belief deserves greater attention from scholars investigating the psychological effects of the Great War. Even if the contents and applications of beliefs are elusive, historians can uncover the paths of healing pursued by ordinary people by focusing on language in letters and diaries where religion was so ubiquitous. Often in tandem with loved ones at home, front soldiers used religion as an essential prism through which they articulated the impact of the war on the "spirit" and "soul." Further, even if they could not solve psychological and emotional problems through religious concepts, rituals and language, the sheer act of communicating these problems had a therapeutic function. Though contemporary psychologists suggested that many concealed their beliefs and emotions, men still, more often than not, tried to convey the damage inflicted on the deepest imaginable level.

In their writing, front soldiers found a space for experimentation with both emotions and religious beliefs. Narrating their experiences through the lens of religion allowed soldiers to ruminate over feelings that might otherwise be taboo in light of masculine ideals of emotional self-control. Religious language gave men an acceptable way for them to bring "feminine" emotions, especially fear and anxiety, into their narratives about the war experience. In addition to experimenting with emotions, writing also gave men a space for exploring more subjective spiritual-religious tools for dealing with trauma. To cope with the collapse or splintering of the religious self, to borrow from historian Stefanos Geroulanos and anthropologist Todd Meyers, which accompanied the physical and psychological impact of wounds in the Great War, new psychological devices were needed to repair the disintegration of prewar spiritual "wholeness."[7]

It might be tempting to suggest that religious beliefs lessened the impact of psychological stress and ultimately lowered the incidence of "war neurosis" or shell shock. However, this would be oversimplified. Experimentation with more subjective rituals and beliefs did not necessarily solve front soldiers' psychological problems. Men struggled in a kind of ambiguous state between prewar psychological structures and the ever-fluctuating conditions of the front. Engulfed by violence, they were wracked by contradictory impulses. Oscillating between piety and irreverence, repulsion and addiction to killing, desensitization and stimulation, front soldiers struggled to process these extreme experiences and emotions through any spiritual-religious prism that might bring them back into that spiritual "middle ground," which psychologist and combat veteran Paul Plaut said was essential to prevent them from "falling into some kind of dark thing."[8]

With the failure of prevailing religious, military, and state prescriptions for dealing with psychological stress, front soldiers were left on their own. Trapped inside a Sisyphean nightmare in which both old and new beliefs failed to bring psychological homeostasis, many searched for ways not only to cope with trauma but also to overcome it. German soldiers' modification of beliefs and rituals reflect individualized attempts at "revitalization" as described by anthropologists.[9] But we might also use the term "reinvention" to analyze how men reconstructed themselves, perhaps in an effort to transcend otherwise inescapable psychological brutalization, and even transformed themselves into gods or the "new man." From the standpoint of trauma psychology, this can be interpreted as an example of humans, finding themselves in a fluid state severed from preexisting beliefs and identity, searching for spiritual metamorphosis as an antidote to death and destruction.[10]

It is difficult to classify these attempts at reinvention or transformation, and they further complicate the question of whether the war reinforced or eroded religious beliefs. The language and imagery used by traumatized soldiers, which included props appropriated from the trench experience, anthropomorphization of machines, and other forms of dabbling with the supernatural, suggest a fusion of religious concepts (rebirth, renewal) and hypermodernity (internalizing the technology of destruction), which produced "something else" that does not fit cleanly into categories of "reinforcing" or "eroding" religious beliefs. This "something else" was not necessarily a new religious dogma, nor did it necessarily suggest a rejection of traditional beliefs. Rather, it was an effort to create an imaginative landscape that could match their surreal conditions by adapting psychological tools that seemed more relevant to their environment and suitable for fixing their psychological wounds.

The adaptability of frontline beliefs highlights the extent to which religion was a lived experience. Personal trauma histories, more so than prewar dogmas, became the center from which front soldiers derived meaning, whether they bandaged trauma with modified versions of Judeo-Christian faith, popular and "alternative" beliefs ("superstitions") or ad hoc rituals and beliefs. More real than anything their senses had encountered before, war became the fabric and landscape of "lived religion." The war experience became the new God or Devil. Like God, trauma might be feared, hated, or loved. But traumatic experiences and memories colonized the religious imagination.

Notes

Introduction

1. Wilhelm S., letter to his wife, November 18, 1914, in *Feldpostbriefe von Mörfeldern und Walldorfern aus dem Ersten Weltkrieg 1914–1918*, ed. Cornelia Rühlig, Katja Englert, and Dagmar Sesche (Offenbach: Berthold Druck GmbH, 2014), 22.
2. Wilhelm S., letter to his wife and daughters, December 11, 1914, in *Feldpostbriefe von Mörfeldern und Walldorfern*, 24.
3. Wilhelm S., letter to his wife, December 31, 1914, in *Feldpostbriefe von Mörfeldern und Walldorfern*, 26.
4. Ibid.
5. Wilhelm S., letter to his wife, July 15, 1915, in *Feldpostbriefe von Mörfeldern und Walldorfern*, 29.
6. Wilhelm S., letter to his wife and daughters, December 11, 1914, in *Feldpostbriefe von Mörfeldern und Walldorfern*, 24.
7. Wilhelm S., letter to his wife, January 11, 1915, in *Feldpostbriefe von Mörfeldern und Walldorfern*, 27.
8. For a necessarily brief list of recent historiography focusing on the impact of the war primarily on religious institutions and nationalism, theology, and interactions between religious leaders and governments, see Philip Jenkins, *The Great and Holy War: How World War I Became a Religious Crusade* (New York: HarperCollins, 2014); Martin Greschat, *Der Erste Weltkrieg und die Christenheit: Ein globaler Überblick* (Stuttgart: Kohlhammer Verlag, 2014); Gerd Krumeich and Hartmut Lehmann, *"Gott mit Uns!" Nation, Religion und Gewalt im 19. und frühen 20. Jahrhundert* (Göttingen: Vandenhoeck & Ruprecht, 2000); Martin Lätzel, *Katholische Kirche im Ersten Welkrieg: Zwischen Nationalismus und Friedenswillen* (Regensburg: Pustet, 2014); Wilhelm Achleitner, *Gott im Krieg: Die Theologie der österreichischen Bischöfe in den Hirtenbriefen zum Ersten Weltkrieg* (Vienna: Böhlau, 1997); Heinz Hürten, "Die katholische Kirche im Ersten Weltkrieg," in *Der Erste Weltkrieg—Wirkung, Wahrnehmung, Analyse*, ed. Wolfgang Michalka (München: Piper, 1994), 725–35.
9. For excellent studies on chaplains and the crisis of faith, see Edward Madigan, *Faith under Fire: Anglican Army Chaplains and the Great War* (London: Palgrave Macmillan, 2011); Patrick J. Houlihan, "Clergy in the Trenches: Catholic Military Chaplains of Germany and Austria-Hungary during the First World War" (PhD dissertation, University of Chicago, 2011); Benjamin Ziemann, "Katholische Religiosität und die Bewältigung des Krieges: Soldaten und Militärseelsorger in der deutschen Armee, 1914–1918," in *Volksreligiosität und Kriegserleben*, ed. Friedhelm Boll (Münster: Lit, 1997), 116–36; for a comparative overview, see Doris L. Bergen, *Sword of the Lord: Military Chaplains from the First to the Twenty-First Century* (Notre Dame, IN: University of Notre Dame Press, 2004).

10. Recent scholarship on the religiosity of British and American soldiers has been the focus of excellent studies by Jonathan Ebel, *Faith in the Fight: Religion and the American Soldier in the Great War* (Princeton, NJ: Princeton University Press, 2010); Michael Snape, *God and the British Soldier: Religion and the British Army in the First and Second World Wars* (New York: Routledge, 2005); Richard Schweitzer, *The Cross and the Trenches: Religious Faith and Doubt among British and American Great War Soldiers* (Westport, CT: Praeger, 2003).
11. Benjamin Ziemann, *Violence and the German Soldier in the Great War—Killing, Dying, Surviving*, trans. Andrew Evans (London: Bloomsbury, 2017), 9–11.
12. One of the most important scholars on "lived religion" is David Orsi. See, for example, Orsi's *The Madonna of 115th Street: Faith and Community in Italian Harlem, 1880–1950* (New Haven, CT: Yale University Press, 2002), xxxiv; see also David Hall, *Lived Religion in America* (Princeton, NJ: Princeton University Press, 1997). Scholars of early modern Europe have also been instrumental in defining "lived religion." See the introduction to Jenni Kuuliala, Rose-Marie Peake, and Päivi Räisänen-Schröder, eds., *Lived Religion and Everyday Life in Early Modern Hagiographic Material* (New York: Palgrave Macmillan, 2019), 1–25.
13. Some of the most influential scholarship on the importance of religion providing a psychological coping mechanism in the trenches include Patrick J. Houlihan's *Catholicism and the Great War: Religion and Everyday Life in Germany and Austria-Hungary, 1914–1922* (Cambridge: Cambridge University Press, 2015), esp. ch. 4; Alexander Watson, *Enduring the Great War: Combat, Morale and Collapse in the German and British Armies, 1914–1918* (Cambridge: Cambridge University Press, 2008); Benjamin Ziemann, *War Experiences in Rural Germany, 1914–1923* (Oxford: Berg, 2007; first published in 1997 as *Front und Heimat: Ländliche Kriegsfahrungen im südlichen Bayern, 1914–1923* by Klartext).
14. See Adrian Gregory and Annette Becker, "Religious Sites and Practices," in *Capital Cities at War: Paris, London, Berlin*, vol. 2, ed. Jay Winter and Jean-Louis Robert (Cambridge: Cambridge University Press, 2007), 383–427; Susan Grayzel, *Women and the First World War* (New York: Longman, 2002).
15. On front soldiers yearning for and incorporating "feminine" characteristics of love and compassion into their language and war experience, see Thomas Kühne, "'… aus diesem Krieg werden nicht nur harte Männer heimkehren'— Kriegskameradschaft und Männlichkeit im 20. Jahrhundert," in *Männergeschichte— Geschlechtergeschichte: Männlichkeit im Wandel der Moderne*, ed. Thomas Kühne (Frankfurt: Campus,1996), 174–91; see also Jason Crouthamel, *An Intimate History of the Front: Masculinity, Sexuality and German Soldiers in the First World War* (New York: Palgrave Macmillan), esp. ch. 3.
16. Erika Kuhlman, *Reconstructing Patriarchy after the Great War: Women, Gender and Postwar Reconciliation between Nations* (New York: Palgrave Macmillan, 2008), 3–4. This was also the case with postwar battles over pensions, where men's sacrifices were privileged while women's sacrifices were perceived as secondary. See Silke Fehlemann and Nils Löffelbein, "Gender, Memory and the Great War: The Politics of War Victimhood in Interwar Germany," in *Psychological Trauma and the Legacies of the First World War*, ed. Jason Crouthamel and Peter Leese (New York: Palgrave Macmillan, 2016), 141–64.
17. On the psychological problems suffered by German women on the home front, see Silke Fehlemann, "Die Nerven der 'Daheimgebliebenen': Die Familienangehörigen der Soldaten in emotionshistorischer Perspektive," in *Nerven*

und Krieg: Psychologische- Mobilisierungs und Leidenserfahrungen in Deutschland, 1900–1939, ed. Gundula Gahlen, Ralf Gnosa, and Oliver Janz (Frankfurt/New York: Campus, 2020), 227–52.
18. One of the most important works that explores the collapsing boundaries between fronts is Karen Hagemann and Stefanie Schüler-Springorum, eds., *Home/Front: The Military, War and Gender in Twentieth Century Germany* (Oxford: Berg, 2002).
19. A fascinating overview of the broad range of superstitions and popular beliefs can be found in Owen Davies, *A Supernatural War: Magic, Divination and Faith during the First World War* (Oxford: Oxford University Press, 2018). On spiritualism, see Jay Winter, *Sites of Memory, Sites of Mourning: The Great War in European Cultural History* (Cambridge: Cambridge University Press, 1995), 64–77; for an excellent overview of diverse belief systems, see Adrian Gregory, "Beliefs and Religion," in Jay Winter, *The Cambridge History of the First World War, Volume 2: Civil Society* (New York: Cambridge University Press, 2014), 418–44. For comparative scholarship on "superstition," see Ralph Winkle, "Connaître à fond de l'âme du soldat: Französische Aberglaubensforschung während des Ersten Weltkrieges," in *Alliierte im Himmel. Populare Religiosität und Kriegserfahrung*, ed. Gottfried Korff (Tübingen: Tübinger Vereinigung für Volkskunde, 2006), 349–70.
20. Eric Kurlander, *Hitler's Monsters: A Supernatural History of the Third Reich* (New Haven, CT: Yale University Press, 2018).
21. Jay Winter called for greater attention to religious faith as a coping mechanism for psychological trauma in "The Language of Shell Shock," keynote presentation at conference, "Aftershock: Post-Traumatic Cultures since the Great War," University of Copenhagen, May 22, 2013.
22. This has been stressed by Jay Winter, *War Beyond Words: Languages of Remembrance from the Great War to the Present* (Cambridge: Cambridge University Press, 2017).
23. For an insightful analysis of semantics and diverse languages in British and German soldiers' letters, see Aribert Reimann, *Der grosse Krieg der Sprachen: Untersuchungen zur historischen Semantik in Deutschland und England zur Zeit des ersten Weltkriegs* (Essen: Klartext, 2000). On the importance of soldiers' letters in British culture, see Samuel Hynes, *A War Imagined: The First World War and English Culture* (London: Bodley Head, 1990).
24. This tension between language and practice has been noted by gender historians. For example, see Kathleen Canning, *Gender History in Practice—Historical Perspectives on Bodies, Class and Citizenship* (Ithaca, NY: Cornell University Press, 2006), 101–20.
25. Roger Chickering, *Imperial Germany and the Great War*, 3rd ed. (Cambridge: Cambridge University Press, 2014), 5–6, 151–2.
26. This book uses collections of letters from a number of archives including the Bundesarchiv-Militärarchiv, Freiburg; the Württembergische Landesbibliothek, Stuttgart, Feldpostbriefe, Sondersammlung Zeit der Weltkriege; the Hauptstaatsarchiv Baden-Württemberg, Stuttgart; and the Bayerisches Hauptstaatsarchiv-Kriegsarchiv, Abteilung IV, Munich. Published collections of letters from local or regional archives are also utilized.
27. On some of the challenges inherent in using letters to reconstruct life experiences, see Robert Blobaum, "Registers of Everyday Life in Warsaw during the First World War: The Uses and Limitations of Ego-Documents," in *Inside World War One? The First World War and Its Witnesses*, ed. Richard Bessel and Dorothee Wierling (New York: Oxford University Press, 2018), 29–55; Gerald Lamprecht, *Feldpost und Kriegserlebnis. Briefe als historisch-biografische Quelle* (Innsbruck: Studien

Verlag, 2002); Peter Knoch, "Erleben und Nacherleben. Das Kriegserlebnis im Augenzeugenbericht und im Geschichtsunterricht," in *"Keiner fühlt sich hier mehr als Mensch…". Erlebnis und Wirkung des Ersten Weltkriegs*, ed. Gerhard Hirschfeld, Gerd Krumeich, and Irina Renz (Essen: Klartext, 1993); Brian K. Feltman, "Letters from Captivity: The First World War Correspondence of the German Prisoners of War in the United Kingdom," in *Finding Common Ground: New Directions in First World War Studies*, ed. Michael Neiberg and Jennifer Keene (Leiden & Boston: Brill, 2011), 87–110. Gender historians have spearheaded analysis of the advantages and disadvantages of letters as sources. See, for example, Christa Hämmerle and Edith Sauerer, eds., *Briefkulturen und ihr Geschlecht—Zur Geschichte der privaten Korrespondenz vom 16. Jahrhundert bis heute* (Vienna: Böhlau, 2003). See also Bernd Ulrich, *Die Augenzeugen. Deutsche Feldpostbriefe in Kriegs- und Nachkriegszeit 1914–1933* (Essen: Klartext, 1997), 40–52.

28. For an intriguing exploration of some of the challenges facing historians working on epistolary culture and letters between soldiers and civilians, see Ilari Taskinen, "Social Lives in Letters: Finnish Soldiers' Epistolary Relationships, Intimate Practices, and Emotionality in World War II" (PhD Dissertation, Tampere University, Finland, 2021).
29. Ulrich, *Die Augenzeugen*, 40, 78.
30. On war diaries as an essential source for understanding the psychological effects of the war, see Marilyn Shevin-Coetzee and Frans Coetzee, *Commitment and Sacrifice: Personal Diaries of the Great War* (Oxford: Oxford University Press, 2015).
31. The complexity inherent in ego-documents, and the diverse discourse employed by men to process trauma, is expertly analyzed by Ziemann in *Violence and the German Soldier in the Great War*, 19–20.
32. Michael Roper, *The Secret Battle—Emotional Survival in the Great War* (Manchester: Manchester University Press, 2009). For an excellent study of the emotions and religious beliefs shared between a French soldier and his wife, see Martha Hanna, *Your Death Would Be Mine: Paul and Marie Pireaud in the Great War* (Cambridge, MA: Harvard University Press, 2009).
33. This book uses front newspapers collected at the Bundesarchiv-Militärarchiv, Freiburg (BArch-MA), which holds an extensive and diverse collection of issues. There were over 100 front newspapers published on the Western and Eastern Fronts.
34. See, for example, the excellent study by Robert L. Nelson, *German Soldier Newspapers of the First World War* (Cambridge: Cambridge University Press, 2011). On representations of gender roles in front newspapers, see also Crouthamel, *An Intimate History of the Front,* esp. ch. 4.
35. Anne Lipp, *Meinungslenkung im Krieg—Kriegserfahrungen deutscher Soldaten und ihre Deutung, 1914–1918* (Göttingen: Vandenhoeck & Ruprecht, 2002), 273–5.
36. Ibid., 27–30; see also Nelson, *German Soldier Newspapers,* ch. 1; for further background on the newspapers, albeit published for propaganda purposes after 1933, see Karl Kurth, *Die deutschen Feld- und Schützengrabenzeitungen des Weltkrieges* (Leipzig: Universität Leipzig, 1937); for a comparison with French trench newspapers, see Stéphane Audoin-Rouzeau, *Men at War 1914–1918: National Sentiment and Trench Journalism in France during the First World War* (Oxford: Berg, 1992).
37. Keith Thomas, *Religion and the Decline of Magic* (London: Penguin Books, 1991), 27.
38. Ibid.

39. Clifford Geertz, *The Interpretation of Cultures* (orig. 1973, New York: Basic Books, 2017), 93–5; see also Robert N. Bellah, *Religion in Human Evolution, From the Paleolithic to the Axial Age* (Cambridge, MA: Belknap Press, 2011).
40. Geertz, *The Interpretation of Cultures,* Ch. 5. On reading rituals and their multifaceted meanings, see also the classic work by Mary Douglas, *Purity and Danger: An Analysis of Concepts of Pollution and Taboo* (New York: Routledge, 1966).
41. For an anthropological approach to revitalization, see Anthony Wallace, *Revitalizations and Mazeways: Essays in Cultural Change*, volume 1, ed. R. M. Grumet (Lincoln: University of Nebraska Press, 2003).
42. Snape, *God and the British Soldier,* 22–3.
43. This has been observed by gender historians, in particular. For example, see Sían Hawthorne, *Gender: God* (New York: Palgrave Macmillan, 2018), xvi.
44. On the weaponization of religious belief to motivate soldiers, see Angela Kallhoff and Thomas Schulte-Umberg, "The Committed Soldier. Religion as a Necessary Supplement to a Moral Theory of Warfare," in *Politics, Religion & Ideology* 16:4 (2015): 434–48; Alexander Watson and Patrick Porter, "Bereaved and Aggrieved. Combat Motivation and the Ideology of Sacrifice in the First World War," in *Historical Research* 83:219 (2010): 146–64; Claudia Schlager, *Kult und Krieg: Herz Jesu - Sacré Cœur - Christus Rex im deutsch-französischen Vergleich 1914-1925* (Tübingen: Tübinger Vereinigung für Volkskunde e.V., 2011). For a transnational comparison of how religion is used to motivate soldiers, see Ron E. Hassner, *Religion on the Battlefield* (Ithaca, NY: Cornell University Press, 2016).
45. Sociologist Martin Riesebrodt synthesizes a wealth of scholarship on this in *The Promise of Salvation—A Theory of Religion* (Chicago, IL: University of Chicago Press, 2010). For a more empirical approach to the appeal of transcendence in the context of German history, and in diverse modern German religious communities, see Michael Geyer and Lucien Hölscher, eds., *Die Gegenwart Gottes in der modernen Gesellschaft: Transzendenz und religiöse Vergemeinschaftung in Deutschland* (Göttingen, Wallstein, 2006).
46. Stefanos Geroulanos and Todd Meyers, *The Human Body in the Age of Catastrophe: Brittleness, Integration, Science and the Great War* (Chicago. IL: University of Chicago Press, 2018), 316–17. One of the earliest and most innovative scholars on the First World War to incorporate an anthropological approach to wounds and identity is Robert Whalen, *Bitter Wounds—German Victims of the Great War, 1914-1939* (Ithaca, NY: Cornell University Press, 1984).
47. Davies, *A Supernatural War,* 1.
48. Patrick J. Houlihan, "Religious Mobilization and Popular Belief," in *1914-1918 online. International Encyclopedia of the First World War,* ed. Ute Daniel, Peter Gatrell, Oliver Janz, Heather Jones, Jennifer Keene, Alan Kramer, and Bill Nasson, issued by Freie Universität Berlin, Berlin, August 26, 2015, https://encyclopedia.1914-1918 online.net/article/religious_mobilization_and_popular_belief.
49. Cathy Caruth, *Unclaimed Experience: Trauma, Narrative, and History* (Baltimore, MD: Johns Hopkins University Press, 1996, revised edition 2016).
50. See Peter Leese, Julia B. Köhne, and Jason Crouthamel, eds., "Introduction," in *Languages of Trauma: History, Memory, and Media* (Toronto: University of Toronto Press, 2021), 3-27. Early versions of some of my ideas in this book were presented in my chapter "Religious Languages in German Soldiers' Narratives of Traumatic Violence," in *Languages of Trauma*, 46-69. On medical constructions of psychological trauma in the age of total war, see Mark S. Micale and Paul Lerner,

eds., *Traumatic Pasts. History, Psychiatry and Trauma in the Modern Age, 1870-1930* (Cambridge: Cambridge University Press, 2001); Paul Lerner, *Hysterical Men— History, Psychiatry and the Politics of Trauma in Germany, 1890-1930* (Ithaca, NY: Cornell University Press, 2003); on the genealogy of PTSD from shell shock to the present, see Allan Young, *The Harmony of Illusions: Inventing Post-Traumatic Stress Disorder* (Princeton, NJ: Princeton University Press, 1997).

51. Leading critics of "cultural trauma" as a category of analysis include Wulf Kansteiner, "Genealogy of a Category Mistake: A Critical Intellectual History of the Cultural Trauma Metaphor," *Rethinking History* 8:2 (2004): 193-221; see also Jeffry C. Alexander, Ron Eyerman, Bernard Giesen, Neil J. Smelser, and Piotr Sztompka, *Cultural Trauma and Collective Identity* (Berkeley: University of California Press, 2004).
52. The need for scholars to be sensitive to subjective narratives and contexts is emphasized by Cathy Caruth, *Listening to Trauma: Conversations with Leaders in the Theory and Treatment of Catastrophic Experience* (Baltimore, MD: Johns Hopkins University Press, 2014).
53. On the history of emotions, see Jan Plamper, *The History of Emotions: An Introduction* (Oxford: Oxford University Press, 2015), 12. See also Joanna Bourke, "Fear and Anxiety: Writing about Emotion in Modern History," *History Workshop Journal*, 55:1 (2003): 111-33; Ute Frevert, "Forum—History of Emotions," *German History*, 28:1 (2010): 67-80.
54. See Shafquat Towheed, Francesca Benatti, and Edmund G. C. King, "Readers and Reading in the First World War," *The Yearbook in English Studies* 45 (2015): 239-61; Debbie McCullis, "Bibliotherapy: Historical and research perspectives," *Journal of Poetry Therapy* 25: 1 (2012): 23-38; Jesse Miller, "Medicines of the Soul: Reparative Reading and the History of Bibliotherapy," *Mosaic: An Interdisciplinary Critical Journal* 51:2 (June 2018): 17-34. Thanks to Peter Leese for sharing his insights on bibliotherapy.
55. Elaine Showalter, "Rivers and Sassoon: The Inscription of Male Gender Anxieties," in *Behind the Lines: Gender and the Two World Wars*, ed. Margaret Randolph Higonnet et al. (New Haven, CT: Yale University Press, 1987), 61-9.
56. Joanna Bourke, *The Story of Pain: From Prayer to Painkillers* (Oxford: Oxford University Press, 2014), 95.
57. Ibid., 111-12.
58. Annette Becker, *War and Faith: The Religious Imagination in France, 1914-1930*, trans. Helen McPhail (Oxford: Berg, 1998).
59. Watson, *Enduring the Great War*, 92-7.
60. Ibid., 97-100.
61. Houlihan, *Catholicism and the Great War*, 10.
62. Ibid., ch. 4.
63. Ibid., 10.
64. Stéphane Audoin-Rouzeau and Annette Becker, *14-18: Understanding the Great War* (New York: Hill & Wang, 2002), 1-11.
65. See Joanna Bourke, *An Intimate History of Killing* (New York: Basic Books, 2000); Ziemann, *Violence and the German Soldier in the Great War*, ch. 2.
66. See Jenkins, *The Great and Holy War*, 5-7; see also Philip Jenkins, "Angels and Horsemen: The Great War as an Apocalyptic Struggle," in *Remembering Armageddon—Religion and the First World War*, ed. Philip Jenkins (Waco: Institute for Studies of Religion, Baylor University, 2014), 71-92.

67. One of the most challenging and sensitive topics in trauma studies is the question of whether perpetrators can also experience their deeds as traumatizing. Different theoretical approaches to "perpetrator trauma" or "post-atrocity perpetrator symptoms" have recently been explored by Raya Morag, "Perpetrator Trauma and Current American War Cinema" and Julia Barbara Köhne, "Aesthetic Displays of Perpetrators in *The Act of Killing* (2012): Post-atrocity Perpetrator Symptoms and Re-enactments of Violence," both in *Languages of Trauma: History, Memory, and Media*, ed. Peter Leese, Julia Barbara Köhne, and Jason Crouthamel (Toronto: University of Toronto Press, 2021).
68. On Jünger's constructions of the war experience, see Ziemann, *Violence and the German Soldier in the Great War*, 63–4.
69. Ursula Wirtz, *Trauma and Beyond: The Mystery of Transformation* (New Orleans: Spring Journal Books, 2014), 45–6. Here Wirtz is heavily influenced by Carl Jung, especially *Memories, Dreams and Reflections* (New York: Pantheon Books, 1963).
70. On "moral injury," see Susan Derwin, "Moral Injury: Two Perspectives," in *Traumatic Memories of the Second World War and After*, ed. Peter Leese and Jason Crouthamel (New York: Palgrave Macmillan, 2016), 47–65; on feelings of betrayal and moral injury, see also Jonathan Shay, *Achilles in Vietnam* (New York: Scribner, 1994), 9–10.

1 "*Gott mit Uns*": Hegemonic Religious Ideals, Emotions, and Mobilizing for War

1. Unteroffizier Georg Guertler, "Der Sieg des Glaubens im Felde," in *Liller Kriegszeitung*, ed. Hauptmann d. L. Hoecker and Rittmeister a.D. Frh. Von Ompteda (Berlin: Verlag von W. Vobach & Co., 1914), 133. This is a collected volume of articles from the army newspaper, *Liller Kriegszeitung*, located in PH 23/181, Bundesarchiv-Militärarchiv Freiburg (henceforth BArch-MA).
2. Ibid.
3. On German Catholic theologians who welcomed the chance to proclaim their nationalism and reinforce religious faith, see Houlihan, *Catholicism and the Great War*, 51–3.
4. On the Catholic church's prewar show of loyalty to national ideals, see Rebecca Ayako Bennette, *Fighting for the Soul of Germany: The Catholic Struggle for Inclusion after Unification* (Cambridge, MA: Harvard University Press, 2012).
5. On home/combat front gender dichotomies, see Hagemann and Schüler-Springorum, "Introduction—Home/Front: The Military, Violence and Gender Relations in the Age of the World Wars," in *Home/Front*, 1–42; on domesticity and national ideals, see Nancy R. Reagin, *Sweeping the German Nation: Domesticity and National Identity in Germany, 1870–1945* (Cambridge: Cambridge University Press, 2006). On these ideals through the eyes of Jewish women in imperial Germany, see Marion A. Kaplan, *The Making of the Jewish Middle Class: Women, Family, and Identity in Imperial Germany* (Oxford: Oxford University Press, 1991).
6. On the militarization of German society, see Roger Chickering, "Militärgeschichte als Totalgeschichte im Zeitalter des totalen Krieges," in *Was ist Militärgeschichte?* ed. Thomas Kühne and Benjamin Ziemann (Paderborn: Schöningh, 2002), 301–12.

7. This is not unique to Germany in the First World War. For a comparative context, see Michael Snape, *God and Uncle Sam: Religion and America's Armed Forces in World War II* (Suffolk: Boydell Press, 2015).
8. Jenkins, *The Great and Holy War*, 11; on the German Protestant church's enthusiastic support for the war, see Karl Hammer, "Der deutsche Protestantismus und der Erste Weltkrieg," *Francia*, 2 (1974): 398–414.
9. See Houlihan, *Catholicism and the Great War*, 29–33 and 51–4. See also Roger Chickering, *Imperial Germany and the Great War*, 51.
10. Heinrich Missalla, *"Gott mit uns": Die deutsche katholische Kriegspredigt, 1914–1918* (Munich: Kösel Verlag, 1968).
11. Anne Lipp, *Meinungslenkung im Krieg*, 273–5.
12. For an excellent overview of front newspapers, see Robert L. Nelson, *German Soldier Newspapers of the First World War*.
13. Author not given, "Kameraden!" *Liller Kriegszeitung*, ed. Hauptmann d.L. Hoecker and Rittmeister a.D. Frh. Von Ompteda (Berlin: Verlag von W. Vobach & Co., 1915), 73, PH 23/181, BArch-MA.
14. Jenkins, *The Great and Holy War*, 85.
15. Author not given, "Kaiserlied in Weltkriege," poem, *Kriegszeitung der 4 Armee*, Nr. 11, January 26, 1915, PH/5/II, BArch-MA.
16. "Ansprache," *Liller Kriegszeitung*, ed. Hoecker and Ompteda, preface, PH 23/181, BArch-MA.
17. Feldpredigter August Jaeger, "Gruess Gott zum Neuen Jahr," and "Bis zum Sieg – Ein Neujahr Gebet," in *Liller Kriegszeitung*, No. 6, January 11, 1915, PH 23/197, BArch-MA.
18. Author given as simply "H.v.R.," "Wir halten durch," *Die Somme-Wacht*, Nr. 14, 4 February 1917, p. 3, PH/5/II/1086, BArch-MA. English-language translation is the author's own.
19. Evangelische Gemeindeblatt, Bietigheim, September 1915 (from the Evang. Pfarramt I, Archiv, Bietigheim), in Christa Lieb, ed., *Zwischen Heimat und Front—Feldpost: Die Kriegsjahre 1914–1918 in Bietigheim, Bissingen, Metterzimmern und Untermberg*, Schriftenreihe des Archivs der Stadt Bietigheim-Bissingen, Band 8 (Stuttgart: Stadt Bietigheim-Bissingen Stadtarchiv, 2009), 16–17.
20. This tension is discussed by Andrea Hofman, "'Kämpfet Recht!' Themen einer evangelischen 'Soldatenethik' im Deutschen Reich während des ersten Weltkriegs," *Interdisciplinary Journal for Religion and Transformation*, 6:1 (2018): 88–105.
21. Julius Schiller, "Der deutsche Hass," *Kriegs-Zeitung der 4. Armee*, No. 13, February 2, 1915, PH/5/II, BArch-MA.
22. Will Vesper, *Kämpfer Gottes-Gesamtausgabe der historische Erzählungen* (Gütersloh: Bertelsmann, 1938).
23. Will Vesper, "Liebe oder Hass?" *Liller Kriegszeitung*, ed. Hoecker and Ompteda, 126, PH 23/181, BArch-MA. English-language translation is the author's own.
24. No author given, "Die sittliche Macht im Kriege," *Liller Kriegszeitung*, No. 36, April 3, 1915, PH 23/197, BArch-MA.
25. Evangelische Gemeindeblatt, Bietigheim, January 1915 (from the Evang. Pfarramt I, Archiv, Bietigheim), in Christa Lieb, ed., *Zwischen Heimat und Front*, 53–4.
26. Ibid.
27. On Jewish soldiers' shared experiences with trauma and brutalization, see Tim Grady, *A Deadly Legacy: German Jews and the Great War* (New Haven, CT: Yale University Press, 2017); for a fascinating overview of diverse German Jewish experiences in the

war, see Ulrike Heikaus and Julia B. Köhne, eds., *Krieg! Juden zwischen den Fronten 1914–1918* (Berlin: Hentrich und Hentrich, 2014).
28. On Jewish front soldiers' complex experiences with integration and discrimination, see Michael Geheran, "Rethinking Jewish Front Experiences," in *Beyond Inclusion and Exclusion: Jewish Experiences of the First World War in Central Europe*, ed. Crouthamel, Geheran, Grady, and Köhne (New York: Berghahn Books, 2018), 111–43; see also in the same volume Jason Crouthamel," 'My Comrades are for the Most Part on My Side': Comradeship between Non-Jewish and German Jewish Front Soldiers in the First World War," 228–56.
29. On case studies of Jewish chaplains' experiences, and the hope for inclusion despite the reality of antisemitism, see Sabine Hank, Hermann Simon, and Uwe Hank, *Feldrabbiner in den deutschen Streitkräften des Ersten Weltkrieges* (Berlin: Hentrich und Hentrich Verlag, 2010); Peter C. Appelbaum, *Loyalty Betrayed: Jewish Chaplains in the German Army During the First World War* (London: Valentine Mitchell, 2014).
30. Feldrabbiner Dr. Baerwald, "Krieg und Religion," *Liller Kriegszeitung*, No. 17, February 4, 1915, PH 23/197, BArch-MA.
31. Ibid.
32. Feldpfarrer Arnold, "Der brave Mann denkt an sich selbst zuletzt," *Kriegszeitung der 4. Armee*, No. 336, March 24, 1918, PH/5/II, BArch-MA.
33. Will Vesper, "Deutscher Kinder Kriegsgebet," *Liller Kriegszeitung*, ed. Hoecker and Ompteda, 40, PH 23/181, BArch-MA.
34. Letter from Sunday school class to Wilhelm W., September 29, 1914, MSG 2/18672, BArch-MA.
35. Letter from Maria H. to Wilhelm W., September 30, 1914, MSG 2/18672, BArch-MA.
36. Letter from Wilhelm W. to his students, May 2, 1915, MSG 2/18672, BArch-MA.
37. See Karen Hagemann, "Of 'Manly Valor' and 'German Honor,' Nation, War and Masculinity in the Age of the Prussian Uprising against Napoleon," *Central European History* 30 (1997): 187–220; on dominant images of militarized masculinity, see Ute Frevert, "Soldaten, Staatsbürger: Überlegungen zur historischen Konstruktion von Männlichkeit," in *Männergeschichte—Geschlechtergeschichte*, 82–5.
38. Andrew Donson, *Youth in the Fatherless Land—War Pedagogy, Nationalism, and Authority in Germany, 1914–1918* (Cambridge, MA: Harvard University Press, 2010), 49–51.
39. See George L. Mosse. *The Image of Man: The Creation of Modern Masculinity* (Oxford University Press, 1996), 86–90; Jason Crouthamel, "Male Sexuality and Psychological Trauma: Soldiers and Sexual 'Disorder' in World War I and Weimar Germany," *Journal of History of Sexuality*, 17:1 (January 2008): 60–84.
40. See also Ute Frevert, *A Nation in Barracks: Modern Germany, Military Conscription and Civil Society* (New York: Berg, 2004), 170–99.
41. George L. Mosse, "Shell Shock as a Social Disease," *Journal of Contemporary History*, 35:1 (2000): 101–8; see also Lerner, *Hysterical Men*.
42. On "muscular Christianity" in Britain, see Donald E. Hall, *Muscular Christianity: Embodying the Victorian Age* (Cambridge: Cambridge University Press, 2006).
43. Pfeilschifter is quoted in Paul Plaut's essay, "Psychographie des Kriegers," in *Beihefte zur Zeitschrift für angewandte Psychologie*, No. 21, ed. William Stern and Otto Lipmann (Leipzig, 1920), 71.
44. Ibid.
45. See Sían Hawthorne, "Introduction," *Gender: God*, xvi.

46. Felddivisionspfarrer Berchewitz, "Kriegerstand und Christenstand, Betrachtungen über die Kriegsleute im Neuen Testament," *Kriegszeitung der 4. Armee*, No. 240, April 15, 1917, PH/5/II, BArch-MA.
47. Ibid.
48. Thomas Kühne, *The Rise and Fall of Comradeship* (Cambridge: Cambridge University Press, 2017), 30–1. See also George L. Mosse, *Fallen Soldiers*, 24–8.
49. B. Pfister, Feldpredigter Inf.-Reg. 14, "Sei getrost und sei ein Mann," *Der Dienstkamerad—Feldzeitung der 3. Division*, No. 2, December 1916, PH8-I/896, BArch-MA.
50. Ibid.
51. Wilhelm Pressel, *Die Kriegspredigt 1914–1918 in Der Evangelischen Kirche Deutschlands* (Göttingen: Vandenhoeck & Ruprecht, 1967), 238–43, quoted from (and translated by) Philip Jenkins, *The Great and Holy War*, 85.
52. K. Kirmse, "Kriegers Nachtgebet," *Kriegszeitung der 4. Armee*, No. 190, October 15, 1916, PH/5/II, BArch-MA.
53. David Raub Snyder, *Sex Crimes in the Wehrmacht* (Omaha: University of Nebraska Press, 2009), 22.
54. Ernst Moritz Arndt, "Von der Manneszucht," excerpted from *Katechismus für den deutschen Wehrmann*, in *Kriegszeitung der 4. Armee*, No. 347, May 2, 1918, PH/5/II, BArch-MA.
55. Ibid.
56. Dechantpfarrer Heinrich Freiherr von Hausen, "Soldatentugenden," *Die Somme-Wacht*, No. 21, February 18, 1917, 1, PH/5/II/1086, BArch-MA.
57. Ibid., 2.
58. This idea that God was an antidote to nervous stress was not unique to German theologians, see Charlotte Methuen, "'The Very Nerve of Faith is Touched': British Preaching during the Great War," in *Predigt im Ersten Weltkrieg*, ed. Irene Dingel, Matthieu Arnold (Göttingen: Vandenhoeck & Rupprecht, 2017), 63–74.
59. Joachim Radkau, "Die Wende zur 'Willenskultur' in der Nerventherapie und das nervöse Doppelgesicht des Krieges Joachim Radkau" in *Nerven und Krieg* 37–52.
60. Von Hausen, "Soldatentugenden," *Die Somme-Wacht*, No. 21, February 18, 1917, 1, PH/5/II/1086, BArch-MA.
61. Ibid., 2–3.
62. Rebecca Ayako Bennette, *Diagnosing Dissent: Hysterics, Deserters, and Conscientious Objectors in Germany during World War One* (Ithaca, NY: Cornell University Press, 2020), 109. See also Guido Grünewald, *Zur Geschichte der Kriegsdienstverweigerung* (Essen: Deutsche Friedensgesellschaft, 1982).
63. Bennette, *Diagnosing Dissent*, 114–17.
64. Robert Gaupp, "Dienstverweigerung aus religiösen (und politischen) Gründen und ihre gerichtsärztliche Beurteilung," *Medizinisches Correspondenz-Blatt* 88 (1918): 167–9.
65. Patrick J. Houlihan, *Catholicism and the Great War*, 91–2.
66. Ibid.
67. Patrick J. Houlihan, "The Churches," in *1914–1918-online. International Encyclopedia of the First World War*, ed. Ute Daniel et al., issued by Freie Universität Berlin, Berlin. https://encyclopedia.1914-1918-online.net/article/the_churches?version=1.0
68. Felddivisionspfarrer Wilhelm Z. to the *Lahrer Zeitung*, Masuren (Eastern front), 15 March 1915, in Marcel Kellner und Knud Neuhoff, eds., "*Solange die Welt steht, ist soviel Blut nicht geflossen*": *Feldpostbriefe badischer Soldaten aus dem Ersten*

Weltkrieg 1914 bis 1918, Schriftenreihe der Badischen Heimat, Landesverein Badische Heimat e.V. und dem Landesverband Baden-Württemberg im Volksbund Deutsche Kriegsgräberfürsorge (Freiburg: Rombach, 2014), 122.

69. On the image versus the reality of the *Burgfrieden*, see Jeffrey Verhey, *The Spirit of 1914: Military, Myth and Mobilization in Germany* (Cambridge: Cambridge University Press, 2000); Steffan Bruendel, *Volksgemeinschaft oder Volksstaat: Die "Ideen von 1914" und die Neuordnung Deutschlands im Ersten Weltkrieg* (Berlin: DeGruyter, 2003).
70. Freiherr von Berlepsch's narrative is quoted within the article by Dr. Joannes Kleinpaul, "Religiöser Burgfriede," *Kriegszeitung der 4. Armee*, No. 195, November 2, 1916, PH/5/II, BArch-MA. On the resonance of Luther's famous hymn in wars since the nineteenth century, see Michael Fischer, *Religion, Nation, Krieg: Der Lutherchoral 'Ein feste Burg ist unser Gott* (Münster: Waxmann Verlag, 2014).
71. Ibid.
72. Rudolf V., letter to his wife, August 30, 1914, MsG2/2901, BArch-MA.
73. Willy L.'s file includes his *Feldgesangbuch für die evangelischen Mannschaften des Heeres*, MSG 2/5051 BArch-MA.
74. See David J. Fine, "Jüdische Soldaten und Religion an der Front," in *Krieg! Juden zwischen den Fronten, 1914–1918*, 133–54.
75. On Jewish women's auxiliary organizations and home front work, see Sabine Hank, "The Social Engagement of Jewish Women in Berlin during the First World War," in *Beyond Inclusion and Exclusion*, 203–28. On Jewish women's experiences with antisemitism on the home front, see Andrea Sinn, "In the Shadow of Antisemitism: Jewish Women and the German Home Front during the First World War," in *Beyond Inclusion and Exclusion*, 170–202.
76. Plaut's personal belongings were studied by Julia Barbara Köhne for her detailed analysis of Plaut's study of the war's traumatic effects. See Köhne, "Paper Psyches: On the Psychography of the Front Soldier According to Paul Plaut," in *Beyond Inclusion and Exclusion*, 331.
77. For more on sermons delivered by military chaplains, see Andrea Hofmann, "'Jesus im Schützengraben'—Kriegspredigten in Nachlässen pfälzischer und hessischer Pfarrer," in *Predigt im Ersten Weltkrieg*, ed. Irene Dingel, Matthieu Arnold, unter Mitarbeit (with help from) von Andrea Hofmann (Göttingen: Vandenhoeck & Ruprecht, 2017), 31–44.
78. Felddivisionspfarrer Otto Riemann, "Gottes Wort im Felde," *Liller Kriegszeitung*, No. 9, January 10, 1915, PH23/188, BArch-MA.
79. Gefr. Nickel, "Die Feldpredigt—Bei granatfeuer gehalten," *Kriegszeitung der 4. Armee*, No. 25, March 15, 1915, PH/5/II, BArch-MA.
80. Walter Bloem, "Deutscher Soldaten—Gottesdienst in Sainte Gudule," *Kriegszeitung der 4. Armee*, No. 31, April 5, 1915, PH/5/II, BArch-MA.
81. Oblt. Engelmann, "Gottesdienst," poem, *Liller Kriegszeitung—Sommerlese 1916*, ed. Hauptmann d.L. Hoecker, Dritter Band, Druck, and Verlag der Liller Kriegszeitung, 1916, 182.
82. Feldpfarrer Arnold, "Wenn Ihr fastet, sollt Ihr nicht sauer sehen—Eine Feldpredigt von Feldpfarrer Arnold" *Kriegszeitung der 4. Armee*, No. 263, July 3, 1917, BArch-MA, PH/5/II. Because the full name of this chaplain is not given, it is not certain whether this is Eberhard Arnold, who before the war was part of the German Student Christian Movement. Eberhard Arnold became critical of organized religion after the war and founded the Bruderhof Community, an international movement committed to peace.

83. For more extensive analysis of this war diary, see Jason Crouthamel, "Paul Lebrechts Kriegstagebuch," *Krieg! Juden zwischen den Fronten*, 105–32.
84. Paul Lebrecht Kriegstagebuch, September 24, 1916, Bayerisches Armeemuseum, made available by the Jüdisches Museum, München, thanks to Ulrike Heikaus and Julia B. Köhne.
85. Paul Lebrecht Kriegstagebuch, September 17, 1917.
86. Paul Lebrecht Kriegstagebuch, December 3, 1916, and January 18, 1917.
87. Paul Lebrecht Kriegstagebuch, September 19, 1917.
88. Paul Lebrecht Kriegstagebuch, September 16–17, 1917.
89. Paul Lebrecht Kriegstagebuch, December 3, 1916.
90. Kaspar G., May 24, 1915, letter, MSG 2/4563, BArch-MA.
91. Kaspar G., July 30, 1915, letter, MSG 2/4563, BArch-MA.
92. Kaspar G., September 5, 1915, letter to his mother, MSG 2/4563, BArch-MA.

2 God and the "Spirit of 1914": Religiosity of Ordinary Soldiers and Civilians at the Outbreak of the War

1. On image versus reality during those August 1914 days, see Verhey, *The Spirit of 1914*, 1–6.
2. On soldierly ideals of fighting to defend the home front and the German family under threat, see Nelson, *German Soldier Newspapers of the First World War*, 155–7.
3. Perhaps the most insightful analysis of the significance of fatalistic thinking, often tied closely to religious beliefs, as a mechanism for coping with violence, can be found in Watson, *Enduring the Great War*, 87–9.
4. For an interesting study of Berthold's exploits, see Robert William Rennie, "Privileged Killers, Privileged Deaths: German Culture and Aviation in the First World War: 1909–1925" (PhD dissertation, University of Tennessee, 2017), 155–7.
5. Rudolf Berthold, Kriegstagebuch, transcribed by his sister Franziska in 1928, July 30, 1914, p. 6, MSG 2/10722, BArch-MA.
6. Adolf Hitler, *Mein Kampf* (original 1925), trans. Ralph Manheim (New York: Houghton Mifflin, 1999), 161.
7. Ibid. On Hitler's experience in the Great War, see Thomas Weber, *Hitler's First War* (Oxford: Oxford University Press, 2011).
8. Gustav K., letter to his brother Walter, April 21, 1915, MSG 2/3788, BArch-MA.
9. Gustav K., letter to his parents and siblings, December 19, 1914, MSG 2/3788, BArch-MA.
10. Gustav K., letter to his parents, August 31, 1914, MSG 2/3788, BArch-MA.
11. Letter from Ruth N. to Uta von S., Bremen, October 26, 1914, in *1914- Briefe und Feldpostbriefe von Beginn des Ersten Weltkriegs*, ed. Horst Schöttler (Hamburg: Severus, 2014), 131.
12. Diary of Hedwig V., March 19, 1915, in *Verborgene Chronik, 1915–1918*, ed. Lisbeth Exner and Herbert Kapfer, herausgegeben vom Deutschen Tagesbucharchiv (Berlin: Galiani Verlag, 2017), 41.
13. Diary of Käthe L., January 21, 1916, in *Verborgene Chronik, 1915–1918*, 177.
14. Letter from Hermann T. to Irmagard T., December 1914, MSG 2/6629, BArch-MA.
15. Unknown author, "Gottesruhe im Kampf," *Die Kriegsflugblätter von Christentum und Gegenwart*, No. 5, published by editors Prof. Dr. Rittelmeyer and Frau Vogt [date of publication not given, probably 1914].

16. Ibid.
17. Ibid.
18. Ibid.
19. Hermann T., letter to his mother, January 31, 1915, MSG 2/6629, BArch-MA.
20. Willy L., letter to his parents, October 23, 1914, MSG 2/5051, BArch-MA.
21. Willy L., diary entries, October 16 and 22, 1914, MSG 2/5051, BArch-MA.
22. Letter from Willy L. to his parents, October 23, 1914, MSG 2/5051, BArch-MA.
23. Letter from Willy L. to his parents, March 3, 1915, MSG 2/5051, BArch-MA.
24. Letter from Willy L. to his parents, February 14, 1915, MSG 2/5051, BArch-MA.
25. Unknown soldier, letter to his family, France, November 1914, in "*Solange die Welt steht*," ed. Marcel Kellner und Knud Neuhoff, 72.
26. Letter from unknown *Landwehrmann*, France, November 1914, in "*Solange die Welt steht*," 71.
27. Wilhelm S., letter to his family, October 28, 1914, in "*Solange die Welt steht*," 66-7.
28. Joseph R., letter to his family, November 15, 1914, in "*Solange die Welt steht*," 78–9.
29. War diary of Otto B., August 23, 1914, Oldenburg, Württembergische Landesbibliothek Stuttgart (henceforth, WLS). This source is available on-line: http://www.wlbstuttgart.de/fileadmin/user_upload/sammlungen/BfZ/Themenportal/Tagebuecher/Borggraefe/Ta gebuch_Borggraefe.pdf. The original Tagesbuchheft as well as its transcription can be found in the Bibliothek für Zeitgeschichte, Lebensdokumentensammlung, Bestand N10.3.
30. Unknown soldier's letter, November 17, 1914, Argonne forest in "*Solange die Welt steht*," 81–2.
31. For a remarkable study of the cultural significance of Christmas in Germany, including during wartime, see Joe Perry, *Christmas in Germany—A Cultural History* (Chapel Hill: University of North Carolina Press, 2014), esp. ch. 3.
32. Dr. Aufhauser, "Weihnacht—das Fest treuester Liebe," *Liller Kriegszeitung*, No. 48, December 21, 1916, PH 23/200, BArch-MA.
33. See Perry, *Christmas in Germany*, 1–12.
34. Füsilier Bach to unknown recipient, France, December 25, 1914, in "*Solange die Welt steht*," 95.
35. For a narrative approach to the "Christmas Truce," see Stanley Weintraub, *Silent Night: The Story of the World War I Christmas Truce* (New York: Penguin, 2002).
36. Josef Peterhans, "Das Christkind will durch unsere Reihen gehen…", *Liller Kriegszeitung*, December 21, 1916, PH 23/200, BArch-MA.
37. Ibid.
38. Wilhelm L., letter to his pastor Johann M., December 23, 1915, in "*Solange die Welt steht*," 178.
39. Bruno C., letter to his wife, December 20, 1915, MSG 2/5903, BArch-MA.
40. Landsturmann FL to his wife December 20, 1915, in "*Solange die Welt steht*," 176–7.
41. Franz W., letter to an unknown recipient, December 19, 1915, in "*Solange die Welt steht*," 175–6.
42. Hermann S., letter to his wife Elly, December 19, 1914, MSG 2/13819, BArch-MA.
43. Hermann S., letter to his wife Elly, January 11, 1915, MSG 2/13819, BArch-MA.
44. Karl H., letter to his pastor, January 2, 1916, in "*Solange die Welt steht*," 185–6.
45. See Roper, *The Secret Battle*, xi.
46. Max M., diary entry, April 1915, in "*Solange die Welt steht*," 44–5.
47. Max M., diary entry, October 30, 1914, in "*Solange die Welt steht*," 36.
48. Max M., diary entry, April 17, 1915, in "*Solange die Welt steht*," 45.

49. Ulrich, *Die Augenzeugen*, 40, 78.
50. Letter from Minna F. to her husband, June 8, 1916, in *Was Tun Wir Hier: Soldatenpost und Heimatbriefe aus zwei Weltkriegen*, ed. Frank Schumann (Berlin: Verlag Neues Leben, 1989), 72-3.
51. Letter from Harry S. to Ida, Bazancow, March 17, 1915, Harry S. file, Bd. 1, Württembergische Landesbibliothek, Stuttgart, Feldpostbriefe, Sondersammlung Zeit der Weltkriege (henceforth, WLS/SZdW).
52. Letter from Hans S. to parents, August 3, 1918, Hans S. file, Bd. 2, WLS/SZdW.
53. Letter from David A. to his pastor, October 26, 1914, in "Solange die Welt steht," 65.
54. Letter from Schwester Gisela, October 5, 1914, im Lazarett to Frau K. [mother of soldier tended to by Gisela] in *1914—Briefe und Feldpostbriefe vom Beginn des Ersten Weltkriegs*, 111.
55. Letter from Rudolf V. to his wife, Julie, August 30, 1914, MsG 2/2901, BArch-MA.
56. Letter from Rudolf V. to his wife, Julie, October 17, 1914, MsG 2/2901, BArch-MA.
57. Ibid.
58. Letter from Rudolf V. to his wife, Julie, the handwritten poem was included in October 28, 1914 letter, MsG 2/2901, BArch-MA.
59. Ibid.
60. Peter Knoch, "Erleben und Nacherleben," in *"Keiner fühlt sich hier mehr als Mensch…,"* 209.
61. Watson, *Enduring the Great War*, 95.
62. Letter from Eduard F. to an unnamed priest, December 10, 1914, in "Solange die Welt steht," 90-1.
63. Historian Patrick J. Houlihan also argued that Catholic rituals and belief systems were particularly reassuring to front line soldiers. See Houlihan's *Catholicism and the Great War*, 1-2.
64. Franz H., letter to his parents, August 1914 [exact date not given], BArch-MA, MSG2/4563.
65. Sterbebild, Franz Xaver Heudorfer, von Schönebürg, fürs Vaterland gestorben am 7. Februar 1917, personal collection of the author.
66. Brian K. Feltman has closely examined family cultures of mourning in conference papers and will explore the topic further in the forthcoming *Sacrifice on Display: The Culture of Everyday Remembrance in Germany, 1914-1933*.
67. Letter from Ambrosius S. to Elisabeth B., Lenkirch, April 2, 1915, in "Solange die Welt steht," 128-9.
68. Anton K., letter to his wife, from Château-Salines, September 26, 1914, MSG2/4563, BArch-MA.
69. Ibid.
70. Max M., diary entry for June 29, 1915, in *Kasseler Soldaten im Ersten Weltkrieg— Tagebücher und Feldpostbriefe*, ed. Bettina Dodenhoeft (Kassel: Scribeo Verlag, 2014), 81.
71. Max M., diary entry for December 31, 1915, in *Kasseler Soldaten im Ersten Weltkrieg*, 93.
72. Ernst H., December 24, 1914, and February 8, 1915, letters to his grandmother and parents, respectively, MSG2/4101, BArch-MA.
73. Ernst H., letter to his mother, March 5, 1915, MSG2/4101, BArch-MA.
74. Ernst H., letter to his parents, May 20, 1915, MSG2/4101, BArch-MA.
75. Ernst H., letter to his grandmother, May 30, 1915, MSG2/4101, BArch-MA.

76. Ernst H., letter from the Depot des Prisonniers de Guerre, Plonignean, October 5, 1917, MSG2/4101, BArch MA. On the damaged masculine image of prisoners of war, see Brian K. Feltman, *The Stigma of Surrender: German Prisoners, British Captors, and Manhood in the Great War and Beyond* (Chapel Hill: University of North Carolina Press, 2015).

3 Processing Trauma: Nerves, Religious Language, and Coping with Violence

1. Letter from Georg G. to his wife, October 14, 1914, MsG2/3600, BArch-MA.
2. Letter from Georg G. to his wife, November 4, 1914, MsG2/3600, BArch-MA.
3. Letter from Georg G. to his wife, November 25, 1914, MsG2/3600, BArch-MA.
4. David Freis, "Psyche, Trauma, und Kollektiv—Der psychiatrische Diskurs über die erschütterten Nerven der Nation," in *Nerven und Krieg,* 53–76.
5. Quoted from Lerner, *Hysterical Men,* 40.
6. Showalter, "Rivers and Sassoon: The Inscription of Male Gender Anxieties," 61–9.
7. Psychologists have spearheaded studies on the appeal of religion's promise of salvation and redemption. See, for example, Riesebrodt, *The Promise of Salvation.*
8. For a particularly sensitive analysis of the complex ways in which emotions and religious language intersect, see Graham Dawson, "The Meaning of 'Moving On': From Trauma to the History of Emotions and Memory of Emotions in 'Post-Conflict' Northern Ireland," *Irish University Review* 47:1 (2017): 82–102.
9. The therapeutic effects of writing have been explored by literary scholars including Towheed, et al., "Readers and Reading in the First World War," 239–61; McCullis, "Bibliotherapy: Historical and research Perspectives," 23–38; Miller, "Medicines of the Soul," 17–34; on the diverse languages used to express trauma, including writing, see also the Introduction to *Languages of Trauma: History, Memory and Media,* ed. Peter Leese, Julia B. Köhne, and Jason Crouthamel (Toronto: University of Toronto Press, 2021).
10. On the diagnosis of "war neurosis," see Paul Lerner, *Hysterical Men*; Hans-Georg Hofer, *Nervenschwäche und Krieg—Modernitätskritik und Kriegsbewältigung in der österreicheschen Psychiatrie, 1880–1920* (Wien: Boehlau Verlag, 2004); on representations of "war hysterics" as unmanly, see Julia Barbara Köhne, *Kriegshysteriker: Strategische Bilder und mediale Techniken militärpsychiatrischen Wissens, 1914–1920* (Husum: Matthiesen, 2009).
11. For the best overview of medical debates over the origins of "war hysteria," see Lerner, *Hysterical Men,* ch. 3.
12. On statistics for psychiatric patients in the regular army, see Whalen, *Bitter Wounds,* 53.
13. Unknown author, "Geistege Gesundheitspflege," *Liller Kriegszeitung,* No. 4, August 11, 1915, PH23/198, BArch-MA.
14. Ibid.
15. On fighter pilots as the embodiment of warrior masculinity, see Stefanie Schüler-Springorum, "Flying and Killing—Military Masculinity in German Pilot Literature, 1914–1939," in *Home/Front—The Military, War and Gender in Twentieth-Century Germany,* ed. Karen Hagemann and Stefanie Schüler-Springorum (Oxford: Berg, 2002), 223–4.

16. On Boelcke's significance in inventing fighter tactics and becoming one of Germany's most famous heroes, see Peter Fritzsche, *A Nation of Fliers—German Aviation and the Popular Imagination* (Cambridge, MA: Harvard University Press, 1992), 70–3.
17. Dr. Georg Wegener, "Boelcke," originally published in the *Kölnischer Zeitung*, reprinted in *Der Flieger*,
No. 2, December 3, 1916, 1, PH 21/215, BArch-MA.
18. Feldgeistlicher Dr. Aufhauser, "Das Fest des Gottesgeistes," *Liller Kriegszeitung*, No. 105, June 9, 1916, PH23/199, BArch-MA.
19. Feldgeistlicher Dr. Aufhauser, "Gott und Selbstvertrauen," No. 1, August 1, 1917, PH/23/202, BArch-MA.
20. *Oberleutnant* Heydemarck, "Minus 30°," in *Der Flieger*, No. 17, March 24, 1917, PH 21/215, BArch-MA. This is an excerpt from a chapter that would be published in his memoir *Doppeldecker "C666"* (Berlin: Verlag August Scherl, 1916).
21. Mark Hewitson, *Germany and the Causes of the First World War* (Oxford: Berg, 2004), 95.
22. Heinrich M., "Die Kraft der Seele," *Kriegszeitung der 4. Armee*, No. 239, April 8, 1917, PH/5/II. BArch-MA.
23. Von der Goltz, "Die Menschenseele—Das Wunder," *Liller Kriegszeitung*, 4. Kriegsjahr, No. 25, October 12, 1917, PH 23/201, BArch-MA.
24. Ibid.
25. Bernt Hüfner, "Draußen," *Kriegszeitung der 4. Armee*, No. 335, March 21, 1918, PH/5/II, BArch-MA. English-language translation is the author's own.
26. Letter from Friedrich B. to his wife, November 2, 1914, MsG 2/4739, BArch-MA.
27. Ibid.
28. Ibid.
29. Johannes W., letter to his family, June 6, 1915, 3.2009.0064, Museumsstiftung Post und Telekommunikation, Feldpost 1914–1918 Sammlung, http://www.museumsstiftung.de/briefsammlung/feldpost-erster-weltkrieg/feldpost.html.
30. Ibid.
31. Baroness von Richthofen, *Mother of Eagles—The War Diary of Baroness von Richthofen*, ed. and trans. Susanne Hayes Fischer (Atglen, PA: Schiffer, 2001; orig. Baroness von Richthofen, *Mein Kriegstagebuch*, 1937), 167. Edited and condensed for publication in 1937, the original manuscript of the Baroness von Richthofen's wartime diaries must be seen in the context of National Socialist propaganda, which was preparing a new generation for another world war. Nevertheless, the mother's candid references to her son's psychological problems are striking. On this point, see Fehlemann, "Die Nerven der 'Daheimgebliebenen,'" 245–6.
32. Ibid., 169.
33. Ibid.
34. Ibid., 168–70.
35. Diary of WW in Bettina Dodenhoeft, ed., *Kasseler Soldaten im Ersten Weltkrieg—Tagebücher und Feldpostbriefe* (Kassel: Scribeo Verlag, 2014), 10.
36. Ibid., 51–2.
37. Letter from Berthold B. to his parents, October 28, 1914, in *Zwischen Heimat und Front*, 37.
38. Letter from Berthold B. to his pastor, January 1, 1915, in *Zwischen Heimat und Front*, 57.

39. Moritz R. letter to *Fräulein Pfaadt*, September 24, 1915, 3.2002.9085, Museumsstiftung Post und Telekommunikation, Feldpost 1914–1918 Sammlung, http://www.museumsstiftung.de/briefsammlung/feldpost-erster-weltkrieg/feldpost.html.
40. Elise K. to her husband Paul K., January 7, 1915, Bd. 1, Feldpostbriefe, WL/SZdW.
41. Fusilier Karl W. to Herr Herbst, Todtmoos, Res. Inf. Rgt Nr. 203, Belgiumn, May 4, 1915, in "*Solange die Welt steht,*" 137.
42. Von H. to Gisela, August 24, 1914, in *1914—Briefe und Feldpostbriefe vom Beginn des Ersten Weltkriegs*, 60–2.
43. Ibid.
44. Letter from Ludwig W. to his fiancée, Fräulein Kätchen W., September 10, 1914, in *1914—Briefe und Feldpostbriefe vom Beginn des Ersten Weltkriegs*, 84–5.
45. Musketier Joseph W., diary entry October 14, 1916, in "*Solange die Welt steht,*" 223–4.
46. Ibid.
47. Letter from AK, Labenville, March 20, 1915, in "*Solange die Welt steht,*" 124–5.
48. Unknown author, "Weissagung im Weltkrieg," *Kriegszeitung der 4ten Armee*, No. 384, September 8, 1918, PH/5/II, BArch-MA.
49. Wilhelm S., letter from November 15, 1914, Alexandrowo, to his wife and daughters, in *Feldpostbriefe von Mörfeldern und Walldorfern aus dem Ersten Weltkrieg 1914–1918*, 21.
50. Wilhelm S., letter from November 18, 1914, to his wife, in *Feldpostbriefe von Mörfeldern und Walldorfern aus dem Ersten Weltkrieg 1914–1918*, 22.
51. Wilhelm S., letter to his wife and daughters, December 11, 1914, in *Feldpostbriefe von Mörfeldern und Walldorfern aus dem Ersten Weltkrieg 1914–1918*, 24.
52. Wilhelm S., letter to his wife, December 31, 1914, in *Feldpostbriefe von Mörfeldern und Walldorfern aus dem Ersten Weltkrieg 1914–1918*, 26.
53. Ibid.
54. Jason Crouthamel, "Male Sexuality and Psychological Trauma," 60–84.
55. Wilhelm S., letter to his wife, July 15, 1915, Russia, in *Feldpostbriefe von Mörfeldern und Walldorfern aus dem Ersten Weltkrieg 1914–1918*, 29.
56. Wilhelm S., letter to his wife, January 11, 1915, Russia, in *Feldpostbriefe von Mörfeldern und Walldorfern aus dem Ersten Weltkrieg 1914–1918*, 27.
57. Antonia Helming, October 18, 1915, diary entry, which includes transcription of a October 15, 1915, letter from her son Hans, sent from the front, in Antonia Helming, "*Mutters Kriegstagebuch*"—*Die Aufzeichnungen der Antonia Helming, 1914–1922*, ed. Stephanie Fredewess-Wenstrup (Münster: Waxmann, 2005), 96.
58. Antonia Helming, November 1, 1915, diary entry, in Helming, "*Mutters Kriegstagebuch,*" 99.
59. Letter from Hermann sent on November 14, 1915, transcribed by Antonia Helming into her diary, November 21, 1915, in Helming, "*Mutters Kriegstagebuch,*" 103.
60. Ibid.
61. Antonia Helming, diary entry, December 26, 1915, in Helming, "*Mutters Kriegstagebuch,*" 109–10.
62. Antonia Helming, diary entry, March 3, 1918, in Helming, "*Mutters Kriegstagebuch,*" 234.
63. Antonia Helming, diary entry, August 20, 1918, in Helming, "*Mutters Kriegstagebuch,*" 252.
64. Letter from Hans W. to his mother, October 10, 1915, MSG 2/18172, BArch-MA.
65. Letters from Hans W. to his parents, January 10, 1916 and January 13, 1916, MSG 2/18172, BArch-MA.

66. Letter from Hans W. to his parents, January 23, 1916, MSG 2/18172, BArch-MA.
67. Letter from Hans W. to his parents, April 5, 1916, MSG 2/18172, BArch-MA.
68. Letter from Hans W. to his parents, December 24, 1916, MSG 2/18172, BArch-MA.
69. Letter from Hans W. to his parents, September 8, 1917, MSG 2/18172, BArch-MA.
70. Letter from Hans W. to his parents, December 14, 1917, MSG 2/18172, BArch-MA.
71. Letter from Hans W. to his parents, July 19, 1918; in this letter he mentions that one of his recent letters was returned to him by military censors, MSG 2/18172, BArch-MA.
72. Letters from Hans W. to his parents, July 26, 1918 and October 1918, MSG 2/18172, BArch-MA.
73. See Hans Wulf August 5, 1914 and August 8, 1914 entries, in Ilse Hoffmann (geb. Wulf), ed., *Hans Wulf—Briefe und Tagebuch eines Rendsburger Soldaten im Ersten Weltkrieg* (Rendsburg: Druckerei Albers, 2003), 22.
74. Letter from Hans Wulf's mother to Hans Wulf, October 25, 1914, in *Hans Wulf*, 43.
75. Letter from Hans Wulf to his mother, December 10, 1914, in *Hans Wulf*, 49.
76. Letter from Hans Wulf to his brother, January 19, 1915, in *Hans Wulf*, 60.
77. Letter from Hans Wulf to his mother, April 22, 1915, in *Hans Wulf*, 75.
78. Letter from Hans Wulf to his mother, April 23, 1919, in *Hans Wulf*, 103.

4 "Where Is God?" The Brutalization of Faith in the Front Experience

1. Musketier Emil Z., letter to his parents, December 4, 1915, in *Zwischen Heimat und Front*, 124–5.
2. Musketier Emil Z., letter to his sister Mathilde, December 12, 1916, in *Zwischen Heimat und Front*, 180.
3. Musketier Emil Z., letter to his sister Mathilde, January 3, 1917, in *Zwischen Heimat und Front*, 185.
4. In a recent overview on the historiography of trauma, and suggestions for new trajectories for scholarly research, Mark Micale observed that trauma to religious values is an avenue of research that still needs historians' attention. Mark S. Micale, "Beyond the Western Front: Studying the Trauma of War in Northern and East Central Europe," keynote given at the conference "Aftershocks: War-related Trauma in Northern, Eastern, and Central Europe," University of Tampere, Finland, October 25, 2018.
5. See Edward Madigan, *Faith under Fire—Anglican Army Chaplains and the Great War*, ch. 5.
6. On diverse approaches to "moral injury," see Susan Derwin, "Moral Injury: Two Perspectives," 47–65.
7. Letter from Maximilan J. to Kurt B., student in Dissen, September 6, 1916, the Somme, Bd. 1, Feldpostbriefe, WLS/SZdW. Thanks to Irina Renz for making this collection available and for her help in finding sources.
8. Letter from Maximilian J. to Kurt B., Lille, September 26, 1916, Bd. 1, Feldpostbriefe, WLS/SZdW.
9. Letter from Maximilian J. to Kurt B., November 12, 1916, Bd. 1, Feldpostbriefe, WLS/SZdW.
10. Letter from Maximilian J. to Kurt B., January 18, 1917, Bd. 1, Feldpostbriefe, WLS/SZdW.

11. Ibid.
12. Letter from Maximilian J. to Kurt B., February 22, 1917, Bd. 1, Feldpostbriefe, WLS/SZdW.
13. Letter from Maximilian J. to unknown, February 10, 1918, Bd. 1, Feldpostbriefe, WLS/SZdW.
14. Letter from Maximilian J. to Kurt B., August 25, 1918, Bd. 1, Feldpostbriefe, WLS/SZdW.
15. Letter from Maximilian J. to Kurt B., June 20, 1918, Bd. 1, Feldpostbriefe, WLS/SZdW.
16. Letter from Heinrich G. to his father, December 20, 1914, MSG 2/2735, BArch-MA.
17. Letter from Heinrich G. to his father, December 11, 1914, MSG 2/2735, BArch-MA.
18. Ibid.
19. Ibid.
20. Letter from Heinrich G., at Vimy/Arras, to his father, November 4, 1915, MSG 2/2735, BArch-MA.
21. Ibid.
22. Letter from Heinrich G. to his father, December 1915 (no exact date given), Vimy/Arras, MSG 2/2735, BArch-MA.
23. See, for example the *Berliner Illustrirte Zeitung*, XXVI Jahrgang, No. 15, April 5, 1917.
24. Leonhard Müller, *Fliegerleutnant Heinrich Gontermann—Nach seinen Auszeichnungen und Briefen* (Barmen-U.: Verlag des Westdeutschen Jünglingsbundes, 1919), 2. Staatsbibliothek Berlin.
25. Ibid., 5.
26. Heinrich Gontermann letter to his parents, March 18, 1916, in Leonhard Müller, *Fliegerleutnant Heinrich Gontermann*, 65–6.
27. Heinrich Gontermann letter to his mother, February 15, 1915, in Leonhard Müller, *Fliegerleutnant Heinrich Gontermann*, 29.
28. Ibid., 64.
29. Heinrich Gontermann letter to his parents, October 5, 1916, in Leonhard Müller, *Fliegerleutnant Heinrich Gontermann*, 70–1.
30. Ibid., 72–3.
31. Lee Kennett, *The First Air War, 1914–1918* (New York: Macmillan, 1991), 145–7.
32. Heinrich Gontermann letter to his parents, February 10, 1917, in Leonhard Müller, *Fliegerleutnant Heinrich Gontermann*, 79–80.
33. Heinrich Gontermann letter to his parents, March 28, 1917, in Leonhard Müller, *Fliegerleutnant Heinrich Gontermann*, 82.
34. Heinrich Gontermann letter to his parents, June 20, 1917, in Leonhard Müller, *Fliegerleutnant Heinrich Gontermann*, 96.
35. Heinrich Gontermann letter to his parents, July 10, 1917, in Leonhard Müller, *Fliegerleutnant Heinrich Gontermann*, 99–100.
36. Leonhard Müller, *Fliegerleutnant Heinrich Gontermann*, 100.
37. Heinrich Gontermann letter to his parents, July 16, 1917, in Leonhard Müller, *Fliegerleutnant Heinrich Gontermann*, 101.
38. Leonhard Müller, *Fliegerleutnant Heinrich Gontermann*, 103.
39. Ernst Udet, *Ace of the Iron Cross* (originally *Mein Fliegerleben*, 1935, trans. Richard K. Riehn, New York: Doubleday, 1970), 41.
40. Ibid., 51.
41. Ibid., 51–2.
42. Heinrich Gontermann letter to his parents, September 29, 1917, in Leonhard Müller, *Fliegerleutnant Heinrich Gontermann*, 106.

43. Heinrich Gontermann letter to unnamed young woman, October 28, 1917, in Leonhard Müller, *Fliegerleutnant Heinrich Gontermann*, 111.
44. Leonhard Müller, *Fliegerleutnant Heinrich Gontermann*, 137–8.
45. Ibid., 127–30.
46. Ibid., 138.
47. Edwin Halle, "Kriegsinnerungen mit Auszügen aus meinem Tagebuch, 1914–1916," April 10, 1915 entry, p. 11 of the manuscript, ME 250.MM31, Leo Baeck Institute Archive, New York (henceforth LBINY).
48. Ibid.
49. Ibid., 9–10.
50. Ibid.
51. Edwin Halle, "Kriegsinnerungen," July 25, 1915 entry, p. 15 of the manuscript, ME 250.MM31, LBINY.
52. Edwin Halle, "Kriegsinnerungen," September 10, 1915 entry, pp. 21–2 of the manuscript, ME 250.MM31, LBINY.
53. Ibid.
54. Edwin Halle, "Kriegsinnerungen," September 19, 1915 entry, p. 24 of the manuscript. Halle's diary only goes through September 1915, ME 250.MM31, LBINY.
55. Edwin Halle, "Kriegsinnerungen," undated, p. 25 of the digital file, ME 250.MM31, LBINY.
56. Verleihung des Ehrenkreuzes an Nichtarier (Paragraph 6), "Zweite Zusammenstellung der vom Reichsministerium des Innern zur Durchführung des Verfahrens bei der Verleihung des Ehrenkreuzes des Weltkrieges herausgegebenen Richtlinien," R1501/125280a/b, Bundesarchiv Berlin-Lichterfelde (henceforth BArch) Thanks to my generous colleague Michael Geheran for sharing this source.
57. Edwin Halle, "Kriegsinnerungen mit Auszügen aus meinem Tagebuch, 1914–1916," undated, p. 25 of the digital file, ME 250.MM31, LBINY.
58. Ibid. English-language translation is the author's own.
59. Karl B., to an unknown recipient, August 24, 1916, in *"Solange die Welt steht,"* 213–14.
60. Georg G., letter to his wife, November 13, 1914, MSG2/3600, BArch-MA.
61. Georg G., letter to wife, November 13, 1914, MSG2/3600, BArch-MA.
62. Georg G., letter to wife, January 11, 1915, MSG2/3600, BArch-MA.
63. Georg G., letter to wife, January 20, 1915, MSG2/3600, BArch-MA.
64. Leutnant Mundschick's letter [undated—from early 1916] to Otto von R., enclosed in Otto von R.'s June 7, 1916, letter to his sister, MSG 2/11374, BArch-MA.
65. Ibid.
66. Ibid.
67. Letter from Otto von R. to his sister, June 7, 1916, MSG 2/11374, BArch-MA.
68. Letter from Otto von R. to his family, September 22, 1915, MSG 2/11374, BArch-MA.
69. Letter from Otto von R. to his family, September 26, 1915, MSG 2/11374, BArch-MA.
70. Ibid.
71. Friedel H. to Hellmuth B., October 12, 1916, in *Zwischen Heimat und Front*, ed. Christa Lieb, 172–3.
72. Letter from Ernst to August S., September 2, 1915, MSG2/19075, BArch-MA.
73. Letter from August S. to Ernst, S., September 2, 1915, MSG2/19075, BArch-MA. English-language translation is the author's own.
74. Feldwebel Rudolf H. to an unknown pastor, November 16, 1917, in *"Solange die Welt steht,"* 293.
75. Ibid.

76. Landsturmann SL to an unknown recipient, March 22, 1917, in "*Solange die Welt steht,*" 260–1.
77. Ibid.
78. Ibid.
79. Siegfried E., May 15, 1915, diary entry, in *Verborgene Chronick, 1915–1918,* 66–7.
80. Ibid.
81. Ibid.
82. Siegfried E., January 6, 1916, diary entry, in in *Verborgene Chronick, 1915–1918,* 171.
83. Siegfried E., March 13, 1916, diary entry, in *Verborgene Chronick, 1915–1918,* 202.
84. Siegfried E., April 13, 1916, diary entry, in *Verborgene Chronick, 1915–1918,* 213.
85. Siegfried E., 11 April 1916, diary entry, in *Verborgene Chronick, 1915–1918,* 212.
86. Siegfried E., March 28, 1916, diary entry, in *Verborgene Chronick, 1915–1918,* 207.
87. Siegfried E., February 6, 1917, diary entry, in *Verborgene Chronick, 1915–1918,* 329.
88. Siegfried E., May 13, 1917, diary entry, in *Verborgene Chronick, 1915–1918,* 357.
89. Siegfried E., May 30, 1917, diary entry, in *Verborgene Chronick, 1915–1918,* 375.
90. Siegfried E., October 25, 1918, diary entry, in *Verborgene Chronick, 1915–1918,* 638.
91. Siegfried E., December 1918, diary entry, in *Verborgene Chronick, 1915–1918,* 699.
92. Artur H. Boer, *The Great War from the German Trenches: A Sapper's Memoir, 1914–1918,* ed. and trans. Bertil van Boer and Margaret L. Fast (Jefferson, NC: McFarland, 2016), 107.
93. Ibid.
94. Hans F., March 16, 1916, diary entry, MSG 2/2735, BArch-MA.
95. Letter from Rudolf G. to his parents, December 2, 1915, in *Kasseler Soldaten im Ersten Weltkrieg,* 115.
96. From Rudolf G's memoirs, written in 1917, exact date not given, in *Kasseler Soldaten im Ersten Weltkrieg,* 132–3.
97. Ibid.
98. Marlene Dietrich, *Marlene,* trans. Salvator Attanasio (New York: Grove Press, 1989), 11.
99. Ibid., 9.
100. Ibid., 10.
101. Ibid., 11.
102. Ibid., 25.

5 Diagnosing Religious Beliefs: Contemporary Scientific and Popular Debates over the Spiritual-Psychological Effects of the War

1. Georg Willers, "Der Krieg und Gottesglaube," in *Der Flieger,* No. 29, June 24, 1917, PH 21/215, BArch-MA.
2. Ibid.
3. Sources on George Willers' biographical data are scarce. After the war, he continued to pursue language study and eventually completed his PhD in 1923 and then taught high school for ten years. In 1933, he gave prodemocratic lectures and published articles critical of Adolf Hitler's militaristic rhetoric until he was fired from his teaching job and placed under Gestapo surveillance. Impoverished and socially marginalized, he was only able to resume teaching after 1945, and he returned

to English instruction at the University of Kiel until his retirement in the 1960s. This basic biographical information comes from a genealogy maintained by his family: http://www.lyndonirwin.com/willersn.htm (accessed May 11, 2020).
4. On Sigmund Freud's analysis of the war's implications for religious life, see Todd Dufrese, *The Late Sigmund Freud: Or, The Last Word on Psychoanalysis, Society, and All the Riddles of Life* (Cambridge: Cambridge University Press, 2017), 68–70. For an overview on prevailing interwar psychiatric discourse on the sexual impact of the war, see Crouthamel, "Male Sexuality and Psychological Trauma," 60–84.
5. For in-depth background and analysis of Stern and Lipmann's Institute for Applied Psychology, see Köhne, "Paper Psyches: On the Psychography of the Front Soldier According to Paul Plaut," 319–23.
6. Köhne, "Paper Psyches," 318–20.
7. Much of the material in the original surveys is missing. See Ulrich, *Die Augenzeugen*, 295.
8. Plaut Paul, "Psychographie des Kriegers," in *Beihefte zur Zeitschrift für angewandte Psychologie*, No. 21, ed. William Stern and Otto Lipmann (Leipzig: Johann Ambrosius Barth, 1920), 1–123, questionnaire: 111–18.
9. Köhne, "Paper Psyches," 325, 331.
10. Ibid., 319, 350.
11. Plaut, "Psychographie des Kriegers," 70.
12. Ibid., 72.
13. Ibid., 72–3.
14. Ibid., 73.
15. Ibid.
16. Ibid., 73.
17. Ibid., 73–4.
18. Ibid.
19. Ibid., 74.
20. Ibid.
21. Ibid., 75.
22. Ibid.
23. Ibid.
24. Ibid.
25. Ibid., 76.
26. Ibid.
27. Ibid., 77.
28. Ibid. To support his argument, Plaut cites Albert Hellwig's dissertation, "Zur Psychologie des Aberglaubens," University of Kiel, 1910, 14–15.
29. Plaut, "Psychographie des Kriegers," 78.
30. Ibid., 79.
31. Ibid.
32. Watson, *Enduring the Great War*, 236.
33. Jörn Leonhard, *Pandora's Box: A History of the First World War*, trans. Patrick Camiller (Cambridge, MA: Harvard University Press, 2020), 496.
34. Watson, *Enduring the Great War*, 236.
35. Walter Ludwig, "Beiträge zur Pychologie der Furcht im Kriege," in William Stern and Otto Lipmann, eds., *Beihefte zur Zeitschrift für angewandte Psychologie* 21 (Leipzig: Johann Ambrosius Barth, 1920), 168.
36. Ibid., 168–9.

37. Ibid., 169.
38. Quoted from Leonhard, *Pandora's Box*, 496-7, translation by Patrick Camiller, originally from Walter Ludwig, *Beiträge zur Psychologie der Furcht im Kriege. Inaugural-Dissertation zur Erlangung der Doktorwüde einer hohen Philosophischen Fakultät der Universität Tübingen* (Leipzig: J.A. Barth, 1919), 7.
39. Ludwig, "Beiträge zur Psychologie der Furcht im Kriege," 172.
40. Ibid., 170.
41. Ibid.
42. Ibid., 171.
43. Ibid.
44. Ibid., 172.
45. E. Schiche, "Über Todesahnungen im Felde und ihre Wirkung," in William Stern and Otto Lipmann, eds., *Beihefte zur Zeitschrift für angewandte Psychologie* 21 (Leipzig: Johann Ambrosius Barth, 1920), 173.
46. Ibid.
47. Ibid., 173-4.
48. Ibid., 177.
49. Ibid., 175-6.
50. Ibid., 176.
51. Ibid., 175.
52. Ibid., 176.
53. Ibid., 177-8.
54. Gary Stark, *Entrepreneurs of Ideology: Neoconservative Publishers in Germany, 1890-1933* (Chapell Hill: University of North Carolina Press, 1981), 43.
55. Ibid.
56. Ibid., 46-8.
57. Ibid., 46.
58. From Erich Everth, Sächsische Biografie: https://saebi.isgv.de/biografie/Erich%20Everth%20 (1878-1934).
59. Hesse published his review of Everth in the December 12, 1915, edition of the *Neue Zürcher Zeitung*, which is cited by Josef Mileck, *Hermann Hesse* (Berkeley: University of California Press, 1977), 42.
60. Erich Everth, *Von der Seele des Soldaten im Felde—Bemerkungen eines Kriegsteilnehmers,* Tat-Flugschriften 10 (Jena: Eugen Diedrichs, 1915), 1.
61. Ibid., 17.
62. Ibid., 2.
63. Ibid., 5.
64. Ibid., 23-4.
65. Ibid., 32-4.
66. Ibid. 44.
67. Ibid.
68. Ibid., 44-5.
69. Ibid., 45.
70. Ibid., 47.
71. Ibid.
72. Ibid., 45.
73. Ibid.
74. Ibid., 48.

75. Erik Koenen, "Ein 'einsamer' Wissenschaftler? Erich Everth und das Leipziger Institut für Zeitungskunde zwischen 1926 und 1933. Ein Beitrag zur Bedeutung des Biographischen für die Geschichte der Zeitungswissenschaft," *Medien & Zeit*, 20:1 (2005): 38–50.
76. Paul Göhre, *Wie ein Pfarrer Sozialdemokrat wurde* (Berlin: Vorwärts, 1906).
77. Paul Göhre, "Der Krieg und die Geschlechter," *Der Flieger*, No. 2, 2. Jahrgang, 30 Dez. 1917, PHD 18/6, BArch-MA.
78. The three essays included "Religionspsychologisches aus dem Schützengraben," which first appeared in *Deutsche Politik*, Jahrgang 1, Heft 26, June 23, 1916; "Front und Politik," *Deutsche Politik*, Jahrgang 2, Heft 14, April 6, 1917; and "Der Krieg und die Geschlechter," *Die Tat*, Jahrgang 9, Heft 4, July 1917.
79. Paul Göhre, *Front und Heimat—Religiöses, Politisches, Sexuelles aus dem Schützengraben*, Tat-Flugschriften 22 (Jena: Eugen Diedrichs, 1917), 1.
80. Ibid., 2.
81. Ibid.
82. Ibid., 3.
83. Ibid.
84. Ibid., 4.
85. Ibid.
86. Ibid.
87. Ibid., 7.
88. Ibid.
89. Ibid., 7–8.
90. Ibid., 8.
91. Ibid., 9.
92. Ibid., 10.
93. Ibid., 11–12.
94. Ibid., 13.
95. Ibid.
96. Paul Göhre, *Der unbekannte Gott—Versuch einer Religion des modernen Menschen* (Leipzig: Verlag von Fr. Wilh. Grunow, 1919), 16.

6 Alternative Beliefs in the Trenches: Superstitions, Gods and Monsters, and Religious Humor

1. Patrick J. Houlihan, "Religious Mobilization and Popular Belief," in *1914–1918 online. International Encyclopedia of the First World War*, ed. Ute Daniel, Peter Gatrell, Oliver Janz, Heather Jones, Jennifer Keene, Alan Kramer, and Bill Nasson, issued by Freie Universität Berlin, Berlin, August 26, 2015. doi: 10.15463/ie1418.10716.
2. This dilemma has been noted by a number of historians, including Owen Davies, *A Supernatural War*, 13; Annette Becker, "Faith, Ideologies, and the "Cultures of War," in *A Companion to World War I*, ed. John Horne (Chichester: Wiley-Blackwell, 2010), 234–47; Friedrich Wilhelm Graf, "'Dechristianisierung': Zur Problemgeschichte eines kulturpolitischen Topos," in *Säkularisierung, Dechristianisierung, Rechristianisierung im neuzeitlichen Europa*, ed. Hartmut Lehmann (Göttingen: Vandenhoeck & Rupprecht, 1997), 32–66.

3. Patrick J. Houlihan, "Religious Mobilization and Popular Belief," in *1914–1918 online. International Encyclopedia of the First World War*.
4. On the problems with terms like 'popular belief,' see Laura A. Smoller, "'Popular' Religious Culture(s)," in *The Oxford Handbook of Medieval Christianity*, ed. John H. Arnold (Oxford: Oxford University Press, 2014).
5. Houlihan, *Catholicism*, 11.
6. See Houlihan, *Catholicism*, 128. Houlihan refers to Karl Egger's *Seele im Sturm: Kriegserleben eines Feldgeistlichen* (Innsbruck: F. Rauch, 1936), 141–4.
7. On the persistence of working-class traditional culture into the industrial age, see E. P. Thomspon, *Customs in Common: Studies in Traditional Popular Culture* (New York: New Press, 1993); on rural traditions providing continuity with prewar life, see Benjamin Ziemann, *War Experiences in Rural Germany*, 124–5.
8. Jay M. Winter, *The Experience of World War I* (London: Macmillan, 1988), 149.
9. Davies, *A Supernatural War*, 1.
10. Hanns Bächtold, *Deutscher Soldatenbrauch und Soldatenglaube*, herausgegeben vom Verband deutscher Vereine für Volkskunde (Straßburg: Verlag von Karl J. Trübner, 1917), 1–2. For more background on Bächtold, see Jenkins, *The Great and Holy War*, 121.
11. Ibid., 32. Over 60,000 POWs from various nations, many of them wounded or ill, were interned in Switzerland during the war as a result of humanitarian efforts. See Thomas Bürgisser, "Internees (Switzerland)," in *1914–1918 online. International Encyclopedia of the First World War*, issued by Freie Universität Berlin, Berlin September 29, 2015.
12. See Benjamin Ziemann, *War Experiences in Rural Germany*, esp. ch. 4.
13. Bächtold, *Deutscher Soldatenbrauch und Soldatenglaube*, 9–10.
14. Ibid., 12–14.
15. Ibid., 25–7.
16. Davies, *A Supernatural War*, 1.
17. Dr. P. Sünner, "Berichte über Spontanphänomene," *Zeitschrift für Parapsychologie*, 7. Jahrgang, 5. Heft, Mai 1932, 204. P. Sünner was the director of a hospital in the Herzberge, and the journal included contributions from professors of psychology and medicine at the University of Zürich, University of Bonn, University of Vienna, and other leading institutions.
18. Press coverage and summaries of the supernatural activity at Großerlach are summarized by Bruno Grabinski in *Spuk—und Geistererscheinungen oder was sonst?—eine kritische Untersuchung* (Hildesheim: Franz Borgmeyer Verlag, 1922), 204–24.
19. Bruno Grabinski, *Neuere Mystik—Der Weltkrieg im Aberglauben und im Lichte der Prophetie* (Hildesheim: Verlag von Franz Borgmeyer, 1916), vii. Grabinski was quite prolific in producing numerous studies of the paranormal with Franz Borgmeyer's popular press, including *Das Übersinnliche im Weltkriege: Merkwürdige Vorgänge im Felde und allerlei Kriegsprophezeiungen* (Hildesheim: Verlag von Franz Borgmeyer, 1917).
20. Grabinski, *Neuere Mystik*, 330–3.
21. Ibid., 18–21.
22. Ibid., 459.
23. Letter from Minna F. to her husband, July 16, 1915, in Frank Schumann, ed. *Was Tun Wir Hier: Soldatenpost und Heimatbriefe aus zwei Weltkriegen* (Berlin: Verlag Neues Leben, 1989), 50. Quoted (translation) from Patrick J. Houlihan, "Religious

Mobilization and Popular Belief," in *1914–1918 online. International Encyclopedia of the First World War*.
24. Letter from Minna F. to her husband, January 1, 1915, in Frank Schumann, ed., *Was Tun Wir Hier*, 24–5.
25. Heinz T., 24.12.15 entry, Kriegstagebuch, MSG 2/1130, BArch-MA.
26. Heinz T., 13.11.18 entry, Kriegstagebuch, MSG 2/1130, BArch-MA.
27. Ibid. His note about his return to the Verdun battlefield appears at the end of this file.
28. Plaut, "Psychographie des Kriegers," 79–80.
29. Lothar von Richthofen, "Memories of My Brother," in Manfred von Richthofen, *The Red Baron*, trans. Peter Kilduff (originally published in 1920 as *Ein Heldenleben*, 1920, New York: Charter, 1969), 119.
30. Lothar von Richthofen, "Berichte von Manfreds Bruder," from Manfred von Richthofen, *Ein Heldenleben* (Berlin: Verlag Ullstein & Co., 1920) quoted (and translation) from Lance J. Bronnenkant, *The Blue Max Airmen*, vol. 8 (Reno: Aeronaut Books, 2016), 82.
31. Lothar von Richthofen, quoted from Manfred von Richthofen, *Ein Heldenleben* (Berlin: Verlag Ullstein, 1920), 222.
32. Author given as "Sp," "Das Amulett," *Der Flieger*, No. 30, May 19, 1918, PH 21/216, BArch-MA.
33. Ibid.
34. Edmund Scheibener, "Soldaten-Aberglaube," *Kriegszeitung der 4. Armee*, No. 31, November 5, 1915, PH/5/II, BArch-MA. Scheibener also published before the war, *Das Gewitter und seine Begleiterscheinungen im Aberglauben des deutschen Volkes* (1913). On *Himmelsbriefe*, see also Houlihan, *Catholicism and the Great War*, 148–9.
35. Letter from Minna F. to her son, January 15, 1915, in Frank Schumann, ed., *Was Tun Wir Hier*, 27.
36. Scheibener, "Soldaten Aberglaube."
37. Fritz Mack, "Zufall, Ahnung, Aberglaube," in *Kriegszeitung der 4. Armee*, No. 119, February 7, 1916, PH/5/II, BArch-MA.
38. Gefreiter Ernst Oehrlein, "Soldaten und Aberglaube," *Kriegszeitung der 4. Armee*, No. 380, August 25, 1918, PH/5/II, BArch-MA. This article by Oehrlein also appeared in the *Liller Kriegszeitung*, No. 5, August 13, 1918, PH23/203, BArch-MA.
39. Ibid.
40. Davies, *A Supernatural War*, 54–5.
41. Ibid., 75.
42. "Der Eigenbrödler" is difficult to translate. "Der Eigenbrötler" is slang for a "loner" or a "maverick" (literally "one who bakes one's own bread"). It is used to describe someone who is unconventional. Thanks to Julia B. Köhne for her expertise in translating this term.
43. Kanonier F. Schiefer, "Die Geisterhand," *Der Eigenbrödler*, No. 19, August 30, 1918, PH22-I/51, BArch-MA.
44. Ibid.
45. On the demonization of 'foreign women,' see Robert L. Nelson, "German Comrades-Slavic Whores," in *Home/Front—The Military, War and Gender in Twentieth Century Germany*, 69–86.
46. Gefreiter Rust, "Seele," *Liller Kriegszeitung*, No. 104, July 7, 1917, PHD 23/201, BArch-MA.
47. Rudolf Stark, *Wings of War: An Airman's Diary of the Last Year of World War One* (originally *Die Jagdstaffel unsere Heimat: Ein Flieger-Tagebuch aus dem*

letzen Kriegsjahr), trans. Claud W. Sykes (Leipzig: Verlag von K.F. Koehler, 1932; London: Greenhill Books, 1993), 46.
48. See, for example, in the original edition of Rudolf Stark, *Die Jagdstaffel unsere Heimat: Ein Flieger-Tagebuch aus dem letzen Kriegsjahr* (Leipzig: Verlag von K.F. Koehler, 1932), 36.
49. Karl Außerhofer, September 18, 1914 diary entry, in Sigrid Wisthaler, ed., *Karl Außerhofer—Das Kriegstagebuch eines Soldaten im Ersten Weltkrieg* (Innsbruck: Innsbruck University Press, 2010), 91.
50. Karl Außerhofer, August 3, 1915 diary entry, in *Karl Außerhofer*, 103.
51. See for example Karl Außerhofer diary entries, August 27, 1915 and August 4, 1916, in in *Karl Außerhofer*, 131 and 161, respectively.
52. Letter from Ernst R. to August S., September 3, 1915, MSG 2/19075, BArch-MA. English-language translation is the author's own.
53. Ibid.
54. Letter from Ernst R. to August S., March 9, 1916, MSG 2/19075, BArch-MA.
55. Letter from Ernst R. to August S., May 12, 1916, MSG 2/19075, BArch-MA.
56. Letter from Ernst R. to August S., October 2, 1916, MSG 2/19075, BArch-MA.
57. Letter from Ernst R. to August S., November 8, 1917, MSG 2/19075, BArch-MA.
58. Letter from Heinrich S. to August S., Wangeresen, November 21, 1917, MSG 2/19075, BArch-MA.
59. Arnold (artist), "Der Beherrscher des Meeres," *Liller Kriegszeitung*, No. 29, October 25, 1916, PH/23/200, BArch-MA.
60. Carl Wilhelm Marscher, "Der deutsche Schrecken," *Liller Kriegszeitung*, ed. Hoecker und von Ompteda (Berlin: Berlag von W. Voback, 1917), 134, BArch-MA, MSG 2/8183.
61. O. J. Olbertz (artist), "Die verfluchte Aufraemearbeit," *Liller Kriegszeitung*, No. 105, June 10, 1917, BArch-MA, PH/23/201.
62. O. J. Olbertz (artist), "Englands Hexenkessel," *Liller Kriegszeitung*, No. 50, December 27, 1916, BArch-MA, PH/23/200.
63. E. George (artist), "Trommelfeuer," *Liller Kriegszeitung*, No. 82, April 1, 1918, PH/23/202, BArch-MA.
64. Gefreiter Gustav Schoedon, "Sturm," *Liller Kriegszeitung*, ed. Hoecker und von Ompteda (Berlin: Verlag von W. Voback, 1917), 114–15, BArch-MA, MSG 2/8183. English-language translation is the author's own.
65. Ibid.
66. An exhibit about these A7V tanks, including "Wotan" on display, can be found at the Deutsches Panzermuseum in Münster, https://daspanzermuseum.de/.
67. Gefechtsbericht, Abschrift, Leutnant d.Res. Jacobs, May 14, 1918, University of Texas-Dallas, George H. Williams Aviation Library, A. E. Ferko World War I special collection, Box 14.1.
68. Stephen T. Lawson, "Jasta 7 under 'Kobes,'" *Cross & Cockade International Journal—The First World War Aviation Historical Society*, 25:3 (1994): 115.
69. This is recounted by aviation historian Bruno J. Schmäling, based on his personal correspondence with Jacobs in the decade before Jacobs died in 1978. See Bruno J. Schmäling, *Jasta Colors*, vol. 1 (Reno: Aeronaut Books, 2020), 65.
70. Jacobs' rosary and leather pouch is on display at the Deutsches Technikmuseum in Berlin. The artifact was part of a collection owned by aero historian Neal W. O'Connor, who donated his collection to the museum.

71. From the war diary of Josef Jacobs, 3 October 1918, cited by William R. Puglisi, "Jacobs of Jasta 7," *Cross & Cockade Journal*, 6:4 (1965): 333.
72. See Bruno J. Schmäling and Peter Kilduff, "In Memorium, Josef Jacobs, 1894–1978," *Cross & Cockade Journal*, 20:1 (Spring 1979), 87. Toward the end of his life, the German tabloid *Bild* did a feature on Jacobs, where they also mentioned his dislike for the Nazis, antagonism with Göring, and subsequent brief arrest. See Heinz Sünder, "Am 80. Geburtstag fliegt der 'Alte Adler' Aus, *Bild*, May 15, 1974, p. 6.
73. The "Brünhilde"-painted CL.II aircraft appeared on Sanke series postcard No. 1071, "Startbereite Schlachtstaffel—Die Flugzeuge sind mit Maschinengewhren, Signalpatronen und Handgranaten ausgerüstet," 1918. Author's personal collection.
74. In *The Nibelungenlied*, Brünhilde was a warrior queen, skilled in weaponry, who is wooed by the hero Siegfried. See *The Nibelungenlied*, trans. A.T. Hatto (New York: Penguin, 1969), 53. In Wagner's opera and other versions of the saga, she is also a Valkyrie.
75. The pentagram crops up in many different cultures and forms with diverse meanings. The symbol was ubiquitous in Christian popular culture in medieval and early modern central Europe. See Owen Davies, *The Oxford Illustrated History of Witchcraft and Magic* (Oxford: Oxford University Press, 2017), 178–9. There is an amazing example the use of this symbol in sixteenth-century drawings on a wooden wall in a farmhouse at the *Schwarzwälder Freilichtmuseum Vogtsbauernhof* in Gutach, Germany, where peasants drew multiple pentagrams over scenes of everyday life.
76. Beckhardt's machine appears in a photo on the cover of Felix A. Theilhaber, *Jüdische Flieger im Weltkrieg* (Berlin: Verlag der Schild, Reichsbund jüdischer Frontsoldaten, 1924).
77. Adolf Auer, Personal-Bogen, cited in Peter Kilduff, *Black Fokker Leader—The First World War's Last Airfighter* Knight (London: Grubstreet, 2009), 132.
78. Ibid. For more on Willy Rosenstein in the context of German-Jewish experiences in the First World War, see Jason Crouthamel, "'My Comrades Are for the Most Part On My Side': Comradeship between Non-Jewish and German Jewish Front Soldiers in the First World War," in *Beyond Inclusion and Exclusion: Jewish Experiences of the First World War in Central Europe*, ed. Jason Crouthamel, Michael Geheran, Tim Grady, and Julia Barbara Köhne (New York: Berghahn Books, 2019).
79. Paul Orlamuender, *Volksmund und Volkshumor: Beiträge zur Volkskunde* (Bremen: Carl Schünemann, 1908).
80. Paul Orlamuender, "Humor," *Liller Kriegszeitung*, No. 112, June 30, 1918, PH/23/202, BArch-MA.
81. Excerpt from *National Review*, July 1918, published in "Offener Brief des Teufels an seinen Geschäftsfreund John Bull," *Kriegszeitung der 4. Armee*, No. 387, September 19, 1918, PH/5/II, BArch-MA.
82. "Offener Brief des Teufels an seinen Geschäftsfreund John Bull," *Kriegszeitung der 4. Armee*, No. 387, September 19, 1918, PH/5/II, BArch-MA.
83. Gefreiter Joseph Mauder, "Hiasls Himmel- und Hoellenfahrt," *Liller Kriegszeitung*, No. 108, June 18, 1918, PH/23/202, BArch-MA.
84. Georg Quert, "Der bayerische Flieger," *Der Flieger*, No. 20, April 22, 1917, PH 21/215, BArch-MA.
85. Cartoon of St. Peter giving a gas mask to an angel, *Kriegszeitung der 4. Armee*, No. 209, Weihnachten 1916, PH/5/II, BArch-MA.

86. For more background on the often bizarre humor found in trench newspapers, especially in relation to gender roles, see Crouthamel, *An Intimate History of the Front*, ch. 4.
87. Drawing "Und Friede auf Erden," *Die Scheuner Kriegszeitung*, 2. Jahrgang, Dezember 1915, PH/10/III/96, BArch-MA.
88. "Lotte ist tot," *Die Scheuner Kriegszeitung*, 3. Jahrgang, No. 18, 1916, PH/10/III/96, BArch-MA.
89. Hans Glückstein, "Fiedelmann Tod," in *Der Drahtverhau*, No. 20, 3. Jahrg., April 1918, PHD 12/40, BArch-MA.

7 Spiritual Subjectivities: Constructing New Beliefs Out of Total War

1. Adolf Ritter von Tutschek, *Stürme und Luftsiege* (Berlin: Verlag Gustav Braunbeck, 1918), 134–5.
2. Ibid.
3. See Anthony Wallace, "Revitalization Movements," *American Anthropologist*, 58 (1956): 265–6.
4. On the powerful spiritual bonds cemented by comradeship, see Thomas Kühne, *The Rise of Comradeship*, especially chapters 2 and 3.
5. On tensions between hegemonic masculine ideals and the broader spectrum of masculine identities found in the trenches, see Crouthamel, *An Intimate History of the Front*, especially ch. 4.
6. On postwar constructions of the image of a "new man," see Bernd Hüppauf, "Langenmarck, Verdun and the Myth of the New Man in Germany after the First World War," *War and Society* 6:2 (September 1988): 70–103; Mosse, *The Image of Man*.
7. Perpetrators traumatized by the violence they performed is a sensitive and complex topic. Different theoretical approaches to "perpetrator trauma" have recently been explored by Raya Morag, "Perpetrator Trauma and Current American War Cinema" and Julia Barbara Köhne, "Aesthetic Displays of Perpetrators in *The Act of Killing* (2012): Post-atrocity Perpetrator Symptoms and Re-enactments of Violence," both in Peter Leese, Julia Barbara Köhne and Jason Crouthamel, eds., *Languages of Trauma: History, Memory, and Media* (Toronto: University of Toronto Press, 2021).
8. See George L. Mosse, *Fallen Soldiers*, especially 182–90. On Jünger's experiences with killing, see Ziemann, *Violence and the German Soldier in the Great War*, especially 75–82.
9. On Jünger's concepts of masculinity, see Bernd Weisbrod, "Military Violence and Male Fundamentalism: Ernst Jünger's Contribution to the Conservative Revolution," *History Workshop Journal* 49 (2000): 69–93; see also Ziemann, *Violence and the German Soldier in the Great War*, 63–4.
10. Bourke, *The Story of Pain—From Prayer to Painkillers*, 122.
11. Letter from Theodor K. to his wife, December 17, 1914, Band 372, WLS/SZdW.
12. Letter from Theodor K. to his wife, December 12, 1914, Band 372, WLS/SZdW.
13. Letter from Theodor K. to his wife, December 17, 1914, Band 372, WLS/SZdW.
14. Hans F., November 2, 1915, diary entry, MSG 2/2735, BArch-MA.
15. On Toller's life and literary transformations, see Steven Schouten, "Ernst Toller," in *1914–1918 online. International Encyclopedia of the First World War*, ed. Ute

Daniel, Peter Gatrell, Oliver Janz, Heather Jones, Jennifer Keene, Alan Kramer, and Bill Nasson, issued by Freie Universität Berlin, Berlin June 8, 2018. DOI: 10.15463/ie1418.11272.
16. Vernon L. Lidtke, "Introduction," Ernst Toller, *I Was a German—The Autobiography of a Revolutionary*, trans. Edward Crankshaw (originally, *Eine Jugend in Deutschland*, 1933). (New York: Paragon House, 1991), xi.
17. Toller, *I Was a German*, 39–40.
18. Ibid., 51.
19. Ibid., 80–2.
20. Ibid., 85–6.
21. Ibid., 86.
22. Ibid., 87.
23. Tom Fecht, *Käthe Kollwitz: Works in Color* (New York: Random House, 1988), 6.
24. Käthe Kollwitz, September 30, 1914 diary entry, in Marilyn Shevin-Coetzee and Frans Coetzee, eds., *World War I and European Society: A Sourcebook* (New York: DC Heath, 1995), 330.
25. Käthe Kollwitz, October 11, 1914 diary entry, in *World War I and European Society*, 332.
26. Jay Winter, *Remembering War* (New Haven, CT: Yale University Press), 147.
27. Käthe Kollwitz, April 22, 1917 letter to Hans Kollwitz, in *World War I and European Society*, 332.
28. Karl Bröger, "Begegnungen mit Gott—Ein Kapitel Kriegsfrömmigkeit," *Neue Hamburger Zeitung*, No. 449, September 3, 1917.
29. Siegfried Kett, Manfred Scholz, Harald Zintl, and Michael Ziegler, eds., *Karl Bröger: Arbeiterdichter, Journalist und Politiker—Documentation zum Symposium am 4. Oktober 2008 in Nürnberg* (Regensburg: Friedrich Ebert Stiftung, 2008), 26–39, http://library.fes.de/pdf-files/bueros/regensburg/14214.pdf.
30. Bröger, "Begegnungen mit Gott—Ein Kapitel Kriegsfrömmigkeit."
31. Ibid.
32. Ibid.
33. Ibid.
34. Ibid.
35. Ibid.
36. Ibid.
37. Ibid.
38. Ibid.
39. Letter from Ernst Emmerich to his parents, January 25, 1915, file 3.2011.3530, Museumsstiftung Post und Telekommunikation, Feldpost 1914–1918 Sammlung, https://www.museumsstiftung.de/briefsammlung/feldpost-erster-weltkrieg/feldpost.html.
40. Letter from Ernst Emmerich to his parents, March 31, 1915, file 3.2011.3530, Museumstiftung Post und Telekommunikation, Feldpost 1914–1918 Sammlung, https://www.museumsstiftung.de/briefsammlung/feldpost-erster-weltkrieg/feldpost.html.
41. "Friedrich Nietzsche: Vom Kriege," *Liller Kriegszeitung*, No. 23, February 22, 1915, PH 23/197, BArch-MA. This included aphorism 477 from Nietzsche's *Menschliches, Allzumenschliches* (1878). The translation here is from Friedrich Nietzsche, *Human, All Too Human* (originally *Menschliches, Allzumenschliches*), trans. R. J. Hollingdale (Cambridge: Cambridge University Press, 1986), 176.

42. Ibid. Here the *Liller Kriegszeitung* quotes from Nietzsche's *Also Sprach Zarathustra*. The translation is by the author.
43. This postcard with Hans Müller's personal inscription is in the possession of the author. The postcard was manufactured by Poskartenvertrieb W. Sanke, Series number 446. The handwritten inscription reads: "Wer nichts fürchtet ist nicht weniger mächtig als der den alle fürchten!—H. Müller." The quote is from Friedrich Schiller, *Die Räuber*, 1. Akt, 1. Szene (1781).
44. The definitive work on comradeship and its sociological significance as a central element in German masculine identity is Thomas Kühne's, *The Rise of Comradeship*.
45. This is a central point made by Thomas Kühne, "'... aus diesem Krieg werden nicht nur harte Männer heimkehren'—Kriegskameradschaft und Männlichkeit im 20. Jahrhundert," 174–91; see also Jason Crouthamel, *An Intimate History of the Front*, esp. ch. 3.
46. See Claudia Bruns, *Politik des Eros—Der Männerbund in Wissenschaft, Politik und Jugendkultur, 1880–1934* (Köln: Böhlau Verlag, 2008), 388–403. Bruns focuses on Hans Blüher, who openly touted homoeroticism and his vision of elite male leadership. See Hans Blüher, *Die Rolle der Erotik in der männlichen Gesellschaft* (Jena: E. Diederichs, 1917).
47. Letter from Alfred S., October 18, 1914, to his mother, Mathilde, in Horst Schöttler, ed., *1914—Briefe und Feldpostbriefe vom Beginn des Ersten Weltkriegs* (Hamburg: Severus, 2014), 124–5.
48. Carl Degelow, "Das Seelenleben des Fliegers im Flug und im Luftkampf," in *Mit dem weissen Hirsch durch Dick und Dünn—Erlebnisse und Betrachtungen eines Kampffliegers* (Altona Ottensen: Verlag von Chr. Adolff, 1920), 41–9.
49. Ibid., 47.
50. Carl Degelow, *Mit dem weissen Hirsch durch Dick und Dünn*, 111.
51. This copy of Degelow's memoir is in the possession of the author.
52. Samuel Jacobs, *Gedanken und Erinnerungen aus dem Weltkriege*, p. 3 of the manuscript (digital file), ME 328. MM41, LBINY.
53. Samuel Jacobs, *Gedanken und Erinnerungen aus dem Weltkriege*, p. 5 of the manuscript (digital file), ME 328. MM41, LBINY.
54. Samuel Jacobs, *Gedanken und Erinnerungen aus dem Weltkriege*, p. 18 of the manuscript (digital file), ME 328. MM41, LBINY.
55. Samuel Jacobs, *Gedanken und Erinnerungen aus dem Weltkriege*, p. 11 of the manuscript (digital file), ME 328. MM41, LBINY.
56. Samuel Jacobs, *Gedanken und Erinnerungen aus dem Weltkriege*, p. 25 of the manuscript (digital file), ME 328. MM41, LBINY.
57. Samuel Jacobs, *Gedanken und Erinnerungen aus dem Weltkriege*, p. 28 of the manuscript (digital file), ME 328. MM41, LBINY. Consistent with Orthodox tradition, he wrote "G-tt."
58. [author unknown], "Unsere erfolgreichsten Kampfflieger," *Der Flieger*, No. 21, April 29, 1917, PH 21/216, BArch-MA.
59. Richard Volker, "Kameraden," in *Der Kamerad*, No. 1, 1918, PH 22-I/50, BArch-MA.
60. [author unknown], "Manfred von Richthofen," in *Der Kamerad*, No. 6, 1918, PH 22-I/50, BArch-MA.
61. See, for example, Andreas Killen, *Berlin Electropolis: Shock, Nerves and German Modernity* (Berkeley: University of California Press, 2006); see also Lerner, *Hysterical Men*, 18–23.

62. Unteroffizier Kauer, August 9, 1914 letter to "den Stammtisch 'Deutsche Futuristen'; Rom, Via della Croce," in Horst Schöttler, *1914—Briefe und Feldpostbriefe vom Beginn des Ersten Weltkriegs* (Hamburg: Severus, 2014), 39–40.
63. Ibid.
64. Tucholsky published this under the pseudonym "Theobald Tiger," "August First" (Zum ersten August), *Die Weltbühne,* August 1, 1918, from Kurt Tucholsky, *Prayer After the Slaughter—The Great War: Stories and Poems from World War I,* trans. Peter Appelbaum and James Scott (New York: Berlinica Publishing, 2015), 33.
65. Ibid.
66. See Bernd Huppauf, "Schlachtenmythen und die Konstruktion des 'Neuen Menschen,'" in *"Keiner fühlt sich hier mehr als Mensch,"* 43–84; On right-wing constructions of the "new man," see Mosse, *The Image of Man,* ch. 8.
67. [unknown author], "Das neue Geschlecht," *Der Flieger,* No. 24, May 20, 1917, PH 21/216, BArch-MA.
68. [author unknown], "Maschine und Geist—Eine Kriegsbetrachtung," *Liller Kriegszeitung,* No. 113, July 3, 1919, PH/23/202, BArch-MA.
69. Ibid.
70. Ibid.
71. Ibid.
72. Ibid.
73. Rudolf Stark, *Wings of War: An Airman's Diary of the Last Year of World War One* (originally *Die Jagdstaffel unsere Heimat: Ein Flieger-Tagebuch aus dem letzen Kriegsjahr*), trans. Claud W. Sykes (Leipzig: Verlag von K.F. Koehler, 1932; London: Greenhill Books, 1993), preface.
74. Ibid., 12.
75. Ibid., 172.
76. Ibid., 158.
77. Edgar von Spiegel von und zu Peckelsheim, *U Boat 202- The Diary of a German Submarine* (originally *Kriegstagebuch U.202*) (Berlin: Verlag August Scherl, first published in 1916; trans. Barry Sommerville, London: A. Melrose, 1919), 40.
78. Ibid., 44.
79. Ibid., 112.
80. Ibid., 133.
81. Ibid.
82. See Klaus Theweleit, *Male Fantasies,* vol. 1 (Minneapolis: University of Minnesota Press, 1987).
83. Von Tutschek, *Stürme und Luftsiege,* 183.
84. See Ernst Jünger, *Der Kampf als inneres Erlebnis* (Berlin: E. S. Mittler, 1922).
85. Ernst Jünger, *Copse 125—A Chronicle from the Trench Warfare of 1918,* trans. Basil Creighton (originally *Das Wäldchen 125,* 1930) (New York: Howard Fertig, 2003), 56–7.
86. An excellent overview of Jünger's approach to writing about killing and surviving can be found in Ziemann, *Violence and the German Soldier in the Great War,* 60–6.
87. Thomas Nevin, *Ernst Jünger and Germany: Into the Abyss, 1914–1945* (Durham, NC: Duke University Press, 1996), 218.
88. Ernst Jünger, *Copse 125,* 2.
89. Ibid., 3–4.
90. Ibid., 41.
91. Ibid., 168.

92. See Mosse, *Fallen Soldiers,* ch. 10; Helmuth Kiesel, *Ernst Jünger. Die Biographie* (Munich: Siedler, 2007), 303–9.
93. Fritzsche, *A Nation of Fliers,* 82.
94. Von Richthofen's additions were published in interwar versions of memoir, including Manfred Freiherr von Richthofen, *Der Heldenleben* (Berlin: Ullstein, 1920). The passage here is from Manfred von Richthofen, *The Red Baron,* trans. Peter Kilduff (New York: Doubleday, 1969), 112. For interesting analysis of von Richthofen's memoirs as a useful documents despite propaganda censorship, see Robert Wohl, *A Passion for Wings: Aviation and the Western Imagination* (New Haven, CT: Yale University Press, 1994), 226–7.
95. Baroness von Richthofen, *Mother of Eagles—The War Diary of Baroness von Richthofen* (originally Kunigunde von Richthofen, *Mein Kriegstagebuch,* 1937), ed. and trans. Susanne Hayes Fischer (Atglen, PA: Schiffer, 2001), 157.
96. Jonathan Shay, *Achilles in Vietnam,* 83–6.

Epilogue: Defeat, Revolution, and Aftermath

1. Samuel Jacobs, *Gedanken und Erinnerungen aus dem Weltkriege,* pp. 32–3 (digital file), ME 328. MM41, LBINY.
2. Samuel Jacobs, *Gedanken und Erinnerungen aus dem Weltkriege,* p. 36 (digital file), ME 328. MM41, LBINY.
3. Ibid.
4. Ibid. On Samuel Jacobs, and other Jewish veterans' experiences during the Weimar and Nazi periods, see Michael Geheran, *Comrades Betrayed: Jewish World War I Veterans under Hitler* (Ithaca, NY: Cornell University Press, 2020), 40, 46.
5. The "stab-in-the-back" legend was eagerly disseminated by nationalistic Protestant circles in particular, according to Boris Barth, *Dolchstoßlegenden und politische Desintegration: Das Trauma der deutschen Niederlage im Ersten Weltkrieg* (Düsseldorf: Droste Verlag, 2003), 150–5.
6. On the "stab-in-the-back" legend, see Wilhelm Deist, "Der militärische Zusammenbruch des Kaiserreichs: Zur Realität der 'Dolchstosslegende,'" in *Militär, Staat und Gesellschaft—Studien zur preussisch-deutschen Militärgeschichte,* ed. Wilhelm Deist (Munich: R. Oldenbourg, 1991), 211–33.
7. Rudolf Berthold, Kriegstagebuch, January 29, 1919, p. 78, MSG 2/10722, BArch-MA.
8. Rudolf Berthold, Kriegstagebuch, January 24, 1919, pp. 76–7, MSG 2/10722, BArch-MA.
9. Ibid.
10. Hitler, *Mein Kampf,* 231.
11. Ibid., 234.
12. Mary Young-Rißmann, "Der verlorene Krieg und die Sittlichkeitsfrage, als Vortrag von Frau Young-Rißmann gehalten zu Freiburg i.B. am September 30, 1923 zur Tagung des Weißes Kreuzes" (Dinglingen: St. Johannes Druckerei, 1930), 1–2.
13. Ibid., 2.
14. Pamphlet from Evangelische Gemeindeblatt, Bietigheim, January 1919 (from the Evang. Pfarramt I, Archiv, Bietigheim), in *Zwischen Heimat und Front,* 24.
15. See James M. Diehl, *Paramilitary Politics in Weimar Germany* (Bloomington: Indiana University Press, 1977).

16. Antonia Helming, August 20, 1918, diary entry, in *"Mutters Kriegstagebuch,"* 252.
17. Antonia Helming, November 13, 1918, diary entry, in *"Mutters Kriegstagebuch,"* 269.
18. Antonia Helming, December 6, 1918, diary entry, in *"Mutters Kriegstagebuch,"* 272.
19. Antonia Helming, December 25, 1918, diary entry, in *"Mutters Kriegstagebuch,"* 273.
20. Antonia Helming, January 17, 1919, diary entry, in *"Mutters Kriegstagebuch,"* 278.
21. Kurlander, *Hitler's Monsters*, 20–2.
22. Ibid.; for more background on the nineteenth-century roots of the Thule Society, see David Luhrssen, *Hammer of the Gods: The Thule Society and the Birth of Nazism* (Washington, DC: Potomac Books, 2012), 20–9; Nicholas Goodrick-Clarke, *The Occult Roots of Nazism* (New York: New York University Press, 1993), 145.
23. Jenkins, *The Great and Holy War*, 160.
24. Kurlander, *Hitler's Monsters*, 39–40.
25. Ibid., 46.
26. Ibid., 42.
27. Ibid., 47; See also Richard Evans, "The Emergence of Nazi Ideology," in *Nazi Germany*, ed. Jane Caplan (Oxford: Oxford University Press, 2009), 42.
28. See Sabine Behrenbeck, *Der Kult um die toten Helden: Nationalsozialistische Mythen, Riten und Symbole, 1923–1945* (Vierow: SH-Verlag, 1996), 412–13.
29. Letter from Otto W. to his wife, Luisle, August 18, 1918, Feldpost Sammlung, Museumstiftung Post und Telekommunikation, http://www.museumstiftung.de/briefsammlung/feldpost-erster-weltkrieg/feldpost.html.
30. Ibid.
31. Antonia Helming, December 24, 1918, diary entry, in *"Mutters Kriegstagebuch,"* 275.
32. Antonia Helming, December 24, 1919, diary entry, in *"Mutters Kriegstagebuch,"* 283.
33. Antonia Helming, October 20, 1920 letter, in *"Mutters Kriegstagebuch,"* 299.
34. Max Goβner, "Erinnerungen an Oberleutnant d. R. Fritz von Röth," in *In der Luft unbesiegt—Erlebnisse im Weltkrieg erzählt von Luftkämpfern*, ed. Georg Neumann (München: J.F. Lehmanns Verlag, 1923), 118. For more praise from is comrades, see also Report IIa/Nr 1471, April 13, 1920, by Hauptmann Schleich, MMJO VK 17 11, Bayrisches Hauptstaatsarchiv, Abteilung IV Kriegsarchiv (henceforth BHStArch, Abt. IV).
35. Goβner, "Erinnerungen an Oberleutnant d. R. Fritz von Röth," 115–17.
36. From a personal interview with Theodor Rumpel in the 1970s given to historian Bruno Schmäling, which Mr. Schmäling was kind enough to convey to the author.
37. *Leutnant d. Reserve* Röth, Jagdstaffel 23, Bitte um Aufnahme in die Ritterklasse (Max-Josef-Orden), April 24, 1918, MMJO VK 17 11, BHStArch, Abt. IV.
38. *Fränkischer Kurier*, January 14, 1919, quoted from Immanuel Voigt, *Stars des Krieges – Eine biografische und erinnerungskulturelle Studie zu den deutschen Luftstreitkräften des Ersten Weltkrieges* (Oldenbourg: De Gruyter, 2019), 271.
39. Kriegsstammrollen 18004: Rangliste Jagdstaffel 16, BayHstA, Abt. IV. Quoted from Voigt, *Stars des Krieges*, 271.
40. "Vermischte Nachrichtung aus Bayern," *Münchener Neueste Nachrichten*, January 4, 1919, MMJO VK 17 11, BHStArch, Abt. IV.
41. "Vermischte Nachrichtung aus Bayern," *Münchener Neueste Nachrichten*, January 9, 1919, MMJO VK 17 11, BHStArch, Abt. IV.
42. Oskar Döbeli, "Ein bayerischer Kampfflieger -- Oberstleutnant Fritz Roeth, die 'Fesselballonkanone,'" *Münchener Neueste Nachrichten*, 15/16 July 1933, MMJO VK 17 11, BHStArch, Abt. IV.

43. Bruno Schmäling summarizes his conversation with Hedwig Röth in his biographical sketch of her brother in his book written with Winfried Bock, *Royal Bavarian Jagdstaffel 23*, trans. Adam M. Wait (Reno: Aeronaut Books, 2018), 294–5. Schmäling cites his notes for this conversation with Hedwig Röth in his biographical sketch of her brother on p. 335. Thanks to Mr. Schmäling for his feedback and correspondence where he further shared his recollections with the author about these conversations.
44. See Sabine Behrenbeck, *Der Kult um die toten Helden*.
45. On Nazism as a secular religion, see Michael Burleigh, *Sacred Causes: The Clash of Religion and Politics, from the Great War to the War on Terror* (New York: Harper Perennial, 2007), 94–5; Philippe Burrin, "Die politischen Religionen: Das Mythologische-Symbolische in einer säkularisierten Welt," in *Der Nationalsozialismus als politische Religion*, ed. Michael Ley and Julius H. Schoeps (Mainz: Philo Verlags, 1997), 181–2; Richard Steigmann-Gall, "Was National Socialism a Political Religion or a Religious Politics?" in *Religion und Nation, Nation und Religion. Beiträge zu einer unbewältigen Geschichte*, ed. Michael Geyer and Hartmut Lehmann (Göttingen: Wallstein, 2004).
46. Alon Confino, "Death, Spiritual Solace, and Afterlife: Between Nazism and Religion," in *Between Mass Death and Individual Loss—The Place of the Dead in Twentieth-Century Germany*, ed. Alon Confino, Paul Betts, and Dirk Schumann (New York: Berghahn Books, 2008), 218–31.
47. Karl Neureuther and Claus Bergen, eds., *U-Boat Stories—Narratives of German U-boat Sailors*, trans. Eric Sutton (London: Constable, 1931), vi.
48. Heinrich T., diary, pp. 41–3, MSG 2/1130, BArch-MA.
49. Heinrich T., diary, p. 125, MSG 2/1130, BArch-MA.
50. Ibid.
51. For more background on this memorial, see Jay Winter, *Remembering War*, 148–9.
52. Käthe Kollwitz, January 4, 1920 diary entry, in Hans Kollwitz, ed., *The Diary and Letters of Kaethe Kollwitz*, trans. Richard and Clara Winston (Evanston, IL: Northwestern University Press, 1988), 96.
53. Käthe Kollwitz, April 21, 1922, diary entry, in Kollwitz, ed., *The Diary and Letters of Kaethe Kollwitz*, 103.
54. Käthe Kollwitz, December 8, 1918, diary entry, in *The Diary and Letters of Kaethe Kollwitz*, 89–90.
55. Käthe Kollwitz, January 1, 1920, diary entry, in *The Diary and Letters of Kaethe Kollwitz*, 95.
56. Käthe Kollwitz, April 1921, diary entry, in *The Diary and Letters of Kaethe Kollwitz*, 98.
57. Käthe Kollwitz, January 1, 1920, diary entry, in *The Diary and Letters of Kaethe Kollwitz*, 96.
58. Käthe Kollwitz, May 1943, diary entry, in *The Diary and Letters of Kaethe Kollwitz*, 130. Kollwitz died in April 1945.

Conclusion

1. Outstanding scholarship on the war experience shared between men and women reveals how much more work there is to do in this direction. See Martha Hanna, *Your Death Would Be Mine* (Cambridge, MA: Harvard University Press, 2006);

Dorothee Wierling, *Eine Familie im Krieg: Leben, Sterben und Schreiben 1914–1918* (Göttingen: Wallstein Verlag, 2013).
2. Jenkins, *The Great and Holy War*, 11.
3. See Madigan, *Faith under Fire*; and Becker, *War and Faith*.
4. See Siegfried Sassoon, *Memories of an Infantry Officer* (London: Faber and Faber, 1930); T. E. Lawrence, *Seven Pillars of Wisdom* (orig. 1935, New York: Wordsworth, 1999); Henri Barbusse, *Under Fire* (orig. *Le Feu*, 1916, New York: Penguin, 2003); on British and French literary responses to the front experiences, see Winter, *Remembering War*, ch. 5.
5. On anti-war literature published during the Weimar Republic, see Ziemann, *Violence and the German Soldier in the Great War*, ch. 10.
6. See Mosse, *Fallen Soldiers*, ch. 10; Winter, *Remembering War*, 246–52; Benjamin Ziemann, *Contested Commemorations: Republican War Veterans and Weimar Political Culture* (Cambridge: Cambridge University Press, 2013).
7. Geroulanos and Meyers, *The Human Body in the Age of Catastrophe*, 316–17.
8. Plaut, "Psychographie des Kriegers," 75.
9. For example, see Wallace, *Revitalizations and Mazeways*.
10. Wirtz, *Trauma and Beyond*, 45–6.

Bibliography

Archives

Bayerisches Armeemuseum
    Paul Lebrecht Kriegstagebuch
Bayrisches Hauptstaatsarchiv, Abteilung IV, Kriegsarchiv (BHStArch, Abt. IV)
Bibliothek für Zeitgeschichte, Stuttgart
    Lebensdokumentensammlung
Bundesarchiv Berlin-Lichterfelde (BArch)
    Reichsministerium des Innern
Bundesarchiv-Militärarchiv, Freiburg i.Br. (BArch-MA)
    Feldpostbriefe und Tagebücher Sammlung (MSG 1 and MSG 2)
    Soldatenzeitungen Sammlung (PH)
Leo Baeck Institute Archive, New York (LBINY)
Museumsstiftung Post und Telekommunikation, Feldpost 1914–1918 Sammlung, http://www.museumsstiftung.de/briefsammlung/feldpost-erster-weltkrieg/feldpost.html
Staatsbibliothek Berlin
    Krieg 1914–1918 Sammlung
University of Texas-Dallas, George H. Williams Aviation Library
    A. E. Ferko World War I special collection
Württembergische Landesbibliothek, Stuttgart (WLS)
    Feldpostbriefe, Sondersammlung Zeit der Weltkriege (WLS/SZdW)

Published Primary Sources

Bächtold, Hanns. *Deutscher Soldatenbrauch und Soldatenglaube*, herausgegeben vom Verband deutscher Vereine für Volkskunde. Straßburg: Verlag von Karl J. Trübner, 1917.
Barbusse, Henri. *Under Fire* (orig. *Le Feu*, 1916). New York: Penguin, 2003.
Berliner Illustrirte Zeitung, XXVI Jahrgang, No. 15, April 5, 1917.
Blüher, Hans. *Die Rolle der Erotik in der männlichen Gesellschaft*. Jena: E. Diederichs, 1917.
Boer, Artur H., *The Great War from the German Trenches: A Sapper's Memoir, 1914–1918*, translated and edited by Bertil van Boer and Margaret L. Fast. Jefferson, NC: McFarland, 2016.
Borgmeyer, Franz. *Das Übersinnliche im Weltkriege: Merkwürdige Vorgänge im Felde und allerlei Kriegsprophezeiungen*. Hildesheim: Verlag von Franz Borgmeyer, 1917.
Bröger, Karl. "Begegnungen mit Gott—Ein Kapitel Kriegsfrömmigkeit," *Neue Hamburger Zeitung*, No. 449, September 3, 1917.

Degelow, Carl. "Das Seelenleben des Fliegers im Flug und im Luftkampf." In *Mit dem weissen Hirsch durch Dick und Dünn—Erlebnisse und Betrachtungen eines Kampffliegers*. Altona Ottensen: Verlag von Chr. Adolff, 1920.

Dietrich, Marlene. *Marlene*, translated by Salvator Attanasio. New York: Grove Press, 1989.

Dodenhoeft, Bettina, ed., *Kasseler Soldaten im Ersten Weltkrieg—Tagebücher und Feldpostbriefe*. Kassel: Scribeo, 2014.

Egger, Karl. *Seele im Sturm: Kriegserleben eines Feldgeistlichen*. Innsbruck: F. Rauch, 1936.

Everth, Erich. *Von der Seele des Soldaten im Felde—Bemerkungen eines Kriegsteilnehmers*, Tat-Flugschriften 10. Jena: Eugen Diedrichs, 1915.

Exner, Lisbeth, and Herbert Kapfer, eds., *Verborgene Chronik, 1915–1918*, herausgegeben vom Deutschen Tagesbucharchiv. Berlin: Galiani, 2017.

Gaupp, Robert. "Dienstverweigerung aus religösen (und politischen) Gründen und ihre gerichtsärztliche Beurteilung," *Medizinisches Correspondenz-Blatt* 88 (1918): 167–9.

Göhre, Paul. *Der unbekannte Gott—Versuch einer Religion des modernen Menschen*. Leipzig: Verlag von Fr. Wilh. Grunow, 1919.

Göhre, Paul. *Front und Heimat—Religiöses, Politisches, Sexuelles aus dem Schützengraben*, Tat-Flugschriften 22. Jena: Eugen Diedrichs, 1917.

Göhre, Paul. *Wie ein Pfarrer Sozialdemokrat wurde*. Berlin: Vorwärts, 1906.

Goβner, Max. "Erinnerungen an Oberleutnant d. R. Fritz von Röth." In *In der Luft unbesiegt—Erlebnisse im Weltkrieg erzählt von Luftkämpfern*, edited by Georg Neumann. München: J. F. Lehmanns, 1923.

Grabinski, Bruno. *Neuere Mystik—Der Weltkrieg im Aberglauben und im Lichte der Prophetie*. Hildesheim: Verlag von Franz Borgmeyer, 1916.

Grabinski, Bruno. *Spuk—und Geistererscheinungen oder was sonst?—eine kritische Untersuchung*. Hildesheim: Franz Borgmeyer, 1922.

Hellwig, Albert. "Zur Psychologie des Aberglaubens." Dissertation, University of Kiel, 1910.

Helming, Antonia. *"Mutters Kriegstagebuch"—Die Aufzeichnungen der Antonia Helming, 1914–1922*, edited by Stephanie Fredewess-Wenstrup. Münster: Waxmann, 2005.

Heydemarck, Oberleutnant. *Doppeldecker "C666."* Berlin: Verlag August Scherl, 1916.

Hitler, Adolf. *Mein Kampf* (original 1925), translated by Ralph Manheim. New York: Houghton Mifflin, 1999.

Hoecker, Hauptmann d.L., and Rittmeister a.D. Frh. Von Ompteda, eds., *Liller Kriegszeitung*. Berlin: Verlag von W. Vobach, 1914.

Hoecker, Hauptmann d.L., and Rittmeister a.D. Frh. Von Ompteda, *Liller Kriegszeitung*. Berlin: Verlag von W. Vobach, 1915.

Hoecker, Hauptmann d.L., and Rittmeister a.D. Frh. Von Ompteda, *Liller Kriegszeitung*. Berlin: Verlag von W. Voback, 1917.

Hoffmann, Ilse, ed., *Hans Wulf—Briefe und Tagebuch eines Rendsburger Soldaten im Ersten Weltkrieg*. Rendsburg: Druckerei Albers, 2003.

Jünger, Ernst. *Copse 125—A Chronicle from the Trench Warfare of 1918*, translated by Basil Creighton (originally *Das Wäldchen 125*, 1930). New York: Howard Fertig, 2003.

Jünger, Ernst. *Der Kampf als inneres Erlebnis*. Berlin: E. S. Mittler, 1922.

Kellner Marcel, and Knud Neuhoff, eds., *"Solange die Welt steht, ist soviel Blut nicht geflossen": Feldpostbriefe badischer Soldaten aus dem Ersten Weltkrieg 1914 bis 1918*, Schriftenreihe der Badischen Heimat, Landesverein Badische Heimat e.V. und dem Landesverband Baden-Württemberg im Volksbund Deutsche Kriegsgräberfürsorge. Freiburg: Rombach, 2014.

Koenen, Erik. "Ein 'einsamer' Wissenschaftler? Erich Everth und das Leipziger Institut für Zeitungskunde zwischen 1926 und 1933. Ein Beitrag zur Bedeutung des Biographischen für die Geschichte der Zeitungswissenschaft" *Medien & Zeit*, 20:1 (2005): 38–50.

Kollwitz, Hans, ed., *The Diary and Letters of Kaethe Kollwitz*, translated by Richard and Clara Winston. Evanston, IL: Northwestern University Press, 1988.

Kurth, Karl. *Die deutschen Feld- und Schützengrabenzeitungen des Weltkrieges* Leipzig: Robert Noske, 1937.

Lawrence, T. E. *Seven Pillars of Wisdom* (original 1935). New York: Wordsworth, 1999.

Lieb, Christa, ed., *Zwischen Heimat und Front—Feldpost: Die Kriegsjahre 1914-1918 in Bietigheim, Bissingen, Metterzimmern und Untermberg*, Schriftenreihe des Archivs der Stadt Bietigheim-Bissingen, Band 8. Stuttgart: Stadt Bietigheim-Bissingen Stadtarchiv, 2009.

Ludwig, Walter. "Beiträge zur Pychologie der Furcht im Kriege." In *Beihefte zur Zeitschrift für angewandte Psychologie* 21, edited by William Stern and Otto Lipmann. Leipzig: Johann Ambrosius Barth, 1920.

Müller, Leonhard. *Fliegerleutnant Heinrich Gontermann—Nach seinen Auszeichnungen und Briefen.* Barmen-U.: Verlag des Westdeutschen Jünglingsbundes, 1919.

Neureuther, Karl, and Claus Bergen, eds., *U-Boat Stories—Narratives of German U-boat Sailors*, translated by Eric Sutton. London: Constable, 1931.

Nietzsche, Friedrich. *Human, All Too Human* (original *Menschliches, Allzumenschliches*), translated by R. J. Hollingdale. Cambridge: Cambridge University Press, 1986.

Orlamuender, Paul. *Volksmund und Volkshumor: Beiträge zur Volkskunde.* Bremen: Carl Schünemann, 1908.

Peckelsheim, Edgar von Spiegel von und zu. *U Boat 202—The Diary of a German Submarine* (originally *Kriegstagebuch U.202*). Berlin: Verlag August Scherl (first published in 1916; translated by Barry Sommerville, London: A. Melrose, 1919).

Plaut, Paul. "Psychographie des Kriegers." In *Beihefte zur Zeitschrift für angewandte Psychologie*, No. 21, edited by William Stern and Otto Lipmann. Leipzig: Johann Ambrosius Barth, 1920, 1–123.

Richthofen, Baroness von. *Mother of Eagles—The War Diary of Baroness von Richthofen* (original Kunigunde von Richthofen, *Mein Kriegstagebuch*, 1937), edited and translated by Susanne Hayes Fischer. Atglen, PA: Schiffer, 2001.

Richthofen, Lothar von. "Memories of My Brother," in Manfred von Richthofen, *The Red Baron*, translated by Peter Kilduff (originally published in 1920 as *Ein Heldenleben*). New York: Charter, 1969.

Richthofen, Manfred von. *Ein Heldenleben.* Berlin: Verlag Ullstein, 1920.

Rühlig, Cornelia, Katja Englert, and Dagmar Sesche, eds., *Feldpostbriefe von Mörfeldern und Walldorfern aus dem Ersten Weltkrieg 1914-1918.* Offenbach: Berthold Druck GmbH, 2014.

Sassoon, Siegfried. *Memories of an Infantry Officer.* London: Faber and Faber, 1930.

Schiche, E. "Über Todesahnungen im Felde und ihre Wirkung." In *Beihefte zur Zeitschrift für angewandte Psychologie* 21, edited by William Stern and Otto Lipmann. Leipzig: Johann Ambrosius Barth, 1920.

Schöttler, Horst, ed., *1914—Briefe und Feldpostbriefe von Beginn des Ersten Weltkriegs.* Hamburg: Severus, 2014.

Schumann, Frank, ed. *Was Tun Wir Hier: Soldatenpost und Heimatbriefe aus zwei Weltkriegen.* Berlin: Verlag Neues Leben, 1989.

Stark, Rudolf. *Die Jagdstaffel unsere Heimat: Ein Flieger-Tagebuch aus dem letzen Kriegsjahr*. Leipzig: Verlag von K. F. Koehler, 1932.
Sünner, P. "Berichte über Spontanphänomene," *Zeitschrift für Parapsychologie*, 7 Jahrgang, 5. Heft, May 1932.
Theilhaber, Felix A. *Jüdische Flieger im Weltkrieg*. Berlin: Verlag der Schild, Reichsbund jüdischer Frontsoldaten, 1924.
Toller, Ernst. *I Was a German—The Autobiography of a Revolutionary*, translated by Edward Crankshaw (original *Eine Jugend in Deutschland*, 1933). New York: Paragon House, 1991.
Tucholsky, Kurt. *Prayer after the Slaughter—The Great War: Stories and Poems from World War I*, translated by Peter Appelbaum and James Scott. New York: Berlinica, 2015.
Tutschek, Adolf Ritter von. *Stürme und Luftsiege*. Berlin: Verlag Gustav Braunbeck, 1918.
Vesper, Will. *Kämpfer Gottes-Gesamtausgabe der historische Erzählungen*. Gütersloh: Bertelsmann, 1938.
Wisthaler, Sigrid, ed. *Karl Außerhofer—Das Kriegstagebuch eines Soldaten im Ersten Weltkrieg*. Innsbruck: Innsbruck University Press, 2010.
Young-Rißmann, Mary. "Der verlorene Krieg und die Sittlichkeitsfrage, als Vortrag von Frau Young-Rißmann gehalten zu Freiburg i.B. am 30 September 1923 zur Tagung des Weißes Kreuzes." Dinglingen: St. Johannes Druckerei, 1930.

Secondary Sources

Achleitner, Wilhelm. *Gott im Krieg: Die Theologie der österreichischen Bischöfe in den Hirtenbriefen zum Ersten Weltkrieg*. Vienna: Böhlau, 1997.
Alexander, Jeffry C., Ron Eyerman, Bernard Giesen, Neil J. Smelser, and Piotr Sztompka. *Cultural Trauma and Collective Identity*. Berkeley: University of California Press, 2004.
Appelbaum, Peter C. *Loyalty Betrayed: Jewish Chaplains in the German Army during the First World War*. London: Valentine Mitchell, 2014.
Audoin-Rouzeau, Stéphane. *Men at War 1914-1918: National Sentiment and Trench Journalism in France during the First World War*. Oxford: Berg, 1992.
Audoin-Rouzeau, Stéphane and Annette Becker. *14-18: Understanding the Great War*. New York: Hill & Wang, 2002.
Barth, Boris. *Dolchstoßlegenden und politische Desintegration: Das Trauma der deutschen Niederlage im Ersten Weltkrieg*. Düsseldorf: Droste Verlag, 2003.
Becker, Annette. "Faith, Ideologies, and the 'Cultures of War.'" In *A Companion to World War I*, edited by John Horne. Chichester: Wiley-Blackwell, 2010, 234-47.
Becker, Annette. *War and Faith: The Religious Imagination in France, 1914-1930*, translated by Helen McPhail. Oxford: Berg, 1998.
Behrenbeck, Sabine. *Der Kult um die toten Helden: Nationalsozialistische Mythen, Riten und Symbole, 1923-1945*. Vierow: SH-Verlag, 1996.
Bellah, Robert N. *Religion in Human Evolution, From the Paleolithic to the Axial Age*. Cambridge, MA: Belknap Press, 2011.
Bennette, Rebecca Ayako. *Diagnosing Dissent: Hysterics, Deserters, and Conscientious Objectors in Germany during World War One*. Ithaca, NY: Cornell University Press, 2020.
Bennette, Rebecca Ayako. *Fighting for the Soul of Germany: The Catholic Struggle for Inclusion after Unification*. Cambridge, MA: Harvard University Press, 2012.

Bergen, Doris L. *Sword of the Lord: Military Chaplains from the First to the Twenty-First Century*. Notre Dame, IN: University of Notre Dame Press, 2004.

Blobaum, Robert. "Registers of Everyday Life in Warsaw during the First World War: The Uses and Limitations of Ego-Documents." In *Inside World War One? The First World War and Its Witnesses*, edited by Richard Bessel and Dorothee Wierling. New York: Oxford University Press, 2018, 29–55.

Bourke, Joanna. *An Intimate History of Killing*. New York: Basic Books, 2000.

Bourke, Joanna. "Fear and Anxiety: Writing about Emotion in Modern History." *History Workshop Journal*, 55:1 (2003): 111–33.

Bourke, Joanna. *The Story of Pain: From Prayer to Painkillers*. Oxford: Oxford University Press, 2014.

Bruendel, Steffan. *Volksgemeinschaft oder Volksstaat: Die "Ideen von 1914" und die Neuordnung Deutschlands im Ersten Weltkrieg*. Berlin: DeGruyter, 2003.

Bruns, Claudia. *Politik des Eros—Der Männerbund in Wissenschaft, Politik und Jugendkultur, 1880–1934*. Köln: Böhlau, 2008.

Burleigh, Michael. *Sacred Causes: The Clash of Religion and Politics, from the Great War to the War on Terror*. New York: Harper Perennial, 2007.

Burrin, Philippe. "Die politischen Religionen: Das Mythologische-Symbolische in einer säkulariserten Welt." In *Der Nationalsozialismus als politische Religion*, edited by Michael Ley and Julius H. Schoeps. Mainz: Philo, 1997, 181–2.

Canning, Kathleen. *Gender History in Practice—Historical Perspectives on Bodies, Class and Citizenship*. Ithaca, NY: Cornell University Press, 2006.

Caruth, Cathy. *Listening to Trauma: Conversations with Leaders in the Theory and Treatment of Catastrophic Experience*. Baltimore, MD: Johns Hopkins University Press, 2014.

Caruth, Cathy. *Unclaimed Experience: Trauma, Narrative, and History*. Baltimore, MD: Johns Hopkins University Press, 1996 (revised edition 2016).

Chickering, Roger. *Imperial Germany and the Great War*, 3rd edn. Cambridge: Cambridge University Press, 2014.

Chickering, Roger. "Militärgeschichte als Totalgeschichte im Zeitalter des totalen Krieges." In *Was ist Militärgeschichte?* edited by Thomas Kühne and Benjamin Ziemann. Paderborn: Schöningh, 2002, 301–12.

Confino, Alon. "Death, Spiritual Solace, and Afterlife: Between Nazism and Religion." In *Between Mass Death and Individual Loss—The Place of the Dead in Twentieth-Century Germany*, edited by Alon Confino, Paul Betts, and Dirk Schumann. New York: Berghahn Books, 2008.

Crouthamel, Jason. *An Intimate History of the Front: Masculinity, Sexuality and German Soldiers in the First World War*. New York: Palgrave Macmillan, 2014.

Crouthamel, Jason. "Male Sexuality and Psychological Trauma: Soldiers and Sexual 'Disorder' in World War I and Weimar Germany," *Journal of History of Sexuality*, 17:1 (January 2008): 60–84.

Crouthamel, Jason. "Paul Lebrechts Kriegstagebuch," *Krieg! Juden zwischen den Fronten*, edited by Ulrike Heikaus and Julia B. Köhne. Berlin: Hentrich und Hentrich Verlag, 105–32.

Davies, Owen. *A Supernatural War: Magic, Divination and Faith during the First World War*. Oxford: Oxford University Press, 2018.

Davies, Owen. *The Oxford Illustrated History of Witchcraft and Magic*. Oxford: Oxford University Press, 2017.

Dawson, Graham. "The Meaning of 'Moving On': From Trauma to the History of Emotions and Memory of Emotions in 'Post-Conflict' Northern Ireland." *Irish University Review* 47:1 (2017): 82–102.

Deist, Wilhelm. "Der militärische Zusammenbruch des Kaiserreichs: Zur Realität der 'Dolchstosslegende.'" In *Militär, Staat und Gesellschaft—Studien zur preussisch-deutschen Militärgeschichte*, edited by Wilhelm Deist. Munich: R. Oldenbourg, 1991, 211–33.

Derwin, Susan. "Moral Injury: Two Perspectives." In *Traumatic Memories of the Second World War and After*, edited by Peter Leese and Jason Crouthamel. New York: Palgrave Macmillan, 2016, 47–65.

Diehl, James M. *Paramilitary Politics in Weimar Germany*. Bloomington: Indiana University Press, 1977.

Donson, Andrew. *Youth in the Fatherless Land—War Pedagogy, Nationalism, and Authority in Germany, 1914–1918*. Cambridge, MA: Harvard University Press, 2010.

Douglas, Mary. *Purity and Danger: An Analysis of Concepts of Pollution and Taboo* New York: Routledge, 1966.

Dufrese, Todd. *The Late Sigmund Freud: Or, The Last Word on Psychoanalysis, Society, and All the Riddles of Life*. Cambridge: Cambridge University Press, 2017.

Ebel, Jonathan. *Faith in the Fight: Religion and the American Soldier in the Great War*. Princeton, NJ: Princeton University Press, 2010.

Evans, Richard. "The Emergence of Nazi Ideology." In *Nazi Germany*, edited by Jane Caplan. Oxford: Oxford University Press, 2009.

Fecht, Tom. *Käthe Kollwitz: Works in Color*. New York: Random House, 1988.

Fehlemann, Silke. "Die Nerven der 'Daheimgebliebenen': Die Familienangehörigen der Soldaten in emotionshistorischer Perspektive." In *Nerven und Krieg: Psychologische Mobilisierungs- und Leidenserfahrungen in Deutschland, 1900–1939*, edited by Gundula Gahlen, Ralf Gnosa, and Oliver Janz. Frankfurt: Campus Verlag, 2020, 227–52.

Fehlemann, Silke, and Nils Löffelbein. "Gender, Memory and the Great War: The Politics of War Victimhood in Interwar Germany." In *Psychological Trauma and the Legacies of the First World War*, edited by Jason Crouthamel and Peter Leese. New York: Palgrave Macmillan, 2016, 141–64.

Feltman, Brian K. "Letters from Captivity: The First World War Correspondence of the German Prisoners of War in the United Kingdom." In *Finding Common Ground: New Directions in First World War Studies*, edited by Michael Neiberg and Jennifer Keene. Leiden: Brill, 2011, 87–110.

Feltman, Brian K. *The Stigma of Surrender: German Prisoners, British Captors, and Manhood in the Great War and Beyond*. Chapel Hill: University of North Carolina Press, 2015.

Flint, Valerie. *The Rise of Magic in Early Medieval Europe*. Princeton, NJ: Princeton University Press, 1991.

Freis, David. "Psyche, Trauma, und Kollektiv—Der psychiatrische Diskurs über die erschütterten Nerven der Nation." In *Nerven und Krieg: Psychische Mobilisierungs- und Leidenserfahrungen in Deutschland, 1900–1939*, edited by Gahlen, Gundula, Ralf Gnosa, and Oliver Janz. Frankfurt: Campus Verlag, 2020, 53–76.

Frevert, Ute. *A Nation in Barracks: Modern Germany, Military Conscription and Civil Society*. New York: Berg, 2004.

Frevert, Ute. "Forum—History of Emotions," *German History*, 28:1 (2010): 67–80.

Frevert, Ute. "Soldaten, Staatsbürger: Überlegungen zur historischen Konstruktion von Männlichkeit." In *Männergeschichte—Geschlechtergeschichte: Männlichkeit im Wandel der Moderne*, edited by Thomas Kühne. Frankfurt: Campus Verlag, 1996, 69–87.

Fritzsche, Peter. *A Nation of Fliers—German Aviation and the Popular Imagination*. Cambridge, MA: Harvard University Press, 1992.

Gahlen, Gundula, Ralf Gnosa, and Oliver Janz, eds., *Nerven und Krieg: Psychische Mobilisierungs- und Leidenserfahrungen in Deutschland, 1900–1939*. Frankfurt: Campus Verlag, 2020.

Geertz, Clifford. *The Interpretation of Cultures* (original 1973). New York: Basic Books, 2017.

Geheran, Michael. *Comrades Betrayed: Jewish World War I Veterans under Hitler*. Ithaca, NY: Cornell University Press, 2020.

Geheran, Michael. "Rethinking Jewish Front Experiences." In *Beyond Inclusion and Exclusion: Jewish Experiences of the First World War in Central Europe*, edited by Jason Crouthamel, Michael Geheran, Tim Grady, and Julia Barbara Köhne. New York: Berghahn Books, 2018, 111–43.

Geroulanos, Stefanos, and Todd Meyers. *The Human Body in the Age of Catastrophe: Brittleness, Integration, Science and the Great War*. Chicago, IL: University of Chicago Press, 2018.

Geyer, Michael, and Lucien Hölscher, eds., *Die Gegenwart Gottes in der modernen Gesellschaft: Transcendenz und religiöse Vergemeinschaftung in Deutschland*. Göttingen: Wallstein, 2006.

Geyer, Michael, and Hartmut Lehmann. *Religion und Nation, Nation und Religion. Beiträge zu einer unbewältigen Geschichte*. Göttingen: Wallstein, 2004.

Goodrick-Clarke, Nicholas. *The Occult Roots of Nazism*. New York: New York University Press, 1993

Graf, Friedrich Wilhelm. " 'Dechristianisierung': Zur Problemgeschichte eines kulturpolitischen Topos." In *Säkularisierung, Dechristianisierung, Rechristianisierung im neuzeitlichen Europa*, edited by Hartmut Lehmann. Göttingen: Vandenhoeck & Rupprecht, 1997.

Grady, Tim, *A Deadly Legacy: German Jews and the Great War*. New Haven, CT: Yale University Press, 2017.

Grayzel, Susan. *Women and the First World War*. New York: Longman, 2002.

Gregory, Adrian. "Beliefs and Religion." In *The Cambridge History of the First World War—Civil Society*, Volume 3, edited by Jay Winter. New York: Cambridge University Press, 2014, 418–44.

Gregory, Adrian, and Annette Becker. "Religious Sites and Practices," In *Capital Cities at War: Paris, London, Berlin*, vol. 2, edited by Jay Winter and Jean-Louis Robert. Cambridge: Cambridge University Press, 2007, 383–427.

Greschat, Martin. *Der Erste Weltkrieg und die Christenheit: Ein globaler Überblick*. Stuttgart: Kohlhammer, 2014.

Grünewald, Guido. *Zur Geschichte der Kriegsdienstverweigerung*. Essen: Deutsche Friedensgesellschaft, 1982.

Hagemann, Karen, and Stefanie Schüler-Springorum, eds. *Home/Front: The Military, War and Gender in Twentieth Century Germany*. Oxford: Berg, 2002.

Hagemann, Karen. "Of 'Manly Valor' and 'German Honor,' Nation, War and Masculinity in the Age of the Prussian Uprising against Napoleon." *Central European History* 30 (1997): 187–220.

Hall, David. *Lived Religion in America*. Princeton, NJ: Princeton University Press, 1997.

Hall, Donald E. *Muscular Christianity: Embodying the Victorian Age.*
Cambridge: Cambridge University Press, 2006.
Hammer, Karl. "Der deutsche Protestantismus und der Erste Weltkrieg," *Francia*, Bd. 2 (1974): 398–414.
Hämmerle, Christa, and Edith Sauerer, eds. *Briefkulturen und ihr Geschlecht—Zur Geschichte der privaten Korrespondenz vom 16. Jahrhundert bis heute.*
Wien: Böhlau, 2003.
Hank, Sabine, Hermann Simon, and Uwe Hank. *Feldrabbiner in den deutschen Streitkräften des Ersten Weltkrieges.* Berlin: Hentrich und Hentrich, 2010.
Hanna, Martha. *Your Death Would Be Mine: Paul and Marie Pireaud in the Great War.*
Cambridge, MA: Harvard University Press, 2006.
Hassner, Ron E. *Religion on the Battlefield.* Ithaca, NY: Cornell University Press, 2016.
Hawthorne, Sían. *Gender: God.* New York: Palgrave Macmillan, 2018.
Heikaus, Ulrike, and Julia B. Köhne, eds., *Krieg! Juden zwischen den Fronten 1914–1918.*
Berlin: Hentrich und Hentrich, 2014.
Hewitson, Mark. *Germany and the Causes of the First World War.* Oxford: Berg, 2004, 95.
Hirschfeld, Gerhard, Gerd Krumeich, and Irina Renz, eds., *"Keiner fühlt sich hier mehr als Mensch…". Erlebnis und Wirkung des Ersten Weltkriegs.* Essen: Klartext, 1993.
Hofer, Hans-Georg. *Nervenschwäche und Krieg—Modernitätskritik und Kriegsbewältigung in der österreicheschen Psychiatrie, 1880–1920.* Wien: Boehlau Verlag, 2004.
Hofmann, Andrea. "'Jesus im Schützengraben'—Kriegspredigten in Nachlässen pfälzischer und hessischer Pfarrer." In *Predigt im Ersten Weltkrieg*, edited by Irene Dingel and Matthieu Arnold. Göttingen: Vandenhoeck & Ruprecht, 2017, 31–44.
Hofmann, Andrea. "'Kämpfet Recht!' Themen einer evangelischen 'Soldatenethik' im Deutschen Reich während des ersten Weltkriegs." *Interdisciplinary Journal for Religion and Transformation* 6:1 (2018): 88–105.
Houlihan, Patrick J. *Catholicism and the Great War: Religion and Everyday Life in Germany and Austria-Hungary, 1914–1922.* Cambridge: Cambridge University Press, 2015.
Houlihan, Patrick J. "Clergy in the Trenches: Catholic Military Chaplains of Germany and Austria-Hungary during the First World War." PhD dissertation, University of Chicago, 2011.
Houlihan, Patrick J. "Religious Mobilization and Popular Belief," in *1914–1918 online. International Encyclopedia of the First World War*, edited by Ute Daniel et al., issued by Freie Universität Berlin, Berlin. August 26, 2015. DOI: 10.15463/ie1418.10716.
Hüppauf, Bernd. "Langenmarck, Verdun and the Myth of the New Man in Germany after the First World War." *War and Society* 6:2 (September 1988): 70–103.
Hüppauf, Bernd. "Schlachtenmythen und die Konstruktion des 'Neuen Menschen.'" In *Keiner fühlt sich hier mehr als Mensch….: Erlebnis und Wirkung des Ersten Weltkriegs.* edited by Gerhard Hirschfeld et al. Essen: Klartext, 1993.
Hürten, Heinz, "Die katholische Kirche im Ersten Weltkrieg." In *Der Erste Weltkrieg—Wirkung, Wahrnehmung, Analyse*, edited by Wolfgang Michalka. München: Piper, 1994, 725–35.
Hynes, Samuel. *A War Imagined: The First World War and English Culture.*
London: Bodley Head, 1990.
Jenkins, Philip. "Angels and Horsemen: The Great War as an Apocalyptic Struggle." In *Remembering Armageddon—Religion and the First World War*, edited by Philip Jenkins.
Waco: Institute for Studies of Religion, Baylor University, 2014, 71–92.
Jenkins, Philip. *The Great and Holy War: How World War I Became a Religious Crusade.*
New York: HarperCollins, 2014.

Kallhoff, Angela, and Thomas Schulte-Umberg. "The Committed Soldier. Religion as a Necessary Supplement to a Moral Theory of Warfare." *Politics, Religion & Ideology* 16 (2015): 434–48.

Kansteiner, Wulf. "Genealogy of a Category Mistake: A Critical Intellectual History of the Cultural Trauma Metaphor," *Rethinking History* 8:2 (2004): 193–221.

Kaplan, Marion A. *The Making of the Jewish Middle Class: Women, Family, and Identity in Imperial Germany*. Oxford: Oxford University Press, 1991.

Kennett, Lee. *The First Air War, 1914–1918*. New York: Macmillan, 1991.

Kiesel, Helmuth. *Ernst Jünger. Die Biographie*. Munich: Siedler, 2007.

Kilduff, Peter. *Black Fokker Leader—The First World War's Last Airfighter Knight*. London: Grubstreet, 2009.

Killen, Andreas. *Berlin Electropolis: Shock, Nerves and German Modernity*. Berkeley: University of California Press, 2006.

Knoch, Peter. "Erleben und Nacherleben. Das Kriegserlebnis im Augenzeugenbericht und im Geschichtsunterricht." In *"Keiner fühlt sich hier mehr als Mensch…". Erlebnis und Wirkung des Ersten Weltkriegs*, edited by Gerhard Hirschfeld, Gerd Krumeich, and Irina Renz. Essen: Klartext, 1993.

Köhne, Julia Barbara. "Aesthetic Displays of Perpetrators in *The Act of Killing* (2012): Post-atrocity Perpetrator Symptoms and Re-enactments of Violence." In *Languages of Trauma: History, Memory, and Media*, edited by Peter Leese, Julia Barbara Köhne, and Jason Crouthamel. Toronto: University of Toronto Press, 2021.

Köhne, Julia Barbara. *Kriegshysteriker: Strategische Bilder und mediale Techniken militärpsychiatrischen Wissens, 1914–1920*. Husum: Matthiesen, 2009.

Köhne, Julia Barbara. "Paper Psyches: On the Psychography of the Front Soldier According to Paul Plaut." In *Beyond Inclusion and Exclusion: Jewish Experiences of the First World War in Central Europe*, edited by Jason Crouthamel, Michael Geheran, Tim Grady, and Julia Barbara Köhne. New York: Berghahn Books, 2018, 317–61.

Krumeich, Gerd, and Hartmut Lehmann, *"Gott mit Uns!" Nation, Religion und Gewalt im 19. und frühen 20. Jahrhundert*. Göttingen: Vandenhoeck & Ruprecht, 2000.

Kuhlman, Erika. *Of Little Comfort: War Widows, Fallen Soldiers, and the Remaking of the Nation after the Great War*. New York: New York University Press, 2012.

Kuhlman, Erika. *Reconstructing Patriarchy after the Great War: Women, Gender and Postwar Reconciliation between Nations*. New York: Palgrave Macmillan, 2008.

Kühne, Thomas. *The Rise and Fall of Comradeship*. Cambridge: Cambridge University Press, 2017.

Kühne, Thomas. "'…aus diesem Krieg werden nicht nur harte Männer heimkehren'—Kriegskameradschaft und Männlichkeit im 20. Jahrhundert." In *Männergeschichte—Geschlechtergeschichte: Männlichkeit im Wandel der Moderne*, edited by Thomas Kühne. Frankfurt: Campus Verlag, 1996, 174–91.

Kurlander, Eric, *Hitler's Monsters: A Supernatural History of the Third Reich*. New Haven, CT: Yale University Press, 2018.

Kuuliala, Jenni, Rose-Marie Peake, and Päivi Räisänen-Schröder, eds., *Lived Religion and Everyday Life in Early Modern Hagiographic Material*. New York: Palgrave Macmillan, 2019.

Lamprecht, Gerald, *Feldpost und Kriegserlebnis. Briefe als historisch-biografische Quelle*. Innsbruck: Innsbruck University Press, 2002.

Lätzel, Martin, *Katholische Kirche im Ersten Welkrieg: Zwischen Nationalismus und Friedenswillen*. Regensburg: Pustet, 2014.

Lawson, Stephen T., "Jasta 7 under 'Kobes,'" *Cross & Cockade International Journal—The First World War Aviation Historical Society*, 25:3 (1994): 115–35.

Leonhard, Jörn, *Pandora's Box: A History of the First World War*, translated by Patrick Camiller. Cambridge, MA: Harvard University Press, 2020.

Lerner, Paul, *Hysterical Men—History, Psychiatry and the Politics of Trauma in Germany, 1890–1930*. Ithaca, NY: Cornell University Press, 2003.

Leese, Peter, Julia B. Köhne, and Jason Crouthamel, *Languages of Trauma: History, Memory, and Media*. Toronto: University of Toronto Press, 2021.

Lipp, Anne. *Meinungslenkung im Krieg—Kriegserfahrungen deutscher Soldaten und ihre Deutung, 1914–1918*. Göttingen: Vandenhoeck & Ruprecht, 2002.

Luhrssen, David. *Hammer of the Gods: The Thule Society and the Birth of Nazism*. Washington, DC: Potomac Books, 2012.

Madigan, Edward. *Faith under Fire: Anglican Army Chaplains and the Great War*. London: Palgrave Macmillan, 2011.

McCullis, Debbie. "Bibliotherapy: Historical and Research Perspectives." *Journal of Poetry Therapy* 25: 1 (2012): 23–38.

Methuen, Charlotte. "'The Very Nerve of Faith is Touched': British Preaching during the Great War." In *Predigt im Ersten Weltkrieg*, edited by Irene Dingel and Matthieu Arnold. Göttingen: Vandenhoeck & Ruprecht, 2017, 63–74.

Micale, Mark S., and Paul Lerner, eds., *Traumatic Pasts. History, Psychiatry and Trauma in the Modern Age, 1870–1930*. Cambridge: Cambridge University Press, 2001.

Mileck, Josef. *Hermann Hesse*. Berkeley: University of California Press, 1977.

Miller, Jesse. "Medicines of the Soul: Reparative Reading and the History of Bibliotherapy." *Mosaic: An Interdisciplinary Critical Journal* 51:2 (June 2018): 17–34.

Missalla, Heinrich. "*Gott mit uns*": *Die deutsche katholische Kriegspredigt, 1914–1918*. Munich: Kösel Verlag, 1968.

Morag, Raya. "Perpetrator Trauma and Current American War Cinema." In *Languages of Trauma: History, Memory, and Media*, edited by Peter Leese, Julia Barbara Köhne, and Jason Crouthamel. Toronto: University of Toronto Press, 2021.

Mosse, George L. *Fallen Soldiers*. Oxford: Oxford University Press, 1991.

Mosse, George L. *The Image of Man: The Creation of Modern Masculinity*. Oxford University Press, 1996.

Mosse, George L. "Shell Shock as a Social Disease." *Journal of Contemporary History*, 35:1 (2000): 101–8.

Nelson, Robert L. *German Soldier Newspapers of the First World War*. Cambridge: Cambridge University Press, 2011.

Nevin, Thomas. *Ernst Jünger and Germany: Into the Abyss, 1914–1945*. Durham, NC: Duke University Press, 1996.

Orsi, David. *The Madonna of 115th Street: Faith and Community in Italian Harlem, 1880–1950*. New Haven, CT: Yale University Press, 2002.

Perry, Joe. *Christmas in Germany—A Cultural History*. Chapel Hill: University of North Carolina Press, 2014.

Plamper, Jan. *The History of Emotions: An Introduction*. Oxford: Oxford University Press, 2015.

Puglisi, William. "Jacobs of Jasta 7." *Cross & Cockade Journal—Society of World War 1 Aero Historians*, 6:4 (Winter 1965): 325–44.

Radkau, Joachim. "Die Wende zur 'Willenskultur' in der Nerventherapie und das nervöse Doppelgesicht des Krieges." In *Nerven und Krieg: Psychische Mobilisierungs- und*

Leidenserfahrungen in Deutschland, 1900–1939, edited by Gundula Gahlen, Ralf Gnosa, and Oliver Janz. Frankfurt: Campus Verlag, 2020, 37–52.

Reagin, Nancy R. *Sweeping the German Nation: Domesticity and National Identity in Germany, 1870–1945*. Cambridge: Cambridge University Press, 2006.

Reimann, Aribert. *Der grosse Krieg der Sprachen: Untersuchungen zur historischen Semantik in Deutschland und England zur Zeit des ersten Weltkriegs*. Essen: Klartext, 2000.

Rennie, Robert William. "Privileged Killers, Privileged Deaths: German Culture and Aviation in the First World War: 1909–1925," PhD dissertation, University of Tennessee, 2017.

Riesebrodt, Martin. *The Promise of Salvation—A Theory of Religion*. (Chicago, IL: University of Chicago Press, 2010.

Roper, Michael. *The Secret Battle—Emotional Survival in the Great War*. Manchester: Manchester University Press, 2009.

Schlager, Claudia. *Kult und Krieg: Herz Jesu—Sacré Cœur—Christus Rex in deutsch-französischen Vergleich 1914–1925*. Tübingen: Tübinger Vereinigung für Volkskunde, 2011.

Schmäling, Bruno J. *Jasta Colors*, vol. 1. Reno: Aeronaut Books, 2020.

Schmäling, Bruno J., and Peter Kilduff, "In Memorium, Josef Jacobs, 1894–1978." *Cross & Cockade Journal*, 20:1 (Spring 1979): 87–91.

Schmäling, Bruno J., and Winfried Bock, *Royal Bavarian Jagdstaffel 23*, translated by Adam M. Wait; Reno: Aeronaut Books, 2018.

Schouten, Steven. "Ernst Toller." In *1914–1918 online. International Encyclopedia of the First World War*, edited by Ute Daniel, et al., issued by Freie Universität Berlin, Berlin June 8, 2018. doi: 10.15463/ie1418.11272.

Schüler-Springorum, Stefanie. "Flying and Killing—Military Masculinity in German Pilot Literature, 1914–1939." In *Home/Front—The Military, War and Gender in Twentieth-Century Germany*, edited by Karen Hagemann and Stefanie Schüler-Springorum. Oxford: Berg, 2002,

Schumann, Frank, ed., *Was Tun Wir Hier: Soldatenpost und Heimatbriefe aus zwei Weltkriegen*. Berlin: Verlag Neues Leben, 1989.

Schweitzer, Richard. *The Cross and the Trenches: Religious Faith and Doubt among British and American Great War Soldiers*. Westport, CT: Praeger, 2003.

Shay, Jonathan. *Achilles in Vietnam*. New York: Scribner, 1994.

Shevin-Coetzee, Marilyn, and Frans Coetzee. *Commitment and Sacrifice: Personal Diaries of the Great War*. Oxford: Oxford University Press, 2015.

Showalter, Elaine. "Rivers and Sassoon: The Inscription of Male Gender Anxieties." In *Behind the Lines: Gender and the Two World Wars*, edited by Margaret Randolph Higonnet, et al. New Haven, CT: Yale University Press, 1987, 61–9.

Sinn, Andrea. "In the Shadow of Antisemitism: Jewish Women and the German Home Front during the First World War." In *Beyond Inclusion and Exclusion: Jewish Experiences of the First World War in Central Europe*, edited by Jason Crouthamel, Michael Geheran, Tim Grady, and Julia Barbara Köhne. New York: Berghahn Books, 2018, 170–202.

Smoller, Laura A. "'Popular' Religious Culture(s)." In *The Oxford Handbook of Medieval Christianity*, edited by John H. Arnold. Oxford: Oxford University Press, 2014.

Snape, Michael. *God and the British Soldier: Religion and the British Army in the First and Second World Wars*. New York: Routledge, 2005.

Snape, Michael. *God and Uncle Sam: Religion and America's Armed Forces in World War II*. Suffolk, UK: Boydell Press, 2015.

Snyder, David Raub. *Sex Crimes in the Wehrmacht*. Omaha: University of Nebraska Press, 2009.

Stark, Gary. *Entrepreneurs of Ideology: Neoconservative Publishers in Germany, 1890–1933*. Chapell Hill: University of North Carolina Press, 1981.

Steigmann-Gall, Richard. "Was National Socialism a Political Religion or a Religious Politics?" In *Religion und Nation, Nation und Religion. Beiträge zu einer unbewältigen Geschichte*, edited by Michael Geyer and Hartmut Lehmann. Göttingen: Wallstein, 2004.

Taskinen, Ilari. "Social Lives in Letters: Finnish Soldiers' Epistolary Relationships, Intimate Practices, and Emotionality in World War II," PhD Dissertation, Tampere University, Finland, 2021.

Theweleit, Klaus. *Male Fantasies*, vol. 1, translated by Stephen Conway. Minneapolis: University of Minnesota Press, 1987.

Thomas, Keith. *Religion and the Decline of Magic*. London: Penguin Books, 1991.

Thomspon, E. P. *Customs in Common: Studies in Traditional Popular Culture*. New York: The New Press, 1993.

Towheed, Shafquat, Francesca Benatti, and Edmund G. C. King. "Readers and Reading in the First World War." *The Yearbook in English Studies* 45 (2015): 239–61.

Ulrich, Bernd. *Die Augenzeugen. Deutsche Feldpostbriefe in Kriegs- und Nachkriegszeit 1914–1933*. Essen: Klartext, 1997, 40–52.

Verhey, Jeffrey. *The Spirit of 1914: Military, Myth and Mobilization in Germany*. Cambridge: Cambridge University Press, 2000.

Voigt, Immanuel. *Stars des Krieges—Eine biografische und erinnerungskulturelle Studie zu den deutschen Luftstreitkräften des Ersten Weltkrieges*. Oldenbourg: De Gruyter, 2019.

Wallace, Anthony. *Revitalizations and Mazeways: Essays in Cultural Change*, Volume 1, edited by R. M. Grumet. Lincoln: University of Nebraska Press, 2003.

Wallace, Anthony. "Revitalization Movements." *American Anthropologist*, 58 (1956): 264–81.

Watson, Alexander. *Enduring the Great War: Combat, Morale and Collapse in the German and British Armies, 1914–1918*. Cambridge: Cambridge University Press, 2008.

Watson, Alexander, and Patrick Porter, "Bereaved and Aggrieved. Combat Motivation and the Ideology of Sacrifice in the First World War." *Historical Research* 83: 219 (2010): 146–64.

Weber, Thomas. *Hitler's First War*. Oxford: Oxford University Press, 2011.

Weintraub, Stanley. *Silent Night: The Story of the World War I Christmas Truce*. New York: Penguin, 2002.

Weisbrod, Bernd. "Military Violence and Male Fundamentalism: Ernst Jünger's Contribution to the Conservative Revolution." *History Workshop Journal* 49 (2000): 69–93.

Whalen, Robert. *Bitter Wounds—German Victims of the Great War, 1914–1939*. Ithaca, NY: Cornell University Press, 1984.

Wierling, Dorothee. *Eine Familie im Krieg: Leben, Sterben und Schreiben 1914–1918*. Göttingen: Wallstein, 2013.

Winkle, Ralph. "Connaître à fond de l'âme du soldat: Französische Aberglaubensforschung während des Ersten Weltkrieges." In *Alliierte im Himmel. Populare Religiosität und Kriegserfahrung*, edited by Gottfried Korff. Tübingen: Tübinger Vereinigung für Volkskunde, 2006, 349–70.

Winter, Jay. *Remembering War*. New Haven, CT: Yale University Press, 2006.
Winter, Jay. *Sites of Memory, Sites of Mourning: The Great War in European Cultural History*. Cambridge: Cambridge University Press, 1995.
Winter, Jay. *The Experience of World War I*. London: Macmillan, 1988.
Winter, Jay. *War Beyond Words: Languages of Remembrance from the Great War to the Present*. Cambridge: Cambridge University Press, 2017.
Wirtz, Ursula. *Trauma and Beyond: The Mystery of Transformation*. New Orleans, LA: Spring Journal Books, 2014.
Wohl, Robert, *A Passion for Wings: Aviation and the Western Imagination*. New Haven: Yale University Press, 1994.
Young, Allan. *The Harmony of Illusions: Inventing Post-Traumatic Stress Disorder*. Princeton, NJ: Princeton University Press, 1997.
Ziemann, Benjamin. *Contested Commemorations: Republican War Veterans and Weimar Political Culture*. Cambridge: Cambridge University Press, 2013.
Ziemann, Benjamin. "Katholische Religiosität und die Bewältigung des Krieges: Soldaten und Militärseelsorger in der deutschen Armee, 1914–1918." In *Volksreligiosität und Kriegserleben*, edited by Wolfgang Michalka. Münster: Lit, 1997, 116–36.
Ziemann, Benjamin. *Violence and the German Soldier in the Great War—Killing, Dying, Surviving*, translated by Andrew Evans. London: Bloomsbury, 2017.
Ziemann, Benjamin. *War Experiences in Rural Germany, 1914–1923*, translated by Alex Skinner. Oxford: Berg, 2007.

Index

afterlife (*see also* 'heaven' and 'hell') 10, 16, 40, 71–2, 119, 131, 133, 174
aircraft (*see* 'flying')
alcohol 27, 61, 186
Amiens, Battle of 189
amulets (charms, *see also* 'talismans') 116, 141–2
angels 19, 50–2, 89, 100, 119, 147, 156–8, 161, 187
anthropomorphization of technology 149, 154, 179, 200
AntiChrist, the (*see also* 'Satan') 65
antisemitism (*see also* 'Jew Count') 22, 54, 93–4, 96, 155, 172–3, 183, 185, 187–8
apocalypse 85, 188
arisophism 187–8
Army newspapers (including divisional and base newspapers)
  Der Eigenbrödler 144
  Kriegszeitung der 4. Armee (*War Newspaper of the Fourth Army*) 6, 17, 25–6, 66, 142–3, 153
  Liller Kriegszeitung (*War Newspaper of Lille*) 6, 17–18, 21–2, 45–6, 63, 143, 149–50, 170, 176
  Die Somme-Wacht 19, 27
atheism (or unbelief) 100, 103–6, 112–14, 126–8, 165

Bächthold, Hanns 138–9
Baeck, Leo 95–6
Beethoven, Ludwig van 194–5
Berthold, Rudolf 37, 185
Bible Student Movement, 29
Biblical scripture (*see also* 'gospels') 27, 30, 41, 43, 65, 93–4, 104, 130, 140, 148, 168, 175
Binswanger, Otto 124
Bittel, Karl 123
Boelcke, Oswald 63, 141, 174

Bolshevism 187
Bröger, Karl 167–8

Catholicism
  clergy (*see also* chaplains) 28–30, 32, 137
  coping with trauma 10, 16, 24, 55, 72–3, 76
  and nationalism 15, 17, 43–4
  rituals 11, 42, 48, 55, 76, 131, 137, 146–7, 153
  and superstition 137
  worship services 16, 28–9, 32, 42–3, 93, 131
censorship 5–6, 78
chaplains (*see also* 'Catholicism' and 'Protestantism')
  coping with stress 31, 63, 102
  criticism of 81, 93–4, 103, 114, 164
  and field services 28–30, 32, 44, 95
  front experiences 101–2
  and propaganda 17, 19–20, 22–3
  and superstitions, 137, 144
charlatanism 136, 139, 141–4
Christianity (*see* 'Jesus', 'Protestantism' and 'Catholicism')
Christmas
  Christmas truce 47
  iconography 44, 157
  services 28–9
  spiritual connection to *Heimat* 32, 36, 44–9, 59, 77, 86
civilians (enemy)
  Belgian 43, 144–5
  French 41–3
  Romanian 31
  women 144–5
clairvoyant, 144
Communist Party, German 123, 187, 194
comradeship (*see also* 'masculinity')
  and Jesus 26–7, 45

and religion 25, 54
  as spiritual experience 54, 86, 129, 132, 162, 171–3, 180, 193
concentration camp 95, 167
conscientious objectors, 27–9
crusade (*see also* 'holy war) 11, 78, 101, 156, 186

defeat
  and religion 185–6, 188–9
  and trauma 102–3, 183, 185–6, 192
Degelow, Carl 172–3
demons 149, 152
Devil, the (or devilry, *see also* 'Satan' and 'the AntiChrist') 65, 99, 152, 152–3, 156, 172
diaries (*see* 'writing')
Diedrichs, Eugen 122–3
Dietrich, Marlene 105–6
Drexler, Anton 188
drug addiction (*see also* 'alcohol') 105, 118

Easter bunny 148
Eastern front (Russia) 29–32, 48, 170, 175
education (Christian), 10, 23–4, 105–6, 148–9
emotions (*see also* 'resilience')
  anxiety 10, 16, 40–1, 50, 55, 62, 68, 76, 80, 88, 105, 141, 195
  fear 12–13, 19, 40, 53, 62, 66, 87, 96, 115, 116–21, 169–70
  and 'femininity' 10, 16, 26, 36, 62, 199–200
  hate 20–2, 84
  helplessness 45, 55, 61, 80, 88, 156
  managing 15–16
  and 'masculinity' 16, 24–6
  pain and suffering 10–11, 31, 52, 57, 62, 70–1, 85, 163–4
Everth, Erich 123–7

faith (*see* 'God')
fatalism 54–9, 117
femininity (*see also* 'women')
  and emotions 10, 16, 36, 62, 199
  and religion 24
field (or front) services (*see also* 'chaplains') 28–31, 41–4, 140

flying
  fighter pilots 37, 64, 88–93, 146–7, 152–5, 161, 172–3, 177
  and stress 65, 90–2, 161, 170, 190
folk beliefs (*see also* 'popular beliefs') 135–6, 138–9, 156
Frank, Hans 188
Freikorps 187
Freud, Sigmund 110, 111
front newspapers (*see* 'army newspapers' and 'trench newspapers')
Futurism 175

Gaupp, Robert, 28
Geist (*see* 'spirit')
German Christian Church 103
ghosts 139, 144, 152, 177
God
  anger at 83, 194
  bridge between two fronts, 49–51
  capriciousness 36, 55–6, 58, 146
  and comradeship 30, 45, 64
  consolation or comfort 39, 53, 57, 69, 72–5, 92–3, 95
  and defeat 186–7, 189
  divine justice 71, 101
  and doubt 58, 75, 79, 82, 103–6, 113, 126–7, 165
  existence of 82, 87, 104, 165
  feminine 130
  Holy Spirit 19, 21, 62, 64–5
  laws of (commandments) 12–13, 28, 94, 96, 99, 107, 148, 168, 190
  and masculinity 25, 164
  and morality 83, 85, 101–2, 126
  nation, 15, 17–19, 22, 37–8
  nerves 67–73, 77–8, 89–90, 98
  protector 39, 50, 71, 77, 99, 125
  resilience 68, 126, 98, 163
  subjective notions of 40, 113, 125, 131, 145–6, 168–9
  unknowability (remoteness) 40, 58, 85–6, 92–3, 95, 104–6, 132, 167–8, 172, 194–5
  will of 17, 22, 30, 36, 38, 45–6, 55, 130, 146, 168, 189
Goethe, Johann Wolfgang von 170, 195
Göhre, Paul, 127–33

Göring, Hermann 153
gospels (*see also* 'Biblical scripture') 27, 30, 41, 43, 93, 104, 130
Grabinski, Bruno 139–40

heaven 38, 42, 57, 69, 71–2, 131–2, 147, 156–7, 187
hell 113, 152, 156–7, 159
Hess, Rudolf 188
Hesse, Hermann 123
Himmler, Heinrich 187
Hirschfeld, Magnus 110
Hitler, Adolf 37–8, 96, 185–6, 188, 193–4
Holy Spirit (*see also* 'God') 19, 21, 62, 64–5
holy war (*see also* 'crusade') 11
Horneffer, August 122
Horneffer, Ernst 122
humor 114, 121, 124, 133, 144–5, 155–9
hybridization of beliefs 135, 145–8

Institute for Applied Psychology, Potsdam 111
Institute of Psychology, Kiel 109
intercession 146–7
Israel 186–7

Jacobs, Josef 152–3, 197
Jesus (*see also* 'God')
  Christmas, 45–7, 157
  and comradeship 30, 45
  Last Judgment (*see also* 'apocalypse') 85–6
  and masculinity 26
  and resilience 19, 31
  and salvation 41, 86–7, 102, 133
  suffering and sacrifice 10, 21, 23, 27, 32, 41
'Jew Count' (*Judenzählung*, *see also* 'antisemitism') 22, 173
Jews (or Jewish)
  front rabbis (*Feldrabbiner*) 22–3, 95–6
  front soldiers 31–2, 71, 93–6, 112, 173–4, 175–6, 183
  Jewish-Christian relations, 31–2, 54, 94
  liberal (reform) 31
  orthodox 173–4
  persecution of (*see also* 'antisemitism') 23, 96, 155
  prayer books 30

worship services 28–9, 95–6
  Sabbath, 29
jinx 121
Judaism (*see* Jews)
Jünger, Ernst 12, 163, 180–1, 197

Kaiser Wilhelm II 17–18, 29, 61
killing, the act of 11, 19, 27–8, 41, 163, 179–82, 188
Kollwitz, Käthe 127, 166–7, 194–5

letters from the front (*Feldpostbriefe, see* 'writing')
'letters from heaven' (*Himmelsbriefe*) 142–3
Liebknecht, Karl 187
Lipmann, Otto 111
'lived religion' 3, 182
Ludendorff, Erich 189
Ludwig, Walter, 116–20
Luther, Martin 142–3
Luxemburg, Rosa 187

magic 8, 142
Mann, Heinrich 127
Männerbünde (male associations) 173
Mary, mother of God 72–3, 143
masculinity
  breakdown 75, 164
  and comradeship 25–7, 171–3
  crisis of 161–2
  degenerate (or 'unmanly') 24, 28, 63, 75
  disillusionment with 164
  and emotions 25–6
  muscular Christianity 25
  and religion 24–5
  warrior ideal, 24–5, 27, 88, 97, 127, 171, 181, 193
memory
  politics of 181, 183
  trauma and 12, 166, 184
  of the war experience 25, 173–4
miracles 42, 66, 73, 176
Monism 122, 128
Monist League 122
monsters 148–55
moral injury (*see also* killing) 12, 41, 82–3, 190
morality organizations 186
Munchener Neueste Nachrichten 192

mysticism 139–40
mythology (*see also* 'Norse mythology')
   Greek and Roman 152, 155, 179
   Norse 8, 136, 146, 152, 154, 160

National Socialism 96, 103, 127, 153–4, 185, 187–8, 193–4
Nauhaus, Walter 187
nerves (*see also* 'war hysteria' and 'war neurosis')
   and God 27, 61, 67–75, 77
   language of 61–3, 67, 77
Neue Hamburger Zeitung 167
'new man', the 162, 174–7, 180–1, 200
Nibelungs, Song of the 142, 154–5
Nietzsche 112, 121–2, 148, 165, 169–70
Norse (Nordic) mythology 8, 146, 152, 154–5, 160, 174, 187
numerology 116, 137–8, 141

occult (*see* 'spiritualism' and 'superstitions')
Odin (*Wotan*) 146, 152, 174, 180, 187
Omens (*see also* 'premonitions') 136–8
Orlamuender, Paul, 156

paganism (*see also* 'Norse mythology') 99, 135–7, 141, 146, 148–52
pain (*see* 'emotions')
paranormal activities, 139
pentagram 155
Pfeilschifter, Georg 24
pilots (*see* 'flying')
Plaut, Paul 30, 111–16, 141
poltergeist 139
popular beliefs (*see also* 'folk beliefs') 8, 116, 135–6, 138–40, 160
pornography 102
prayer
   and agency 43, 49, 62, 70, 74, 99
   prayer books 29–30, 95
   as protection 23–4, 50
   satirical 175–6
   and stress ('nerves') 15, 23, 26–7, 58, 62, 68, 77–8, 152
   as therapy 68, 77–8, 97
   useless, 130–1
   and victory 19, 64
premonitions (*see also* 'omens') 120–2
prisoner of war (POWs) 58–9, 169–70, 178

Protestantism
   clergy 15, 19–21, 27, 101–3, 127–8, 142–3, 166
   coping with trauma 10–11, 19–21, 131, 191–2
   media 15–16, 19, 21, 26, 64
   mobilization and militarization 16, 23
   prayer and hymn books 29–30
   worship services 28–9, 31, 93
Prussian tradition 26, 69
Psalms, the (*see also* 'Biblical scripture') 23, 81, 95, 140, 175
psychologists
   study of religion 12, 111–16, 120–3
   study of superstition, 115–16, 121
psychiatrists
   diagnosis of mental illness 28, 63, 67, 124
   and religion, 24, 111–16, 120–3
   skepticism towards 62, 76–7
psychic powers 140
psychological trauma (*see* 'war neurosis or war hysteria' and PTSD)
psychotechnics 111–12
PTSD (Post Traumatic Stress Disorder) 9

racism (*see also* 'antisemitism') 94, 173, 183, 185, 187–8
redemption (*see also* 'salvation')
   anxiety over 41, 87
   and nationalism 16, 70, 102
   and Nazi ideology, 193
   overcoming pain 163, 168
   as a reward 38, 177
Reichsbanner 167
Remarque, Erich Maria 199
renewal or rebirth 15, 112, 123, 126, 163–6, 168
resilience
   and comradeship 83, 162–4, 171
   criticism of resilience 93–4
   outside religious faith 119, 126, 136
   and religious faith 1, 10–11, 15–16, 19, 40–2, 61–8. 71–3, 76, 93–7
Revelation, Book of 65
Richthofen, Baroness von 69, 182
Richthofen, Lothar 141
Richthofen, Manfred von 69, 146, 174, 181
Rosenstein, Willy 155, 172–3

Rosh Hoshanah 71, 95
Röth, Friedrich 190–3
Rupp, Julius, 166

salvation (*see also* 'Jesus' and 'redemption')
  anxiety over 99, 133
  hope for 19, 30, 37, 40–1, 62, 65, 68, 70–6
  outside Christian thought 168, 193
Satan (*see also* 'demons' and 'the Devil') 65, 156, 197
Schiche, E. 120–2
Schiller, Friedrich 170
Schopenhauer, Arthur 148
secular religion 198
Seele (*see* 'soul')
self-therapy (*see also* 'writing')
  and art 194
  religion as 9, 63, 68, 79, 199
sexuality 24, 27, 102, 186
shell shock (*see* 'war neurosis or war hysteria')
sin 10, 12, 19, 21, 41, 83, 85, 87, 172, 180
Social Democratic Party (SPD) 74, 101, 127–8, 166–7, 175
socialism 24, 166–8, 195
soldiers' newspapers (*see* 'army newspapers' and 'trench newspapers')
Somme, Battle of the 72, 83–4, 119, 139
Sonderweg ('special path' of history) 198
soul (*Seele*) 62–3, 66, 69, 79, 112, 123–4, 139
spells 140
spirit (*Geist*) 27, 50, 62–4, 79, 89, 139, 172, 176
'spirit of 1914' 35, 41, 54
spiritualism 144–5
Spring 1918 Offensive 83, 149, 176
St. Peter 157–8
'stab-in-the-back' legend 183–6
Stark, Rudolf 146–7, 177–8
Star of David 155
Stern, William 111
Storm of Steel (*see* 'Ernst Jünger')
suicide 99, 120, 148, 164, 190–3
supernatural
  environment 87
  forces 7, 62, 113, 115, 143
  phenomena 115–16, 139–41, 149–52, 177
  powers 121, 139–40
superstitions
  anxieties about 136, 142, 143
  coping with stress 112, 115–16, 121, 136, 140–1
  definitions 135, 137
  potential harm 143–4
  practices 115–16, 137–8, 140–1
Supreme Army Command (OHL, *Oberste Heeresleitung*) 5
swastika (*Hakenkreuz*) 155
symbolism 146, 155–6, 188

talismans 137–8, 141–2, 153
tanks, 152
Tat, Die 122–3
Ten Commandments (*see* 'God's laws')
Teutonism 142
Thule Society 187–8
Toller, Ernst 12, 164–6, 199
Trench newspapers (*Schützengrabenzeitungen*)
  Der Drahtverhau 159
  Der Flieger 64, 142, 157, 174–6
  Der Kamerad, 174
  Die Scheuner Kriegszeitung 157
Tucholsky, Kurt 175–6
Tutschek, Adolf *Ritter* von 161, 179–80

U-boats 149, 178, 193
Udet, Ernst 91–2

Valhalla 174
Valkyrie 8, 136, 154
Verdun, Battle of 72, 97, 112, 141, 164
Vietnam War (*see also* 'moral injury') 12, 82, 182
Vikings (*see also* 'Norse') 174
völkisch nationalism 187
Vorwärts 175

Wagner, Richard 154
War Ministry 111
'war neurosis' or 'war hysteria'
  diagnosis 61, 63, 67, 164, 199
  stigmatization 28, 63, 77, 110

war newspapers (*see* 'army newspapers' and 'trench newspapers')
war worship 175–80
Weimar Republic 12, 103, 184
Weltbühne, Die 175
women
  accusations of betrayal, 185
  enemy civilians ('foreign') 144–5
  gender roles and religiosity, 16, 23–4, 32, 35–6, 69–70, 99
  nurses 53, 109
  and religious language (*see also* 'writing') 38–9, 63
  spiritual power 69–70
  and trauma 69, 76–8, 186–7, 189

worship services (*see* 'field services' and 'chaplains')
writing
  coded or self-referential 148
  diaries as sources, 4–6, 9
  letters (*Feldpostbriefe*) as sources 4–6, 9, 12
  as self-therapy 9, 63, 199
  women's writing, 37–9, 49, 69, 76–8, 105–6, 166–7, 186–7, 194–5

Young-Rißmann, Mary 186
Ypres, Battle of 67–8, 83, 85, 173

Zeppelins 149

www.ingramcontent.com/pod-product-compliance
Lightning Source LLC
Chambersburg PA
CBHW062125300426
44115CB00012BA/1814